D1290072

THE DECORATIVE ARTS AND CRAFTS OF NANTUCKET

THE DECORATIVE ARTS AND CRAFTS OF NANTUCKET

by Charles H. Carpenter, Jr.
and Mary Grace Carpenter

with photographs by Arthur d'Arazien

DODD, MEAD & COMPANY • *New York*

Published in cooperation with
the Nantucket Historical Association and
the Nantucket Historical Trust

Published by Dodd, Mead & Company, Inc.
71 Fifth Avenue, New York, New York 10003
Manufactured in the United States of America.
Designed by Claire Counihan
First Edition

1 2 3 4 5 6 7 8 9 10

Library of Congress Cataloging-in-Publication Data

Carpenter, Charles Hope, 1916-
The decorative arts and crafts of Nantucket.

Bibliography: p.
Includes index.
1. Decorative arts—Massachusetts—Nantucket Island.
2. Decoration and ornament—Massachusetts—Nantucket Island. I. Carpenter, Mary Grace. II. D'Arazien, Arthur. III. Title.
NK835.M42N33 1987 745'.09744'97 87-16178
Trade Edition: ISBN 0-396-08488-5
Limited Edition: ISBN 0-396-09255-1

To
Susan and Richard, Shelley and Rick,
Philip and Karen, and our grandchildren,
Matthew, Benjamin, Peter, Faith,
Michael, Philip, and Mary Hope.

CONTENTS

ACKNOWLEDGMENTS

Because of the broad scope of this book, covering as it does the whole spectrum of Nantucket's decorative arts and crafts, we felt that every chapter should be reviewed by people who were most familiar with the particular areas involved. We thank all of them and resist the facetious suggestion of a scholarly friend that we should blame all the errors in the book on these individuals, and claim all the good things as ours alone!

Chapter 1, "Introduction," was first read by Joanne Polster, librarian, American Crafts Council. Howard Schless, professor of English, Columbia University, read the introduction and three other chapters. Historians Thomas Drake, emeritus professor of history, Haverford College, and Arthur J. Worrall, professor of history, Colorado State University, helped sharpen our statements about Quakerism in Nantucket's past. Helen Winslow Chase and Elizabeth A. Little, with their encyclopedic knowledge of Nantucket history and prehistory, helped us avoid mistakes and misjudgments.

Chapter 2, "At Home in Nantucket: Life-Styles, 1700–1900," was read by Helen Winslow Chase, Thomas Drake, Elizabeth A. Little, and Howard Schless. Parts of the chapter were read by Mrs. W. S. Archibald, Jr., Dr. Pamela J. Annas, Mrs. H. Crowell Freeman, and Clay Lancaster. Mrs. Archibald made available much of the material about her grandfather, H. O. Underwood, "The Summer Resident"; Mrs. Freeman reviewed the section on her ancestors involved in the Middle Brick, Joseph and Matthew Starbuck; Dr. Annas, associate professor and director of the Nantucket Program, University of Massachusetts, Boston, read the section on the Indian weaver, Netowa; Clay Lancaster, author and architectural historian, furnished valuable information on the "typical Nantucket house."

Chapter 3, "Furniture in the Home," was developed with the help of Harry Hilbert, antiquarian and cabinetmaker. The final draft of the chapter was meticulously critiqued by Gerald W. R. Ward, furniture and silver scholar and assistant editor of the *Winterthur Portfolio.* Chapter 4, "Mariners' Things, Boxes, Toys, Woodenware," was read by Helen Winslow Chase and Howard Schless. Chapter 5, "Textiles," was nurtured by Susan Burrows Swan, associate curator, Winterthur Museum. Drafts of the textile chapter were read by Sarah Lowengard, textile consultant; Patsy Orlofsky, author and director of the Textile Conservation Institute; and Delmar Swan, textile technologist. Our advisers for Chapter 6, "Ceramics, Glass, and Lighting Devices," were Ellen Denker, consultant and author, and Bert Denker, author and photographic librarian, Winterthur Museum, and Donald L. Fennimore, associate curator, Winterthur Museum. Chapter 7, "Silver," was reviewed by Martha

Gandy Fales, scholar and author, and Donald L. Fennimore. Some of the material in the section "Paul Revere and the Union Lodge" was furnished by Lynwood Proctor of Nantucket. Chapter 8, "Iron, Pewter, Copper and Brass, Tin," was read by Donald L. Fennimore. Chapter 9, "Scrimshaw," was read by Helen Winslow Chase; Nancy Chase, Nantucket ivory carver; Richard Kugler, director of the New Bedford Whaling Museum; Ian M. G. Quimby, editor, *Winterthur Portfolio;* Howard Schless; and by Paul Winfisky, assistant curator, and Peter Fetchko, director, The Peabody Museum of Salem. Pamela Annas read the section "The Pequod as Scrimshaw." Chapter 10, "Baskets," was read by Marianne Carlano, curator, Wadsworth Atheneum, Elizabeth A. Little, William A. Severns, who has been making Nantucket baskets since the 1920s; and Harry Hilbert, basketmaker. Chapter 11, "Carvings and Drawings," was reviewed by Helen Winslow Chase. Part of the section on decoys was contributed by Donald C. O'Brien, Jr., chairman of the board, National Audubon Society and longtime collector of Nantucket decoys. Chapter 12, "Souvenirs From Far-away Places," was read by Helen Winslow Chase.

The cooperation of the Nantucket Historical Association was essential to the writing of this book. Many of the objects are from the Association's collections, and their extensive research holdings were invaluable. We wish to thank John N. Welch, administrator, H. Flint Ranney, president, and members of the council of the Association for their help, advice and encouragement. We particularly want to thank Victoria Hawkins, curator of collections, who worked with us from the beginning, and we are grateful for the help of Jacqueline Haring, Louise Hussey, Peter MacGlashan, Edouard Stackpole, Leroy True, and Elizabeth Tyrer.

We wish to thank Mrs. Ann B. Oliver and Walter Beinecke, Jr., and the Nantucket Historical Trust for their assistance and encouragement in the preparation of the book.

Miss Barbara P. Andrews, librarian, and Mrs. Janice O'Mara, assistant librarian, Nantucket Atheneum, were most helpful, as was Laura Evans of the Maria Mitchell Association. Phyllis J. Visco and Sylvia M. Chadwick of the Nantucket Probate Court and Sandra M. Chadwick, Carole E. Corkish, and Margaret C. Pignato, of the Nantucket Registry of Deeds office, helped us through the maze of Nantucket court records.

The reference librarians of the New Canaan, Connecticut, Library answered dozens of questions with unfailing patience: Mrs. Indu Arya, Mrs. Nancy Halpert, Mrs. Phebe Kirkham, and Mrs. Barbara Rosett.

In addition to those already mentioned, the people in the following list (which is surely not complete) contributed in one way or another to the making of this book: Albert Brock; Michael K. Brown, Museum of Fine Arts, Houston; Henry Carlisle; Janis W. Carlson, Winterthur Museum; Alcon Chadwick, Alma Coffin, Virginia Clark; Wendy Cooper, Colonial Williamsburg; David Cross; Brian Cullity, Heritage Plantation Museum; Edward Dougan, Mr. and Mrs. John P. Elder; Nancy Goyne Evans, Winterthur Museum; Barbara Franco, Museum of Our American Heritage; Fred Gardner, Patricia Gardner, Elizabeth Gilbert, Nina Hellman; Ronald L. Hurst, Colonial Williamsburg; Joyce Jakula, Laura Lovett, Walt Lucas, Paul Madden; Christopher Monkhouse, Museum of Art, Rhode Island School of Design; Paul Morris; Christina H. Nelson, Saint Louis Art Museum; Margareta Grandin Nettles, Virginia Newhouse; Andy Oates, Merle Orleans, Rafael Osona, Robert Ray, Dr. Edward Richardson, Jane Ray Richmond; Rodris Roth, Smithsonian Institution; Harold Sack, David Schorsch; Judith I. Selleck, Heritage Plantation Museum; Peter Sprang, Old Deerfield; Richard Sylvia,

Charles and Mickey Sayle, Eva Marie Tausig, Jack Weinhold, Stephen Wise; Rodrick S. and Marjorie K. Webster, The Adler Planetarium, Chicago; Erica Wilson; and Stan Whippy, Suva, Fiji.

In memoriam, we would like to remember island residents who contributed to our knowledge of Nantucket: Nancy Grant Adams, William Coffin, Nelson O. Dunham, Catherine Defrieze Fitzpatrick, Michael Gardine, and Earl S. Ray.

Lastly, we thank Arthur d'Arazien, who did most of the photography for the book. Arthur, considered to be the father of modern industrial photography, has an international reputation, and we feel we were fortunate indeed to have had his services.

Notes on the Illustration Captions

Figure numbers of captions are indicated by the numbers set off to the left of the captions. Dimensions, when available, are given in inches (in.) and in centimeters (cm.). The last line in the caption indicates the present owner or the origin of the photograph. The abbreviation "NHA" is for the Nantucket Historical Association.

The names of the objects in this book are based, wherever possible, on the names used in contemporary records. For example, Nantucket inventories use the terms "four back" and "three back" chair, instead of the more usual present-day terms of slat-back or ladder-back chair, and "round" chair for roundabout or corner chair.

The Value of Money in the Eighteenth Century

In the seventeenth and eighteenth centuries, monetary values in Nantucket records were expressed in terms of English pounds, shillings, and pence. A pound sterling (£) was equal to twenty shillings (s), and a shilling was equal to twelve pence (d). Thus, £10–12–2 signifies ten pounds, twelve shillings and two pence.

There was considerable inflation in the eighteenth century. A measure of this inflation is demonstrated by the appraised value of the *same* silver tankard in the inventories of successive generations of the Swain family:

1718	£12–10–00
1737	21–00–00
1744	61–00–00

In 1750, "old tenor" money was revalued by dividing by a factor of seven and a half. However, most Nantucket records continued to make valuations in old tenor right up to the Revolutionary War.

THE DECORATIVE ARTS AND CRAFTS OF NANTUCKET

1. Introduction

This book strives to give a broad and accurate picture of what people had in and around their homes in Nantucket, a small sandspit of an island thirty miles out in the Atlantic Ocean off the coast of Massachusetts. The focus is on the decorative arts and the crafts of the eighteenth and nineteenth centuries, although twentieth-century objects are included. While the book emphasizes things made by Nantucketers, it also encompasses things made elsewhere with an island history.

Chapter 2, "At Home in Nantucket: Life-Styles, 1700–1900," gives the social background and framework for the rest of the book and provides a basis for tying together the material culture and the history of the island. We sketch nine representative life-styles: six of the eighteenth century, two of the nineteenth century; and one, "The Summer Resident," represents an important aspect of the twentieth century. Throughout the book are thumbnail sketches of Nantucketers associated with specific artifacts.

Chapters 3 through 8 deal primarily with those household furnishings usually classified as the decorative arts: furniture, boxes, woodenware, textiles, ceramics and glass, silver, and other metals. Chapters 9 and 10 describe the characteristic Nantucket crafts of scrimshaw and lightship baskets. Chapter 11, "Carvings and Drawings," includes weather vanes, carvings of whales and animals, decoys and gravestones, drawings of family trees, hand-drawn maps, and drawings in whaling logs. Chapter 12, "Souvenirs from Far-Away Places," tells of the astonishing array of things brought back to Nantucket by the whalers and other seamen from all over the world: sailors' valentines, boxes from China and Pitcairn Island, tapa cloth and war clubs from Fiji and Samoa, and an eighteenth-century doll depicting the French dauphin.

We should state briefly what we do *not* attempt to do in this book. It is not a history of Nantucket, at least not a history in the conventional sense of the word. Many books have been written on various phases of the island's history,[1] and more will no doubt be written in the future. Such "standards" as Obed Macy's *The History of Nantucket,*[2] first published in 1835, and Alexander Starbuck's book of the same name, first published in 1924,[3] are indispensable to an understanding of the island's past. Macy and Starbuck may be updated, revised and supplemented, but they have never been superseded.

We deal only peripherally with the architecture of Nantucket, primarily in relation to furnishings. Clay Lancaster's *The Architecture of Historic Nantucket* (New York, 1972), is the most comprehensive book in the field. Other valuable books on this topic include:

Everett U. Crosby, *Ninety Five Per Cent Perfect* (Nantucket, 1953)
Henry Chandlee Forman, *Early Nantucket and Its Whale Houses* (New York, 1966)
George Allen Fowlkes, *A Mirror of Nantucket, An Architectural History of the Island* (Nantucket, 1959)

Robert diCurcio's *Art on Nantucket* (Nantucket, 1982) chronicles the painters and paintings of the island.

Although today Nantucket is a thriving resort (some would say *too* thriving), with the pleasures, aches, and pains of other New England coastal resort areas, we believe it is fair to say that in the past the island was not really a microcosm of an eastern seaboard town of America. Nantucket was different, even from its nearby neighbors, Martha's Vineyard and Cape Cod. Visitors to the island in the eighteenth and nineteenth centuries often spoke of this difference. Obed Macy put it this way:

> A community situated like that of Nantucket, and pursuing a business almost as insulated as their location, must have some peculiarities. Their manners and customs have often been noticed by travelers, and, it may be, placed in a more striking contrast with those of the continent than comports with strict truth.[5]

Crèvecoeur,[6] in his classic *Letters from an American Farmer,* first published in England in 1782, pictured Nantucket as a quiet, idyllic, set-apart Eden, "this happy settlement":[7]

> Would you believe that a sandy spot, of about twenty-three thousand acres, affording neither stones nor timber, meadows nor arable, yet can boast of an handsome town, consisting of more than 500 houses, should possess above 200 sail of vessels, constantly employ upwards of 2000 seamen, feed more than 15,000 sheep, 500 cows, 200 horses; and has several citizens worth 20,000£ sterling![8]

Benjamin Franklin, writing to his sister, Mrs. James McCom, *knew* his Nantucket relatives were different:

> *Phila. Aug. 3, 1789*
>
> Dear Sister: I think our Family were always subject to being a little Miffy. By the way, is our Relationship in Nantucket quite worn out? I have met with none from there of late years who were disposed to be acquainted with me except Captain Timothy Foulger. They are wonderfully shy. But I admire their honest plainness of speech. About a year ago I invited two of them to dine with me. Their answer was, that they would, if they could not do better. I suppose they did better, for I never saw them afterwards and so had no opportunity of showing my Miff if I had one.[9]

John James Audubon, soon after an 1840 visit to Nantucket to sell copies of his famous work, *The Birds of America,* wrote his wife:

> My visit to Nantucket was perhaps a fruitful one, in as much I have procured 18 names while there and now have 20 subscribers on that *truly curious island.*[10] [Our italics].

Although part of Nantucket's difference in the past was certainly due to its isolation (even today a winter storm can cut the island off from the mainland for two or three days), the essential difference was the result of two factors, whaling and Quakerism. Both started about the same time—whaling about 1690 and Quakerism formally in 1708—and both ended about the same time, in the last third of the nineteenth century.

Brief sketches of Nantucket whaling and Quakerism will suggest why both of these influences were crucially important in forming the character of the island and the artifacts made and used there.

Whaling[11]

The economic emphasis of Nantucket in the seventeenth century was not whaling, but the raising of sheep and the production of wool. Even before the first European settlers arrived in 1659, the island had been used as pastureland by Thomas Mayhew and others from Martha's Vineyard. Although the first generation of Nantucketers subsisted on sheep raising, it soon became obvious that the sandy glacial soil would not allow enough farming to support a large population. The English Woolens Act of 1699, which curtailed cloth manufacture in America, was an additional incentive to find other ways to earn a living.

As early as 1672 the town voted to grant land and sheep commons to encourage men to come to the island to develop whaling and codfishing,[12] although whaling did not become an organized activity until about 1690. By the first quarter of the eighteenth century, whaling had become a thriving industry, and for a hundred years, from 1725 to 1825, Nantucket was the leading whaling port in America, and eventually, the world.

Prior to 1775, the whaling trade was an important source of income, not only for Nantucket, but for the colonial Northeast. A measure of its importance can be gleaned from colonial export statistics which show that between 1768 and 1772, the five-year period for which records of colonial trade are most complete, whaling products (whale oil and spermaceti candles) accounted for 15 percent of all sterling earned from direct exports from New England. Whale oil exports to Great Britain add up to almost two-thirds of the total, the remainder being spermaceti candles and whale oil to the West Indies and southern Europe.[13] Since Nantucket represented at least half of the total whaling trade in America,[14] it means that the island whalers were generating about 8 percent of the *total* export income from New England to all areas during the 1768–1772 period.

The maritime tradition of whaling and fishing surely had an effect on how Nantucketers built their houses and what they put in them.[15] Houses tended to be snug, with shiplike storage places and steep back stairs with rope handholds. Furniture was compact and simple and often multipurpose.

Whaling gave men from the island extraordinarily extensive contacts overseas. By 1740, Nantucketers knew the whole coast of America from Labrador to the Caribbean.[16] By 1775, they had traveled the coasts of South America and Africa,[17] and sold their precious whale oil and whalebone in Boston and Philadelphia and London. After the Revolutionary War, when the Pacific Ocean was opened up to whaling, vast new parts of the globe were seen and experienced by Nantucket whalers. They were true internationalists. Mixed with locally made furnishings were English furniture and furniture from Newport and Boston, dinner services from China, tapa cloth from South Sea islands, and whalebone swifts, all of which gave a cosmopolitan and sometimes exotic look to the interiors of Nantucket houses.

Nantucket was a one-industry town. There was no backcountry to encourage other trades besides whaling as there was in the mainland ports of Boston and Salem and Providence. Whaling, with all its support activities of cooperage, ropewalks, candle making and so on, was the town's and the island's only real business.

For over a century and a half, whaling was the lifeblood of Nantucket. When the last whaler, the bark *Oak,* William B. Thompson, master, sailed from the island on November 16, 1869, for the Pacific Ocean,[18] it was indeed the end of an era.

Whaling died rather quickly in Nantucket. The periods of the French and Indian War, the Revolution, and the War of 1812 all saw drastic cutbacks in whaling, but Nantucket made quick recoveries from these upheavals. The final decline of Nantucket whaling became evident in the late 1820s and in the 1830s when the larger whaleships needed for the long Pacific voyages could no longer sail over the bar that barricaded the Nantucket harbor. The ingenious "camel,"[19] a floating drydock, helped ferry the heavier vessels in and out of the harbor in the early 1840s, but it couldn't stop the inevitable. New Bedford, with a deep-water harbor that could handle the largest whaleships, took over from Nantucket as the leading whaling port after 1825. The great fire of 1846, which destroyed the wharves and the entire business district of the town, was the beginning of the end of Nantucket as a whaling port; a second blow came three years later, in 1849, when more than 600 men (from a population of about 9,000) left Nantucket for the gold fields of California.[20] The discovery of oil in Pennsylvania and the invention of oil refining about the time of the Civil War sounded the death knell of whaling, even though it continued (and continues) in the twentieth century on a very different basis.

The effect of all this on the island was calamitous. From a population of almost 10,000 in the early 1840s, the town shrank to 3200 people by 1875.[21] The average house was by that time worth $300 to $400. Moor's End, the redbrick mansion on Pleasant Street, built for Jared Coffin in 1829, was sold in 1867 for $2350 and resold for the same amount in 1873. That Nantucket real estate was depressed throughout the rest of the nineteenth century is reflected in the fact that Moor's End changed hands again in 1899 for $2500.[22] This is a property that was sold in 1986 for $3,400,000.

It wasn't until Nantucket was discovered and promoted in the 1870s and 1880s as a summer resort that the town and the island began slowly to come back. The fact that no other industry, such as large-scale textile manufacture, had come after the Civil War to replace whaling undoubtedly saved hundreds of the town's early houses. It was too expensive to tear them down and build new ones. People "made do" in the old houses. Some were modernized, some were renovated and turned into stores and inns and changed beyond recognition, but many survived, virtually intact. Today there are 800 houses on Nantucket built before the Civil War.[23]

The Quakers

A powerful motive of the first Nantucket settlers was freedom, political and religious. The Massachusetts Puritans, who also came to America in the name of religious freedom, had, from the beginning, been intolerant of any religious view that varied from their own. People of different religions and those who felt no need of any religion at all began to chafe under the rule of the Puritan majority. Thomas Macy was one such man. He did not leave his home in Salisbury, Massachusetts, for economic reasons; indeed, with 1000 acres of land, a good house, and "considerable stock,"[24] he seemed to have had every reason for staying put. In 1659 Macy was arrested, put on trial and fined thirty shillings and "admonished by the Governo'r"[25] for what the Puritans had deemed an illegal activity: giving shelter to four Quakers who stopped at his house to get out of a rainstorm. Soon afterwards Macy left Salisbury with his family for an unknown future in Nantucket. There is no evidence that Macy was a Quaker or even a Quaker sympathizer, but it is clear that he was driven away by the stifling authoritarian climate of the time.

Macy's reason for leaving the mainland for an isolated island home may be more dramatic than most, but there is evidence[26] that others of the first settlers of Nantucket were uncomfortable with the heavy-handed rule of the Puritans and meant to distance themselves from it. The island was their refuge.

There does not seem to have been any organized religious group in the Nantucket English community in the seventeenth century. Obed Macy remarks that "during the first fifty years after the settlement, the people were mostly Baptists; there were some Presbyterians, a few of the Society of Friends."[27] There were, no doubt, religious services of some kind held on Sundays at that time, probably in homes. Sunday, or First Day, was a day set apart in Nantucket as it was in the rest of New England.[28]

The first religious group to formally organize in Nantucket was the Society of Friends, called Quakers. The founding of the first Quaker Meeting in 1708 was a direct outgrowth of the missionary visits of Friends from off-island. Among others, Thomas Chalkley, a Quaker missionary-merchant from Philadelphia, visited the island twice, in 1693 and again in 1704. John Richardson, a well-known English Friend, came in 1701. Between 1704 and 1708 a number of other Friends visited Nantucket from Rhode Island, Long Island, Philadelphia, and England.[29]

Mary (Coffin) Starbuck, with her husband, Nathaniel, and her blacksmith son, Nathaniel, led the Quaker movement in Nantucket. At a time when women were second-class citizens, the position of Mary Starbuck (1645–1717) was truly remarkable. She was widely recognized as a leading person on the island. A contemporary, John Richardson, wrote of her as "Mary Starbuck, who the islanders esteemed as a Judge among them for little of Moment was done without her, as I understood."[30] Richardson called her "the great woman." A later source states that although her husband, Nathaniel Starbuck, was "a man of no mean parts, she far exceeded him in soundness of judgment, clearness of understanding, and in the elegant and natural way of expressing herself."[31]

It is perhaps difficult for us today to realize the depth of religious fervor that existed at the time of the first Friends meetings in Nantucket. Richardson wrote of a meeting in "Parliament House," Mary Starbuck's home, at which Mary

> spoke trembling . . . Then she arose, and I observed that she and as many as could well be seen, were wet with Tears from their Faces to the fore-skirts of their Garments and the floor was as though there was a Shower of Rain upon it.[32]

Quakerism, in its beginnings in Massachusetts in the 1650s,[33] was a radical departure from mainstream Puritan thought. In contrast to the quiet, inward-looking Friends of the eighteenth century, the first generation of Quakers in the seventeenth century were activists; they fought the established church, holding its clergy in scorn, they practiced civil disobedience; the men refused to remove their hats in church or in the presence of rank, and they refused to take oaths.[34] The Quaker belief in the "Inner Light" and in "that of God in all men," and their belief that all could experience God directly without the help and guidance of priests and ministers appealed to many, but it was a doctrine that was a threat to the established church. And, of course, the Quaker resistance to paying any kind of church taxes was a problem for the authorities.

The Puritan-dominated government of Massachusetts took the strongest measures to suppress Quakerism. Quakers' ears were cropped, Quakers were flogged out of towns, dozens were jailed, and four were hanged.[35] The most famous case was that of Mary Dyer, who was hanged on Boston Common because she returned to Boston after she had been banished from that town for her Quaker beliefs. It wasn't until 1661, when Charles II, newly restored to the English throne, sent a strong letter to the Massachusetts authorities ordering all future trials of Quakers to be transferred to courts in England,[36] that the pressure was let up on Friends in the colony. They were still harassed, but no more were sent to the gallows and many were released from prison.

Quakerism began to spread into rural areas and small towns of New England, and by the 1670s Rhode Island, already liberal in its tolerance of different religions, had enough members of the Society of Friends to elect one of their own as Governor and to control the provincial government. By the beginning of the eighteenth century, the Quakers were pretty much accepted all over New England, even by the establishment in Massachusetts.[37]

The Nantucket Friends Meeting, formed in 1708 with Mary Starbuck's son Nathaniel as clerk, obviously filled a need, for the Meeting grew rapidly. In a forty-year period, it outgrew a series of meetinghouses and expansions. By the late 1750s, the Friends' meetinghouse at the corner of Pleasant and Main Streets served 1500 persons, 835 women and 665 men, and in 1762 the great meetinghouse was enlarged again, the Quaker community on the island having grown to almost 2400 persons.[38]

That was the peak of Quakerism in Nantucket. Quakers were strong politically and financially. Their devotion to simplicity and their strict adherence to traditional ways influenced architecture, home furnishings, clothing, and social behavior.

The Revolutionary War and the War of 1812 were disastrous to Nantucket as a community and particularly to Quakerism. The Friends' long-standing and unyielding stance against war led them to read out of the Meeting dozens of Friends who had supported and/or participated in the American cause. To the agonizing trials of wartime was later added the Hicksite division in Quakerism,[39] which had a devastating effect on American Quakerism in general. The Nantucket Meeting broke into two factions, with the older Quakers unable to accommodate to changing times. After 1830 Quakerism in Nantucket started to fall apart rapidly. Almost every month the Meeting recorded the disownment of members for one reason or another. Common reasons were marrying out of the Meeting (that is, a Friend marrying a non-Friend) and members' nonattendance at meetings. By the 1840s the number of Friends on the island had shrunk drastically. By the late 1860s there were only a few Quakers, and by 1900 it was said none were left. It was not until the 1930s that an informal Friends Meeting was reestablished on the island.

However, the Quaker heritage remained strong, even in the Victorian era. Most of the larger Main Street houses of the 1830s and 1840s probably continued to be more simply furnished than comparable houses on the mainland, and the exteriors of the houses had a Quaker simplicity. It was only in the two white-columned Hadwen mansions built in the 1840s on Main Street opposite the Three Bricks, and the later Victorian houses of Charles Robinson on Broad and Fair Streets, that Nantucket really threw off the Quaker influence.

Quakerism, particularly in the eighteenth

century, produced a kind of egalitarianism in Nantucket. Although, as will be seen in Chapter 2, the probate records indicate a wide spread in the wealth of individuals, there was a remarkable homogeneity in the architecture of the island and in life-styles. Phebe Folger's 1797 watercolor drawings depicting the town[40] indicate that the overwhelming majority of the houses were of the kind we now label "the typical Nantucket house," a two-and-a-half-story house with the entry usually at one side of the front.[41] We know also from the inventories of the eighteenth century that the household furnishings of the rich did not differ radically from those of their less-affluent neighbors.

Part of this homogeneity was due to intermarriage. It was said that everyone on Nantucket was related to everyone else. Everyone outside the immediate family was a "cousin" or "aunt" or "uncle." For more than a century and a half, from 1660 to 1830, Nantucket was a closed community, united in one main economy, whaling, and dominated by one religious group, the Society of Friends.

Quakers and the Decorative Arts

The early Quakers, with their intense spiritual concerns, were distrustful of the arts, placing severe limitations on all forms of aesthetic expression. Music and the theater were banned. Simplicity was stressed in dress, home furnishings, and architecture. Specific advice was given on household decor:

> As to chests of drawers, they ought to be plain and of one color, without swelling works.
>
> As to tables and chairs, they ought to be all made plain, without carving, keeping out of all new fashions as they come up, and to keep to the fashion that is serviceable.
>
> And as to making great mouldings one above another about press-beds and clock-cases, etc, they ought to be avoided, only what is decent according to Truth.
>
> So that all furniture and wainscoating should be all plain and of one color.[42]

In Philadelphia and Newport many of the leading craftsmen were "of the Friendly persuasion." Philadelphia cabinetmakers William Savery, Thomas Affleck, John Letchworth, and David Evans were Quakers, as were the Richardsons, the leading silversmiths. The now-celebrated cabinetmakers of Newport, the Townsends and the Goddards, were Quakers.

The eighteenth century saw a progressive increase in the wealth of the Quaker communities of Philadelphia and Newport. The furnishings supplied by Quaker craftsmen became more "elegant" with time, showing a drift away from absolute simplicity. In 1764, a Chester County, Pennsylvania Friend complained that the Quakers had discarded much of their earlier simplicity and that "many of the Society were grown rich; that wearing of fine costly garments and with fashionable furniture, silver watches became customary with many."[43]

Nantucket Quakers were probably more conservative than Quakers of Philadelphia and Newport. This is demonstrated by the comparative plainness of the surviving Nantucket houses and furnishings. This did not mean that these houses were poorly furnished. The inventories indicate that eighteenth-century Nantucket Quakers had fine things in their homes, expensive furniture, textiles, and silver.

The attitude of the more affluent Friends of the eighteenth century, both on and off the island of Nantucket, is well expressed by a 1738 letter of John Reynell of Philadelphia, ordering furnishings from London. He requested: "a Handsome plain looking glass . . . and 2 raised Japan'd Black Corner Cubbards, no Red in 'em, of the best sort but Plain." Frederick Tolles, a Quaker historian, felt that the letter of John

Reynell summed up the whole concept of "The Quaker Esthetic," saying: "In that phrase—'of the best sort but Plain'—lies the Quaker merchants' practical resolution of the conflict between his Quaker instincts and his sense of his status in society."[44]

Regional Characteristics

Because of the conservative predilection of most Nantucketers, Quakers and non-Quakers, particularly in the eighteenth and early nineteenth centuries, their home furnishings *were* often understated, sometimes severely simple. Although this simplicity in furnishings could be seen as evidence of poverty, we believe that simplicity and functionality were matters of choice for Nantucketers of the time, a direct result of maritime tradition and Quaker preferences. Of course, simplicity does not necessarily equate with dullness. The best of these simple pieces reflect the bare, austere beauty of the island itself.

However, one must be careful not to carry this idea of a Nantucket plain style too far. By the middle of the eighteenth century quite a few Nantucketers had the resources to own the best of personal and home furnishings in the latest style. The rich variety of textiles in the inventories and the account books, the fact that men had wigs, silver and gold breeches' buttons, silver shoe buckles, the number of high chests of drawers, tall clocks, and fine desks in the inventories, all suggest a high standard of living. Nantucketers may have been isolated and insular, but they knew what was going on in Boston and Philadelphia and London.

As early as the first quarter of the eighteenth century, islanders like Jethro Coffin's wife, Mary, and Captain Stephen Greenleaf had their portraits painted by the Boston artist known today as the Pollard Painter.[45] Both were magnificently costumed. In 1764, Captain Timothy Folger, Benjamin Franklin's cousin, mentioned in his letter on page 2, was painted by John Singleton Copley. The portrait (Figure 1 illustrates Nantucket artist George Gardner Fish's 1876 copy) shows an urbane, self-assured man with a white wig, a silk neckerchief and a rich plum-colored coat and waistcoat.

During the eighteenth and early nineteenth centuries, the most characteristic furniture form made on Nantucket was a series of re-

Figure 1. Timothy Folger, by George Gardner Fish, copied from the original painting by John Singleton Copley. Signed lower left: "J. S. Copley, Pinx. 1766 / Copy by G. G. Fish, 1876." (Copley actually painted the original in 1764.) Oil on canvas, 50 1/2 x 40 3/4 in. (128.3 x 103.5 cm.). (*NHA*).

lated small tables and candlestands. Almost all have two- or three-piece tops. Four of these tables are illustrated in Chapter 3. Several dozen are known to have been made, many of which are still on the island. Windsor chairs and four-back (often called ladder-back) side chairs made in the eighteenth century are local variations of well-known themes. In the folk crafts, sailor-made furniture of the eighteenth and nineteenth centuries was a Nantucket specialty; furniture and boxes inlaid with whalebone, whale ivory, and exotic woods; sea chests with elaborately woven becket-handles. The Nantucket basket is a unique form of the ancient craft of basketry which has long flourished on the island. The words scrimshaw and Nantucket are almost synonymous, although scrimshaw was never limited to Nantucket sailors, or for that matter, even to American sailors. Scrimshaw was truly international. However, because of the extent of Nantucket's involvement in whaling, the scrimshaw produced by Nantucketers is particularly significant.

Other regional characteristics will be pointed out at appropriate places in the book. However, we feel that the whole body of decorative arts and crafts produced on Nantucket, especially in that unselfconscious time before the onslaught of twentieth-century tourism, has the flavor, the character, and the mark of the island.

2. At Home in Nantucket: Life-styles, 1700–1900

Objects divorced from their cultural context become only things—at best, works of art, more often, curiosities. Decorative art and craft objects are enriched and enhanced by knowing where and when they were made, what their use was, and in what kind of environment they existed.

This chapter seeks to give a background for Nantucket's arts and crafts by depicting, however sketchily, a sampling of nine representative life-styles to show how individuals lived in changing times and circumstances, and to evince the variety, and sometimes the complexity, of their lives and their material possessions. The nine life-styles include supplemental material which elaborates and expands certain aspects of the accounts. For example, in "An Indian Weaver: Jeremy Netowa," we describe his work and the things he owned and we also note the passing of the Nantucket Indians. In "Living in a Typical Nantucket House: Peter F. Coffin," we illustrate the island practice of having more than one family making use of a single dwelling by including evidence from the will of Francis Joy.

Certainly, the nineteenth century is more easily accessible than the seventeenth or eighteenth centuries. Many of Nantucket's nineteenth-century furnishings are still on the island today, some in their original houses. We have more sources of information for furnishings and life-styles of the nineteenth century than of the earlier centuries. Nantucket, for example, did not have a newspaper until 1816 when the *Nantucket Gazette* was first published, and although it ceased publication in 1817, *The Nantucket Inquirer,* the forerunner of today's *Inquirer & Mirror,* began publication on June 23, 1821. However, we feel it *is* possible to develop a picture of how people lived on Nantucket in the late seventeenth and eighteenth centuries and how their houses were furnished, although the picture is no doubt distorted by our twentieth-century prejudices and our imperfect knowledge of the past. By studying the existing early houses of the island, the surviving furnishings, probate and other court records, wills, tradesmen's account books, diaries, and printed historical accounts, we can begin to comprehend and understand these life-styles that seem so different from those of the late twentieth century.

Just how different these life-styles were has to be recalled. Consider living in an early Nantucket house: drafty in the winter, with no central heat, no electricity for cooking or heating or lighting or the refrigeration of food; no running water for bathing, for the kitchen, for the toilet; where most of the clothing, the bedding materials, towels, napkins, and tablecloths had to be handwoven and handmade; where the only source of warmth for the house and heat for cooking was the fireplace, which had to be supplied with scarce and expensive firewood, usually from the mainland. (The early fireplaces never had dampers, which meant that when there was no fire burning all the heat escaped up the chimney, chilling the room to near outside temperatures.) One could go on and cite the lack of good roads on the island and the dependence on sailing vessels to get people and materials on and off the island.

Few of us today *have* to grow our own food, or to make our own clothes, or shiver in unheated rooms. The Steamship Authority delivers us (and our automobiles) to the mainland in two and a half hours and an airplane gets us to Hyannis in twenty minutes. However, there is an island mentality, even today. There is a literal sense of isolation, a sense of separateness from the outside world, a feeling that must have been much more intense in the first two hundred years of the island's history.

The Colonial Revival

Our view of the past has long been idealized and sentimentalized by the Colonial Revival movement, a movement that still has a powerful effect on the mores of the late twentieth century. When even brain surgeons and computer engineers come home to new "colonial" homes with "country" or "colonial" interiors and furniture, we know we are dealing with a potent cultural force.

Beginning in the last part of the nineteenth century, there was a widespread interest in the old houses of America and in the furnishings of the colonial era. That this movement was based more on romantic nostalgia than on historical fact is well recognized by historians, museum curators, and independent scholars.

First, there is the difficulty with the word *colonial.* Although the American colonies ceased to be a part of England after the Declaration of Independence in 1776, "colonial" is often extended to describe Federal houses and furnishings of the late eighteenth and early nineteenth centuries, and even Empire furnishings of the second quarter of the nineteenth century. The word colonial was, and still is, used with a lack of precision, fuzzily, to define not only things made in the seventeenth and the first three quarters of the eighteenth century in America, but also those objects made a half century or more *after* 1776.

The second problem involves the correct furnishings of homes and rooms of the colonial period. Many of the period rooms and houses in local museums and historical societies have been furnished with a mixture of things that are often entirely out of period: nineteenth-century ball-top andirons and Sandwich lamps, twentieth-century oriental carpets, nineteenth- and twentieth-century ceramics, and so on. The problem is twofold. There is sometimes a lack of knowledge of what should go into a seventeenth- or eighteenth-century house, and there is the simple lack of appropriate furnishings. There are historical houses open to the public furnished with the wrong things simply because that is all that is available.

The third reason that keeps us from furnishing seventeenth- and eighteenth-century rooms correctly involves more subtle factors: present-day taste and practical considerations. It is probably a fact that we would find correctly furnished rooms of this early period aesthetically dreadful, and, from a practical point of view, quite overcrowded. Early inventories, both on and off the island, indicate that such rooms as the parlor were often filled with furniture.[1] The *parlor* or *best room* of a late seventeenth- and early eighteenth-century Nantucket house was a multipurpose room, quite different from the seldom-used parlor of a Victorian house. It was one of the two main rooms on the first floor of a typical early house, the other often designated the *hall* or *keeping room.* The parlor contained the best furniture of the house and the parents' bedstead, often with hangings which could enclose the bed. It served as a room where company was entertained, and was often used for dining. The hall was furnished similarly to the parlor, usually with the second-best bed.

The six eighteenth-century Nantucketers we discuss in this chapter were of widely different social and economic stations. Five of the six men were in some way or other involved in whaling, underlining the importance of that activity in Nantucket. (A similar sampling of households in Suffolk County, Massachusetts, of the same period would show no involvement of any kind in whaling.[2])

In considering the nineteenth century, the room-by-room inventory of Peter F. Coffin, a ship captain, gives a good idea of what was in the kind of house that is often called "the typical Nantucket house." In the 1830s and early 1840s Nantucket prospered. Ralph Waldo Emerson lectured several times at the Nantucket Atheneum.[3] The building of the great mansions on Main Street in the 1830s and 1840s shows that Nantucket had entered fully into the mainstream of nineteenth-century America. All over town, the old houses were modernized with Greek Revival doorways on the outside and classical mantels added to paneled eighteenth-century fireplace walls inside. The most famous of the Main Street mansions were the "Three Bricks," built by Joseph Starbuck for his three sons in 1838. The Middle Brick, originally occupied by Matthew Starbuck and his family, is the only one of the three houses still in the family of the original owner. This fine house is in no way a museum. It has many of its original furnishings as well as those of successive owners, who have treated the house with love and respect, but who have not been afraid to leave their mark. This kind of house is much more of a rarity in this country than it is in Europe.

The chapter ends with a sketch of a summer resident of the early part of the twentieth century.

It was only in the twentieth century that serious efforts were made to rehabilitate and restore old houses and fill them with appropriate furnishings, a process that has accelerated since World War II. More and more people are becoming aware of Nantucket's heritage.

Tristram Coffin, 1685–1706

The first inventory in Book A, No. 1, of the *Probate Records of Nantucket County,* dated October 17, 1706,[4] is that of Tristram Coffin, great-grandson of Tristram Coffin, the first chief magistrate of the island. The first Tristram died October 2, 1681, three and a half years before the birth of his namesake, who was born April 26, 1685. When the latter died in 1706, at the age of twenty-one, he was married to Hannah Brown. They had no children.

Tristram was a young man of substance. The inventory of his household furnishings makes it clear he was involved in both farming and whaling. He owned a barn and a substantial number of farm animals: two heifers, two oxen, two steers, three cows, two calves, 238 sheep, and a horse. In the barn were 290 pounds of wool and six loads of hay. He was directly involved in whaling. He owned four harping irons (harpoons), two lances, a main warp, a new warp, and a drug. (A warp is a towline; a drug [drogue, drudge] is a block of wood or crossed planks fastened to a whale line that was used to check a whale in its strug-

Figure 2. The Jethro Coffin house, built in 1687, from a photograph of about 1920 before the house was restored.

gle to escape capture. The drug acts against the water exactly as a kite does against the wind.[5]) Coffin's inventory included fifty-one pounds of whalebone, valued at ten pence per pound.

Thus Tristram Coffin, who may have married Hannah Brown only a short time before his premature death, had settled into the kind of life-style that has long been characteristic of the island. A man made a living in a variety of ways, one of which almost always involved the sea. Tristram was a farmer and a whaler. His life varied seasonally, much in the manner of today's island carpenters and house painters, who drop these occupations on November first to become professional scallopers for the season.

We have no record as to whether Tristram owned a house. We do know he owned real estate which was divided between his wife and his three sisters.[6] Tristram's father, Peter Coffin (called sick Peter), had died in 1699 when Tristram was fourteen. Tristram probably continued to live in his father's house to the time of his own death. The house was located on the north shore of the island, just east of Capaum Pond, which in the eighteenth century had access to the sea. The house lots of Peter Coffin and his father, also named Peter, were located just east of the house lot of the original Tristram Coffin.[7]

The Peter Coffin house is long since gone from its original location. It was probably moved a mile or so east to the town of Sherborn, as were most of the other early houses. In 1795 the town of Sherborn was renamed Nantucket, so that the town, the county, and the island all had the same name.

In order to show the kind of house Tristram and his wife would have lived in, we illustrate the house of his uncle, Jethro Coffin, built in 1686 and still standing (Figure 2). It is owned by the Nantucket Historical Association and is

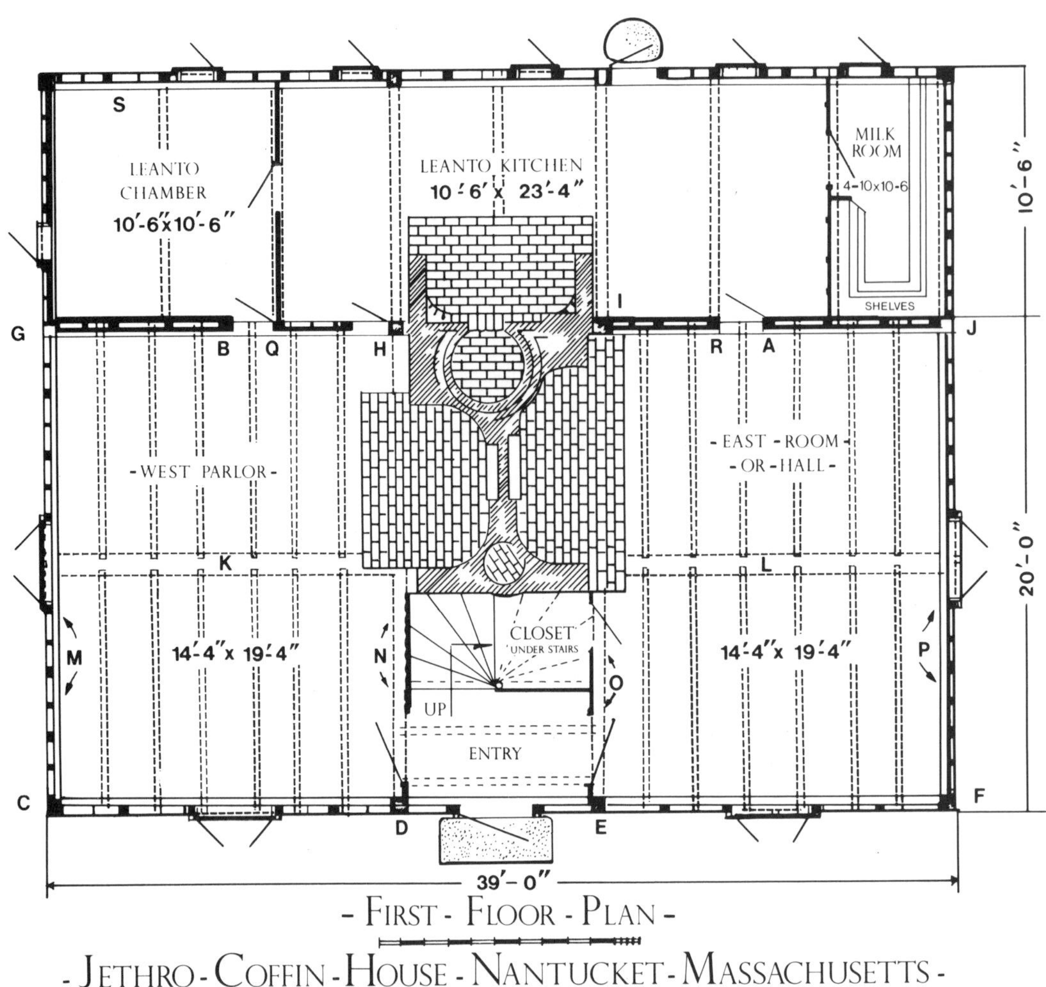

Figure 3. Floor plan drawn by Laura Stover from a 1927 drawing by Alfred F. Shurrocks. *(Original floor plan courtesy of The Society for the Preservation of New England Antiquities.)*

known as "The Oldest House." Facing due south, the Jethro Coffin house is a lean-to house, a story and a half on the front side, its back roof sloping down to a half story in the rear, with the first-floor rooms arranged around a large T-shaped chimney (Figure 3).[8]

The most valuable things in Tristram's house were his textiles, particularly beds and bed furniture. In the eighteenth century the word *bed* had a different meaning than it has today. The bed was the mattress itself, which would have been filled with such materials as feathers, wool, and cotton ("flock"[9]) or straw.[10] The *bedstead* in the inventories was the wooden bedframe. Bedsteads were usually given a much lower value than beds and such bedding as bolsters, sheets, pillows, pillowcases, and bed hangings. Tristram's best bed and bolster were valued at nine pounds while his bedstead was valued at only ten shillings.

Tristram Coffin did not have much household furniture but, after all, he was only twenty-one, recently married, and without children. (We hope it is not too simplistic to note that people usually accumulate things as they grow older, and that, up to a point, the number of possessions tends to be a function of age.) His inventory lists a table, eight chairs, a trunk, and a great chair. Many Nantucket inventories of the eighteenth century list at least one great chair, an unupholstered four-back armchair.

Tristram owned three tablecloths. He and his wife ate from trenchers, small round wooden plates. Food was served at the table from pewter or wooden dishes. He owned two guns and a rapier, presumably inherited from his father. Perhaps because of the Quaker influence, there seem to be fewer guns in Nantucket inventories after about 1710 than there are in mainland inventories of the same time. The one outright luxury item in Tristram's inventory was a silver cup valued at two pounds, ten shillings.

Where did the furnishings in Tristram Coffin's house come from? Who made them? Some of the furniture would have been brought from the mainland, mostly from Boston and the Boston area, but much of the furniture may well have been made on the island. Most of the textiles in Coffin's house would have been woven on the island, although some of the finer pieces may have come from England. Nantucket had weavers from the beginning. Some were Indians, such as Jeremy Netowa, who will be discussed later in this chapter.

The ceramic wares used in Nantucket in the late seventeenth and early eighteenth centuries came mostly from New England, England, and Germany. Utilitarian redware pottery, with green, yellow, brown, or black glazes, was available from Charlestown, Massachusetts, where potters had been practicing their craft since the middle of the seventeenth century. Between 1700 and 1740 at least forty potters were active in Charlestown.[11] Brown Staffordshire salt-glazed stoneware and gray German salt-glazed stoneware were widely available in the Massachusetts Bay Colony.[12]

As far as we know, almost all of the pewter plates, bowls, porringers, and so on in Nantucket before the Revolutionary War were of English origin. No marked pieces of American pewter with a Nantucket association of this period have been located. Pewter spoons were made in Nantucket since spoon molds appear in inventories of the time.

The silver in Nantucket homes before 1725 seems to have been entirely of New England origin, usually Boston. We know of no pieces of English silver with a Nantucket provenance before 1775.

A Nantucket Blacksmith: Nathaniel Starbuck, Jr., 1668–1753

We know that much of the ironwork in Tristram Coffin's time was made by Nathaniel Starbuck, Jr., a blacksmith and merchant. Starbuck's account book of the period 1683–1738 gives an extraordinarily detailed record of his business transactions.[13] The 118-page account book has approximately 6500 entries. Some pages are missing and the bottoms of many pages are partly disintegrated, but even in its fragmented state, and taking into account the illegibility of a number of the entries, it is a fascinating social document.

From the account book we get the feel of everyday business in Nantucket in the late seventeenth and early eighteenth centuries. A blacksmith was an extremely important person in colonial America. In a preindustrial time he made tools and metal articles for the home and the farm. On Nantucket, he was essential to whaling.

A list of the things Nathaniel Starbuck made underlines his importance to the community. For the farmer he shod horses by the dozens; he made plowirons, pitchforks, shovels, hatchets, broadaxes, and chains. For house builders and furniture makers he sharpened nails, made spikes ("great nails"), "brads for barn floor," hand saws, door hinges, desk hinges, and lock hasps. For the home he made flesh forks, tongs, shears, trammels (adjustable potholders for the fireplace), spits, pot hooks, fire shovels, skillet frames, fire slices (a flat shovel for removing coals from ovens), gridirons, pressing irons. However, there is no evidence that Nathaniel Starbuck made either iron or brass pots, kettles or skillets. These items would probably have been imported from England, although the Saugus ironworks made iron pots and skillets in the seventeenth century. Starbuck lists a number of entries of "Legging a pot 2/–" (October 1699), that is, he added legs to an existing iron pot or repaired broken ones. He also made a "baile for a brass kittle" (noted on page ten of his account book).

He made calash boxes and box bands and rings for calash wheels. The calash was a one-horse box wagon that was the main form of land transportation for Nantucketers for the first 250 years of the island's modern history.

Whaling tools were an important part of Nathaniel Starbuck's business. There were many orders for these tools in the 1697–1710 period, showing the great upsurge of whaling activity at that time. He made harping irons, Spanish irons, lances, tow-iron shafts, blubber forks and blubber knives. He also made a number of shark hooks.

Nathaniel Starbuck was directly involved in whaling, as is indicated by a 1699 entry in the account book: "made a harping iron for our crew—06/06." He owned whaleboats, a whale house (1704), and a sloop. There are many entries over a long period of time recording his whaling activities. He seems to have sold his whale oil and whalebone in Boston. However, in 1720 one shipment of six barrels of oil was consigned through Boston directly to Richard Partridge of London.

Although there are many cash transactions mentioned in Starbuck's account book ("cash," "silver money," "pieces of eight"), the evidence is that Nantucket's was then primarily a barter economy. Starbuck received for his wares and services such things as old iron, wool, corn, hogs, barrels, knives, whale oil, whalebone, and sheep-commons shares. He traded goods for mowing and plowing and work for his house.

The account book suggests he may have made some furniture: "2 mo 1730—by an ovil table maple leave calerd [colored—stained?] 2/10/0"; "3 mo 1731—by making a pine desk for brother BS [Barnabas Starbuck] 1/5/0"; "6 mo 1708—a chest for Mary Starbuck 08/—"; "1707—a cubberd for Namasha."

He also bought furniture: "3 mo 1735—by an oak table made by Ramsdale—2/10/0." An undated entry on page forty-eight notes: "Richard Evans—a pair of hinges for a chest—02/06—making me a chest." Thus Starbuck identifies two early eighteenth-century Nantucket cabinetmakers, [Jonathan] Ramsdale and Richard Evans.

Nathaniel Starbuck's account book presents a side of his life that has been ignored by historians. Starbuck is in the history books because of his connection with the Quakers, and because he was town clerk, and clerk of the proprietors of the common and undivided lands. He was also, as mentioned earlier, the first clerk of the Society of Friends, the Quakers, and, with his famous mother, Mary Starbuck, was one of the founders of the Friends Meeting in Nantucket.[14] In his lifetime he saw this Friends Meeting grow from a handful of people to well over a thousand.

A few quotations from Starbuck's account book listing things other than his blacksmithing business include such items as:

> Oct 1697—The sloop—2 times up the harbor—16–00 [From the town up the inner harbor to Wauwinet.]
>
> 1703—money for building whaleboat—09–06
>
> 1707—To Dinah's robbing my house—01–00–00 [We leave it to the reader to guess what this entry meant. Starbuck's wife was named Dinah!]
>
> William Arnold—commissions of 28 lb. bone at Boston—00–02–09 (p. 74).

Page sixty notes a number of marriages Starbuck performed as town clerk in the period 1710–1716.

After 1717 the entries in Starbuck's account book are more concerned with general-store items than with blacksmithing. Mary Starbuck, Nathaniel's mother, had operated a store for the Indians of the island from 1683 to the time of her death in 1717. Nathaniel took over the business which continued until his death.

Nathaniel Starbuck was eighty-five when he died in 1753. The average life span of people in the English-speaking world at the time was only about thirty-five years. However, this average is distorted by the high mortality rate of infants and young children and the loss of women at the time of childbirth. Men who survived until manhood often lived long lives. Of the original proprietors who lived out their lives on the island, and whose birth dates are known, two lived into their seventies and seven into their eighties: Tristram Coffin, Sr., seventy-six; Thomas Macy, seventy; Richard Swain, eighty-one; Peter Coffin, eighty-nine; John Swain, eighty-two; Nathaniel Starbuck, Sr., eighty-four; James Coffin, eighty; Thomas Coleman, eighty-three; Edward Starbuck, eighty-six.

Women who survived the childbearing years could generally look forward to a relatively long life. Dinah (Coffin) Starbuck, Nathaniel's wife, died in 1750 at fifty-nine. Nathaniel's mother, Mary, was seventy-two when she died in 1717. Both women had borne ten children.

John Swain, 1633–1715

John Swain was one of the original proprietors of Nantucket and one of the largest landowners. It is said that he and his father, Richard Swain, also a proprietor, owned almost a third of the island.[15] All Nantucket Swains descend from John Swain and his wife, Mary Dyer. Swain's name appears a number of times in the early annals of the town. In 1673 he was named a selectman and he was involved in negotiations with the Indians in matters of land disputes.[16]

During the first twenty-five years after the island was settled, John Swain, a farmer, lived on one of the original proprietors' house lots north of Hummock Pond, just east of Trott's Swamp.[17] In 1680 he purchased land in Polpis from the Indian sachem Wauwinet, the title of which was confirmed in 1684 and 1686.[18] In about 1687 Swain built a house in Polpis where he lived the rest of his life.[19] His inventory shows that, in addition to his house valued at forty pounds, he had a barn, malt house, and a "long house." His move to Polpis was made because of the good farmland in that part of the island. Where the original house lots were laid out by the proprietors in the Hummock Pond area and north, the meadowlands were satisfactory for grazing, but Swain, after his first quarter of a century on the island, obviously felt that the Polpis area was better for his type of farming.

The inventory of Swain's house, like others of the time in the probate records, was not done on a room-by-room basis, which makes it impossible to know in which rooms the furnishings were placed. However, it is feasible to make some reasonable guesses, since in most cases the authors of the inventories clearly listed the contents of one room before going on to the next. Often, as in the case of Swain's inventory, silver, being valuable and scarce, was listed at the beginning of the inventory. He owned a silver tankard valued at twelve pounds, a silver cup at twenty-five shillings, and a spoon at ten shillings. In Chapter 7, "Silver," we trace the descent of some of John Swain's silver down through later generations of the family.

The configuration of the Polpis house at the time of John Swain's death is not known. If we assume that his house was typical of the early houses of the island, with a floor plan similar to that of the Jethro Coffin house built at about the same time (Figure 3), the furnishings in the inventory fit reasonably well into the plan of a center-chimney house with a parlor on one side, a hall on the other, and a lean-to kitchen at the rear, with a small milk room at one end. A few of the inventory items do not fit neatly into such an arrangement, but, taking into account the fact that the whole probate procedure was quite casual at the time in Nantucket, the following is, we feel, a reasonable conjecture as to the contents of the rooms of John Swain's house:

The Parlor

The parlor would have contained a large fireplace and some of the best furnishings in the house. The "eight leather chairs at 12s" were probably the sturdy Boston-type straight chairs with turned front legs and leather-covered seats and backs.[20] There were sixteen more chairs listed on the next line of the inventory, but, since there were none listed in the other rooms of the house, we assume that the inventory takers simply listed the total for the house in one place. At that time chairs were not stored around tables, or in the middle of the room as we do today, but were lined up along a wall, no doubt to keep the central space available. The parlor also contained a "Chest Draws 45s," a "Closse stool 20s" (a stool fitted with a chamber pot), a "Case 12s," "Chest 4s," a "Looking glass 16s," "hat brush 2s," a "bedstead 10s," "a large table 15s," a "Sugar box 1s," "Two hour glasses 6d," another "Chest Draws 30s," a "Cubberd 15s" and a "bible 6s." Around and in the parlor fireplace was a "Warming pan 4s," "andirons 6s, tongs and firepan 3s," and a "pair of bellows 1s."

The Kitchen

The lean-to kitchen fireplace housed a "back iron 20s," two trammels and a "pair of large andirons 15s." Cooking equipment included a "kettle 10s," "a large Kettel 15s," a "pot 10s," a "Spit 3s," "frying pan 6d," "large brass kettle 45s," two skillets, a "Small brass kettle 3s, one larger 5s," a "Chafing dish 10s," a "Skimmer 6d," and a "Fork 1s." The latter was no doubt a wrought-iron flesh fork of the kind made by Nathaniel Starbuck. In the kitchen was "a small table 3s" and a "table frame 4s." The table frame, with a board top, was a long narrow table, used for dining, which could be dismantled for easy storage. Probably some of the above-mentioned sixteen chairs would have been used in the kitchen.

The Milk Room

The small room off the lean-to kitchen, called a milk room, buttery, or dairy, is where the dairy products were processed. Swain's milk room contained "2 pails 1/6, cheesefat 2s, keeler 1s, 4 dishes 2/6, a large churn 5s, one small 2s, 3 treys 5s, tub 1/6."

The Hall

The other principal room of the house, the hall, contained two beds, the household linens, a number of pieces of ceramic ware, pewter, and a "brass candlestick and Snuffer 8s." The ceramic wares included "a Small Earthen pot

Figure 4. Broad brimmed pewter platter, seventeenth century, unmarked. Diameter: 20³/8 in. (51.8 cm.). (*NHA*).

1s," "3 plates Earthen 1/6, 3 platters Earthen 3s, one Cheny [Chinese] platter 3s, 4 flowered ditto 8s." The pewter included "3 broad brimmed platters 21s [a broad brim is a characteristic of seventeenth-century pewter platters (Figure 4)], 3 narrow brimmed 15s, 4 basons 12s, 8 plates 16s, 2 porringers 3s, Small platter 2s, one Tankard 6s, quart pot 3s." Furniture in the hall were two bedsteads with beds and bolsters, "a white [unpainted] chest 6s," "one Large [?] Chest 5s," and a "fashionable table 15s." The item just before the "white chest" in the inventory was a "lether carpit 2s." Carpets were not used on floors in the early part of the eighteenth century but, as suggested by the inventory, were used as covers for chests or tables. The elegant eighteenth-century table carpet was a "Turkey" carpet, that colorful textile seen in contemporary paintings. It is unusual to find leather carpets in an inventory. Textiles in the hall included "towell 2/6, 6 table Cloths 24s, 3 sheets 30s, napkin 2/6, 3 coverlids 60s, one Smaller 16s, 1 bed rug 10s, 1 duch b[l]anket 16s, 4 b[l]ankets 20s."

John Swain's farm animals constituted a major part of his personal estate: "4 hoggs 12s," "1 brown cow 5 pounds white back 4 pounds 1 Red one 5 po, 1 Noding Cow 3 po–10s 1 black Steer 4 pound 1 bull 3 pound 1 small bull 20s," and "all the sheep is 340 at 8£ a score come to—136–00–00."

John Swain died in 1715 at the age of eighty-two; his will was not probated until 1718.

An Indian Weaver: Jeremy Netowa, ?–1728

It has been estimated that the total Indian population of Nantucket at the time of the arrival of the first white settlers in 1659 was about 3000.[21] When the settlers arrived, Indians had been living on Nantucket for ten and a half millennia, since about 8500 B.C.,[22] more than *thirty times* longer than that of the "modern" white settlement.

By seventeenth- and eighteenth-century standards, the Indians were not treated badly by the Englishmen who settled Nantucket. The land was purchased legally from the natives. There were no serious disturbances between the Indians and the white population on the island, in contrast to the massacres, wars, and bloody revenge raids that erupted so often all over the rest of New England in the seventeenth and eighteenth centuries.

The Indians lived apart from the white population, mostly in the eastern part of the island. Some no doubt kept completely apart, living the life-style of their ancestors. Some were laborers for the white community;[23] a number became expert whalers, carpenters, and weavers; and a few operated within the white economy, supplying needed services and goods, and, for all practical purposes, becoming members of the white community. On the other hand, some Indians were slaves, although the word *slave* does not often appear in eighteenth-century Nantucket records. The probate court records usually referred to them as "servants" or by such term as "the Indian boy." Nevertheless, they were slaves and not indentured servants. Indentured servants of the pre-Revolutionary period may have had no more freedom than slaves, but their indentures were for specific time periods and they were not treated as property in Nantucket probate inventories. The word *slave* is used occasionally in the Book of Records in the Registry of Deeds office. For example, in 1750 Ebenezer Gardner, "Gent.," stated:

> out of Good Will and Respect that I have & bear unto my Servant Pompy & in consideration of my own Mortality it being Appointed for all men once to Die for which Reasons & other Good & Lawful Reasons & Considerations me thereunto Moving I hereby Make And Ordain this Instrument of Manumission and hereby Discharge my old Servant Pompy from being a Slave.[24]

(The next section of this chapter, "Africa, A Free Negro," discusses the freeing of two slaves by William Swain in the 1750s.)

There are six Indian slaves shown in the pre-Revolutionary War Nantucket probate records. The inventory of Thomas Bunker, who died in 1721, listed two: "the Indian boy Peleg—£20–00–00" and "the Indian Girl Dorcas—£10–00–00."[25] The inventory of Joshua Sevolle, who died in 1735, a farmer who was John Swain's son-in-law, included an "Indian boy—£30–00–00."[26] Francis Coffin, mariner, who died in 1738, had "an Indian boy Joseph—£25–00–00";[27] and Daniel Folger, who died in 1748, owned "an indian Servant—£60–00–00."[28] The last Indian slave listed in a Nantucket inventory was that of Daniel Hussey (1751): "An Indian Boy James—£70–0–0." The fact that the slaves owned by Daniel Folger and Daniel Hussey were shown at much higher values than the Indians in earlier inventories reflects the value of money in the middle of the eighteenth century rather than increased worth. By the 1750s the pound sterling had perhaps only fifteen percent of the buying power it had had thirty years earlier.

One Nantucket Indian who operated fully in the white economy was Jeremy Netowa, who died in 1728, a weaver with a wife and three daughters. That only a few Indians did so operate is indicated by the fact that there are only ten detailed inventories of Indians in the Nantucket probate records of the eighteenth century. None of the ten was wealthy. The value of their estates ranged from twenty-eight pounds to two hundred thirty-nine pounds,[29] while Thomas Brock, the white Nantucketer whom we will discuss later in this chapter, had an estate of over 16,000 pounds when he died in 1750.

There are two Netowas (also spelled Notowa, Netowah, Nettawas, Natawar) in seventeenth-century records, which indicate that the Netowa family was well known to and respected by the English community. The first reference in the Nantucket court records is of a Sam Notowa who apparently acted as a police deputy for the whites:

> Nantucket ye 4th of January 1692 Resasumo and Tespagon were examined concerning whale bone lost by Capt Richard Gardner and Company and there being great suspision of thare stealing a part and consorting it. It was concluded they should be bond over to next court held in Sherborn and Sam Notowa engageth in the sum of four pounds for thare apprehension.[30]

There is a 1698 reference to a preacher "Quequenah, Netowa a man greatly esteemed by the English for his sobriety."[31]

Most of what we know about Jeremy Netowa, the weaver, comes from two sources: the inventory of his estate entered in the Nantucket Probate Court records on July 17, 1728,[32] and an account book owned by the Nantucket Historical Association, covering the activities of a weaver from 1711 to 1728, which we feel can be clearly attributed to Netowa.[33]

Netowa's probate inventory indicates that he lived in a simple one-room European-type house, open to the rafters, of the type found in Sconset (Siasconset). The width of the house was probably no more than ten or twelve feet, with a large fireplace on the north wall. The length of the building may have been fifteen to eighteen feet. The furnishings of Netowa's house were minimal: a bedstead, four chairs, a plank table, two chests, and a box, altogether valued at £1–13–08. The tools of Netowa's trade were valued more than his furniture:

Pr looms	£3–10–0
Warping bars	0–10–0
3 slays and harness	0–18–0
Quilling wheel 6/ and a Spezme [?] 2/6	0–8–6
a linnen wheel	0–1–0
a woolen Spinning wheel	0–6–0
	£5–13–6

Figure 5. An eighteenth-century hand-operated loom which had originally been set up by a professional weaver for multi-harness weaving to do fancy patterns. Later, perhaps in the nineteenth century, the loom was converted by a home weaver to make more simple patterns. As shown, the warp is incorrectly set up. Height: 83 in. (211 cm.), length: 67 in. (170 cm.), width: 66½ in. (169 cm.). (*NHA*).

The loom no doubt dominated the small living space, those of the time averaging five by five by six feet (Figure 5). The great open fireplace of Netowa's house was equipped with a trammel, pot hooks, two iron pots, an iron kettle, and a frying pan. There were bellows for fanning new fires or dying embers. The fireplace was the functional center of an eighteenth-century house, large or small, being used for cooking year-round and heat for those damp, often bone-chilling, winter months. Netowa's inventory mentions no eating tools, no spoons or wooden dishes or trenchers, only "a wooden tray—0–1–0." This might have been a hollowed-out eating trough. The whole family may have eaten out of the same vessel, with fingers or perhaps wooden spoons. The only other articles we associate with food and drink in Netowa's inventory are "a Jugg—0–36" and "3 Glass bottles—0–[?]–6." The only personal belongings of Netowa in the inventory are a pair of shoes. The item "his wollen Cloths—3–7–0" could indicate clothing, but more probably was unsold or undelivered cloth from his loom. Perhaps his clothes were buried on him.

Like most early Nantucketers, Indian or English, Netowa did some farming. He had a horse and a hog. His inventory included four and one-quarter bushels of wheat and two and one-quarter bushels of barley. He owned "a wooden harrow—0–2–0." The account book indicates that he did plowing for others, sometimes in March but more often in April. He usually received ten shillings per acre for plowing, but once he charged fifteen shillings for "plowing one acre of hard ground."

Netowa was involved in whaling. The account book records the purchase of "1 harping iron—00–08–06," and he received 00–17–11 "for carting bluber to Lot beach." The last item in his inventory tells us that Netowa made a whaling voyage in 1728, the year he died: "his voyage in the spring—11–13–2."

The forty-seven-page account book documents Netowa's production as a weaver in some detail. The accounts are by customer, of which there are about thirty. The kinds of fabrics included: wide cotton, striped, druggit (drugget, a thin woolen cloth), striped druggit, worsted, carsy (kersey, a coarse woolen cloth of twill weave), shirting, cotton and linen worsted, playn (plain) cloth, worsted shir(t)ing, cotton and linen, fine cloth, and striped worsted shirting. Most of the fabrics brought him six to nine pence per yard. One of the most expensive was striped worsted shirting. Netowa made four yards of this cloth for Robert Watson in 1719 at a cost of 00–13–01, or more than three shillings per yard. During the eighteen years covered by the account book, Netowa wove about 2200 yards of cloth. Most of this was woven during a fifteen-year period, 1712 to 1726. Although the account book shows entries for every month of the year, most of the weaving was done in the winter months, November through March.

In addition to the above-mentioned woven fabrics, the account book records that he made twenty-four coverlets and five cradle rugs. Rugs were used as bedcoverings at this time. The cradle rugs are always listed with a coverlet, suggesting that the woven cradle rugs were made to match a coverlet in color and weave. The twenty-four coverlets included seven checkered coverlets and two four-shuttle (four color) coverlets. No colors are mentioned for any coverlets in the account book. The price of a plain coverlet was ten to twelve shillings, and a four-shuttle coverlet sixteen shillings. The coverlet-cradle rug combinations were sixteen shillings.

We were able to trace some of Netowa's textiles in the probate inventories of his customers. These inventories give us a few hints as to what use these textiles were put. For example, the account book notes under the account of John Coleman:

> "July 6: 1714 to weaving 24 yards cotton and lining—00–12–00".

John Coleman died in 1715. When his will was probated the inventory included:

> "one pair of cotton and Linnen sheets—00–12–00".

John Coleman's pair of sheets would have used no more than half the twenty-four yards of cloth mentioned in Netowa's account book. The fact that both valuations were twelve shillings was probably a coincidence.

Netowa made a number of weavings for John Swain (1664–1739), son of the first John Swain, including:

Mar. 14, 1722	28 yds. playn	01–01–00
	13 yds. fine cloth	00–10–00
Dec. 1724	25 yds. cloth	00–16–08

Swain's 1739 inventory included several textiles that could have used Netowa's cloth: white and green bed curtains, sheets and tablecloths. Netowa made several coverlets and a cradle rug for him in the 1722–1724 period. Four of these coverlets appear in Swain's 1739 inventory, valued at a total of £15–5–0.

From 1722 to 1727, Netowa made 131½ yards of cloth for Thomas Clark. There are no specific items in Clark's 1741 inventory that can be traced directly to Netowa, but Clark's inventory included twelve sheets, eighteen pillowcases, eight tablecloths, eleven napkins, and twelve blankets. Netowa also made a few shirts and pairs of breeches for himself and others. His wife, Abigail, worked with him, according to the listings on page eighteen of the account book: "to my wife's spinning—01–00–07." There are several more entries on the same page for spinning in the years 1721–1726. The only entry that tells us how much wool was being spun is the one for 1726: "to spinning eight pounds yarn—00–16–00."

Netowa seems to have obtained much of his wool from his customers, wool that had been cleaned and carded. (There is no mention of cards in Netowa's inventory.) One entry says: "four pounds of black wool." In almost all cases the value of the wool was credited to the customer's account. There is an occasional mention of flax in the account book.

The one clear indulgence that shows up in the account book is tobacco. For example: "Feb 1713—to 14 pound tobackco—0–17–06." There is no mention of alcoholic beverages in the account book.

When Jeremy Netowa's estate was settled (July 17, 1728) and all his debts paid, there remained £12–07–00 plus his house valued at £33. Jeremy's widow received a third of the personal estate, or £4–02–04. His three daughters each received £2–14–10. In addition, the probate records note:

> The widow shall have the third part of the dwelling house during her life and the three daughters the rest and after the widow's Decease the whole shall be to the daughters equally.[34]

It would be easy to take the known facts about Jeremy Netowa and picture a kind of idyllic life for him, à la Crèvecoeur: the good Indian living peacefully with nature in tune with the ancient folkways of his forefathers, the good Indian living usefully in an Englishman's society, living simply but comfortably in an English-style house instead of a savage wigwam or Indian hut, one season blending into another, with spring plowing, the annual whaling voyage, and the endless pleasure of watching the cloth grow on the busy loom. Evenings were spent by him in front of the great fireplace watching the smoke drifting up from his pipe.

An idyllic picture. But does it jibe with *all* the facts? Does it jibe with the fact that the Indians were treated as natives or domesticated savages? At best they were tolerated as carpenters, whalers, weavers, laborers; at worst as drunken, thieving nuisances. Does it jibe with the fact that twelve Indians and not a single white man were executed on the Island of Nantucket before the Revolutionary War?[35]

The town fathers of Nantucket were quite specific in their aim of keeping the Indians in their place. On May 18, 1726, it was voted "that all Indians, negros and *other suspected persons* [our italics] that shall be found on the wharfs or about the town after nine of the clock at night shall be taken up and carried before some Justice of the Peace who is hereby desired to lay a fine of two shillings a piece on all he finds guilty."[36]

The Indian population steadily decreased during the first century of white occupation. In 1763, before the great "sickness," Obed Macy lists their population as 358.[37] During the sickness, which lasted from August 16, 1763, until February 16, 1764, 222 Indians died of a disease Macy said was "called by some the yellow fever and by some the plague."[38] The disease did not affect the white people of the island. During the time of the sickness six of Jeremy Netowa's descendants and/or relatives died, including a Jeremiah Netowa, as well as his son, also named Jeremiah, and James, Abigail, Sarah, and Jonathan.[39] Apparently that was the end of the Netowa family. We have found no mention of a Netowa in Nantucket records after 1764.

The Indians' lack of resistance to the white

man's diseases, and their inability to handle the white man's rum and gin, which often led to habitual and weakening drunkenness, led also to their final demise on the island. According to Macy, their numbers had decreased to thirty-five in 1784.[40] The last two people recognized as Indians on Nantucket died just after the middle of the nineteenth century. Abram Quary (Abraham Quady) died November 25, 1854, aged eighty-two years and ten months, and less than two months later, on January 12, 1855, Dorcas Honorable died in the town asylum.[41]

Obed Macy mourned the passing of the Nantucket Indians in a noble paragraph in his *History:*

> Thus the existence of a tribe of natives terminated, and their land went to strangers. In the simple charity of nature, they received our fathers. When fugitives from Christian persecution, they opened to them their stores, bestowed on them their lands, treated them with unfailing kindness, tasted their poison, and died. Their only misfortune was their connexion with Christians, and their only crime, the imitation of their manners.[42]

Africa, a Free Negro, ?–1728

The inventory of Africa, a weaver who died in 1728, is the only inventory of a black man identified as such ("Africa, a free Negro") in the records of the Nantucket Probate Court before the Revolutionary War.[43] It is relevant to compare Africa with Jeremy Netowa. Both were weavers who died in the same year, 1728. Africa and Netowa knew each other. An undated entry in Netowa's account book states: "to making on[e] payr of briches for Africa." However, the life-styles of Africa and Netowa must have been quite different. Africa lived in town with the white population, while Netowa lived well out of town with the island Indians.

Africa's inventory indicates that he had, by the standards of the time, a plethora of worldly goods in comparison with the spartan furnishings of Netowa's house. Africa was not wealthy, but he must have lived quite comfortably. He was probably one of the few free black men on the island when he died, although there were others, such as "Jonas, a negro man," who bought a horse in 1719.[44]

We found evidence of eighteen black slaves in the colonial period court records of Nantucket, in addition to the six Indian slaves listed previously. In 1718 Stephen Hussey willed three slaves to his wife and children. Nathaniel Coffin, mariner, who died in 1721, owned three slaves: "George £50–0–0, Sabina £15–0–0, and Phyllis £42–10–0." The inventory of Joseph Coffin (1724) mentions a "negro boy—£35." (To give some idea of the value of money in the 1720s, it can be noted that Africa's horse was valued at £8–10–00, and Netowa's house was appraised at £33.) Nathaniel Gardner (1729) left a "Negro boy Toby—£90." Samuel Barker, yeoman, who died in 1740, had four slaves: Primus, sixty pounds and Zubinah, eighty pounds; a child, Boston, five pounds, and a mulatto, Pico, thirty pounds. Thomas Brock, who will be discussed later, had two slaves. One was listed in his inventory as a "negro woman £120–0–0." The other was mentioned in his will, which was entered in the probate records as of May 4, 1750: "I will that my negro man Rubin shall have his time and be free when he shall arrive at the age of thirty years."

To this list should be added Africa, who was freed before 1710, Pompy, noted on page 20, and the two slaves of William Swain mentioned below who were freed in the 1750s.

The 1790 United States Census listed seventy-six negroes or mulattoes living in Nantucket. In 1800 the total "persons of color" was 228. By 1820 there were 132 free colored males and 142 free colored females on the island.

There appear to have been relatively few blacks in Nantucket before the Revolutionary

War, and only a handful of slaves after the middle of the eighteenth century. One would like to think that this was due, at least in part, to the strong stand the Quakers had taken against slavery.[45] In 1716 the Dartmouth Friends Meeting sent a query to the Quarterly Meeting, of which Nantucket was a part, asking "wheather itt be agreeable to truth to purchase slaves and keep them term of life?"[46]

Thomas Drake, Quaker historian, summarized the responses to this query:

> The Dartmouth people answered their own question by condemning the slave trade, but said nothing as to slavery itself. Over in South County, Greenwich Friends agreed that no more slaves ought to be brought "from foreign parts." Quaker Newport, most affected by the Query, made no reply. But Nantucket Friends, as one might expect from their remoteness from contact with slavery, unequivocally declared it was the "sense and judgement" of their Meeting that it was "not agreeable to truth for Friends to purchase slaves and keep them term of life."[47]

The Nantucket Quaker position on the slavery question was supported by the anti-slavery pamphlet of Elihu Coleman written in 1729 and published in 1733, titled *A Testimony Against That Antichristian Practice of Making Slaves of Men.*

Although the Nantucket Friends Meeting took a position against slavery, even members of their own Meeting who owned slaves did not immediately free them. It was not until the 1750s that Quaker William Swain (1688–1770),[48] son of John Swain, Jr., freed two slaves, one in 1751:

> These May Certify that Boston a Negro Man lately my servant is a free man and not a Slave but hath free Liberty to trade and trafick with any body and to go where he pleaseth as Witness my Hand at Nantucket the Twenty Third Day of November Annoque Domini 1751.
>
> William Swain.[49]

Eight years later the second was recorded:

> To all people to whom these Presents shall come Greetings know ye that whereas Essex, a Negro man in Sherburn in the county of Nantucket being my Slave, hath to me always been a faithful Servant and behaved himself well for which consideration I do by these presents manumett and Set free the said Essex to be a free men both from me and my heirs and assigns from hence forth forever so that my self my Heirs and assigns from henceforth Shall have no Demands on the said Essex in any shape than they would have had if the said Essex had been free born and Never under Bondage as Witness my hand and seal at Sherburn aforesaid the seventeenth Day of May in the Thirty second year of his Majesties Reign Annoque Domini 1759
>
> William Swain
>
> Signed Sealed and Delivered
> in presence of
> Caleb Bunker
> Abishai Folger[50]

We know nothing more of Essex, but feel Africa must have been an exceptional man. He had been owned by William Gayer, who freed him before 1710. When Gayer made his will on September 21, 1710, "being sick and weak in body but of sound mind and memory," he divided his considerable holdings of Nantucket land between his son William and his two daughters, Damaris Coffin and Dorcas Starbuck, but he gave life rights to parts of his house to his housekeeper, Patience Foot, and to Africa. The clause in Gayer's will referring to Africa states:

> I give to Africa a Negro once my servant twenty sheep and commonage for them and for one horse as also the East Chamber of my now dwelling house and half the leanto and all the other half of my barn and try house with the half of all the lands and fence about my house and the half of the lot toward Monomoy to hold all the sd. lands and other the premises to him the sd. Africa during his na-

turall life and I will that my daughter Damaris Coffin shall have the use of the rest of my Dwelling house if she should come hither to live.[51]

The Gayer house, which was built in 1684, was located on Center Street on a site now occupied by the three-story Folger house.[52] Presumably, Africa continued to live in Gayer's house after the latter's death in 1710.

Africa's inventory indicates he had some learning. The fact that he owned a Bible and at least three other books places him in a kind of elitist category when we look coolly at the intellectual life of the first hundred years of the white man's occupation of the island. Books were not plentiful in Nantucket in the seventeenth and early eighteenth centuries. Of the forty-five inventories recorded in the Nantucket Probate Court records in the first half of the eighteenth century, only half (twenty-two) listed books of any kind. The total number of books in these inventories was about sixty. (We do not know the *exact* number because two of the inventories list an item "books," which we assume to be at least two.) Of the total of sixty books, twenty-seven were Bibles and four were dictionaries. Africa was one of only seven men listed in the probate records before 1750 who owned books other than Bibles and dictionaries!

After the Revolutionary War more books began to appear in Nantucket inventories. A few men had real libraries. Zeebulon Butler, whose estate was probated September 13, 1790, had ninety-eight books, including books in French, Latin, and Greek, plus some odds and ends such as *Customs and Manners.*

Dr. Benjamin Tupper, physician, who died in 1794, had fifty-six volumes, many of which were medical books. He owned a copy of Johnson's *Dictionary,* books on religion and history, and something called *Every Man His Own Lawyer.*

Africa was well dressed for his station. His most valuable piece of clothing was his "Jacoat," valued at £2–10–0. He owned two other jackets as well as a hat, leather breeches, and a greatcoat. He had buckles (pewter?) for his shoes. He owned two bedsteads, a bed, five blankets, a coverlet, and two bed rugs. He owned eleven chairs, seven chests, a warming pan valued at one pound sterling, a lamp, and a candlestick. He had a horse and saddle and three guns. The inventory included half the barn left to him by William Gayer which housed a few farming tools. No doubt he had at least a kitchen garden.

There is no loom mentioned in Africa's inventory but there were a number of items of his profession of weaver: "weavers goods £1–14–0." These included a pair of worsted combs, cards (carding combs), slays, wool, and a number of miscellaneous pieces of cloth.

Africa had inherited a share in a tryhouse from William Gayer, and his inventory included tools of his fishing and whaling activities: a lance, a fish and drawing knife, and a compass.

Because of the fact that the *Oxford English Dictionary* lists "looking glass" as a slang variant of chamber pot in the seventeenth and eighteenth centuries, it has been suggested by James Deetz in his book *In Small Things Forgotten* that many of the "looking glasses" in seventeenth-century Plymouth, Massachusetts, inventories were really chamber pots.[53] There is not even a hint that Nantucket appraisers made use of such a euphemism. The looking glasses in Nantucket inventories usually have high values, indicating they were the real thing. Ebenezer Gardner, who made Africa's inventory, certainly had no qualms about coming to the point. He straightforwardly listed "a piss pot—2/6."

The probate court records indicate that Africa's possessions were sold at public auction.

Their value totalled £102–16–11. However, his debts and court and administration charges added up to £103–12–6, wiping out all of his assets. The administration charge alone was eight pounds, much higher than usual. For example, the estate of Eunice Arthur (May 25, 1730) listed "Administration trouble and charge—£2–10–0," and the estate of Prince Coffin (also May 25, 1730) was charged the same amount, £2–10–0, for administration. One wonders whether the amount charged to Africa's estate was arbitrarily set to correspond to the balance of his estate after his debts were paid. After all, he had no heirs.

Thomas Brock, 1698(?)–1750

Thomas Brock, who died in 1750 at the age of about fifty, is listed in the family records as a "Scotchman and a Distiller."[54] We have ample evidence of his distilling activities. His inventory, taken February 1, 1750, lists a "still house and Land—£630," and there is today in the Brock family a handsome black-green glass bottle with a seal marked "T / BROCK / 1744" (Figure 6). Brock purchased property for his distillery in 1730 from E. Gardner. The deed[55] notes that "there hath lately been erected and set up a still house in Wesco in Sherborne." Brock's rise in the world in the 1730–1750 period is reflected in the occupations listed after his name in the Nantucket land records. In 1730 he was called a "marriner," in 1738 a "distiller,"[56] and in 1746 he was listed as a "merchant."[57] Toward the end of his life, in 1750, the Registry of Deeds rated Brock as a gentleman, listing him as "Thomas Brock, Esqr."[58]

When Brock died in 1750 he was one of the richest men on the island. His estate totaled 16,192 pounds. Brock's wealth was symbolic of the great increase in prosperity which whaling brought to Nantucket in the second quarter of the eighteenth century. The size of estates, as shown in probate inventories, increased dramatically in the 1730s and 1740s, both in terms of real monetary value, the amount of property, and the amount and richness of household furnishings.

Figure 6. Blown glass bottle of English manufacture, dark black-green, applied seal with inscription "T / BROCK / 1744" in a raised circle. Height: 9¼ in. (23.5 cm.), diameter: 5 in. (12.7 cm.). (*Courtesy Albert G. Brock*). Seal fragment in foreground from a similar bottle. (*Courtesy Mrs. John P. Elder*).

Brock's house, which is reputed to have been the building that now houses a shop at the northwest corner of Center and Quince Streets, was valued at 1600 pounds. He also owned an "old house & land & fencing—£500," a shop, cow commons, half of a Tuckernuck house and a share of the wharf (Straight Wharf). But it was Brock's holdings in shipping that represented a major source of his wealth. He owned the sloop *Jemima,* appraised at 560 pounds, and parts of nine other vessels:

3/8 Sloop Nantucket	£1125
1/2 Sloop Tryall and boat	1150
5/16 Sloop Golden Hind	525
1/4 Sloop Susanna	400
1/4 Sloop Content	250
1/4 Sloop Hannah	525
1/5 Sloop Pearl	166
1/6 of 5/6 Sloop Fortune	135
3/8 Sloop Fame	975

The practice of owning fractions of a number of different vessels rather than having full ownership of one or a relatively few seagoing vessels was standard in Nantucket. It spread the risk. Whaling was a hazardous business and the loss of a vessel owned by one individual could be disastrous. In addition, there was the ever-present danger of attack by French and Spanish privateers that had been prowling the Atlantic since the early 1740s.[59] In 1750 sloops were usually fifty to seventy-five tons in size; they were used interchangeably for whaling, cod fishing, and freighting cargoes.[60] At that time the Nantucket whaling fleet consisted of about sixty sloops. By 1775 it had doubled in the number of vessels and tripled in tonnage. During this period Nantucket had about half of the total number of vessels of all of New England involved in whaling.[61]

There is some confusion as to where and when Thomas Brock was born. One record indicates he was born in Nantucket in 1698 and another gives his birth as 1700 in Paisley, Scotland.[62] In 1725 he married Patience Gardner, daughter of Joseph and Ruth (Coffin) Gardner.[63] Between 1728 and 1749 Patience bore him ten children, six sons and four daughters, five of whom lived into the nineteenth century.

Brock's business interests were extensive. He must have been an energetic man, a first-rate entrepreneur, to have been involved in so many quite different businesses. In addition to owning and operating the distillery, Brock's long, detailed inventory indicates he had a store stocked with everything from dry goods to ship supplies; he was actively involved in whaling, and, no doubt, coastal shipping, and was, like so many Nantucketers, a part-time farmer. He owned a barn, three cows, seven horses, and six cow commons.

Brock's store had materials for whaling voyages: lances, harpoons, tow irons, tackle blocks, oars, cordage, boat rope, and salt-pork and salt-beef by the barrel. He had "2 boats at the shore," and a third interest in a tryhouse where the whale blubber was rendered to recover whale oil, plus the above-mentioned share in the wharf. At the time of his death he owned 158 pounds of whalebone in Nantucket plus another 100 pounds at Philadelphia. The total value of the 258 pounds of whalebone was £526. The high value of whalebone (and whale oil) in the middle of the eighteenth century was a powerful incentive to expand and extend whaling voyages to the further reaches of the Atlantic, from Greenland to grounds off southern Africa and the southern shores of South America.

Brock's store primarily handled dry goods, with some hardware items. Many of the textiles he sold have names which are long since obsolete:[64] "cambet" (camlet, a plain woven cloth of wool, linen, or goat's hair, used for clothing, bed hangings, and furniture upholstery), "Bengal" (silks from India, usually striped), "garlick" (a linen cloth imported from Holland or Germany), "shalloon" (a cheap twill-woven worsted cloth), "calamink" (calimanco, a tightly woven glossy worsted cloth), "russels" (a worsted damask), "ozne" (osnaburg, a coarse, unbleached linen cloth first made in Osnabruck, Germany) and "fuschin" (fustian, usually a twill-woven cotton and linen cloth). There were twelve and a half dozen handkerchiefs in the inventory, probably from England, and eight "cotton Romals" (handkerchiefs from India). There were tapes, laces, bags, duck, "baze" (baise or bay, a coarse, open, woolen cloth), drugget, ribbons, thread, broadcloth, pins, knitting needles, thimbles, buttons, mohair, muslin, "lawn" (a fine, plainwoven linen), and many yards of "cloth" and "silk." In addition to yard goods and sewing supplies, Brock stocked shirts, jackets, tablecloths, and feathers for pillows and mattresses.

Nontextile items in the store included brooms, sickles, brimstone, knives, finishing nails, shingle nails, clapboard nails, and red lead.

There were, of course, other stores in Nantucket in 1750.[65] Account books from some of these stores give a clear idea of the kinds of goods handled. For example, Cromwell Coffin's account book,[66] covering the period 1738–1765, tells us his store dealt in groceries, dry goods, and a few hardware supplies such as nails, jackknives, tin cups, mugs, and stone pots. Coffin sold some of the same textiles as Brock but he had less variety and more commonplace yard goods, such as osnaburg, kersey, and muslin. Coffin's food and grocery line included such things as flour, coffee, tea, molasses, tobacco, apples, butter, cheese, chocolate, corn, beans, salt, a number of spices, oatmeal, gingerroot, bread, and mustard. Incidentally, there seem to have been "chocoholics" in the eighteenth century! There are repeated entries in Coffin's account book of chocolate purchases by Joseph Coffin and James Coffin.

Coffin's account book names an eighteenth-century Nantucket cabinetmaker: "Bought a table of Stephen Kidder—£6" (October 2, 1758).

Although the inventory of Thomas Brock's house was not made on a room-by-room basis, it is clear that the appraiser listed items in one room at a time. The first room in the inventory was the parlor, or best room, the room that housed the parents' four-post bed, six four-back chairs, a great chair, a high case of drawers (highboy), a round table, and a trunk. On the walls were seven pictures and a looking glass.

The high case of drawers in the parlor, appraised at thirty-two pounds, had only a third the value of the bed and bedding in the same room, but Brock obviously considered it to be an important part of his estate. His will, entered into the probate records as of May 4, 1750, singled it out:

> I give and bequeath to Patience my beloved wife my Great Bible and one high Chest of Draws . . .

His will also mentions another high chest of drawers:

> To my daughter one high chest of Draws which she has had in possession for some time past.

The fact that Brock's will singled out the two high chests of drawers suggests that these pieces of furniture were more important than indicated by their appraised values.

The bed and bedding in the parlor was valued at more than 100 pounds, the most valuable in the house. As noted before, the actual four-post bed (the bedstead) was valued at much less than the mattress, bedding, and bed hangings. The high value of "Bed No. 1" suggests it was a down-filled mattress:

	£ s d
Bed No. 1	38– 2–6
Bedstead & curtain rods	8– 0–0
White Curtains	15– 0–0
Tester & head cloth	6– 0–0
2 pillowcases & bolsters	4–16–0
2 sheets	5– 0–0
3 blankets	11– 0–0
A quilt	14– 0–0
	101–12–6

The round table in the parlor must have been occasionally used for entertainment. In the inventory were three punch bowls and six "smaller bowls," plus a "China bowl," a "Delft bowl," and a glass bowl.

Perhaps the most surprising thing in the room was the bountiful supply of linens:

20 sheets
50 pillowcases
10 towels
33 napkins
13 tablecloths

At a time when it was customary for two and even three people to sleep in one bed, the Brock household contained the relatively large total of eleven beds. Four were four-posters fully equipped with curtains, testers and headcloths. If we can assume that the "negro woman," a slave valued at 120 pounds, used one of the beds and the parents used the one in the parlor, there were nine beds for the ten children. Beds number two and three had blue calico curtains in contrast with the white curtains of the parents' bed. Most beds in the eighteenth century had both pillows and bolsters. People slept in a more upright position than we do today, a practice that is still common in Europe.

By Nantucket standards Brock owned a substantial amount of silver. Silver was not nearly as common in eighteenth-century Nantucket as it was in such cities as Boston and Philadelphia. There is little evidence that silverware was ever considered a form of money in Nantucket, as it was said to have been in other parts of the American colonies.[67] Nantucketers put their money into real estate, and in ships, tryhouses, wharves, and whale boats—the tools of whaling and fishing. The sea was the main source of their wealth.

Brock's inventory included the following pieces of silver:

	£ s d
17 spoons [large]	103– 4– 6
1 doz. teaspoons & tongs	18– 0– 0
1 spout cup	35– 0– 0
2 porringers	60– 0– 0
1 tankard	86– 0– 0
1 pepper box	7– 0– 0
1 set breeches buttons	9–18–11
1 two-handled cup	19– 0– 0
	338– 3– 5

Silver was no doubt a status symbol. Only the most affluent of the islanders owned anything more than a silver spoon or two. Certainly Brock's silver breeches buttons were a form of conspicious consumption. They were public proof of his success.

We do not know where the silver was kept in the house. It is listed after the living rooms and bedchambers, just before the inventory of the kitchen. It may have been kept there in winter. The kitchen fire was probably the only one that was kept burning almost continuously, which meant that the kitchen was in winter the only really comfortable room in the house.

The last room in the house to be inventoried

was the kitchen, really a kitchen-living-dining-room. In it were twelve chairs, two tea tables, two square tables and a large amount of cooking equipment. When all twelve of the Brock family were together it must have been a bright, active and busy room.

There was much pewter:

	£ s d
Pewter 75 lbs at 10/0	37–10–0
15 old hard metal plates	8– 0–0
9 "shoal" [shallow] small metal plates	4– 0–0
1 Doz square hard plates	9– 0–0
1/2 Doz Deep hard mettel [plates]	4–10–0
10 old plates	3– 0–0
2 gallen basons	5– 0–0
1 bason 18/ 2 wash basons 55/	3–13–0
8 porringers	3– 0–0
	76–13–0

The Brock family would have eaten from pewter plates and been served from pewter bowls and platters. There are no pewter spoons in the inventory. Such spoons would have been included in the seventy-five pounds of pewter shown above. There is only one fork listed. It was probably a large flesh fork of the kind made by Nathaniel Starbuck. There are two dozen knives in the inventory, probably with English steel blades and handles of wood, ivory, or bone. There was one brass candlestick, one iron candlestick, and a candle box.

There was a variety of iron, copper, and brass tools and utensils in the kitchen:

3 brass kettles	1 spit
4 tea kettles	1 spit & fender
1 kettle iron	1 roasting iron
5 skillets	3 skimmers
3 basons	2 ladles
1 copper teapot	1 chafing dish
4 pots	1 trammel
1 dripping pan	andirons

One wonders what happened to Thomas Brock. His life was cut off when he was in what should have been his prime, when he had realized great material success. His youngest child, Walter, was less than a year old when Brock died. His wife was left with ten children, eight of whom were under eighteen. In addition, she had to deal with a variety of businesses: the distillery, the store, the farm, the shipping interests.

The level of material wealth Brock enjoyed persisted in Nantucket until the time of the Revolutionary War. The island's population rose to 3320 in 1765 and to 4412 in 1776. Two inventories of this period give us a glimpse of life on the island at the time, a glimpse that suggests that, although the Quakers ruled the island, life was by no means austere and dull.

The inventory of David Baschard, who died in 1770 and who is listed as an innkeeper in the *Nantucket Vital Records* and as a "Trader" in the probate records, gives us a very complete account of what was in his store and in his inn. His store dealt primarily in yard goods, spices, and hardware. The inn contained, among other things, twenty-three pictures, twenty-four teapots, ninety-seven punch bowls (cups? —they were valued at only eight pence each), twenty-five dozen white stone cups and saucers, and eleven chamber pots.

John Clark, who died on December 24, 1768, must have been a bit of a dandy. His inventory lists no furniture, but a rather dazzling array of clothing, including:

2 beaver hats
pr. silver shoe buckels
pr. large shoe buckels

pr. silver sleeve buckels
pr. new shoes (plus old shoes)
pr. silk garters
blue broadcloth suit (coat, breeches, waistcoat)
3 pr. blue breeches
7 pr. worsted stockings
2 striped Holland shirts
2 checked Holland shirts
2 white Holland shirts
4 waistcoats [one of which was of "fine red Broad Cloth, Gold lace")
1 blue jacket
1 light blue coat

Living in a Typical Nantucket House: Peter F. Coffin, 1779–1823

Peter Fosdick Coffin was born October 5, 1779. His middle name came from his mother, Lydia Fosdick. Peter had no sisters and one brother, who died in 1799. His father, Henry Coffin (1748–1828), is listed in nineteenth-century court records as a yeoman. Peter's grandfather, also named Henry Coffin (1716–1756), had been a mariner. Peter Coffin was called a mariner in Nantucket records as early as 1808,[68] and, although we have no specific knowledge of his having been on a whaling voyage, it is probable that he had been, since whaleships were the standard training ground for most Nantucket seafarers.

Coffin was involved in an incident in the War of 1812 that is described in Starbuck's *History of Nantucket.*[69] By the summer of 1814, Nantucket, which had been blockaded for two years by the British navy, was critically short of foodstuffs, and firewood was desperately needed for the coming winter. The town of Nantucket sent the sloop *Hawk,* David Starbuck, master, under a white flag of truce to the Chesapeake Bay to petition the British commander in chief for permission to bring food supplies and firewood to Nantucket from the mainland, unmolested by British warships. Near Cape Henry the Nantucketers boarded the *Asia,* a seventy-four gun frigate, to begin negotiations. To their surprise, they found on board three fellow Nantucketers, Peter F. Coffin, Jacob Barney, and Alexander Russell, who had been captured with the sloop *Earl* of Nantucket, off Fort Henry. Captain Coffin and his associates had been on a voyage to bring supplies back to the island. The three men from the *Earl* were eventually released, but the *Hawk* was apparently unsuccessful in its main mission of obtaining immediate supplies for the island.

In 1808 Peter Coffin had purchased from his father, Henry Coffin, a house in Wesco Hills, on Fair Street, that had been owned originally by his father's father, Captain Henry Coffin.[70] At that time there were three adjoining Coffin houses which formed a kind of family compound on or near Fair Street: the houses of his uncles Thaddeus Coffin and Shubael Coffin, and the house Peter bought from his father.

We do not know the exact location on Fair Street but have surmised it was at the lower end, away from Main Street, perhaps near Lyon or Farmer Streets. From the layout of the house, which can be clearly deduced from the inventory in the probate court records,[71] we know that it was a type of house that existed by the hundreds in late eighteenth- and early nineteenth-century Nantucket and that has become known as a "typical Nantucket house."[72] Many survive today. Figure 7 shows such a house, Number 47 Fair Street, as it was about 1890, a three-quarter house owned then by Peter Folger. (Nantucketers have long designated a two-and-a-half story, center-chimney house with two window bays on one side of the front doorway and one window bay on the other side as a three-quarter house; a house with two window bays on one side of the doorway, and

Figure 7. "Three-quarter" house at 47 Fair Street in about 1890.

none on the other, a half-house; and a symmetrical arrangement of two window bays on each side of the doorway as a full house.)[73]

There is some evidence that by 1821 Peter Coffin knew he might not have too long to live. In 1821, a year and a half before he died, he made a will leaving everything to my "beloved wife Peggy" except twenty shares of "Publick Stock" which he left to "my honorable father Henry Coffin."[74] In 1822 he made several real estate transactions that seem to indicate he was getting his estate in order.

He died July 11, 1823, at the age of forty-four, leaving his wife Peggy, aged thirty-seven, and four children aged three to fourteen, and his father Henry, who was seventy-five years old. When Peter Coffin's estate was probated on October 22, 1823, it was valued at $13,521.60, most of it in the form of securities. The value of his household furnishings totalled $755.60. Coffin's estate was sizable for the time. The value of money has, of course, changed drastically since 1823. One would have to multiply 1823 dollars by a factor of perhaps forty to find an equivalency in 1987 dollars.

Figures 8 and 9 show reconstructed plans of the first and second floors of Coffin's house,

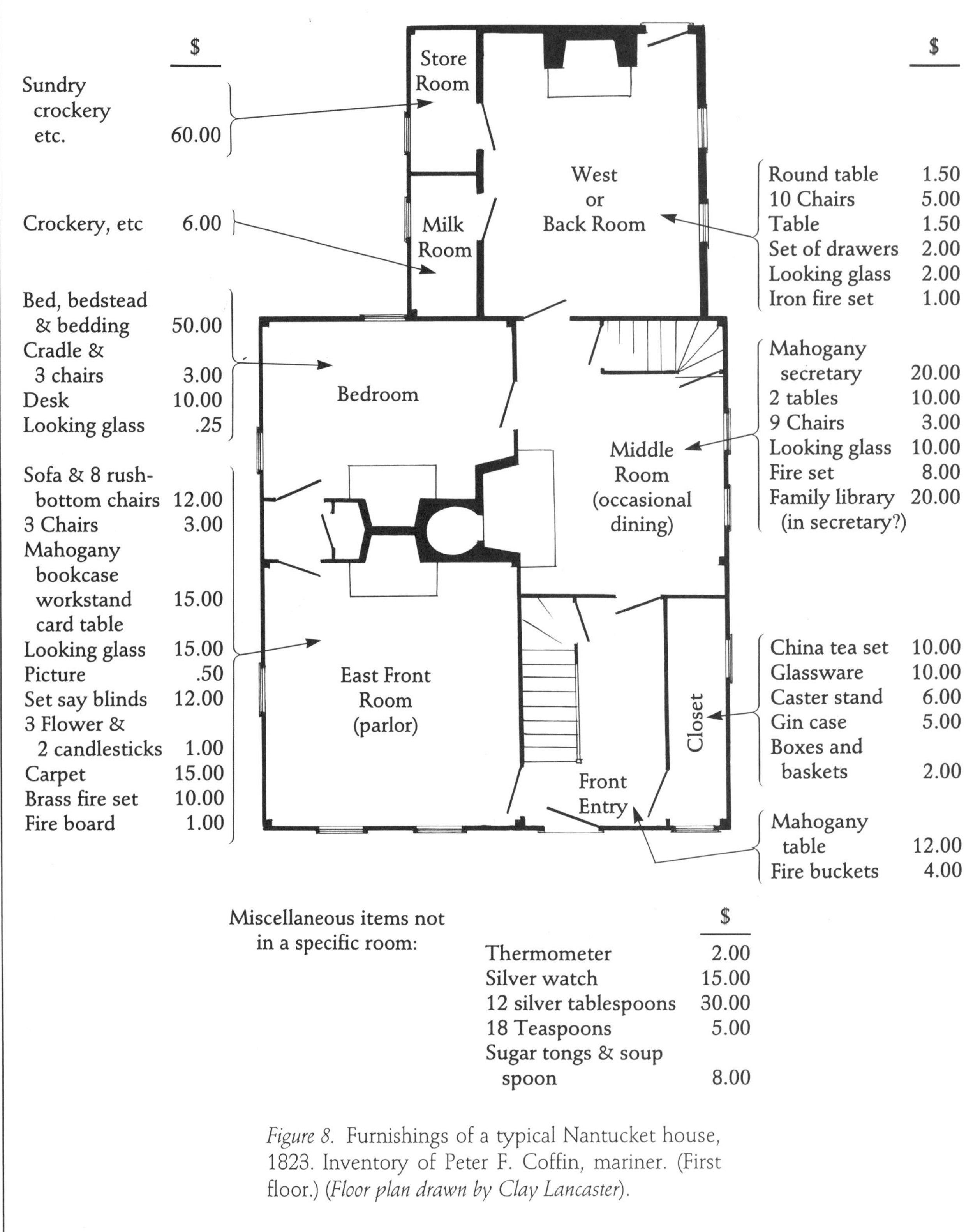

Figure 8. Furnishings of a typical Nantucket house, 1823. Inventory of Peter F. Coffin, mariner. (First floor.) (*Floor plan drawn by Clay Lancaster*).

with a list of furnishings in the various rooms and their appraised values as indicated by the inventory. *Not* included in Figures 8 and 9 are the things in the cellar kitchen and the garret. The cellar kitchen contained:

Three tables	$2.50
Six chairs	1.00
Sundry pieces of furniture	5.00
Lamps and flatirons	1.10
One fire set	1.00
Tea kettle, pans etc.	8.00
Tubs, casks in the inner cellar	6.00

The relatively low valuations of the furniture in the cellar suggests it was a collection of old and well-used pieces. The chairs and tables along with cooking equipment, suggest that the cellar kitchen was used for cooking and for most meals, although the family no doubt occasionally dined on the first floor. The flatirons indicate that ironing was done in the cellar.

The garret, or attic, had, according to the inventory only a bed and "furniture." Perhaps the Coffin family had a hired girl who helped with the cooking and ironing and helped care for the children, her bed being in the garret.

The small front entry of the house was sparsely furnished. There was a nice mahogany table and the usual pair of leather fire buckets hanging beside the stairway. The table in the entry was appraised at twelve dollars, the most valuable table in the house.

We can gain some idea of the quality of the furnishings in Peter Coffin's house by comparing the appraised values of items in different rooms. For example, the looking glass in the east front room, no doubt the "best room," was valued at fifteen dollars, the one in the middle room ten dollars, while the looking glass in the downstairs bedroom was valued at only twenty-five cents. The most expensive looking glass in the house was in the front chamber upstairs, valued at twenty dollars.

Three rooms had carpets, the east front room and the two chamber rooms on the second floor. The only room with curtains was the front room, with its set of say "blinds." (Say is a thin woolen stuff, or serge, of twill weave.) Inside wooden shutters are common in Nantucket houses, obviating the need for curtains, which usually only appeared in the best rooms of the house.

The east front room of the Coffin house was the living room or parlor. It contained the usual seating: a sofa, eight rush-bottom chairs, plus three other chairs. As in the earlier houses, this seems a lot of chairs for a room that was probably no more than fifteen feet square. There were a total of forty-three chairs in the house, plus the sofa in the east front room. In the front room were also a mahogany workstand, a card table, and a mahogany bookcase. The only books mentioned in the inventory were in the middle room. The picture in the front room was valued at fifty cents; it was probably a print. The three flowerpots, the brass fire set, and fire board (with a painted scene?) suggest a bright, cheery room.

The inventory of Peter Coffin's east front room shows that the function of the parlor had changed since the eighteenth century. The parlor had become the living room in the twentieth-century sense. (House plans of the time used both the designations "parlor" and "setting room.") It no longer contained the parents' bed as it would have in the seventeenth and most of the eighteenth century, and it no longer housed a dining table. Rooms were beginning to take on more specific functions, although Coffin's house still did not have a dining room. Many houses did have specific dining rooms by the beginning of the nineteenth century, and almost all had them by the middle of the century.

The parents' bedroom was on the first floor, in back of the front room. The bed, because of its high valuation of fifty dollars, may have

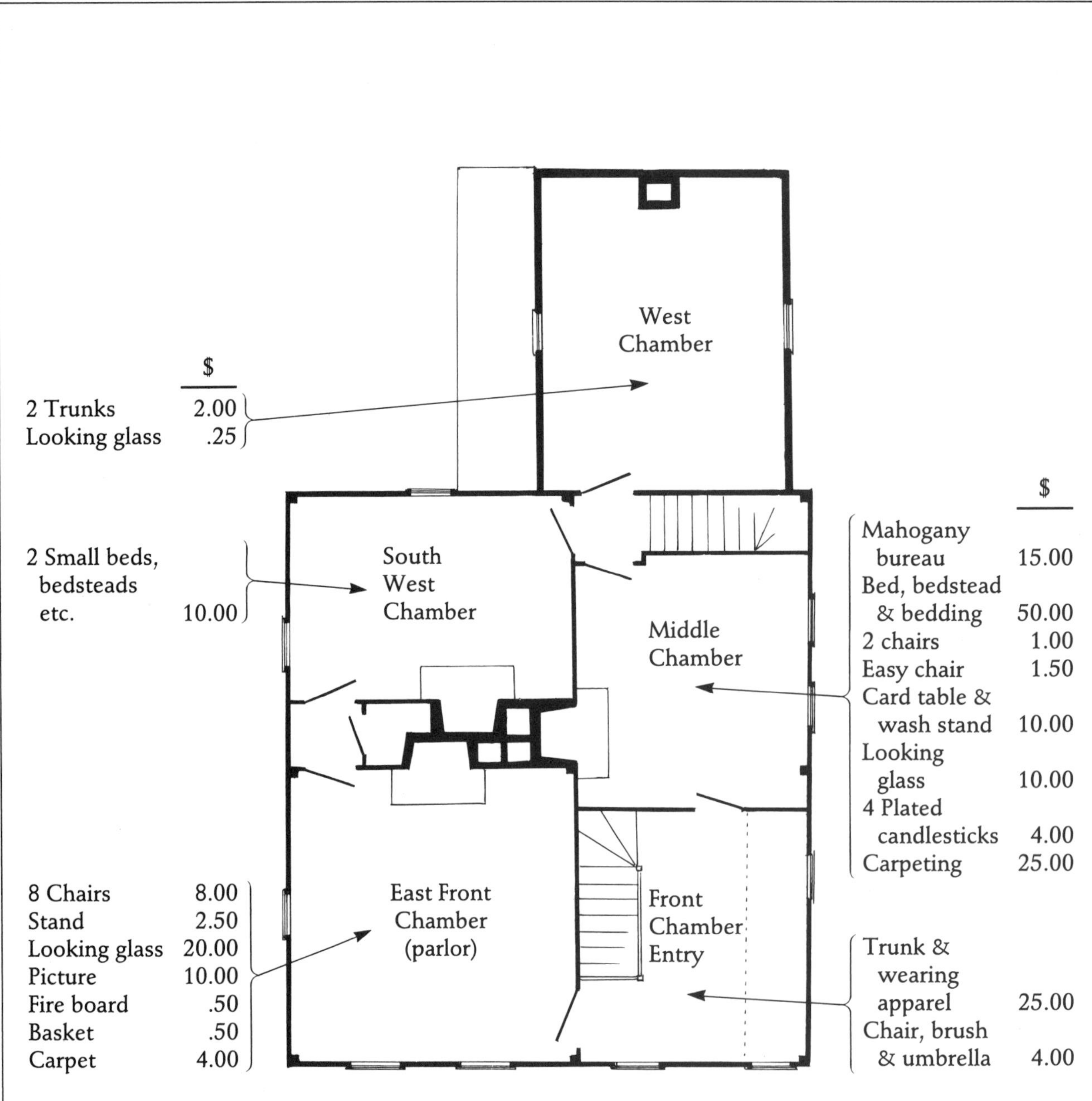

Figure 9. Furnishings of a typical Nantucket house, 1823. Inventory of Peter F. Coffin, mariner. (Second floor.) (*Floor plan drawn by Clay Lancaster*).

been a well-furnished eighteenth century four-poster. The bedroom also had a cradle for the baby, three chairs, and a desk. The middle room may have corresponded to today's family room. It contained a mahogany secretary and the "family library." Both the middle room and the west or back room may have occasionally been used for dining. Both rooms had tables and adequate numbers of chairs.

We have a theory: we believe that Peter Coffin's father, Henry Coffin, was living with them at the time of Peter's death. It is obvious that Peter and his father were close. The first bequest in Peter's will was to his "honored father." They were involved together in several real estate transactions in the years before Peter's death. His father was seventy-five. Peter's mother, Lydia, had been dead for twenty years.

Henry Coffin would have lived upstairs, the east front chamber being his living room. This room contained not only the most valuable looking glass in the house, it contained a picture valued at ten dollars. (The high value suggests a portrait.) His bedroom, the middle chamber, a well-furnished room, contained, among other things, an "easy chair" which we like to think of as a century-old Queen Anne wing chair that may well have been re-covered several times in its useful life.

The children used the south west chamber where the beds were probably set up in dormitory fashion.

The use of the front chamber room upstairs as a living room was common in Nantucket. The second-floor chamber-parlor was almost always treated architecturally as a living room. In eighteenth-century houses, the fireplace wall would be paneled in a manner similar to the front room below. In the nineteenth century, the second-best mantel in the house would likely have been in the front chamber upstairs. A widow or widower, or a woman whose husband was away on a three- or four-year whaling voyage, would use part or all of the second floor as living quarters.

The doubling up of families in Nantucket houses is reflected in the statistics. For example, the 1800 census indicated that there were 5617 people in Nantucket, living in 779 dwellings, which averages over seven persons per dwelling. No figures for the number of dwellings seem to be available for the 1810 and 1820 censuses. In 1820 the population had grown to 7266. This increase of almost 30 percent suggests that the number of people per dwelling was greater than that of 1800.

Many eighteenth- and nineteenth-century Nantucket wills contained instructions for the dividing up of a house, leaving specific rooms or areas of a house to designated individuals. The will of Francis Joy, probated September 11, 1823,[75] spelled out in great detail how his house was to be divided between his wife, Elizabeth Joy, and his daughter-in-law, Judith Joy, widow of his son, Thaddeus Joy. Six pages of the court records give detailed directions and drawings to describe the division. There is a plot plan showing the division of the land around the house. The second plot plan divides the cellar. A third plan shows the division of the first floor of the house. It shows which rooms and closets were to go to his widow, and which to his daughter-in-law, and those areas, such as the entryway and back staircases, that were to be available to both parties. Similar divisions were made for the second floor and the garret.

The Joy house was a "typical" Nantucket house, probably quite similar to the house of Peter F. Coffin, except that the floor plan was reversed, that is, the floor plans were mirror images of each other. There is no mention of household furnishings in Francis Joy's will and there is no inventory in the probate court records.

Figure 10 shows the division of the first floor

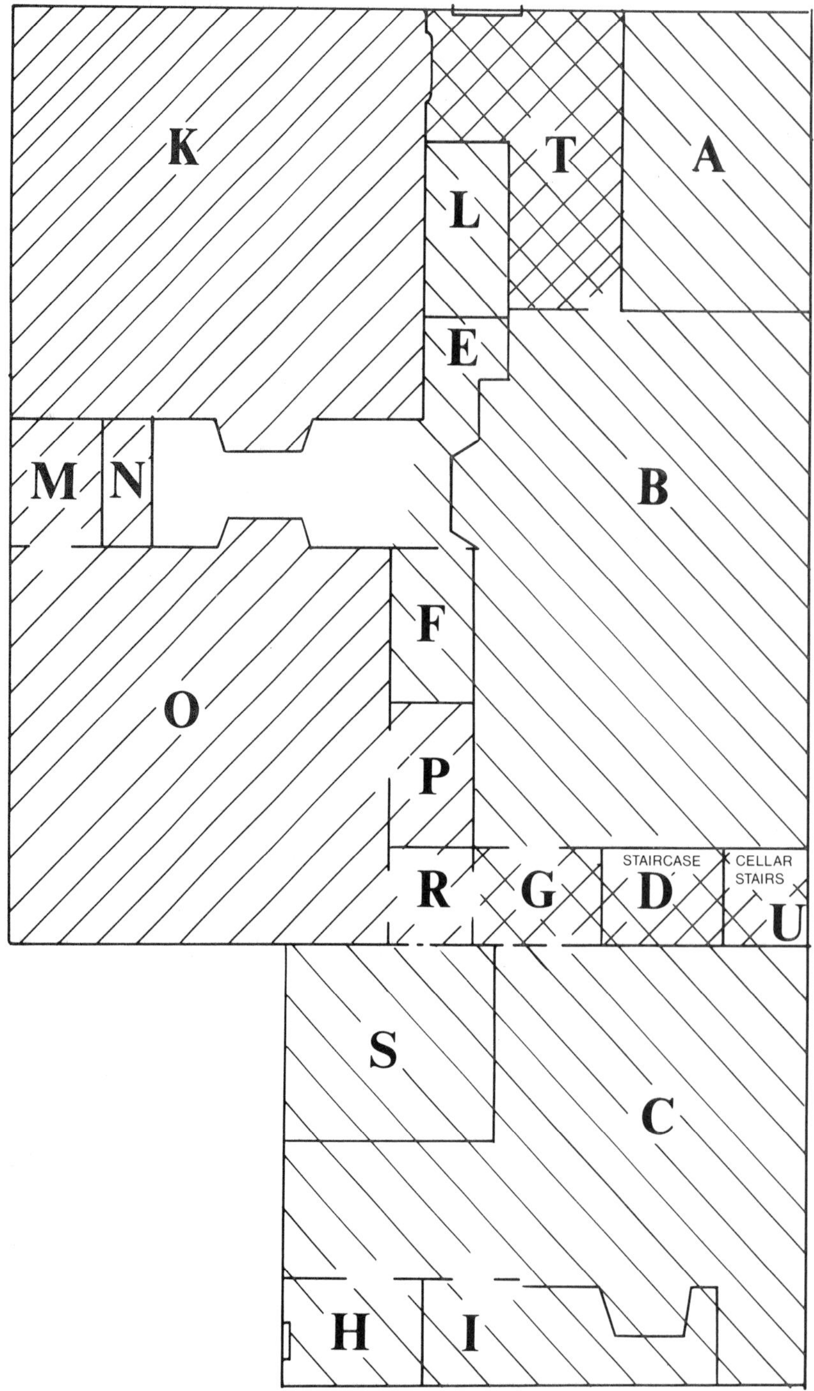

Figure 10. First Floor plan of the Francis Joy house.
(Floor plan drawn by Laura Stover).

of the Joy house. In order to help clarify the division, we have superimposed diagonal lines on the plot plan to designate the various areas. The areas with diagonal lines down to the left (K,M,N,O,P,R) were designated for Elizabeth Joy, his widow. Those areas with diagonal lines down to the right (A,B,C,E,F,H,I,L,S) were for Judith Joy, the daughter-in-law. The front entryway (T), back passage (G), and staircases (D,U) were for the use of both.

The directions for the division of Francis Joy's house are among the most meticulous, specific, and extensive in the Nantucket Probate Court records. However, there does seem to be an explanation for this particular case. Francis Joy was eighty-three years old when his will was drawn up on September 30, 1822. His wife Elizabeth (his second wife) was sixty-two. His son by his first wife, Phebe, Thaddeus Joy, had died the year before, on January 11, 1821, leaving Judith, his widow, and four children, who were living in the house owned by the father-in-law, Francis Joy. He clearly intended that Judith Joy and her children, and Elizabeth Joy, should share the house equally. There is the feeling that Francis Joy, in making his last will and testament, "being weak in body but of sound and perfect mind and memory," felt a deep sense of responsibility to provide equitably for the two parties, his dead son's family and his wife Elizabeth.

The Middle Brick: Joseph Starbuck, 1774–1861; Matthew Starbuck, 1813–1876

The thirty-one year period, 1815–1846, saw profound changes in Nantucket life-styles. It was during this period that the island began to discard its old ways and enter fully into the mainstream of American culture. Although this era saw the end of Nantucket's dominant position as the leading whaling port, it was a time of great growth and prosperity for the island. There was a building boom. Old houses were modernized, new houses were built all over town, and, for the first time, houses were being built that could clearly be called mansions. Fine brick houses began to adorn that part of Main Street west of the business district, establishing it as *the* fashionable street in town, although the brick mansions of Jared Coffin were built not there, but on Pleasant and Broad Streets, respectively. The red-brick houses of Henry Coffin, 75 Main Street, and his brother, Charles G. Coffin, 78 Main Street, built in the early 1830s by James Field, head carpenter, and Christopher Capen, head mason, set the style for the houses built further out Main Street. The Three Bricks, the three identical red-brick mansions lined up in a stately row opposite the end of Pleasant Street, were destined to become landmarks of American architecture. All of these houses were built in a simplified Greek Revival style,[76] mute evidence of the restraining influence of the Quakers, even though the Quaker sect itself was gradually disappearing.

The furnishings of these new houses also reflected a break with the past. The plain vernacular furniture of the Quakers, the Nantucket-style tables, the traditional Windsor chairs, went out of style and were relegated to back rooms and bedchambers. Some of the Windsor chairs were transformed and fitted with chamber pots. People became intrigued with the fashionable Empire furniture. There was a new love of complexity in home furnishings which was to reach its peak in the eclectic historicism of the Victorian era. Nantucket was, of course, not alone in this break with the past. Everywhere in America, Queen Anne, Chippendale, and early Federal furniture, old silver, and other furnishings of the eighteenth century were generally considered old fashioned, to be replaced with up-to-date things.

The man who planned and built the Three Bricks, Joseph Starbuck (Plate III), was a part of both the old and the new Nantucket. He was born of a Quaker family, and although he drifted away from the Friends Meeting, he continued to operate in the blunt, honest, straightforward manner of his Quaker heritage. He was a man of his time, shrewd, hardworking, successful, interested in the world outside Nantucket, and at the same time a conservative. He was interested in architecture. However, it should be noted that, although he designed and built three stylish houses for his sons on Main Street and saw his daughter housed in one of the white-columned mansions across the street from the houses of his sons, Joseph himself lived out his life in a modest house not too different from hundreds of other two-and-a-half story shingled houses on the island.

Joseph was made a partner in his father's business in 1793, when he was nineteen.[77] Although there were difficulties ahead—the Jefferson embargo and the War of 1812—the 1790s were not necessarily the worst of times to enter the whale-oil business in Nantucket. The exodus of the leading whaling merchants, the Rotches, to Europe and then to New Bedford after the Revolutionary War, left something of a vacuum on the island in the whale-oil business, a vacuum that eventually was ably filled by Joseph Starbuck and his sons.

When Joseph built a house for his own family in 1807 on New Dollar Lane, it was a departure from the usual center-chimney, two-and-a-half story house. Outside it was conventional enough in appearance, being two storys front and back, but it had two chimneys, placed to the right and left of the middle of the house, away from the ends, so that each of the four corner rooms of the two floors of the house could have its own fireplace. The center front door opened directly into a wide hall which extended through to the back of the house. In the rear of the New Dollar Lane house was built a tryworks and a candle house, locating Starbuck's place of work right at his back door. However, it meant that his house and those of his neighbors were subject to the stench from the tryhouse when whale oil was being rendered, an odor that by all accounts must have been pungent indeed.

Joseph Starbuck was successful as a manufacturer and merchant and as a shipowner. In his lifetime he and his sons had ownership in twenty-three ships, three schooners, and three sloops.[78] Four of the whaleships, the *President,* the *Hero,* the *Omega,* and the *Three Brothers,* built in the 1811–1833 period, brought back 64,400 barrels of oil valued at almost $2 million.[79] The profits from whaling and shipping enabled Joseph Starbuck to accumulate what at the time was called a "princely fortune."

Early on, Starbuck began to think about the future of his three sons, George, Matthew, and William. After he built the above-mentioned ship *Three Brothers,* named for his sons, he began formulating plans for building houses for them on Main Street. He purchased the old homesteads of Hezekiah Bunker and Gideon Coffin, tore them down, and in 1837 started building. Joseph was the designer and the contractor for the houses. He used the mason who had built the two brick Coffin houses, Christopher Capen, but hired a new head carpenter from the mainland, James Child. The exterior designs of the Three Bricks were similar to the Henry Coffin house down the street, with the addition of one-story white-columned porticoes. The porticoes, with Greek Ionic columns, are said to have been suggested by Starbuck's son-in-law, William Hadwen (Figure 11).

According to Starbuck's records, the two lots on which the houses were built cost $12,800, while the three brick houses themselves cost a total of $27,324, or a bit more than $9100 each.[80] The Starbuck sons were quite young when the houses were finished: George,

Figure 11. The "Three Bricks", Main Street, Nantucket, built in 1838 by Joseph Starbuck for his three sons. (*NHA photograph*).

who married Elizabeth Swain in 1833 and had by 1838 three children, was twenty-seven; Matthew, who married Mary Ann Morton in 1835, was twenty-two; and William, the youngest and unmarried, was only eighteen. We focus our attention on the Middle Brick because it is the only one of the three houses still owned by descendants of the original owner, Matthew Starbuck, and also because it retains many of its original furnishings.

Matthew Starbuck, born in 1813, was educated in island schools until he was fourteen, at which time his father sent him to Boston, to work for the firm of Josiah Bradlee, the countinghouse which marketed much of Nantucket's whale oil at that time. Bradlee was known as a merchant of the old school, stern and demanding, a strict taskmaster. Matthew obviously learned well. He was successful in his business career and meticulous in his account books.

Matthew worked as a clerk in the Bradlee business until he was twenty-one, returning to Nantucket in about 1834 to enter his father's business. His seven-year stint in Boston undoubtedly had a great effect on his life-style.

He learned the ways of commerce of a leading Boston business, and he had regular contacts with whaling captains from Nantucket and other ports who were in Boston selling their cargoes, contacts which would prove valuable later in his career. In addition, he would, as the son of one of the richest men in Massachusetts, have had entrée to fashionable homes in Boston, which surely developed his taste for fine furnishings. Many of the original furnishings of the Middle Brick seem to have come from Boston.

Matthew's first wife, Mary Ann, died of a "violent fever" in October 1838, probably before she had a chance to live in her beautiful new home. Matthew remarried in 1840, his second wife being Catherine Wyer.

In business he followed in the footsteps of his father. The firm G&M Starbuck became one of the foremost businesses on the island. For several decades, Matthew was a leading citizen of the town. Joseph Farnham, writing in 1915 of his youth in Nantucket before the Civil War, remembered Matthew as a man of great style:

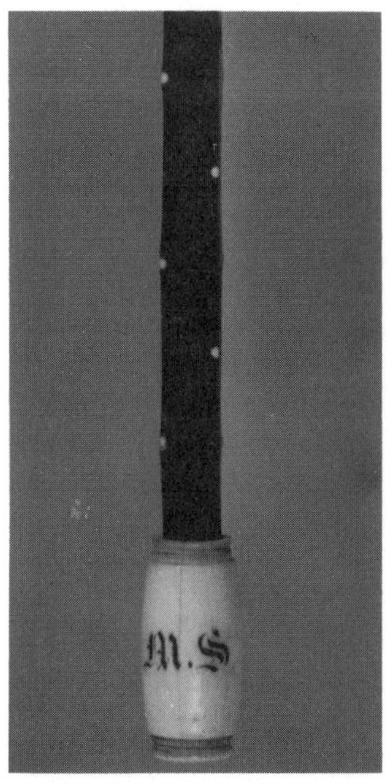

Figure 12. Detail of Matthew Starbuck's riding crop, carved baleen with tiny whale-ivory inlays, ivory handle engraved "MS." Length: 28⅝ in. (72.7 cm.). (*Courtesy of Mrs. H. Crowell Freeman*).

> I remember so well the Starbuck family—Joseph, the father, and the three sons, George, Matthew and William; in combination a material part of the whaling industry of the town. The father lived on New Dollar Lane, while the three brothers occupied the yet remaining three brick mansions on Main Street, nearly opposite Pleasant Street. What a beauty was the "clipper" whale-ship, "Three Brothers," named for those three sons, and which I most distinctly remember. That Starbuck family, father and sons, long since passed to the Great Beyond, in my boyhood constituted a leading and respected part of the elite of the town. The three brothers were all fond of, and most carefully cared for, the horse. Each had one or more of a distinctively fine grade, none anywhere superior. Matthew, who lived in the middle of the three brick houses, was a horse fancier to a rare degree. [His riding crop is shown in Figure 12.] He was particularly fond of a carriage horse of beauty and rapid gait, and drove such with evident pride and delight. Boys of my day will, with me, pleasantly recall what we then knew as "Matt Starbuck's racer." An animal of fine lines, graceful in manner, attractively caparisoned,[81] and if not making a mile in two minutes, or thereabouts, as highly bred horses in these days do, yet he was fleet of foot, and Mr. Starbuck thoroughly enjoyed riding behind that quick-moving "trotter." Individually, it was Mr. Starbuck's sport, yet it was a sport for us boys, as we often witnessed and appreciatively in that way entered into it. "Matt Starbuck's Webster!"—I feel confident that those once boys with me will agree that never before or since was there ever such a fast horse—at least as we then comprehended it with our boy intellect.[82]

During the decline of Nantucket whaling Matthew and his brother George gradually went out of the whale-oil business. Matthew invested heavily in the Cape Cod Railway and was for many years a director of the company. For the last twenty years of his life he was also president of the Nantucket and Cape Cod Steamship Company.[83] He died in 1876 at the age of sixty-three, leaving his wife Catherine alone in the big house. Three of their children lived in Boston, a son in Greenport, New York, and a daughter in San Francisco. Catherine lived in the Middle Brick until her death in 1916 in her ninety-seventh year, leaving the house to her daughter, Maria Mitchell Mackay. In 1920, when Pauline Mackay Johnson, granddaughter of Matthew and Catherine, inherited the house, it was virtually unchanged structurally since it had been built; there was only one bathroom in the house and it had not been wired for electricity.[84] Mrs. Johnson's daughter, Mrs. H. Crowell Freeman, has owned the house since 1958.

The Middle Brick today is a vivid reminder of what has been called Nantucket's golden age. It is filled with possessions of the succeeding generations, which makes it quite different from those carefully restored house-museums with furnishings strictly "of the period." Plates I through VIII give several views of the first floor of this fine house.

The Summer Resident: H. O. Underwood, 1858–1921

Nantucket began to develop as a summer resort in the 1870s and 1880s. In 1871, R. H. Cook published a *Tourist's Guide,*[85] which advertised the Ocean House hotel, boarding houses, and "summer pleasure boats" for hire. New hotels were built, rooming houses proliferated, and people from off-island began to buy and build houses in the towns of Nantucket and Sconset. Few of the summer people of the late nineteenth century came to the island because of antiquarian interests. They came to swim and sail and fish and loaf and get away from it all. Some bought old houses in town and lived in them pretty much as they did back home. Some fixed up small fishermen's houses in Sconset, the kinds of houses that were often spoken of as "quaint." Others built inexpensive, flimsy cottages, leaving wall-studs and rafters exposed, houses that were not designed for year-round living. The latter were often decorated with a wild range of furnishings, from genuine eighteenth- and early nineteenth-century antiques, to reproductions, to wicker and mission oak. None of these cottages was sullied by a professional decorator's touch! Figure 13 shows a cottage (location unknown) "tastefully" furnished with inexpensive furniture, oriental rugs, prints, and photographs, a fishing net drawn around the doorway to give the proper nautical look, and, just beyond, a billiard room for rainy days.

Some of the new cottages were more sturdily built, possibly even with the help of an architect. One such summer house, known as the Underwood cottage (Figure 14), on Brant Point, was built in 1899 by Henry O. Underwood, a Boston businessman (Underwood's Deviled Ham). This is one of the houses lining the shore of the outer harbor that is viewed by boat visitors coming through the jetties toward Nantucket today. The 1881 map *Bird's-eye View of the Town of Nantucket Looking Southward* does not show a single house along this shore, and even by 1900 there were only a few strucures there: a hotel, cottages, and beach houses.

In 1898 and 1899 Mr. Underwood and a close friend from Belmont, Edwin F. Atkins, built two similar cottages for their families side by side on Hulbert Avenue, facing the beach.[86] The two cottages had only living rooms, bedrooms, and bathrooms. A third "kitchen" cottage was built behind the two beach cottages. This cottage housed the dining room, kitchen, laundry room, the maids' sitting room, two pantries, and bedrooms for six servants. The two families shared these kitchen and dining

Figure 13. Nantucket cottage interior, circa 1900. (*NHA photograph*).

facilities. The kitchen cottage, since converted for family living, still has the cast-iron coal stove marked with the name "Walker & Pratt Manufacturing Co. Boston."

The Underwood cottage had a twenty-by-thirty-foot living room overlooking the outer harbor. A corner of the living room as it was in about 1900 is shown in Figure 15. Unpainted tongue-and-groove fir siding was used on both the walls and ceilings of all rooms of the cottage. The living room ceiling was vaulted and had hooks in it to suspend hammocks. To the left of the fireplace, under the window, was a built-in seat. Just below the mantlepiece was a row of brilliantly colored Chinese flower paintings on rice paper under glass. Oriental carpets were on the floor. On the far side of the living room (not pictured) were built-in bookcases, on top of which were displayed golf and sailing trophies. Books originally in the cases in 1901 included *Moby Dick,* Edward Noyes Westcott's *David Harum,* Winston Churchill's *The Crisis,* several of William Dean Howells' novels, Stevenson's *Treasure Island,* Kipling's *Captains Courageous,* Jerome K. Jerome's *Three Men on Wheels,* and books by Frank Stockton and Henry James.

The living room, like the rest of the house, was simply furnished with tables, sofas and hammocks, Hitchcock and wicker chairs, the latter painted black. The six bedrooms had white iron bedsteads with brass knobs, chests

Figure 14. The Underwood cottage, Brant Point, Nantucket, circa 1900.

Figure 15. Northeast corner of living room of the Underwood cottage, circa 1900.

of drawers, a chair or two, a washstand, towel rack, bowl, and pitcher. All the furnishings were brought from Boston. Just off the living room was a small wet bar with an amusing plaque on the wall depicting a jolly Hogarthian figure with glass in hand and the inscription "Honor, Wealth and Fame may desert us. Thirst is Eternal."

The Underwood family with children, servants, and dogs arrived in June for the summer and left in September. Mr. Underwood, with his many business interests in Boston, came to the island only on weekends. Later, when he retired, he spent summers in his cottage. He died there on August 22, 1921.

The Underwoods' eldest daughter, Alice, then fifteen, kept a diary of activities in the summer of 1902. Although the entries in Alice's diary are brief and sometimes telegraphic, they give a warm, nostalgic view of a young girl's uncomplicated, carefree succession of seemingly wonderful days of summer. Some samples:

> Friday, June 27
> Lunched at E. C. Left Boston at 1:38 P.M. HOU, ACU, MCU, DGW, Miss Thurston and Mr. Baldwin. Beautiful day. RJM on boat. Sat up by the pilot house. Arrived in fair time. Had supper in dining room. Fire in dining room that morning, but very little damage done. HCU and JCU at Nantucket already. Isabel and Betty came home.
>
> Monday, June 30
> Sailed all day in "Hanks" with Allen and Duncan. Beautiful day. Easterly wind. Button boots. Nearly fell overboard. Orrin came to call after tea. Played fantan. Mr. Baldwin and HOU court up in Abner.

Friday, July 4

Fishing in Samoset. ACU seasick. No fish. Dead flat calm. Bathing at low tide. Long string of fire crackers for steam boat. After supper, the quartet came down. Sat on beach and watched fire works. Sang, "I've been working on the railroad."

Friday, July 11

Sailed up harbor in Illissus. Good crowd. Put up curtains at Atkins. Marked out tennis court. Played tennis. Bathed. Allen, Lay, Malcolm. Went to boat. HOU, Mr. Cutter, Mr. Hamlen, and Bobbie. Moonlight sailing. Quartet and Bobbie Atkins.

Thursday, July 24

Played tennis in the morning and sailed with Mr. Buckley in the Patsy. Sailed with Orrin in the afternoon. Lang and lip language. Walked up town after tea and sat on steps. Cigaretts, pillow, etc.

Wednesday, August 6

Bathed in morning. Sat on lawn and played with rabbits. Quartet. (Orrin in Nanquit). Sailed with Lay in the Skip. Stiff breeze. Went up town to hear the band after tea.

Monday, August 25

Hot calm day. Canoes in morning. Bathing. Sailing with Malcolm in afternoon. Jenny, Alice, Lay, Rob and Allen. Miss Middlebrook's tea. Canoing after tea. Lay and harmonica. Marga played golf in afternoon. Becalmed and caught in a shower. Rainbow.

Tuesday, August 26

Jenny, Alice, Marga and Lay sailed with Malcolm in morning. Foursome sail in afternoon. Swindled Lang, Allen and Rob. Marga played golf. Walked up town after tea. Sat on bank steps. Grand fight. Malcolm grouchy.

Tuesday, September 9

Flew kites in the morning. Barbara and Mr. Smith went on noon boat. Lay, Rob, Allen, Aunt Emily and Marga played tennis and bathed. Cloudy, began to rain. After tea, played vingt-et-un with Bob and Allen. Poured in the evening. Chilly. Cold bathing. "Fuzzy" went at noon.

Friday, September 12

Craigs packed. After dinner, Lay and Alice sailed in the Skip. After tea, Lang and Allen came over. Lang to say good bye. Bully night and good moon.

Sunday, September 14

ACU and MCU went mushrooming. Craigs went on noon boat. Marga sailed with Bobbie in the Skip and Alice with Lay in the Hanks. Other people in Samoset. After tea, sat around the fire. MCU went to the Wood's. Read poetry.

Friday, September 19

Nothing doing in morning. Good bye sail in Illissus after lunch. Lay, Orrin, Marga and ACU. Stayed out until 6:30. Night boat very late. Mr. and Mrs. Harding, Frank, Mr. and Mrs Swift and Elizabeth (Swift) came. 10 lbs. candy.

3. Furniture in the Home

In the previous chapter we traced the increase in the quantity, and by inference, the quality, of the furnishings in Nantucket inventories of the first half of the eighteenth century. The trend is underlined by other island inventories. For example, Nathaniel Coffin, a mariner who died in 1721, had a clock valued at nineteen pounds, a high figure for the time, indicating it might have been a fine English tall clock. He owned a "great oval table" of the type shown in Plate XII, valued at £1–10–0, a "little oval table," £1–0–0, possibly like the table in Figure 35, a "great looking glass," £4–10–0, and "6 old Turkey work chairs," 12 shillings. This is the kind of furniture which could have graced a fine home in Boston, where Coffin almost certainly sold his whale oil and bought most of his high-style furniture. This seems to have been a pattern for Nantucket for the seventeenth and the first half of the eighteenth century. High-style, fashionable furniture was brought to the island, mainly from Boston, but later also from Newport, Philadelphia, New York, and London. The custom-house records of Providence and Newport, Rhode Island, show that furniture was sold from these towns to Nantucket soon after the Revolution. In the years 1783, 1788, 1792, and 1793, desks, chairs, and tables came from Providence,[1] and in 1788 and 1789 desks and tables were shipped from Newport[2] to the island.

By the middle of the eighteenth century there were enough joiners and chairmakers working on the island to supply much of the local demand. The more utilitarian furniture forms such as turned chairs, cupboards, chests of drawers, plain desks, small tables, and so on, the kind that could be called vernacular furniture, had been made on the island since the late seventeenth century.

Richard Macy, 1689–1779

Richard Macy is the earliest Nantucket furniture maker for which any extensive documentation is available. His account book[3] shows that he made a variety of furniture forms in the 1710–1728 period. Macy had a shop but often worked for others and like most craftsmen of his time, made a living any way he could. He did plowing, mowing of hay, plastering, hauling of clay and rocks; he made bricks, he mended boats and calashes, and tried out oil from "whale fat." An important part of his work was house carpentry (he built a house for Nathaniel Barnard in 1732 for forty-five pounds) and furniture making. Macy's account book lists the following items having been made in the 1710–1719 period:

4 coffins	2 calashes
7 chests	1 ax handle
7 bedsteads	6 window frames
3 tables	5 casements
1 cheese press	19 oars
1 binnacle [housing for ship's compass]	7 wheels
1 "joynt" stool	2 rimming of wheels
1 meal chest	3 yokes
1 closet	1 harrow
1 meal trough	4 drugs

The account book indicates that in 1728 Macy made a spinning wheel.

All of Macy's furniture was priced under one pound sterling: chests, six to ten shillings; bedsteads, fourteen to nineteen shillings (although Macy made one bedstead for Nathaniel Barnard in 1713 for eight shillings); tables, three and a half to eight shillings; coffins, seven to nine shillings; and a binnacle, four shillings.

The Furniture Makers

Furniture makers in eighteenth-century Nantucket were listed in the records in two separate categories: joiners and chairmakers. The joiners made case furniture, tables, clock cases, and joined chairs, the kind of furniture usually associated with cabinetmaking. The chairmakers made the three- and four-back (slat-back) chairs, and Windsor and other turned chairs. The turning lathe was an important piece of equipment for the chairmaker; in fact, one chairmaker, Richard Gardner, is also listed in the land records (1761) as a turner. We identified sixteen joiners and twelve chairmakers working in Nantucket in the colonial period. There is evidence of joiners since the beginning of the eighteenth century:

Joiners in colonial Nantucket

1700–1725	3
1726–1750	3
1751–1776	10

On the other hand, all the chairmakers surfaced in the records after about 1747, suggesting that Windsor chair production might have been rather extensive in the last half of the eighteenth century:

Chairmakers in colonial Nantucket

1700–1725	0
1726–1750	1
1751–1776	11

Chairs

There was an abundance of chairs in eighteenth-century Nantucket inventories: Tristram Coffin (1706) had nine, John Swain (1718), twenty-four, and Thomas Brock (1750), fifty-four. Other typical inventories of the time included many chairs: Nathaniel Gardner (1723), had twenty-two, Joseph Coffin (1724), thirty-two, and Nathaniel Coffin (1728), thirty-five. George Macy's 1776 inventory listed a Windsor chair: "Winsor Chair—3–10–0."

Mary Starbuck must have had quite a few chairs. When John Richardson visited the island in 1701, he told of a Quaker gathering at the Starbuck house:

> The large and bright rubbed Room was set with suitable Seats or Chairs, the Glass Windows taken out of the Frames, and many Chairs placed without very conveniently, so that I did not see anything a wanting, according to the Place, but something to stand on, for I was not free to set my Feet upon the fine Cane Chair, lest I should break it.[4]

Figure 16. Four-back side chair, rush seat, turned maple posts, hickory slats and rungs, painted black, arc-shaped top slat over three arched slats, 1710-1760. Height: $46^{1}/_{2}$ in. (118 cm.). (*NHA*).

The "fine Cane Chair" could well have been a high, cane-backed and cane-seated English Baroque chair.[5]

The turned side chair in Figure 16 is an example of the most common type of seating furniture of the first half of the eighteenth century, both in Nantucket and the rest of New England. Such chairs are usually designated as slat-back or ladder-back chairs, but in Nantucket inventories they are always called "four back" chairs. There is an occasional "three back" chair in an inventory, but they are far outnumbered by the four-back variety. This type of chair was made all over New England for a very long time, from the seventeenth century to at least the time of the Revolutionary War. We have used 1710–1760 as the time period we believe most of these chairs were made on the island. The Nantucket-made chairs are characterized by rather slim, vertical lines, with turnings that seem to be a bit more delicate than those of the mainland. The backs of the Nantucket four-back chairs flair or spread out at the top, that is, the backs are wider at the top—from three-quarters of an inch to one and a half inches—than at the bottom of the stiles or back posts. The front stretchers usually have two raised sections, or "sausages," in the middle, making use of only the center part of the typical seventeenth-century sausage turning, which had raised sections uniformly turned from one end of the stretcher to the other. The finials are usually crisply turned, with a flattened ball, topped with a knob. Figure 17 shows the branded mark "Mo Meeting," which indicates that the chair belonged to the Friends Meeting. It may well have been the clerk's chair for use in the Monthly Business Meeting.

The three round or roundabout chairs in Plate IX and Figures 18 and 19 all have elements in their design that represent variations from what have come to be thought of as "standard" New England furniture forms. Although these chairs are commonly called corner chairs today, they were called roundabout chairs in eighteenth-century Boston.[6] In Nantucket inventories they were called "round" chairs. Andrew Myrick's 1783 inventory listed "1 round leather Bottom Chair—1–4–0." The turnings of the posts and stretchers of the round chair in Plate IX, with their elongated trumpet shapes, the flat arms which terminate in vigorous, out-turning curves, are related to

Figure 17. Detail of finial and top slat of four-back chair, stamped "Mo Meeting," indicating that it had been the property of the Society of Friends Monthly Meeting. (*NHA*).

William and Mary-style furniture of the late seventeenth and early eighteenth centuries. The Queen Anne-style splats, which are quite light and graceful compared to the sturdy, almost ponderous quality of the rest of the chair, suggest that the chair was probably made in the 1730–1760 period. The chair was from the estate of Mrs. Nancy Adams, whose grandmother was Nancy Grant, wife of Captain Charles Grant. After Mrs. Adams died in 1968, the chair, minus the seat, was sold to a local dealer. Several years later the original seat was found in the attic of the Adams house. It had been covered with a half-dozen layers of cloth, representing a series of reupholsterings, which, when removed, revealed the original brown leather-covered seat.

The round chair in Figure 18 is a typical New England Queen Anne-style roundabout chair, almost certainly made in Nantucket. The turned posts, the cabriole front leg with turned pad foot, the arms and the crest rail are typical of chairs usually attributed to eastern Massachusetts. However, the splats are related to plain Chippendale-style splats, suggesting a slightly later date for the chair, somewhere between 1755 and 1770. The authors own a round chair which appears to be a duplicate of the one in Figure 18. Our chair, which came from the Nantucket estate of Earl S. Ray, had the bottom of its legs cut down in the nineteenth century so that the back three legs could be fitted with casters.

The large round chair with carved claw and ball feet in Figure 19, which is now a chamber

Figure 18. Round or roundabout chair, cherry, painted black, 1755–1770. Height: 30 3/4 in. (78.1 cm.), width: 25 in. (63.5 cm.), depth: 24 1/4 in. (62.2 cm.). (*NHA*).

Plate I. Stairway in center hall of the Middle Brick, plain painted balusters, mahogany newel post and hand rail, scrolled brackets on stringers at ends of each step. The plain-turned, vase-shaped newel is in harmony with the rather ponderous woodwork of the house. The hall is the only room that retains its original wallpaper, with repeating large scroll patterns, the condition of which is quite fine considering its age. The carpets in the halls and on the steps are twentieth century. The ceiling height of the first floor rooms is 10 ft., 5 in.

Plate II. Fragment of Brussels carpet which covered the first floor of the house wall to wall; found in the attic. Size: 31½ in. x 27 in.

Plates I–VIII are from the Middle Brick.

Plate III. Fireplace wall of the west parlor, figured marble mantle. Portrait of Joseph Starbuck painted in 1847 by John Bisbee. Argand lamps on mantle are marked: "Manufactured by / H. N. Hooper & Co. / Boston," made about 1840. The steel-shafted andirons with brass finials are earlier than the house, 1790–1810. The firebucket on the left is marked: "J. GORHAM / 1836," the one on the right: "WILLIAM MACKEY / 1803 / AFFLICTIS / CONSOLATION." Josiah Gorham was the husband of Sarah Starbuck, Joseph's first child. William Mackay was the great-great-grandfather of the present owner.

Plate IV. Gas chandelier in west parlor installed in 1854–1855, at which time manufactured gas was first installed in Nantucket, gilt cast bronze, cherubs are patined black, original glass mantels. Diameter: 30 in.

Plate V. Empire mahogany sideboard with Starbuck family plate. Dimensions of sideboard: length 66¾ in., height 49 in., depth 26 in. To the right is a nineteenth-century child's Windsor highchair. The portraits are of Charlotte Langdon Lodge Mackay and Robert Culwell Mackay, grandparents of the present owner.

Plate VI. East wall of dining room. Empire mahogany serving table, dimensions: length 41 in., height 32 in., depth 25½ in. Both the serving table and the sideboard are original to the house. The serving table is set with a collection of Starbuck family pewter, several pieces of which are illustrated in Chapter 8. The Empire mahogany dining room chair is part of a set of eight, one of which bears the label "S B & Son." (Penciled numbers on the chair frames suggest this was part of a larger set.) It is identical to the chair in Plate X which originally came from the Jared Coffin house on Pleasant Street. The painting of the five Starbuck children (28½ in. x 35½ in.) is signed "G. G. Fish 1860." The bell pull on the left is Berlin work embroidery. The Argand wall fixture on the right is original to the house.

Plate VII. Northeast corner of front room of double parlor. The wallpaper was made by Zubba, Alsace-Lorraine, and was installed in 1922. The curtain valences, or lambrequins, are copies of the originals. (There would have been a full set of draperies with the valence, and "glass" curtains.) The mahogany table with black marble top (one of a pair) and mahogany firescreen with Berlin work embroidery date from the middle of the nineteenth century. The plain gilt mirror above the mantle is original to the house. At the time it was customary to have mirrors over a mantle rather than a portrait. The Sinumbra lamp on the table dates from the 1840s, the glass prisms having been added at a later date. The bronze sculpture of Mercury is European, late nineteenth century.

Plate VIII. Empire mahogany sofa, circa 1835, square table on right, twentieth century. The free-standing swift mounted on an octagonal whalebone and whale-ivory inlaid box dates from the second quarter of the nineteenth century. Height: 19 in.

Plate IX. Round or roundabout chair, maple, turned legs, stretchers and arm supports, vase-shaped splats, painted black, original brown leather seat, 1730–1760. Height: 31¼ in. (79.4 cm.), width: 25¼ in. (64.1 cm.), depth: 24½ in. (62.2 cm.). (*Collection of the authors*).

Plate X. Empire side chair, one of a set of eight, mahogany with crotch mahogany veneer on the splat and crest rail, circa 1835. Needlepoint seat cover made in the twentieth century by the granddaughter of the original owner. Five of the chairs bear the penciled initials "BFC" for Benjamin F. Coffin, son of Jared and Hepsabeth (Swain) Coffin. Benjamin F., who was born in 1814, was living in Moors' End on Pleasant Street when he married Mary C. Crosby in 1835. The eight chairs have punched Roman numerals under the seat—II, XV, XVI, XVII, XX, XXI, XXIII, XXIIII—which suggests there had been at least twenty-four chairs in the original set. Height: 32¾ in. (83.2 cm.), depth: 19 in. (48.3 cm.), width: 19¼ in. (48.9 cm.). (*Private collection*).

Plate XI. Windsor high chair, carved ears and arm ends, maple, hickory, and pine, painted black. Painted on the crest rail is the date "1737." The chair was probably made in the last quarter of the eighteenth century. Height: 36 in. (91.4 cm.). (*Private collection.*)

Plate XII. Large drop-leaf table, turned legs and stretchers, dovetailed drawer (not shown), butterfly hinges under top, all maple, old red paint, 1700–1720. Said to have first been owned by Mary Starbuck (1645–1717), daughter of Tristram and Dionis Coffin. Height: 27½ in. (69.9 cm.), width: 49½ in. (125.7 cm.), length: 55½ in. (141 cm.). (*NHA.*)

Plate XIII. Stand with turned pedestal, carved legs, two-piece flat top, cherry, 1750–1800. Formerly owned by Grace Brown Gardner. Height: 26 3/8 in. (67 cm.), top: 16 1/2 x 16 5/8 in. (41.9 x 42.2 cm.). (*Private collection*).

Plate XIV. Dressing table, drawers with opalescent glass handles, pine, grain-painted to imitate curly maple, 1825–1840. Height: $35^3/_4$ in. (90.8 cm.), width: 42 in. (106.7 cm.), depth: $18^3/_4$ in. (47.6 cm.). (*NHA*).

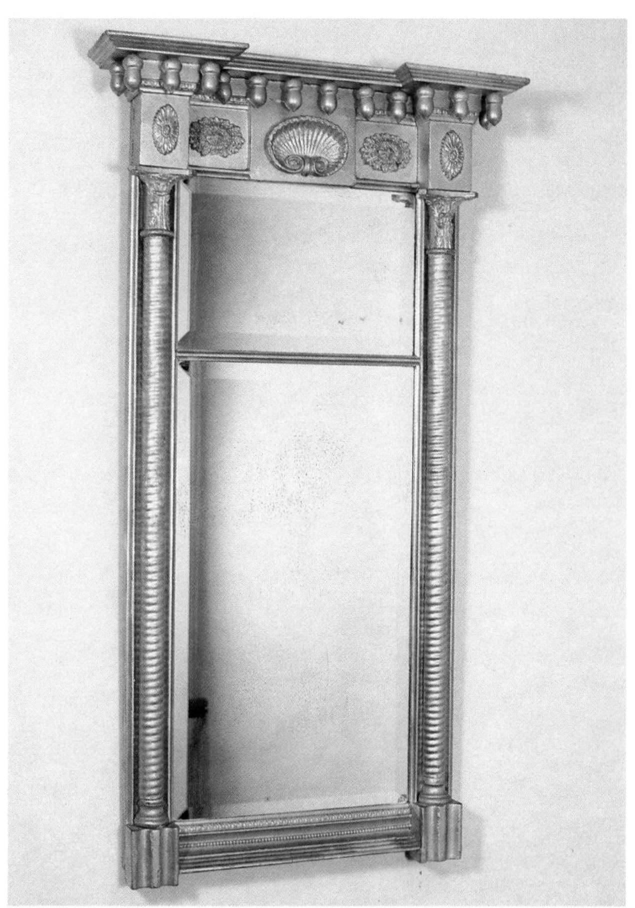

Plate XV. Looking glass, gilt frame, bevelled glass, circa 1830. Height: 42 in. (106.7 cm.), width: $23^1/_2$ in. (59.7 cm.). (*Private collection*).

Plate XVI. Astronomical tall clock, made by Walter Folger, Jr. in 1788–1790. Mahogany clock case with brass stop-fluted quarter columns, silvered dial with the inscription: "Walter Folger / Nantucket." The clock case was made in Boston. Height to top of finial: 101½ in. (257.8 cm.). The portrait of Walter Folger at the left of the clock was painted by William Swain of Newburyport, Massachusetts in 1827–1828. Below the portrait is a plaster bust of Benjamin Franklin, Walter Folger's cousin, and a Windsor chair with Folger's stamp "WF" on the bottom. (*NHA*).

Plate XVII. Piano made by John Osborne, Boston, in 1818, mahogany with rosewood and brass inlays, brass rosettes, drawer pulls, griffin and lyre, collars on tops of legs and cup casters. On the music rack is a painted and gilt shell with the inscription: "J. Osborne. / Manufacturer. / No 12, Orange Stt. / Boston." Height: 33 1/2 in. (85.1 cm.), depth: 25 1/4 in. (64.1 cm.), width: 67 in. (170.1 cm.). Piano stool, grain-painted with original horsehair upholstery on seat. Height: 20 1/4 in. (51.4 cm.), diameter of seat: 12 in. (30.5 cm.). (*Collection of Paul Madden, on loan to the NHA*).

Plate XIX. Dressing case with mirror, mahogany inlaid with ebony, rosewood, whalebone, and whale ivory, whale-ivory feet and knobs, made by Captain James Archer on the whaling bark *Afton,* 1853–1856. Height: 35 1/2 in. (90.2 cm.), width: 29 in. (73.7 cm.), depth: 13 1/8 in. (33.3 cm.). (*NHA*).

Plate XVIII. Sea chest, pine, painted blue, originally owned by Joseph Mitchell, 2nd, master of the Nantucket-built whaleship *Three Brothers*, circa 1835. Length: 46 5/8 in. (118.4 cm.), height: 20 1/8 in. (51.1 cm.), depth: 19 1/4 in. (48.9 cm.). On the sea chest is a horizon glass engraved "Joseph Mitchell, 2nd," Length: 37 1/2 in. (95.3 cm.). (*Private collection*).

Plate XX. Table, inlaid on four sides and around the drawer front with whalebone strips scrimshawed with vine patterns, top inlaid with whalebone. Oak with mahogany pulls on the drawer. Made on board ship for Charlotte Coffin Gardner, wife of William Bunker Gardner, between 1845 and 1855. Height: 26 1/2 in. (67.3 cm.), width: 18 in. (45.7 cm.), depth: 17 1/2 in. (44.5 cm.). (*Private collection*).

Plate XXI. Pipe box, pine, inlaid with whalebone. Masonic symbols, drawer at base, accompanied by a handwritten note "Pipe Box the property of Capt. Obed Worth who died about 1804." Height: 14 in. (35.6 cm.), width: $4^{7}/_{8}$ in. (12.4 cm.), depth $3^{1}/_{4}$ in. (8.3 cm.). Clay pipe marked "T D" on bowl and "McDougal / Glascow, Scotland" on the stem. Length: $6^{1}/_{2}$ in. (16.5 cm.). (*NHA*).

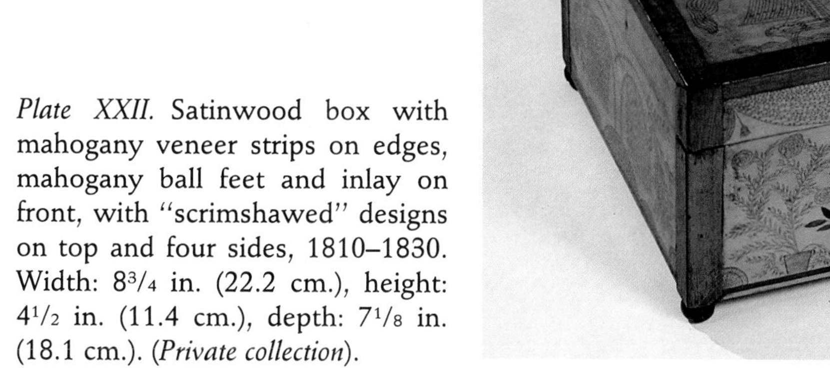

Plate XXII. Satinwood box with mahogany veneer strips on edges, mahogany ball feet and inlay on front, with "scrimshawed" designs on top and four sides, 1810–1830. Width: $8^{3}/_{4}$ in. (22.2 cm.), height: $4^{1}/_{2}$ in. (11.4 cm.), depth: $7^{1}/_{8}$ in. (18.1 cm.). (*Private collection*).

Plate XXIII. Mahogany box, inlaid with ebony, whalebone, and whale ivory, dated 1849. Width: 11 in. (27.9 cm.), height: 4⁷/8 in. (12.4 cm.), depth: 5³/4 in. (14.6 cm.). (*NHA*).

Plate XXIV. Two painted boxes, French, late eighteenth century. The large box on the left has a Macy family history; the smaller box on the right is branded on the bottom: "M JOY / 1799." Left box, width: 16 in. (40.6 cm.), height: 11¹/2 in. (29.2 cm.), depth: 11¹/2 in. (29.2 cm.). Right box: width: 10¹/2 in. (26.7 cm.), height: 7³/8 in. (18.7 cm.), depth: 6³/4 in. (17.1 cm.). (*NHA*).

Plate XXV. Model of the pinky *Eagle*, made by Charles F. Sayle in 1942. Hull carved from poplar, with a scribed deck attached. Painted green and black with a white stripe. Bottom painted "tallow" white. Length: 12¼ in. (31.1 cm.), height over mast: 11⅞ in. (30.2 cm.). (*Courtesy of Mr. and Mrs. Charles F. Sayle*).

Plate XXVI. Mercury barometer and thermometer, inscribed "T. Pool / Son / New York," originally owned by Captain Obed Luce (1768–1846). Mahogany with crotch veneer on front, ebony inlay, ivory knob and finial, 1815–1828. Height: $39\frac{3}{4}$ in. (101 cm.). (*Private collection*).

Figure 19. Round or roundabout chair, mahogany, cabriole legs with claw and ball feet, 1760–1790. Height: 32³/₈ in. (81.4 cm.), width: 27 in. (68.6 cm.), depth: 27 in. (68.6 cm.). (*NHA*).

chair, has the following handwritten note pasted on the frame under the seat:

> This chair belonged to and was used by Rev. Wm. J. Breed pastor of the North Cong. Church of Nantucket. At the sale of his effects in 1839, it was bought for fifty cents by Mrs. Mary W., wife of Capt. Edw W. Coffin. George O. Buck—then a lad of 13 years—carried it home from the auction on his head. Mrs. Coffin concluded she did not want it and gave it to her brother-in-law Capt. Randall Kelley to split up. The latter decided to repair it and kept it as long as he lived. After his widow's death, it came again to Mrs. Coffin and after the death of her daughter Mrs. Susan P. Barrett it came to Capt. George H. Brock. In August 1910 the latter refused an offer of one hundred dollars for the chair.

The side chair in Figure 20, with a Queen Anne-style splat, has turned legs similar to those of the turned four-back chair in Figure 16. The chair in Figure 21 is in the Chippendale style. The pierced splat, which extends to the seat, has a delicate heart-shaped opening at the top. The legs are chamfered, giving a light, delicate effect to the chair, raising it above the average example.

Figure 20. Side chair, rush seat, ebonized maple, 1760–1800. Height: 38³/₄ in. (98.4 cm.), depth: 15 in. (38.1 cm.), width: 19³/₄ in. (50.2 cm.). (*NHA*).

The English side chair of the 1760–1770 period in Figure 22 has an interesting historical association. The accession record of the Historical Association states: "This chair is one of six brought from England by Capt. Hezekiah Coffin on the whaleship *Beaver* loaded with tea from the East India Co. in 1768." A brass plaque on the back of the chair tells a slightly different story: "Brought from England aboard the *Beaver* when involved in The Boston Tea Party" (1773). We have no other evidence as to whether or not the chair was actually on the *Beaver* at the time of that famous event in American history.[7]

Figure 22. English side chair, pierced Gothic-style splat, mahogany, brought to Nantucket on the whaleship *Beaver* by Captain Hezekiah Coffin, circa 1770. Height: 36³/₈ in. (92.4 cm.), depth: 19¹/₄ in. (48.9 cm.), width: 21¹/₂ in. (54.6 cm.). (*NHA*).

Figure 21. Side chair, pierced splat, birch. There are two dates on the original seat frame: "1766" written on the linen lining and "1799" on the frame itself. The chair came from the estate of Catherine Defrieze Fitzpatrick, 1765–1800. Height: 38¹/₂ in. (97.8 cm.). (*Private collection*).

The Empire side chair in Plate X is practically identical to the dining room chairs in the Middle Brick (Plate VI), one of which bears the label "S B & Son." We have not been able to determine whether or not they were made in Nantucket. Although there are a number of such Empire chairs on the island today with long local histories, such chairs were also made in Boston and New York.

The low slipper chair in Figure 23 is a whimsical example of Victoriana that is a variation from the more typical nineteenth-century rococo furniture that one finds in many old houses on the island. There is no evidence that any of these Victorian chairs were Nantucket made.

The baby pen or chair in Figure 24, sometimes called a baby cage, is a simple, functional piece of furniture that could have been made by almost any householder. This was apparently a relatively common piece of Nantucket furniture in the seventeenth and eighteenth centuries.

Figure 24. Baby pen or chair ("baby cage"), pine with blue milk paint, 1700–1800. On the bottom are remnants of a signature in chalk: "Sam S. Barnard (or Barney) 38 Day [?] Street." Height: 14¾ in. (37.5 cm.), depth: 17 in. (43.2 cm.), width: 19 in. (48.3 cm.). (*NHA*).

Figure 23. "Slipper" chair with casters on the front legs, birch with carved cherry splat, circa 1870. Height: 30¼ in. (77.5 cm.), depth: 17 in. (43.2 cm.), width: 19 in. (48.3 cm.). (*Private collection*).

Windsor Chairs

America has had a long-time love affair with Windsor chairs. From the time they were first introduced in this country in the second quarter of the eighteenth century to well into the nineteenth century, it was our most popular seating form. Thomas Jefferson is said to have written the Declaration of Independence on a Windsor writing-arm chair.[8] There were Windsor chairs on the east portico of Mount Vernon for visitors waiting for an audience with the retired commander in chief. Windsor chairs were strong, comfortable, and cheap.

Nantucketers knew about and probably imported Philadelphia Windsors at an early date. From the beginning of the eighteenth century and the visit of Thomas Chockley and others there were close ties between the island Quakers and those of Philadelphia. In addition, there were strong commercial ties. We have already noted that Thomas Brock's inventory listed "100 lb. bone at Philadelphia—£210," graphic evidence that the whalers sold products there.

We believe that Windsor chairs were being made in Nantucket by the early 1760s. In addition to Caleb Stretton, who was working as a chairmaker in 1747, there were four chairmakers, Richard Gardner, Robert Clasby, Christopher Swain, and Stephen Barnard, who were prosperous enough to be involved in land transactions in the years 1761 to 1763, suggesting that there was a flurry of activity in chairmaking at that time in Nantucket. (These chairmakers were no doubt making a variety of chairs, including Windsors.) Unfortunately, at the time of this writing (1986), none of these makers can be connected with specific pieces of furniture. Only two Nantucket chairmakers of the eighteenth century are associated with known Windsor chairs: Charles Chase and Frederick Slade. One chair is attributed to Slade, while a half-dozen chairs branded with Chase's name are known.

Because of the number of chairmakers working on the island, Windsor chairs of the Philadelphia (and later, Boston) types may well have been made in Nantucket early on. The fanback armchair in Figure 25 (also illustrated on the back jacket cover), one of a pair, is a good example of a Philadelphia-type Windsor of what is considered the best period, 1765–1780. There is a great splay to the cylinder-and-ball foot legs, the back and the arm posts are nicely turned. The almost round seat has a tail piece which forms a seat for the two socketed back braces. The arched crest rail has well-carved ears. Except for two features, this chair is similar to a Philadelphia armchair in the Art Institute of Chicago.[9] The features which are different are: the "Nantucket" chair has arms which terminate in sharper, more dramatic back curves, and its center spindle has a bal-

Figure 25. Windsor armchair, crest rail and arms maple, spindles hickory, seat poplar, old green paint, 1765–1780. Height: 40 3/4 in. (103.5 cm.). Candlestand, iron and brass, New England circa 1725. It probably originally had a brass finial on top. Height: 67 3/4 in. (172 cm.). (*NHA*).

uster shape at the top over two turned rings, plus two more turned rings at arm level which line up with the top and bottom of the arms. The other spindles have the remnants of painted rings that line up with the turned rings of the center spindle.

Charles Chase (1731–1815) made some of the island's best-known pieces of furniture, examples of his Windsor chairs being in the Winterthur Museum, Colonial Williamsburg, and the Art Institute of Chicago. In view of his obvious proficiency, it is surprising to find that he was most often listed in the land-court records as a carpenter, and only once, in 1811, was he listed as a "chair maker." Over a fifty-three year period he was called a "carpenter" (1758 and 1783), a "housewright" (1776), and a "house carpenter" (1811). The records suggest that Charles Chase was a carpenter-builder who also made Windsor chairs.

Figure 26. Fan-back Windsor side chair, nine spindles, carved ears. Hickory, maple and poplar, originally painted green. Branded on botton of seat "C. CHASE." Formerly owned by Grace Brown Gardner, circa 1770–1790. Height: 36 in. (91.4 cm.). (*NHA*).

The fan-back Windsor side chair in Figure 26 is branded on the bottom of the seat "C. CHASE." Chase's chair is related to Philadelphia side chairs.[10] The turnings of the back posts, legs, and stretchers are similar. However, the seats of Chase's chairs seem to have been slightly more vigorously carved, the swell in the middle of the crest rail more pronounced, and the notches by the ears deeper and sharper.

The fan-back armchair in Figure 27, also branded "C. CHASE" (Figure 28), in the collection of Colonial Williamsburg, gives additional evidence of Charles Chase's mastery of the Windsor chair form, a chair that has been described as "majestic" by Charles Santore, author of *The Windsor Style in America.*[11] There is an almost identical armchair made by Chase in the collection of the Winterthur Museum.[12] The Chase chairs were made in a style that is usually dated 1765–1780, but we believe that the time span of Chase's production should be widened a bit, to 1760–1800. The earlier date is because of the aforementioned close and frequent contacts between Nantucket and Philadelphia, and the later date because of the well-known predilection of craftsmen away from the urban centers to continue working longer in established styles. There was probably a hiatus in most chairmaking activities in the 1776–1783 Revolutionary War period, a time when the commercial life of the island came nearly to a halt.

Figure 27. Windsor armchair, maple posts, legs and stretchers. The crest rail, arms and spindles are ash or hickory. The arm scroll is made of a single piece, the arms are pinned at the back of the stiles, and a separate tail piece is tenoned and pinned to the seat at the back to support the braces. Entire chair covered with modern red paint over an earlier black and the original green. Height: $47\frac{3}{4}$ in. (121.3 cm.), width: $22\frac{7}{8}$ in. (58.1 cm.), depth: $21\frac{1}{4}$ in. (54.0 cm.). (*Colonial Williamsburg*).

Figure 28. Brand on chair in Figure 27 beneath seat at front.

Based on those chairs branded with "C. CHASE," the following characteristics can be noted for his chairs: The turnings of the baluster-and-ring legs are more restrained than those of typical Connecticut and Rhode Island examples, the tapered bottom leg sections sometimes having a straight, attenuated taper. Occasionally the taper is accentuated a bit toward the bottom. The top part of the leg is made of two vase-shaped balusters separated by rings. The side stretchers have typical swellings in the middle, while the center stretcher has two vigorously turned rings. The legs of Chase's chairs, particularly those of the large armchairs, have a generous splay. The baluster-and-ring arm supports and the stiles each have two vase-shaped balusters, which, in the case of the armchairs, start above the arm junction. The one-piece arm scroll fits into a squared unturned section of the stile, and is pinned with a nail at the back. The back crest rails of the Chase chairs usually exhibit a good lift in the middle. Ear scrolls are deeply carved, and there is a deeply cut, sharp notch by the ears. The seats have strong vigorous shapes. The armchairs have separate tailpieces in the back, with grain perpendicular to the seat and pinned to the seat to support the back braces. All of Chase's chairs seem to have been painted green originally. The brand "C. CHASE" in a rectangle is usually on the bottom of the seat, at the front (Figure 28).

The highchair in Plate XI has some of the characteristics associated with Chase's chairs, the crest rails with carved ears and deep notches and similar stiles and arms. However, the turnings of the legs and the medial stretcher with a ring turned in the middle, are different. The medial stretcher is related to early Philadelphia Windsors, as is the whole design of the chair. The highchair has the date "1737" painted on the crest rail. It is one of the heirlooms of Matthew Starbuck's Middle

Figure 29. Fan-back Windsor armchair, crest rail and arms maple, spindles hickory, seat poplar, greenish-black paint decorated with gold lines and light green trim. On the bottom is nailed a cardboard note with the inscription "This chair was made by Fredrick Slade in 1799." Height: 42¼ in. (107.3 cm.), seat depth: 16⅝ in. (42.3 cm.), seat width: 21⅝ in. (54.9 cm.). (*Private collection*).

Brick. The chair certainly dates later than 1737, possibly as late as the last quarter of the eighteenth century. We searched the records for a Starbuck relative who might have been born in 1737. No luck.

The fan-back armchair in Figure 29 is the only known Windsor attributed to Frederick Slade. We do not know the date of Slade's birth, but it would not have been before 1777, since his parents, Benjamin and Rhoda (Coleman) Slade, were married in Nantucket November 21, 1776. Frederick died, unmarried, in July 1800, "coming from Havana."[13]

Slade's armchair has certain details in common with the chairs of Charles Chase and other Nantucket Windsors: the squared-off section of the stiles at the place where the arms are joined in, and the brace-block attached to the back of the seat with grain running perpendicular to the grain of the seat. (Slade's block is squared off at the corners, while Chase's blocks have rounded corners.) Points of difference are: the carved scrolled ears of the crest rail are larger and more vigorously carved than those of the Chase chairs; the stylized knuckle-ends of the arms are broader and quite different from the more conventional knuckles of the Chase chairs; the turnings of the legs and stretchers of the Slade chair are simpler than those of the Chase chairs (the medial stretcher does not have turned rings); finally, the turnings of the stiles are different, the curves of Slade's baluster shapes being less pronounced.

Late Windsors

The bow-back rocker, with a rather high comb-back, in Figure 30, has cross stretchers and bamboo-turned legs. Windsor rockers are rare, most of those we see today having been converted from armchairs by the addition of rockers. The rockers on the chair in Figure 30 are definitely original, which suggests it was made late, probably in the nineteenth century.

The rod-back side chair in Figure 31 and the rocker in Figure 32 are both branded "WF" for Walter Folger, Jr., the maker of the famous astronomical clock in Plate XVI. The question is whether the chairs were made by Folger or simply branded as possessions, a common practice of the time. There seems to be nothing in Folger's account books and other records now in the library of the Nantucket Historical Association to indicate he made the chairs, even though he was fully capable of doing so. He was a first-rate mechanic, a man with highly capable hands. However, he did not attempt to make the case for his famous clock, ordering it instead from Boston. The fact that the chair in Figure 32 has both the brand mark "WF" for Walter Folger, Jr., and "EKF" for Edward K. Folger, youngest son of Walter Folger, Jr., seems to strengthen the case for ownership since it is unlikely that both men would have been involved in the making of such chairs. The rod-back chair in Figure 31, with straight bamboo-turned legs, stretchers, stiles, and crest rail, is a type known as a "double bowed"

Figure 30. Windsor rocker, legs and rockers maple, stiles hickory, seat pine, painted black, 1795–1810. Height: 43¼ in. (109.9 cm.). (*NHA*).

Figure 31. Rod-back Windsor side chair (one of four), painted green. Branded on bottom "WF" for Walter Folger, Jr., (1765–1849), early nineteenth century. Height: 33½ in. (85.1 cm.). (*NHA*).

Figure 32. Rocking chair, painted red with black outline. Earlier stenciling can be seen through the red paint. Branded on bottom "WF" for Walter Folger, Jr. and "EKF" for Edward K. Folger, youngest son of Walter Folger, Jr. Said to have been made in 1789 for Anna Folger, wife of Walter Folger, Jr. The date 1789 seems too early, more likely 1820–1840. Height: 38¾ in. (98.4 cm.). (*NHA*).

Windsor in the nineteenth century and today as a "birdcage" Windsor. The chair in Figure 32 is sometimes called a "Salem" rocker. The caption notes that the rocker was said to have been made in Nantucket in 1789, although, as pointed out in the caption, this date seems too early.

The oversized late Windsor in Figure 33, made in Boston in 1884, is a survival copy of a mid-nineteenth-century style of chair. Its ample size (twenty-eight and one-fourth inches wide, twenty-eight inches deep) indicates it was designed for a big man. Captain Charles W. Fisher, Nantucket master of the whaling bark *Alaska,* out of New Bedford in 1880, reported taking on May 4, 1884, a sperm whale which yielded 162 barrels and twenty-two gallons of oil, a record up to that time. On his return from the voyage, several of his brother

Figure 33. Windsor armchair, made in 1884 for Captain Charles W. Fisher, to commemorate his taking of a record-breaking sperm whale. Stamped on bottom of seat: "J. C. Hubbard / Boston." Height: 35¼ in. (89.5 cm.), depth: 28¼ in. (71.8 cm.), width: 28¼ in. (71.8 cm.). (*NHA*).

whaling captains had the chair made for him and presented it to him as the holder of the record.

Tables

The descriptions of tables in eighteenth-century Nantucket inventories are not very useful in identifying specific examples of furniture. The descriptions are too general. John Swain's 1718 inventory lists "a large table 15s," "a small table 3s," "a table frame 4s," and "a fashionable table 15s." The "large table" may have been an oval-topped drop-leaf table with turned legs of the type shown in Plate XII; the "small table" could have been either an oval-topped stand as in Figure 34, or an oval-topped table like the one in Figure 35. The "table frame" was no doubt a trestle table with a one- or two-board top which could be dismantled for compact storage. The "fashionable table" could have been an oval-topped Queen Anne-style drop-leaf table with cabriole legs, two of which swing out to support the leaves. The tables in Thomas Brock's inventory are even less specifically described, five of which are merely noted with the description "round table." The values of these "round tables" vary from one

Figure 35. Small oval table, splayed turned legs, all maple, 1710–1770. Height: 22¾ in. (57.8 cm.), top: 22¾ x 25½ in. (57.8 x 64.8 cm.). (*NHA*).

Figure 34. Stand with turned pedestal shaft, oval top, hard pine top and pedestal, maple feet and top support, 1700–1725. Height: 22¾ in. (57.8 cm.), top: 15¼ x 18 in. (38.7 x 45.7 cm.). (*NHA*).

pound to a high of fourteen pounds. Perhaps the table valued at fourteen pounds was also a large drop-leaf table of the type shown in Plate XII.

The three late seventeenth- or early eighteenth-century tables illustrated in Figures 34 and 35, and Plate XII have long Nantucket histories. The stand in Figure 34 could well have been made on the island. The turned pedestal shaft is related to the turnings of the stiles of the four-back chair shown in Figure 16. The chairmaker who made the four-back chairs could easily have made the stand.

The oval table with turned legs in Figure 35 is today often designated as a tavern table, a term not used in eighteenth-century inventories. A Nantucket inventory would have listed it as an "oval table" or "small oval table." The large oval-topped table in Plate XII, with its turned legs and stretchers, was probably made in Boston in the latter part of the seventeenth or early eighteenth century. These large, impressive tables fold for convenient storage along a wall. When open they have a commanding presence, comfortably seating eight people for dining. This particular table has evidence of powderpost beetle attack in its legs, but otherwise it is in good condition. The table retains much of its original red paint; the feet are original. It has a single drawer (not shown). The outer edge of the top is slightly rounded. Later tables of this type have ovolo-type edges.

The Typical Nantucket Table

We mentioned earlier that the single most characteristic Nantucket furniture type of the eighteenth and early nineteenth centuries is a series of small stands or tables of the kind sometimes designated as "candlestands," with shaped legs, a turned center post, and a round or shaped top. Although tables with top diameters of thirty inches or more are known, most are smaller. Almost all have two-piece tops, although we illustrate one with a three-piece and one with a one-piece top. The reason for these two- and three-piece tops is not known. It has been suggested that such tops would be more resistant to warping in the damp sea atmosphere of the island, but this idea seems to have little validity. A more likely explanation is that such tops were cheaper to make. Furniture woods had to be imported to the island and narrower pieces were less expensive. Nantucket furniture makers were always carefully saving in their use of materials.

The small round-topped stand in Plate XIII, which has a Gardner family provenance,[14] is an excellent example of the earliest type of these tables. The flat two-piece top is tapered to an edge thickness of only fifteen thirty-seconds of an inch. The slim shaft with a ring approximately in the middle, the ball at the bottom of the shaft, which is really an egg-shaped swelling, the tapered, carved legs, which have a considerable lift, are all characteristic of the typical Nantucket table. The design of these tables was influenced by the Quaker aesthetic, just as were the early Shaker tables. (There is a definite link between early Shaker furniture and simpler Quaker forms of the eighteenth century that is still to be explored by scholars.) There are at least twenty-five or thirty of these tables on the island today, most with identical leg contours, which suggests that many were made in the same shop.[15]

The beautifully crafted stand in Figure 36, with a shaped two-piece top, is made of very dense mahogany. The legs are shaped with contours similar to the previous table. The gracefully shaped top, and the plain shaft with urn at the base, are variations on a theme.

The table in Figure 37, with its urn-shaped

Figure 37. Tip-top table, shaped two-piece top, turned pedestal with urn, carved legs with chip carving (Figure 38), all birch, 1775–1810. Height: 27 in. (68.6 cm.), top: 19¼ x 20⅛ in. (48.9 x 51.1 cm.). (*Private collection*).

Figure 36. Stand with turned pedestal, carved legs, two-piece top, mahogany, 1750–1800. From the estate of Catharine Defrieze Fitzpatrick. Height: 27¾ in. (70.5 cm.), top: 17⅝ x 18½ in. (44.8 x 47 cm.). (*Private collection*).

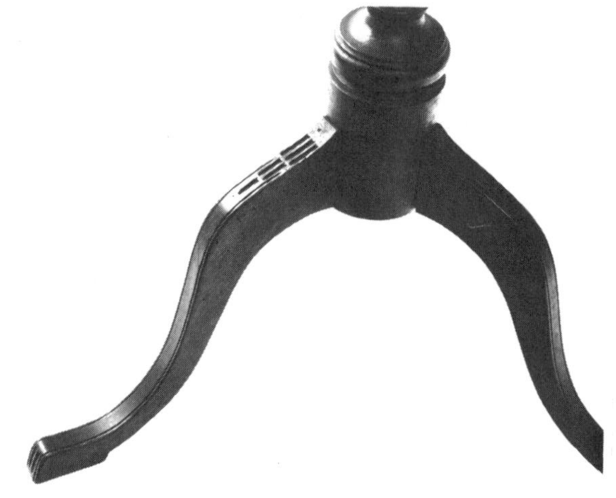

Figure 38. Chip carving on leg of table in Figure 37.

Figure 39. Tip-top table, scrolled three-piece top, turned pedestal with urn, "spider" legs. Top and legs birch, pedestal maple, 1815–1830. Height: 27¼ in. (69.3 cm.), top: 17⅝ x 27¾ in. (44.8 x 70.5 cm.). (*Courtesy Mrs. John P. Elder*).

turnings in the pedestal, has legs that are closely related in shape to the previously discussed tables. The chip carving on the legs and the carved feet (Figure 38) is a characteristic Nantucket touch. The last variant of what we call "the typical Nantucket table," illustrated in Figure 39, has rather abbreviated legs but a handsome scrolled top. It has a nineteenth-century feel, forecasting Victorian exuberance. The four tables shown in Plate XIII and Figures 36, 37, and 39 are representative of the several dozen known examples of this type of table; they show the evolution in style from a purely Quaker version of the Queen Anne style to the nineteenth century, when the plain forms of the past were being discarded, just as Nantucketeers of the time were spiritually turning away from their plain Quaker heritage

The large, severely simple drop leaf table in Figure 40, made of heavy, dense mahogany, speaks of the Quaker taste of its original owner, Joseph Starbuck. This is the kind of plain, undecorated furniture that is seldom illustrated in furniture books. One can note the tapered legs, which are usually later than untapered legs, and the swing legs which support the table leaves. We would guess that Joseph Starbuck acquired this table about 1807, when he built his New Dollar Lane house.

In the second quarter of the nineteenth century grain-painted furniture and woodwork in houses became fashionable. The dressing table in Plate XIV, grained to imitate curly maple, is an attractive example of this genre.

Acanthus carved furniture and newel posts in houses were a common motif of the 1830s in Nantucket. There are so many newel posts of the type illustrated in Figure 41 in Nantucket houses that one suspects they were made on the island. The work table in Figure 42 has similarly carved legs which combine baroque carved acanthus-leaf forms with small areas of geometric cross-hatching.

Figure 40. Drop-leaf table, tapered legs, mahogany, 1790–1820. Belonged to Joseph Starbuck (1774–1861). Height: 29½ in. (74.9 cm.), width: 47⅞ in. (121.6 cm.), length with leaves up: 72⅜ in. (183.8 cm.). (*Private collection*).

Figure 41. Newel post in Fair Street house, Nantucket, mahogany, circa 1836. Height: 42 3/8 in. (107.6 cm.).

Figure 42. Work table, acanthus carved legs, original brass handles and feet, mahogany with crotch mahogany veneer on front, 1825–1840. From the estate of Catharine Defrieze Fitzpatrick. Height: 30 1/2 in. (77.5 cm.), width: 23 1/8 in. (58.7 cm.), depth: 17 in. (43.2 cm.). (*Private collection*).

Furniture Makers and Retailers in the 1820s and 1830s

There were no cabinetmakers advertising in the Nantucket newspapers of the 1820s and 1830s, although several of the Main Street stores advertised that they made furniture to order. The *Nantucket Inquirer* had the following advertisement on January 8, 1831:

> FURNITURE
> CONSTANTLY FOR SALE AT THE
> NANTUCKET FURNITURE WAREHOUSE
> (MAIN STREET, OPPOSITE PACIFIC BANK)
> AN ELEGANT ASSORTMENT OF
> CABINET FURNITURE
> Horse Hair sofas, side boards, Secretaries & Book cases, Grecian and Card tables, Grecian Dining tables; plain do: plain Tea do; Grecian & Plain worktables,—Dressing do, Light stands of every pattern and description; wash stands of all kinds; bedsteads, writing desks, crickets,[16] cribs &c. The above articles are made of the best materials, by experienced workmen, warranted good, and will be sold at as low rates as can be purchased at any regular warehouse in the state. An article made to order, on short notice, and at lowest cash prices.
>
> George Worth, Agent

Two and a half years later, on September 25, 1833, George Worth listed prices in his advertisement in the *Inquirer:*

> The subscriber offers for sale a general assortment of cabinet Furniture (at reduced prices) among which are:

Sofas	from	$ 35	to	$50
Center tables	from	25	to	45
Bureaus	from	7	to	10
Card tables	from	7	to	20
Work tables	from	1.75	"	20
Looking glasses	from	.50	"	30

> some of which have elegant mahogany frames; Chairs from common wood seats at .50 to rich cane seats, Curl maple at 1.00 together with and endless variety of other articles too numerous to mention.
>
> Also 1000 lbs. of Live Geese Feathers sold in lots to suit subscriber
>
> Also English and Straw Entry Carpeting, on consignment 500 yds. of superfine English Carpeting—300 do Straw Entry do—persons wishing to purchase are requested to call and examine for themselves.
>
> George F. Worth

Another merchant, James Tallent, was both a retailer of furniture and a maker of looking glasses. His advertisement in the January 15, 1831, *Nantucket Inquirer* noted:

> Jas. Tallent has on hand, at his store on Pearl Street, an extensive assortment of FURNITURE, of the most fashionable Boston patterns.
>
> Old furniture repaired, varnished and trimmed in the neatest manner. Looking glasses and picture frames of every description at short notice.

James Tallent's advertisement should warn us to beware of present-day claims of "original finish" or "original varnish" on pieces of antique furniture. A Queen Anne table with its "original finish" may have been refinished by a James Tallent a century and a half ago!

Case Furniture

The chest of drawers in Figure 43, in the collection of Historic Deerfield, was made in the first half of the eighteenth century. The Deerfield chest was exhibited in the 1935 Loan Exhibition of Heirlooms at the Charles G. Coffin

ments, and the chest was grain painted in the nineteenth century.

The slant-top mahogany desk in Figure 44, probably made in Boston or the Boston area in the third quarter of the eighteenth century, presently in the Yale University Art Gallery, has a long Nantucket history. Inscriptions on

Figure 43. Chest of drawers, probably made in Nantucket, oak and white pine, grain painted on front, 1700–1750. Height: 33½ in. (85.1 cm.), width: 27½ in. (69.9 cm.), depth: 16½ in. (41.9 cm.). (*Historic Deerfield*).

house on Main Street, Nantucket, then in the possession of Mrs. Abbot Coffin. According to a label pasted inside the upper right-hand drawer, it was owned in 1740 by Micajah Coffin. The only Micajah Coffin in the *Nantucket Vital Records* was born in 1734, making it unlikely he would have been considered the owner of the chest in 1740. However, the *Vital Records* lists a Micah Coffin (1705–1783) who could have been the original owner. It apparently had been in the Coffin family since the eighteenth century. The brasses are replace-

Figure 44. Slant top desk, four graduated drawers, replaced brasses, base of case with molding over cabriole legs terminating in claw and ball feet, mahogany and white pine, circa 1768. On a document drawer are several inscriptions in pencil including: "Wm Butler / September ye 10, 1768; Wm C. Dyer / April 28th, 1838 / Lydia C. Wyer do Do; 1861 / – 1768 / 93; Wm Clisby Desk from / Huldah Crosby June 1830." On another drawer is the note: "Wm Clisby Oct 9 1874 / Nantucket / CW." Height: 44¼ in. (112.4 cm.), width: 44¾ in. (113.7 cm.), depth: 22½ in. (57.2 cm.). (*Yale University Art Gallery, The Mabel Brady Garvan Collection*).

the desk indicate it was owned and possibly acquired in 1768 by William Butler of Nantucket, a housewright born on Martha's Vineyard. Butler married Mary Jenkins of Nantucket in 1742. He died in 1791. His will indicated that he left everything to his wife, who died in 1811. Neither Butler nor his wife have inventories in the probate court records. The desk then belonged to Huldah Crosby (1750–1833), a niece of the Butlers, who apparently sold or gave it to William Clasby in 1830. In 1838 it seems to have been owned by William C. Wyer and his wife Lydia (Coffin) Wyer, who were married in 1823. The desk was acquired in the twentieth century by Jacob Margolis, a New York dealer, who sold it to Francis P. Garvan in 1926.[17]

There are a dozen or so cupboards in eighteenth-century inventories, usually spelled "cubberd" or "cubbard." John Swain (1718 inventory) had one valued at fifteen shillings. The cupboard in Figure 45 has certain affinities with the kas form of cupboard which Nantucketers may have seen in New York or Pennsylvania, but the Nantucket cupboard is more compact than the monumental kases, more reticent in its design, more vertical in its feeling. Most eighteenth-century Nantucket case furniture of this type was painted, usually green. The caption for Figure 45 mentions the fact that the ivory handles on the bottom dovetailed drawer are not original. The practice of adding whalebone and whale-ivory handles to old furniture has been a "beautification" practice in the twentieth century by unscrupulous dealers and naive owners. Unfortunately, such changes take away from, rather than add to, the value of a piece.

Figure 45. Cupboard, pine, originally painted green, H-hinges, brass handle on doors, brass eschutcheon on bottom drawer. The ivory handles on the bottom drawer are not original. Said to have been made in 1770 by Ichabod Aldrich (1733–1821). Height: 62 3/8 in. (158.4 cm.), width: 39 1/4 in. (99.7 cm.), Depth: 19 1/2 in. (49.5 cm.). (*NHA*).

The writing table and desk in Figure 46 was probably made on Nantucket. There are several related desks with local histories still on the island. A similar desk in the Henry Coffin house on Main Street is illustrated in Kenneth Duprey's *Old Houses on Nantucket.*[18] The Coffin desk has acanthus-carved legs, while the desk in Figure 46 has turned legs. The interiors are almost identical. This form of desk was made in several places in the United States. They have been dubbed colloquially as "captain's desks" in coastal areas, but the term has no historical validity. The design of these desks leaves something to be desired. When open, the large shallow shelf spaces seem to invite a clutter of papers. The lid, when down, puts considerable stress on the hinges holding it and almost all such desks at one time or another have had to be repaired. A virtue is that they do not take up too much space when closed.

Figure 46. Writing table and desk with drop lid, one drawer with brass pulls, turned legs, 1820–1840. Sides, back legs, and shelf, cherry, drawer front and front legs, mahogany, crotch mahogany veneer on face of drop-lid. Height: 55 1/4 in. (140.3 cm.), width: 34 1/8 in. (86.7 cm.), depth: 19 7/8 in. (50.5 cm.). (*Collection of the authors*).

Looking Glasses

We counted 145 looking glasses in the Nantucket inventories of the 1680–1776 period, the first appearing in Nathaniel Gardner's 1713 inventory: "Looking glass 20/." Looking glasses were listed in the inventories in three categories: (1) "looking glasses" (2) "great" or "large" looking glasses and (3) "small" looking glasses. Only one entry added another descriptive note: "1 Looking glass gilt case—2–5–0," in Joseph Starbuck's 1761 inventory. The values of looking glasses were usually high in colonial inventories. Thomas Brock (1750) owned two looking glasses valued at twenty pounds and thirty pounds respectively, which compares with a thirty-two pound valuation for the high chest of drawers in his parlor.

Remembering the small panes of glass used in houses at the beginning of the eighteenth century, it is perhaps surprising to learn that quite large pieces of glass were used in looking glasses of the time. The London newspaper, *The Post Man,* February 13, 1700, included an advertisement:

> Large looking-glass Plates, the like never made in England before for size and goodness are now made at the old Glass house at Foxhall, known by the name of the Duke of Buckingham House, where all people may be furnished with rough plates from the smallest sizes to those six feet in length and proportional breath, at reasonable prices.[19]

The phrase "reasonable prices" was of course advertising license, since large looking glasses were always high priced in the eighteenth century.

As noted earlier, there was extensive contact between Nantucket and Philadelphia in the eighteenth and early nineteenth centuries. The Philadelphia looking glass with the label of John Elliott, Jr. in Figure 47 has a long Nantucket history. The looking glass can be dated

Looking Glasses in Nantucket Inventories 1706–1776

	1706–1725	1726–1750	1751–1776
Looking glasses	6	32	61
Great or large looking glasses	2	3	14
Small looking glasses	1	5	21

Figure 47. Looking glass with the label of John Elliott, Philadelphia, mahogany frame, original glass, 1796–1803. From the estate of Catharine Defrieze Fitzpatrick. Height: $34^3/_4$ in. (88.3 cm.), width: $19^1/_2$ in. (49.5 cm.). (*Private collection*).

from the label as having been made in the 1796–1803 period.[20] The label on the back of the looking glass reads:

JOHN ELLIOTT,

> At No. 60, South Front Street, between Chestnut and Walnut Streets,/ Philadelphia,/ Sells by Wholesale and Retail/ Looking Glasses/ In neat Mahogany Frames of American Manufacture:/ Coach Glasses, Window Glass/ Spectacles, Paint-/ ers Colours, Oil, Varnishes, &c.—And a ge-/neral Assortment of / Drugs and Medicines,/ N.B. Old Glasses new quicksilvered and framed as usual,/ and new Glass supplied to People's old Frames.

This relatively plain-looking glass in the Chippendale style was out of date by 1800, but it was the kind of form that would have been completely at home in an island parlor of the time.

The gilt looking glass in Plate XV, with the shell motif on the top rail, may have been made in James Tallent's shop. The beveled glass is possibly a later addition. However, other Empire looking glasses with Nantucket provenances also have beveled glass, which could indicate a local preference, and/or the style of the maker.

Clocks

The Nantucket Historical Association's most famous object, the astronomical clock made by Walter Folger, Jr., a relative of Benjamin Franklin, is an important clock, a real tour de force, made by a man in his early twenties.[21] The clock, shown in Plate XVI, was designed to do much more than tell time. It told the number of the year and day of the month, it tracked the exact motion of the sun and its declination, it showed the exact phases and motion of the moon, and, finally, it gave a regular reading of high tide at Sconset, the town at the east end of the island of Nantucket.[22] Oddly enough, the clock does not have a second hand. Perhaps Walter Folger, in his fabled idiosyncratic way, considered a second hand too mundane for his mechanical masterpiece.

Walter Folger, Jr., who was born in 1765, received a rudimentary education in the Nantucket schools. He taught himself algebra, calculus, surveying, navigation, astronomy, and French. He was mechanically minded and set himself up as a maker and repairer of clocks and watches. He started work on his famous clock in 1788, using a standard brass clock mechanism as his basic building block. He worked two years on the clock, setting it into operation on July 4, 1790. The brass plaque now on the clock states: "Made by the Hon. Walter Folger of Nantucket in the year 1787 at the age of 22," which does not agree with Folger's own account of when he made the clock.[23] It operated well throughout his lifetime. However, after Folger's death in 1849 the complicated mechanism of the clock ceased functioning properly, although it continued to keep good time. It was repaired in 1953 by Dr. Arthur L. Rawlings and again operated well, but soon it reverted to its old problems. Apparently, the clock needs the constant attention of someone like its maker or Dr. Rawlings to keep it operating consistently.

The mahogany case for the clock was made in Boston about 1790, possibly by the same maker who made the Willard clock cases, which it resembles. In Folger's papers there is a receipt for a clock case that was presumably for the astronomical clock, although it is dated almost a year after the clock was said to have been finished. The receipt reads:

> Nantucket June 1st 1791 Received of Walter Folger Junr/ the sum of Eleven Dollars being part pay for a clock-/ case . . . / Cornelius Allen

The fretwork on top the clock had been constricted to fit the low ceiling of Folger's house, but apparently this was not enough, since it was necessary to cut holes in the floor to accommodate the clock.[24]

Folger became well known among contemporary clockmakers as a source for a fine grade of watch oil made from sperm oil. He received orders from as far away as Baltimore. Simon Willard was anxious to get a vial of oil as soon as possible:

> *Boston Dec. 29, 1803*
>
> Dear Sir
> I wish for a little vial of your
> good clock & watch Oil if you
> aney waye get some to me soon
> it would very much oblige your
> most Humble
> Servt Simon Willard
>
> Mr. W. Folger
>
> would it not be a good way
> to send a small vial inclose
> it in a paper and send it
> by Post —

Walter Folger served in the Massachusetts House of Representatives and the Massachusetts Senate, and for four years he served in the House of Representatives in Washington. He was judge of the Court of Common Pleas, and for twenty years an attorney at law. He was interested in science and wrote several scientific papers. In 1819 he made a reflecting telescope and with it discovered spots on Venus. During the War of 1812 he set up a "factory" on Nantucket for carding and spinning cotton and wool with power-driven looms. It is said that everything he wore in court came from his own factory. In view of all this one might assume that Folger was a rich man. He wasn't. It is said that he was quite indifferent about money. Daniel Webster and Ralph Waldo Emerson visited him. Webster wrote:

> On the Island of Nantucket met with a philosopher, mathematician, and astronomer in Walter Folger, worthy to be ranked among the great discoverers in science. He preferred to live quietly in his home town among his old friends.[25]

The tall clock in Figure 48 is located in a typical four-bay Nantucket house at 1 Vestal Street, where Maria Mitchell, the distinguished astronomer, was born. The house was built in 1790 for Hezekia Swain and his brother; it was acquired on January 1, 1818, by William Mitchell and on August 1, 1818, his daughter Maria was born there. Maria Mitchell achieved worldwide fame when she discovered a comet in 1847. Later she became professor of astronomy at Vassar College. The Vestal Street house is now part of the Nantucket Maria Mitchell Association and is open to the public. The house is notable in that it is one of the few "typical" Nantucket houses that has survived relatively intact with many original features and furnishings, as the wood-grain painted walls of the "new" (1825) kitchen, painted floors in the bedroom to simulate carpeting and "astronomical" wallpaper.

Inside the door of the tall clock in Figure 48 is an undated inscription:

> This clock was presented to the Hon. William Mitchell of Nantucket, Mass., by his father on his marriage [to Lydia Coleman], Dec. 12, 1812. It was presented by Mr. Mitchell to his daughter Phebe Mitchell Kendall. She

Figure 48. Tall clock, bonnet top, fluted quarter columns, ogee feet, painted face with the inscription "Jn Deverall / Boston," and maps of the Eastern and Western hemispheres, with rotating "man-in-the-moon" indicating the phases of the moon. The clock case is mahogany with satinwood inlays. Height: 86 in. (218.4 cm.). (*Nantucket Maria Mitchell Association*).

moved to Inman Street, Cambridge, Mass., she left it by will to her son Wm. Mitchell Kendall.

Wm. Mitchell Kendall

The wall clock in Figure 49 is a typical example of a Willard-type banjo, although there is no signature on it. The clock was owned by Miss May Congdon of School Street, Nantucket, in the first half of the twentieth century.

Figure 49. Banjo clock, gilt wood frame, reverse paintings on glass in shaft and base. The clock has a Congdon family history in Newport and Nantucket. Made in the Boston area, circa 1815. Height including finial: 32 3/8 in. (82.2 cm.). (*Private collection*).

A Piano

The piano in Plate XVII was made by John Osborne of Boston in 1818. Osborne's better-known pupil was Jonas Chickering. Some of the history of the piano is written on the sides of the two drawers. On the right-hand drawer: "This Piano bot of John Osborne in Boston 1818," and "C. J. Folger & wife at Sconset Sep. 21, 1852 / U.S. Secty. Folger died / Sept. 4, 1884." On the left drawer: "Sarah M. Barrett moved this to Sconset July 1837" and "This piano taken to town for repairs October 7, 1863." On the bottom of the seat of the piano stool is written: "J. W. Barrett July 17, 1854." The piano was bought by George S. Smith December 22, 1818, and in June 1823 sold to Charles E. Phillips, "dancing master" of Nantucket. In 1836 or 1837, after the sudden death of Charles Phillips at the age of forty, it was acquired by J. W. Barrett, whose daughter moved it to Sconset.[26]

This elegant piano, made by John Osborne, with the glitter of its applied bronzes, is a symbol of the kind of worldly life-style that would have been unthinkable to the orthodox Quakers of the eighteenth century, when even a plain, unadorned piano would have been banned.

4. Mariners' Things, Boxes, Toys, Woodenware

This chapter begins with a miscellany of objects associated with mariners: "nautical" furniture, boxes, sailing vessels, and instruments. The Nantucket furniture discussed in the previous chapter could be characterized as regional variations of New England forms. The furniture and the boxes in this chapter were not part of the mainstream, representing as they do the peculiar and quite characteristic taste of the mariner, both in terms of materials of construction, function, and exuberance. On the other hand, the toys and woodenware we illustrate in the latter part of the chapter would have been at home in many other New England locales.

"Nautical" Furniture. Joseph Mitchell's Sea Chest

The sea chest was an important possession of a seaman, whether he was a common sailor or captain of the ship. Outfitters supplied green hands with a chest and contents for a four-year whaling voyage. The chest typically contained two pairs of underpants, a jacket, two pairs of "thin" pants, two "hickory" shirts, a sou'wester, two pairs of stockings, and a pair of shoes. In addition, there were a jackknife, comb, looking glass, paper of needles, quarter pound of thread, five pounds of tobacco, a keg of oil soap, tin cup and spoon, mattress, pillow, and blankets.[1] The rough textiles of the sailor's outfits were "made of bull's wool and dog's hair woven together by thunder and lightning."[2]

The sea chests of the ship's officers tended to be a bit more elaborate than those of the sailors in the forecastle. The blue-painted chest in Plate XVIII was owned by Joseph Mitchell, 2nd, captain of the Nantucket-built whaleship, the *Three Brothers,* held by George and Matthew Starbuck. When Captain Mitchell left Nantucket on July 12, 1841, he was to spend most of the next ten years at sea. The *Three Brothers* cruised the Pacific Ocean on whaling voyages of four and a third and five years. Captain Mitchell lived out of his sea chest for all but an eight-month home stay between the two voyages.

On the inside right of the sea chest there is a document box with lid, and on the left, four slots for charts. The corners of the chest are dovetailed; the top is hinged with thin, rather elegant strap hinges; the handles, or beckets, on the two ends of the chest are sailor knotwork which had been dipped in tar to stiffen and prevent rotting. Occasionally, the brackets used to fasten the beckets to a sea chest were made of whalebone, or of neatly carved mahogany pieces. Clifford Ashley noted that "the best type of becket cleared the edge of the lid when lifted, thereby sparing the sailor's knuckles."[3] Wallace Nutting apparently thought that *becket* was a very arcane term. In his *Furniture Treasury* he illustrates a becket with this caption:

> By way of surprise, a becket is shown. This is the handle worked by sailors for their chests. The test of an antiquarian is that he knows the name of this and a few other things.[4]

(One wonders what the "few other things" were!)

Few sea chests have survived with their original beckets. Of approximately two dozen such chests in the storage room at the Mystic Seaport Museum in 1985, only two had their original becket-handles. Unfortunately, particularly fine beckets are often sold as independent artifacts, having been removed at one time from sea chests which may have been too plain, or too large, or damaged.

Inlaid Furniture

Inlays have been common throughout the history of American furniture, but the use of small pieces of wood inlays with contrasting colors, and particularly the use of whalebone and whale ivory, seems to have had a special appeal to the mariners of the nineteenth century. Although we know of only a few pieces of furniture of this type with a Nantucket association, there are many such inlaid boxes in public and private collections both on and off the island. Furniture and boxes inlaid with whalebone and whale ivory are usually classified as scrimshaw and are often shown in museums with engraved whales' teeth, jagging wheels, busks, and so on. We have chosen to group them with furniture and box forms because of their functional relationship to these objects.

The dressing table with mirror in Plate XIX is a spectacular example of inlaid furniture. It was made by Captain James Archer for his wife, Mary, during a three-year South Atlantic cruise. Whales had become scarce by the 1850s and Captain Archer's voyage was no doubt considered unsuccessful. His bark *Afton* returned with only 336 barrels of sperm oil and sixty-seven barrels of whale oil.[5] However, the scarcity of whales must have given Captain Archer plenty of time to make this remarkable object.

The small table inlaid with scrimshawed whalebone in Plate XX was obviously not made by a cabinetmaker. Its solid, squat, nononsense look suggests it might have been made by a ship's cooper, or perhaps by Captain Gardner himself. William Bunker Gardner, born in Nantucket in 1811, married Charlotte Coffin in 1839. Captain Gardner was master of the whaleship *South Carolina* out of New Bedford, July 1844, to the Indian Ocean and the Pacific Northwest, returning May 10, 1848.[6] From 1852 to 1854 he was master of the *Sarah Parker,* a trading vessel operating between Nantucket, San Francisco, and the Pacific Northwest. In 1856 Gardner died of yellow fever on his way home from Rio de Janeiro and was buried at sea.

The round-topped inlaid table in Figure 50, an example of patience and flair, takes the idea of inlaid furniture a bit further. It was as if Shadrack Gifford, the maker, set out to see how many pieces he could possibly use in a forty-and-a-half-inch diameter table. The stylized S-shape of the legs of the table is very similar in silhouette to the bracket supports of the mirror of Captain Archer's dressing case in Plate XIX.

Figure 50. Inlaid table with tipping top, drawers on four sides, made in 1852 by Shadrack Gifford of 1384 pieces of wood: mahogany, satinwood, ebony, rosewood, walnut, oak, and curly maple. Height: 27⅝ in. (70.2 cm.), diameter of top: 40½ in. (102.9 cm.). (*NHA*).

Boxes

The earliest American boxes inlaid with whalebone which we know are pipe boxes made in the last part of the eighteenth and early part of the nineteenth centuries. Obed Worth, the original owner of the pipe box in Plate XXI, was born in 1763; he married Janet Townsend in 1790 and died in 1813 "at sea," rather than in 1804, as stated in the handwritten note found in the box.

The most distinctive feature of the satinwood box inlaid with mahogany in Plate XXII is the "scrimshawing" on the top and four sides. We use the word scrimshawing in quotes because the technique of cutting a design in a surface and filling the cuts with ink or other coloring material is usually associated with whalebone and whale-ivory objects. This box displays the same technique as that employed in making scrimshawed whales' teeth and whalebone busks, and uses the same motifs as used in conventional scrimshaw. However, the box allowed its maker to work on a larger scale, to inscribe on the top a seven-and-a-half-inch three-masted ship under full sail with an American flag and a long flowing banner with stars and stripes. On the front are two inlaid hearts, one superimposed on the other, as well as scrimshawed flowerpots. On the two ends are stylized weeping willow trees similar to those in mourning pictures. On the back, under swags on the lid, is a coastal scene with a lighthouse and a two-story, three-quarter house on the right; on the left in the sea are a bark and two coastal schooners.

We illustrate in Figure 51 and Plate XXIII two typical wooden boxes inlaid with whalebone and whale ivory.[7] The rosewood box in Figure 51 is architectural in its design, perhaps with a touch of Quaker reticence, while the design of the box in Plate XXIII, with many small pieces set in the wood, is more exuberant, almost flashy; it is related to such furniture pieces as Captain Archer's dressing case in Plate XIX. There is no history available on either of these two boxes. They were probably made in the 1830–1860 era.

Perhaps this is the place to interject a warning. *There are many fakes made by inlaying old wooden pieces with whalebone and whale ivory.* It is very common to find old boxes "beautified" with such inlays. Some, or perhaps many, such objects were not made with any intent to defraud, but they become true fakes if and when they are passed off as period objects. Examine inlaid pieces critically in a good light, preferably sunlight. If the inlays have been inserted into the surfaces of boxes or other articles with old finishes, one can sometimes detect new finish around the inlays, particularly if the ivory inlays had been sanded to make them even with the old surface. Also, old inlays often do not fit their cut-out spaces exactly, due to the differential shrinkage of the wood over a period of time.

The "Books" box in Figure 52 came from the

Figure 51. Rosewood box, inlaid with satinwood and other tropical woods and whalebone and whale ivory, 1830–1860. Width: 13⁷/₈ in. (35.2 cm.), height: 6¹/₂ in. (16.5 cm.), depth: 10³/₈ in. (26.4 cm.). (*NHA*).

Figure 52. Box, pine, painted grey with black letters "BOOKS" on top and front. Strap hinges, iron handles, circa 1825. Height: 17³/₄ in. (45.1 cm.), width: 21 in. (53.3 cm.), depth: 14⁷/₈ in. (37.8 cm.). (*Private collection*).

attic of 2 Charter Street, Nantucket, in the 1960s. It was originally owned by Captain Nathaniel Fitzgerald, whose only recorded voyage as a whaling master was on the ship *Hero,* out of Nantucket to the Pacific Ocean November 22, 1824, returning April 16, 1827, with 2222 barrels of oil. Captain Fitzgerald, who later operated a store at the corner of Fair and Charter Streets, purchased the house at 2 Charter Street in the 1860s from a descendant of Benjamin Coffin, the Nantucket schoolmaster.

The bottle case or wine chest in Figure 53 was apparently standard equipment in the captain's cabin of most whaling vessels. Even if the captain was a teetotaling Quaker, he would have had brandy, port, and/or madeira wines for his guests during those gams when whaling captains (often neighbors from Nantucket) visited each other in far-distant places, often in the middle of the Pacific Ocean. Eighteenth-century inventories mention such items. Richard Worth's inventory, made February 7, 1763, included "1 Case & Bottles—0–4–0."

The two painted French boxes in Plate XXIV remind us of the Nantucket whalers and their families who lived in France, in and around Dunkirk and Le Havre, from about 1785 to the early years of the nineteenth century. Under the leadership of William Rotch, as many as sixty Nantucket Friends lived in France during this time and many more visited there, since there were some seventy ships and captains associated with the move.[8] These painted boxes are mute evidence of the French connection. In one of these, there is an old handwritten note which says "First of the three Moses Joys." Moses Joy was born in Nantucket April 30, 1781; he married Deborah Macy in Nantucket on January 1, 1801, and died there July 4, 1847.

Another form of decoration in boxes involved the use of decoupage, paper cut-outs pasted on a surface. Decoupage, which flourished in the 1815–1830 period, was applied

Figure 53. Case with bottles, late eighteenth or early nineteenth century. Pine, nailed construction, old dark red paint. Width: 21 in. (53.3 cm.), height: 14½ in. (36.8 cm.), depth: 15½ in. (39.4 cm.). The square dark green bottles, unmarked, vary in height from 11½ to 12½ in. (29.2 to 31.8 cm.). (*NHA*).

also to such furniture as tables and chairs. There are a number of boxes similar to the one in Figure 54 known to have been made on the island. We would suggest that this particular decoupage box, with Anna Fish's name on the bottom, was created by her sometime in the second decade of the nineteenth century, since Anna, who was born in Cotuit, Cape Cod, married Simeon Coffin in Nantucket on September 19, 1819. If she had made the box after her marriage, she would probably have used her married name, Anna Coffin. Other evidence of an early date includes a cut-out fifteen-star American flag on the box.

Boats

At this point in the book we pause for a moment to glance at two sailing vessels which lifted the craft (pun intended) a bit above the level of the usual working sloops and catboats of the island which were primarily designed to get from A to B as efficiently as possible.

Pleasure sailing came with the emergence of Nantucket as a summer resort in the 1870s and 1880s. Figure 55 shows the catboat *Cleopatra* in Nantucket harbor at the turn of the century. The *Cleopatra* was built in 1895 in Osterville, Massachusetts, for a Mr. Russell, summer resident from Cincinnatti, Ohio, where he was a manufacturer of playing cards. Although the *Cleopatra* was a well-designed boat with a tastefully decorated sternboard, her most striking feature was the mainsail made in the form of a large American flag. She must have been a glorious sight when she sailed out of the harbor

Figure 54. Decoupage pine box, brass handles, lined with green paper, ball feet missing, 1810–1820. On the bottom is inscribed "Anna Fish." Width: 14¼ in. (36.2 cm.), height: 6⅝ in, (16.8 cm.). depth: 10 in. (25.4 cm.). (*NHA*).

Figure 55. The catboat *Cleopatra*, Nantucket harbor, circa 1900. Built in 1895 at Osterville, Massachusetts. The American flag mainsail was made for her in 1898. Length: 32 ft. 5 in., beam 15 ft. 2 in. (*Photograph courtesy Charles F. Sayle*).

on the Fourth of July with Old Glory blowing full in the breeze.

The sloop *Argonaut,* Figure 56, which for many years was tied up at Straight Wharf in the Nantucket harbor, was built during the years 1935–1938 by Charles F. Sayle and Clovis Mazerolle in their spare time at Nantucket's Commercial Wharf. The keel was cut in February 1935 and the boat was launched July 28, 1938, at 8 P.M. The *Argonaut,* named for those who sailed with Jason on the *Argo* in search of the Golden Fleece, was originally designed as a working scalloper's boat, but, as she was being built, her form changed. She became a pleasure boat that was meant to sail well and please the eye. The "fly" rail around the stern was pure

Figure 56. Sloop *Argonaut* built on Commercial Wharf, Nantucket by Charles F. Sayle and Clovis Mazerolle, 1935–1938. Length: 25 ft. 10 in., beam 9 ft. 3 in. (*Photograph taken in 1950, courtesy Charles F. Sayle*).

decoration, as were her sternboard and the carved tailboards at the bow which joined at the small carved billet head. The sloop has a small trunk cabin with five-and-a-half-foot headroom which could sleep three.

Charlie Sayle, as he is known to hundreds, was a Gloucester fisherman in the 1920s, before coming to Nantucket in 1929, where he became a builder of ship models and an ivory and wood carver. His miniature ivory whales, half models of whaleship hulls, and maps of Nantucket grace the tops of many lightship basket-purses. Examples of his wood carvings of whales are to be seen in the ground floor rooms of the Jared Coffin House. Sayle has made a number of ship models notable for their painstaking accuracy. The model of the pinky *Eagle* in Plate XXV, made in 1942, is based on a schooner built in Duxbury, Massachusetts, in 1820. The original *Eagle* did fishing and coastal freighting in the nineteenth century; in the first quarter of the twentieth century she was used as a yacht out of Kittery, Maine. During the winter of 1927, when the *Eagle* was 107 years old, she was hauled for the last time, no longer seaworthy.[9] The pinky was always a relatively small boat, never longer than about fifty-eight feet. The pinky *Eagle* was forty-three feet long, with a beam of twelve feet, eight inches. Pinkys, sharp at both ends, like a ship's lifeboat, were very common in the eighteenth and early nineteenth centuries, but few were built after 1840.[10]

Instruments

The Davis quadrant or backstaff, invented by John Davis about 1590, was used by American mariners for determining latitude until about the time of the Revolutionary War. The user kept his back to the sun (hence the term backstaff), projecting a shadow onto the instrument to measure the angle of the sun. The Davis quadrant in Figure 57 was made by Thomas Greenough (1710–1785) for David Macy of Nantucket in 1737. Greenough was a well-known Boston maker of compasses and

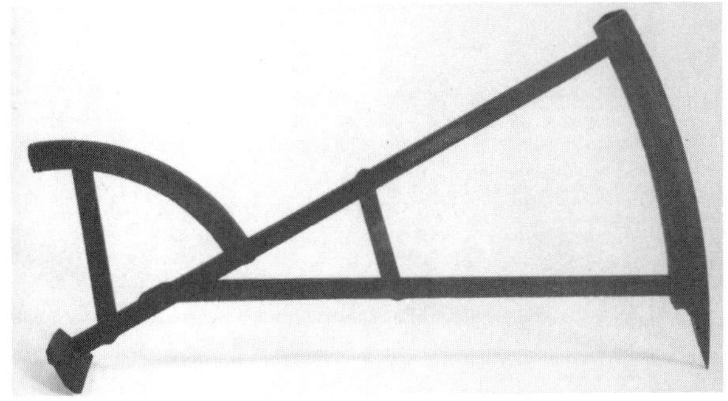

Figure 57. Davis quadrant or backstaff, inscribed: "Made by Thos Greenough 1737 / For David Macy March 28". Part of scroll-end of the sixty-degree arc broken off. Length: 24½ in. (62.2 cm.). (*Courtesy Robert Cary Caldwell*).

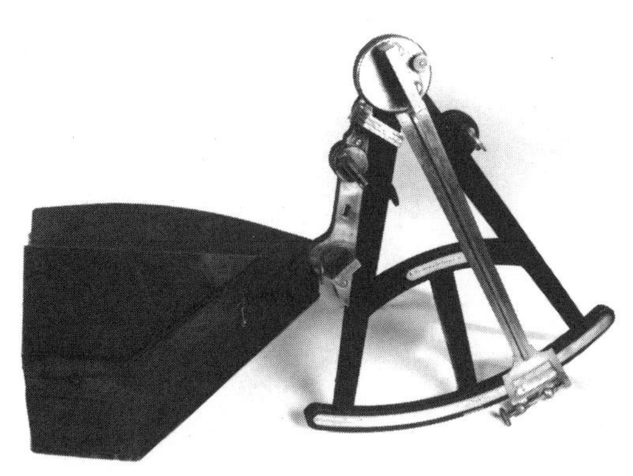

Figure 58. Octant, with mahogany case, ebony frame inset with 0°–110° ivory scale, brass index arm, two sets of filters and mirror, maker's name on ivory plaque: "A Cairns 13 [or 12?] Waterloo Rd Liverpool". Originally owned by Captain Chandler Brown Gardner (1810–1889). Circa 1830. Length of index arm: 11⅞ in. (30.2 cm.). (*Private collection*).

other instruments for mariners and surveyors.[11] Four Davis quadrants made by Greenough are known, the one made for David Macy being the earliest. Greenough's account book listed another Nantucket customer:

> In account with Captain Andrew Mirick of Nantucket: 1772, March 21: For 2 compasses, 1 leaded—£0/16/8.[12]

David Macy, son of John and Judith (Worth) Macy, was born in Nantucket September 12, 1714. He married Dinah Gardner January 6, 1739 and removed to Guilford, North Carolina, April 28, 1771.[13]

The octant in Figure 58 must have been one of Will Gardner's favorite possessions. The popular minister who, after his retirement to Nantucket in 1940, wrote four books on Nantucket history, *Three Bricks and Three Brothers* (1945), *The Coffin Saga* (1949), *The Clock That Talks and What It Tells* (1954), and *The Triumphant Captain John and Gardners and Gardiners* (1958), was photographed on two different occasions with his grandfather's octant.[14] Dr. Gardner was proud of his whaling ancestor, grandfather Chandler Brown Gardner, who was born June 10, 1810. Chandler Gardner first went to sea in 1823, at the age of thirteen, as a cabin boy on the *Diana* out of Nantucket, for a year's cruise in the South Atlantic, returning October 7, 1824. He shipped again in 1825 to the South Atlantic as cabin boy on the *Barclay*, Peter Coffin, master, returning a year later, on June 17, 1826. In 1826, when he was sixteen, he shipped as a boatsteerer or harpooner on a brand-new vessel, the brig *Pacific*, Captain David Baker, leaving Nantucket November 4, 1826, for a two-and-a-half-year cruise to the South Pacific. The *Pacific* returned to Nantucket March 8, 1829, with 2,189 barrels of sperm oil, a full load. In 1830, Gardner received his first rating as an officer, shipping as third mate on the *Congress*, captain Thomas Brock, leaving Nantucket August 23, 1830, and returning October 5, 1831. Three weeks later, on October 27, he married Susan Doolittle Swain, and two and a half months later, on January 13, 1832, he shipped again on the *Congress*, this time as first mate under Captain Charles Abrahams. It was more than three years later, on April 29, 1835, that the *Congress* returned to Nantucket. From 1835 to 1839 Gardner shipped as first mate on the *James T. Stewart*, captain, James T. Stewart.[15] In the latter part of this voyage Gardner became captain of the ship and put down a mutiny at the Bay of Shoals. Captain Gardner went on two more voyages as master: the *Helvetia* out of Hudson, New York, to the Indian Ocean, 1839–1841, and the *Logan* out of New Bedford, 1844–1847.

In 1849 Gardner joined a company of forty Nantucket men who bought the bark *Russell* in order to go to the California gold fields. They sold the bark in California and made their way to the Tuolomne River section, commonly called by the miners "Twarmy River." Gardner was in California on and off for ten years. On Thanksgiving Day 1859 he returned to Nantucket from his last trip to California, reportedly bringing with him $52,000 in gold.

Captain Gardner lived out his life in a small house on the south side of Plumb Lane (number 4), which still stands. There he took care of his wife Susan, who had become totally blind. He also bought a house in Sconset on Broadway which became known as the "House of Lords," where it became a meeting place for retired whaling captains during the fishing season.

Captain Gardner probably would have acquired the octant in Figure 58 by 1831 when he shipped as first mate on the *Congress.* The first mate's job was to make a daily reading of the location of the ship, and to keep the ship's log. Since Captain Gardner's retirement in 1859, the octant has remained much of the time in four nearby houses on the island. In the nineteenth century it was in Captain Gardner's house on Plumb Lane. During the 1940s Will Gardner kept it in his house around the corner at 33 Orange Street. In the 1960s it came to Earl S. Ray at 27 Fair Street, just opposite Plumb Lane, and since Earl Ray's death in 1973, it has been next door at 25 Fair Street. We note this trail of ownerships as an example of how old Nantucket artifacts, over a period of time, travel from house to house on the island, often in the same neighborhood.

The name on Captain Gardner's octant is that of Alexander Cairns, who was a nautical, optical, and "philosophical" instrument maker. The records show he lived at both numbers 12 and 13 Waterloo Road, Liverpool.[16]

The mercury barometer with inlaid thermometer in Plate XXVI, marked "T. Pool Son / New York," was from the estate of Earl Ray. It had been in his family since the nineteenth century, having originally been owned by Obed Luce (1768–1846), a Nantucket whaling captain.[17] Mr. Ray, who, like many of his maritime ancestors, had a great interest in the weather, kept a daily log of barometer and temperature readings, with notes on the weather. During the great hurricane which devastated New England coastal areas in September 1938, Mr. Ray pasted a red strip on the glass housing of the barometer at 27.70 inches of mercury, to mark the lowest level the barometer had reached during his lifetime. The worst of that 1938 hurricane just missed Nantucket, doing extensive damage to Martha's Vineyard, Cape Cod, and the mainland shoreline. There were high winds on Nantucket that September 21, washing away up to fifty feet of the south shore. One house in Madaket, the old Humane House, which had been converted into a summer home, washed into the sea, but otherwise the island escaped with only minor damage to roofs and trees.

The T. Pool / Son barometer dates from the 1815–1828 period, since Thomas Pool, Jr. is listed in New York directories as working independently after 1828 as a thermometer maker, first at 568 Pearl Street and later on Fulton Street and then on Broadway. In the 1835–1836 New York Directory, Pool is listed without the 'Jr.,' which suggests that Thomas Pool, Senior was by then dead.[18]

Toys

The little tin horse in Figure 59 was made by James Austin for one of his sons, probably between 1840 and 1850. Austin, who was born in 1809, married Mary Folger in 1833 and had three sons: Joseph, born in 1834, Charles, 1839, and John Folger, 1844. The toy horse was given to the Maria Mitchell Association in 1946 by James Austin's grandson, C. Warren Austin. We discuss James Austin's work and life in Chapter 8.

The child's version of the Nantucket box wagon, or calash, in Figure 60 was made by Jo-

Figure 59. "Tin" sheet metal toy horse, made by James Austin, Nantucket tinsmith, for one of his sons, 1840–1850. Length: 6½ in. (16.5 cm.), height: 5⅛ in. (13 cm.). (*Maria Mitchell Association*).

Figure 60. Three-wheel toy wagon, made by Josiah C. Brock about 1870. Frame of wagon pine, rear and side panels and bottom mahogany, front panel pine, wheels cherry. Length: 13½ in. (34.3 cm.), width: 7 in. (17.8 cm.), height: 5 in. (12.7 cm.). (*Courtesy of Mrs. John P. Elder*).

Figure 61. Double-head rocking horse, pine and hickory, rocker painted blue with red striping, modelled pine horse heads painted white with black manes and sponge decorations, remains of leather harness. Length: 34½ in. (87.6 cm.), width: 12¾ in. (32.4 cm.), height: 12⅛ in. (30.8 cm.). (*Maria Mitchell Association*).

siah C. Brock, born August 18, 1822. He married Mary Elizabeth Coleman after 1850. Their two sons, Albert G. and Benjamin, were born in 1862 and 1864. The beautifully made box wagon substituted a wheel in front where a horse would have been in a full-sized version. Mr. Brock seems to have used bits of wood he had at hand: pine, mahogany, and cherry.

The double-head rocking horse in Figure 61 was given to the Maria Mitchell Association by Grace Brown Gardner. At a time when horse-drawn carriages were fashionable, many a child must have fantasized over riding behind his very own "pair."

Woodenware

The most common items of woodenware in eighteenth-century Nantucket inventories were trenchers. Few have survived. After years of constant usage they no doubt became worn, cracked, warped, and/or broken and were discarded. We assume that the wooden *dishes* listed in early inventories were larger than trenchers; they had higher values. Africa's inventory lists "two wood Dishes 1/10" and "16 trenchers 2/6." The inventory of Nathaniel Barnard, Jr.,[19] who died in 1718, lists "26 trenchers—0–2–2" and "wooden dishes—0–11–4." The inventory of Samuel Barker,[20] who died in 1739, includes "14 round wooden plates—0–6–0" and "19 Square Trenchers—0–6 & 8 square Do—0–2–6." Mary Earle Gould, in her book *Early American Wooden Ware,* claimed that square trenchers came from England.[21] Other woodenware in the inventories include: milk trays, little trays, cedar tubs, oak tubs, rolling pins, bowls, candle boxes, butter tubs, "Kelars" (keelers, shallow, hooped tubs used to cool milk); pails, spoons, "piggans" (piggins, a small wooden bucket with one stave projecting above the rim for use as a handle); spice mortars, mortars and pestles, kegs, casks, meal troughs, churns. Some bowls were "knot bowls," and a number of bowls and mortars were made of lignum vitae. All of these items could have been fabricated by the island's coopers. We have identified 189 coopers on Nantucket in the 1700–1775 period.

Figure 62. Two eighteenth century mortars and pestles. The left is Nantucket Indian; right is turned lignum vitae, from family of Grace Brown Gardner. Left mortar, height: 8 3/8 in. (21.3 cm.), length of pestle: 9 1/2 in. (24.1 cm.). (*NHA*). Right mortar, height: 8 5/8 in. (21.9 cm.), length of pestle: 12 1/4 in. (31.1 cm.). (*Private collection*).

Wooden mortars and pestles were in almost every eighteenth-century household. Many things had to be ground before being used: salt, sugar, herbs, spices. The two mortars in Figure 62 were both used in eighteenth-century Nantucket. The plain one on the left is an Indian product made by hollowing out a section of a tree trunk. The pestle was turned out on a lathe. The lignum vitae mortar on the right was from the family of Grace Brown Gardner. Lignum vitae, a dense tropical wood, was favored for mortars because the weight gave stability to the object when grinding took place. The tight grain kept the substance being ground from invading the wood, also making it easier to clean. The two shades of the wood, the heart and the sapwood, gave interesting decorative effects. The turnings of the right-hand mortar in Figure 62, with two bands of rings, the lower band with a deep cut, is often seen on examples with an island history.

There are many tankards listed in early inventories, but we have found none specifically designated as wooden tankards. A tankard is a drinking vessel with a lid and handle, used for cider or wine, or hot drinks like toddy or flip. Silver tankards are always designated as such in inventories, as, on occasion, are pewter tankards, but in most cases the word tankard alone in an eighteenth-century inventory would seem to indicate either a wooden or a pewter tankard. The wooden tankard in Figure 63 is a typical cooper's product. With its staves and hoops, the tankard is put together like a barrel. However, the tankard has a handsomely carved handle, which puts it a bit higher on the scale of decorative art than a utilitarian barrel.

Butter churns were used for agitating milk or cream to obtain butter. The pump churn in Figure 64 has a plunger which is propelled up and down in the churn with the arm acting as a fulcrum. The churning action separates out globules of butter which, after straining off the buttermilk, are washed with water (usually salted unless fresh butter is desired) to coagulate the butter.[22] If we are to accept the data on the 1904 note attached to the churn, this churn was probably made about 1734. The more usual type of eighteenth-century churn was the plunger type, which made use of a high, slender, hooped tub with a long-handled plunger which fitted through a hole in the center of the lid.

The cooper-made buckets in Figure 65 are typical of the sturdy, undecorated vessels that were common around Nantucket houses and barns until well into the twentieth century. This is the kind of utilitarian artifact that saw little change in design or method of fabrication in the first two hundred years of the island's history. It wasn't until the nineteenth century, with its inexpensive factory-made products, that metal (tinplated or galvanized sheet steel) began to replace the cooper's woodenware vessels. Paradoxically, many of the old woodenware buckets and tubs are still around, while most of the "late" metal products have been discarded as rusty, broken, and useless.

Figure 64. Pump churn, oak. The attached lable, put on when the Historical Association's Fair Street museum opened in 1904, reads: "Butter churn / used in Nantucket / 170 years old." Height: 25 1/8 in. (63.8 cm.). (*NHA*).

Figure 63. Wooden tankard, carved oak handle and lid, hard pine staves and bottom, hickory hoops, eighteenth century. Height: 8 3/4 in. (22.2 cm.). (*NHA*).

Figure 65. Three cooper-made containers. Left to right are a piggin (handle damaged), height over handle: 15 1/8 in. (38.4 cm.), center, bucket with handle, height over handle: 9 3/4 in. (24.8 cm.), right, blue-green hooped tub without lid, height: 9 1/2 in. (24.1 cm.). (*NHA*).

Figure 66. For wash day. Tub on the left, pine and hickory, is painted "PHOEBE MACY / 1822." Height: 16 3/4 in. (42.5 cm.), diameter 21 1/4 in. (54 cm.). Middle, a plunger; right, one-piece wash board, pine. Height: 15 1/2 in. (39.4 cm.). (*NHA*).

The washtub in Figure 66 is dated 1822 with the name Phoebe Macy. According to the *Nantucket Vital Records,* there were a number of Phoebe Macys on the island in the first part of the nineteenth century. This one could have been Phoebe Gardner Macy who married Silas B. Macy October 21, 1821.

Woodenware played an important role in everyday life in Nantucket in the eighteenth and nineteenth centuries. The islanders stored food and oil in wooden barrels and casks, used wooden tubs for washing and wooden buckets for transport, and for a time early on, ate from wooden trenchers. The strong tradition of craftsmanship fostered by the island coopers gave Nantucketers sturdy, useful, and well-designed wooden vessels and containers that usually outlived their owners.

5. Textiles

The setting aside of common land for the raising of sheep was one of the first orders of business for the white settlers of the island. Sheep were permitted to run wild on the commons. Once a year the sheep were herded together, washed in Washing Pond (adjacent to Capaum Pond), sheared, and the wool allocated according to the owner's brand marks on the sheep. The sheep were then set free for another year. At a town meeting of freeholders on March 19, 1707, a resolution was recorded: "It is agreed that ye 2 day of ye 4 month [April 2nd] next shall be ye day to begin to wash ye sheep."[1] Also recorded at the same meeting: "The town doth choose & appoint James Coffin Jr George Gardner & Stephen Coffin Jr to take account of all the fleeces at ye time of shearing our sheep next ensuing & also adjust the Commons with every man for this year."[2]

A fulling mill was in operation on Nantucket by the end of the seventeenth century. This was a kind of water mill where woven wool cloth was "fulled," that is, scoured, shrunk, and pressed to render it stronger, closer, and finer.[3] The 1680 inventory of Nathaniel Wier listed "5 yd woolen cloth fuld . . . 1–05–0."

Textiles had an importance in the seventeenth and eighteenth centuries that may seem odd in the twentieth century. We have already noted in Chapter 2 the high value placed on such textiles as bedding and bed "furniture" in the inventories of the eighteenth century. For example, in Tristram Coffin's 1706 inventory, his bed and bolster were valued at nine pounds and a suite of bed curtains was valued at £ 3–10–0, while his eight chairs were valued at two shillings, nine pence each and his "great chair" at three shillings. If we consider *only* the furnishings in Tristram Coffin's house, the textiles accounted for forty-three percent of the total appraised, fair market value of everything in his house. (Not included as household furnishings are farm and whaling tools, farm animals, hay, wool, and whalebone.) The textiles in Thomas Brock's 1750 inventory underline their economic importance in both the home and store of a wealthy man. The bedding, bed curtains, sheets, blankets, and so on of his number-one bed were valued at £93–12–6, while the six four-back chairs in the same room were valued at twenty-two shillings each. One of the symbols of Brock's wealth was the fact that he had eleven beds in his house, four of which were fully furnished high beds. The textiles in Brock's store had a total value of about £1,650. Essentially all were imported fabrics, which obviously found a ready market on the island.

Weavers

There were weavers on the island from the beginning of the white settlement. Peter Folger, when he acquired property in 1663, was referred to as a "Weaver, Interpreter and Miller." We found records of fifty-two weavers in colonial Nantucket, all of them men. The number of weavers increased with the population:

Weavers in colonial Nantucket

1660–1700	3
1701–1725	9
1726–1750	14
1751–1776	26

These figures, which represent a summary of the list of weavers on page 223, are based on the dates of first mention in the records. However, many continued in their work for years after the date of first mention. For example, Nathaniel Paddock (1708) was still listed in the records as a weaver in 1752, and Shubal Pinkham (1721) was listed as a weaver in 1753. Many were no doubt weavers *before* the record dates. At any one time in the first three-quarters of the eighteenth century, there were at least two dozen weavers operating on the island.

The seventeenth- and eighteenth-century county records of Nantucket, which tell us that all the weavers on the island were men, also tell us that the spinning of the yarn used by the weavers was all done by women, called spinsters. (We have found no mention of the terms needleworker or needlewoman in either the land or probate court records.) The term *spinster,* as used in the records, refers to the number 1 definition in Samuel Johnson's famous eighteenth-century dictionary:[4] "A woman who spins," and not his number 2 definition: "(In law) The general term for a girl or maiden woman." Damaris Coffin was called both a "widow" and a "spinster" in the land records, and Sarah Pease was called "Spinster & wife to ye sd Seth." An unmarried woman was listed as such in the court records. The statistics on spinsters in Nantucket are distorted by the lack of data before 1750:

Spinsters in colonial Nantucket

1700–1725	1
1726–1750	3
1751–1776	98

The reason there were so few spinsters listed in the first half of the eighteenth century in Nantucket is simple: the list was developed almost entirely from the Nantucket County land records and far fewer women than men were involved in land transactions at that time. There were obviously many women spinning before 1750 whose names never entered into any kind of public record. We assume all the spinsters listed in the records were those who practiced spinning as a regular occupation. They spun for money or bartered their services.

It is a generally accepted fact that it took at least four or five spinsters to supply one full-time weaver.[5] It was only in the 1751–1776 period that Nantucket statistics began to conform to this ratio, there being then ninety-six spinsters and twenty-six weavers, or about four spinsters per weaver.

The great increase in the number of women whose names appeared with their husbands' names in land records after 1750 is evidence of their changing status in Nantucket. A strong factor was the Quaker influence. The idea of equality of men and women stressed by the Society of Friends spilled over into the whole community. A number of women had their own businesses, and seemed to have had considerable control over their lives. Later, after

1790, during the time of the several-year whaling voyages, women *had* to take care of themselves and their families while their husbands were absent from the island. Thus, Quakerism and whaling, in different ways, changed women's position in Nantucket, making them more self-reliant and independent, part of that "difference" noted early in the book.

The Textiles of Eunice Arthur, 1706–1729

The inventory of Eunice Arthur, a single woman who was only in her twenty-third year when she died May 19, 1729, gives a rare glimpse of a woman's personal belongings in the first part of the eighteenth century. Eunice was born June 29, 1706, the daughter of John and Mary (Folger) Arthur. When her estate was settled on May 25, 1730, her six brothers and sisters each received £ 11–4–5. The appraisal of her belongings was made by three women: Ann Coffin, Judith Wilcocks, and Ruth Gardner, an unusual event in itself. Her furnishings included: two chests, a table, a bedstead, a chest of drawers, a tray; and pots, bowls, platters, a cup, and a chafing dish; a Bible and ten and one-fourth ounces of "plate." The fact that she owned silver is an indication of her social status on the island. The textiles in her inventory included:

Clothing

5 shifts	3 gowns
12 aprons	1 pocketbook
9 neck cloths	4 petticoats
24 caps	2 quilted petticoats
1 riding hood	pr gloves
	pr stays
1 bonnet	4 pr stockings
3 pockets	gartering
1 girdle	1 wascoat

Bedding and Linens

3 pr sheets	1 rug
4 pr pillow cases	1 bed
6 bolsters	2 tablecloths
5 blankets	12 napkins
2 coverlets	5 towels

Cloth and Tools

garlix	silk and thread
cloth	thread bobbin
4 1/2 yds cherryderry[6]	a little wheel

Tools

We illustrate a sampling of tools used in the making of textiles and the fabrication of articles using textiles. Other textile-related objects are included elsewhere in the book. A sewing worktable is shown in Chapter 3 with furniture (Figure 42), and such things as whalebone and whale-ivory swifts are grouped with scrimshaw in Chapter 9.

A common perception is that every household in colonial times had a spinning wheel and that practically the whole female population was involved in the making of textiles. This was only partly true in Nantucket. Based on the probate inventories of the 1706–1776 period, only one out of three households listed any kind of spinning wheel. And since many less-affluent estates did not go through the probate court, there were probably *fewer* than a third of the households with spinning wheels on the island. As pointed out, much of the spinning was probably done by "professional" spinsters. Looms for weaving were bulky and expensive and they were obviously not in the average eighteenth-century Nantucket house. Only 6 percent of the inventories up to 1750 included a loom.

It is not known where the spinning wheel in Figure 67, with the signature "D. Thomas"

Figure 67. Linen or flax wheel (left), turned distaff, stamped with the signature "D. Thomas." Height to the top of wheel: 34⅞ in. (88.6 cm.). Yarn winder (right), with clicking mechanism which counts the revolutions for measuring length of yarn. Height: 33¾ in. (85.7 cm.). (*NHA*).

was made.[7] There are two kinds of spinning wheels mentioned in Nantucket inventories, small linen wheels and large wool wheels. Although Jeremy Netowa's inventory lists both a "linnen wheel" and a "woolen spinning wheel," most of the inventories list only "spinning wheel" and/or "linen wheel," which suggests that a "spinning wheel" was a large wool wheel, since the linen wheels are listed as such. Spinning wheels were made by chairmakers, particularly Windsor chairmakers.

The yarn winder in Figure 67 has no maker's name on it. These winders were used to count the yardage of the yarn. There are about 120 yards in a skein. When wool is left on a yarn winder under tension, kinks are removed and the twist is set in the yarn.[8] The tape loom in Figure 68 was used for making trim tape for clothing and such articles as the pocketbooks in Plate XXXII. The so-called "squirrel-cage" swift or yarn winder in Figure 68 has a pair of adjustable cages which hold the yarn vertically rather than horizontally, as does the usual umbrella-type swift or yarn winder. The whale-ivory fitting on the shaft of the winder in Figure 68 is a characteristic Nantucket touch.

The sewing box with revolving spool holder in Figure 69 was made on board ship for Charlotte Coffin Gardner, wife of Captain William Bunker Gardner, between 1845 and 1855.

The chatelaine in Plate XXVII, with a clip to fasten it to the top of an apron, offered a stylish and convenient way for a woman to carry her scissors and pinholder box. Chatelaines continued to be popular through most of the nineteenth century. Gorham and Tiffany and other American silversmiths made expensive, hand-

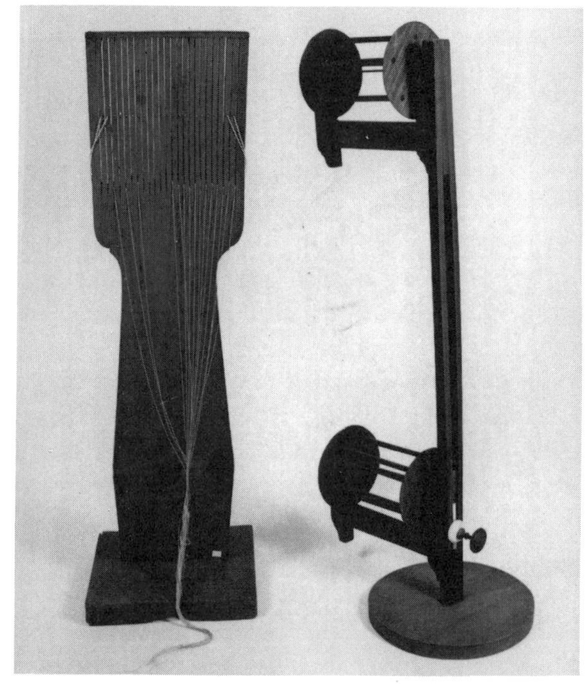

Figure 68. Free-standing tape loom (left), given to the Nantucket Historical Association by R. B. Hussey in 1898. Height: 34⅞ in. (88.6 cm.). On the right: adjustable yarn winder or "squirrel cage" swift. Note the whale-ivory fitting on the shaft next to the bottom cage. Height: 35½ in. (90.2 cm.). (*NHA*).

Figure 69. Sewing box with revolving spool holder, pin cushion on top, made on board the ship *Sarah Parker,* William Bunker Gardner, master, for his wife Charlotte Coffin Gardner. Turned whale-ivory posts, inlays, pulls and cup, inlaid mahogany drawer fronts. Height: 9¾ in. (24.8 cm.). (*NHA*).

somely decorated ones in silver, with three or four attachments.

The quilting template in Plate XXVIII was used as a pattern guide. It was dipped in a chalky powder, then laid on the fabric to be quilted, thus making the pattern for stitching.[9] We assume Diana Gardner was related to the Nantucket Gardners but there is no mention of her in the *Nantucket Vital Records.* There was a John Webster born in Nantucket in 1788, but we have found no record as to whether he was ever married.

Needleholders or Needle Sheaths

Figure 70 illustrates five scrimshaw needleholders or needle sheaths. Another, made of silver, is shown at the left in Plate XXVII. The function of these objects has been obscured by the passage of time. It has been suggested that they were for the storage of sewing needles.[10] However, such a usage does not make sense. The holes in the average American needleholder are far too shallow to make them useful, even temporarily, for the storage of sewing needles. An understanding of their original use comes out of a study of knitting practices of the eighteenth and early nineteenth centuries, a procedure which was quite different from standard practices of the twentieth century. The knitting needles themselves never had knob ends and tended to be thinner:

> The old knitting needles were graded in sizes, much as they are graded today, but in

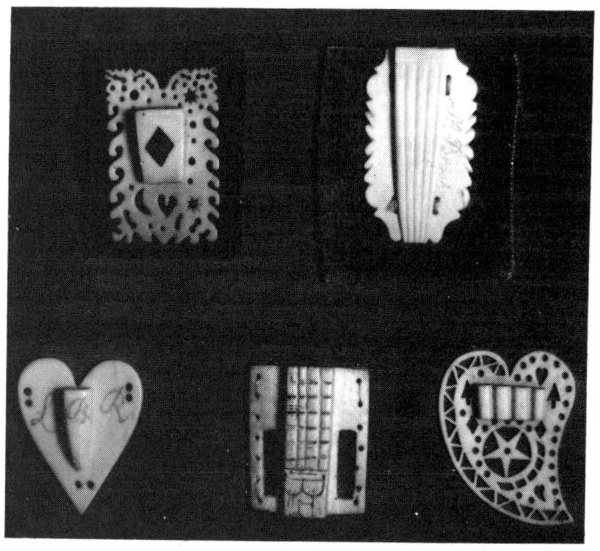

Figure 70. Whale-ivory knitting needleholders. Top left: 1⅞ x 1¼ in. (4.8 x 3.2 cm.); top right: inscribed "M Brooks," 2⅛ x 1¼ in. (5.4 x 3.2 cm.); lower left: heart-shaped with inscription "LBR," 1¾ x 1⅜ in. (4.4 x 3.5 cm.); lower middle: inscribed "JBL," 1⅝ x 1¼ in. (4.1 x 3.2 cm.); lower right: 1⅞ x 1½ in. (4.8 x 3.8 cm.). (*Private collection*).

the 17th and 18th centuries the finer needles were more popular, the finest being no thicker than sewing needles and justly described as "wires."[11]

In the European style of knitting, the lower end of the right needle was anchored in some sort of device such as a needleholder or needle sheath:

> The right needle was placed into the bore hole of the needleholder, and the right hand, thus freed of supporting the needle, was placed close up over the needle point, the forefinger acting as a shuttle, making the least possible movement and attaining a speed of 200-odd stitches a minute.
>
> Balance was maintained with the thumb and other fingers, and these "played" the stitches downward as they were knitted off the left needle with a rhythmical movement, similar to playing a flute, while the left hand in turn played the stitches up to the point of the left needle.[12]

This style of knitting is still practiced in Europe, particularly in the Scandinavian countries and rural Great Britain:

> But, though the use of the knitting sheath may be obsolete to the modern knitter, the idea still survives in the rural districts of Britain and Europe. In northern Scotland the country women will fix their right needle into a bunch of feathers thrust through the belt, while the Devonshire and Cornish women will use a twist of straw tucked through their apron strings, or make a long, narrow straw cushion which they call a knitting cushion or truss.[13]

American needleholders of the eighteenth and early nineteenth centuries usually had holes around their outer edges which were used to sew the holder onto small pieces of cloth, often velvet. Figure 70 shows two with their original cloth supports. These were in turn pinned onto an apron or dress belt, to furnish a firm base for the right knitting needle. (There seems to be no record of them being used on the left hip.[14]) The English designation for such an object was knitting *sheath.* There were also hollow-ended knitting *sticks* which served the same function. Perhaps, to be precise, the American examples should be designated as *knitting needleholders.*

Fancy Needlework

In the eighteenth century, when all textiles were highly valued, a finely executed piece of needlework represented the peak of achievement for young ladies of "good families." The earliest examples of Nantucket fancy needlework we know of are the quilted petticoats or underskirts of the late seventeenth and early eighteenth centuries. Quilted petticoats originated as an English fashion in the seventeenth century and they were worn in England and America until the middle of the eighteenth century.[15] Although these quilted petticoats were made as warm undergarments for winter wear,[16] they were meant to be seen. The skirts of many of the dresses worn over the petticoats were open in front from the waistline to the hem to show off the undergarment. Petticoats were tied at the waist with tapes or drawstrings and often had plain unquilted fabrics attached to their tops.[17] These petticoats, often made of silk, were fully lined and made with enough material to make a full skirt. The elaborately stitched patterns gave a three-dimensional, sculptured look to the surface of the garments.

We have already seen that Eunice Arthur had two of these quilted petticoats in her 1730 inventory, one valued at thirty-five shillings. Two first-rate examples of these interesting garments have survived on the island. One is well documented, while little is known of the history of the other. The blue silk quilted petticoat in Plate XXIX, still in the family of the original owner, has two very old handwritten notes attached to it. The one that appears to be the oldest reads:

> Damaris Gayer stitched and was married in this skirt petticoat to Nathaniel Coffin Grandson of Tristram in 1697[sic].[18]

The other note reads:

> Elizabeth Ramsdall married Levi Starbuck 1793 and was the 5th person married in this skirt her mother & all of her ancestors having worn it before
>
> Given to Eliza Coffin
>
> Children of Eliza Coffin must draw for ownership after I have done with it unless they chose to divide it some other way.
>
> E. C.[19]

This petticoat, clearly of American design, has extra pieces of cloth sewn on at the top, evidence that the garment had been, in the past, fitted to several different waist sizes. Another silk-quilted petticoat, yellow-gold in color, in the collection of the Nantucket Historical Association, a detail of which is shown in Plate XXX, has no recorded history, but could have been made in the first half of the eighteenth century.[20] This yellow-gold petticoat is lined with several fabrics, all linen except one of polished wool. There is a pocket, probably not original, cut into the fabric on the opposite side from the opening. The petticoat is pleated into the waistband. Quilting stitches range from ten to fifteen per inch.

Among the most important pieces of needlework of pre-Revolutionary America is a group of embroidered pictures worked in Boston in the "Young Ladies School" featuring a "Fishing Lady and Boston Common," although the Boston Common locale in many of these pictures had, at best, a tenuous relationship with reality. Such leading museums as Winterthur, Historic Deerfield, and the Museum of Fine Arts, Boston, display examples of these embroideries. The version of this group in the collection of the Nantucket Historical Association (Plate XXXI) is one of the best-preserved examples of the "Fishing Lady" group. The elegantly dressed gentleman and the lady with her arched fishing pole in the picture have an awkward charm as do the five dogs and the fully antlered stag in the background. The house at the upper left in the embroidery is not the usual idea of an eighteenth-century New England house. Perhaps it was copied from an English print or a design provided by the Boston teacher.

Susanna Colesworthy (the *Pollard Papers* list her name as Susan[21]) was born in Boston May 7, 1752. The Colesworthys were neighbors of Paul Revere[22] and her father, Gilbert Colesworthy, took part in the Boston Tea Party. Susanna and other members of the Colesworthy family moved to Nantucket in the last quarter of the eighteenth century;[23] three are listed in the 1790 and the 1800 censuses. The *Nantucket Vital Records* indicate that Susanna was the mother of Persis.[24] We have found no record of Susanna's marriage. She died "single" January 13, 1811.[25]

The pocketbook on the left in Plate XXXII, decorated with silk and wool embroidery, has a pink plain-woven glazed worsted lining. The zig-zag pattern of the pocketbook on the right in Plate XXXII, which is unusually small for an eighteenth-century example, is worked in what would today often be called flame, Florentine, or Hungarian stitch. These are, however, twentieth century terms. The contemporary designation was Irish stitch.[26]

The early nineteenth century saw the flowering (literally) of men's vests or waistcoats. The portraits of Erastus Salisbury Field and others often featured men with these colorful garments. One of the first products made by the Atlantic Silk Company in Nantucket was silk vesting. The ivory-colored satin waistcoat in Figure 71, with its meticulously embroidered

Figure 71. Man's vest or waistcoat, hand-embroidered on ivory satin, first quarter of the nineteenth century. Length: 17½ in. (44.5 cm.). (*NHA*).

undulating vines with green leaves and pink flowers, gave a very elegant touch to the normally sedate attire of the gentleman of the time.

Samplers

Samplers, embroidered needlework designs or pictures, made by schoolgirls in the seventeenth, eighteenth, and nineteenth centuries, are among the most appealing of the artifacts of our past. Since they are usually signed and often give the age of the maker, they seem to speak to us directly, easily bridging the years in between. To quote Susan Swan:

> The sampler is one of the most intriguing forms of early American needlework we have. Certainly, it was a long-popular art form, practiced by the earliest immigrants and still produced well into the nineteenth century. It virtually chronicled needlework styles as they were changing, since the fashionable fancywork of any particular day invariably found its way into samplers.[27]

The eleven Nantucket samplers which we show in this chapter, in approximate chronological order, date from 1797 to 1828, a thirty-one year period. The ages of the girls making the samplers ranged from eight to fifteen, with an average of 11.9 years. Samplers were made under the supervision of a teacher, usually in a school. The fact that two of the samplers state that they were made at the *Nantucket Friends School,* kept by Lydia Gardner (Figure 76 and Plate XXXIV), enables us to attribute eight samplers, made in the 1797–1808 period, to this school. The features that are characteristic of these Nantucket samplers will be pointed out in the discussion of specific examples. The verses on the Nantucket samplers are not peculiar to the island. These verses, which range from sentimental couplets to absolute doggerel, with occasional flashes of unconscious humor, are very much like the verses on other American samplers of the time. It was a time when it was fashionable to dwell on death and the life hereafter. Little eight-year-old Susan Hall used one of the many versions of the "Roses are red" quatrain:

> The Grass is Green The Sky is Blue
> The Roses fade And so must you

By the way, Susan did not fade for some time. According to the *Nantucket Vital Records*[28] she was married four times, to Joseph Millwood, Charles G. Coffin, Joseph Holmes, and George Wood. The verses on Mary Starbuck's 1808 sampler tell us that we must not only *live* a pure life, we must *think* it. Sinful visions must be banished from the mind since "God can see and hear and write down every thought."

We do not mean to poke fun at these verses. It was a sentimental time. Even the poetry of well-known poets of the time dwelt on melancholy, death, and the purity of the soul.

Workers of samplers often made mistakes in spelling, letters were left out of alphabets, sometimes they had trouble getting everything on one line, putting words or syllables at the end below or above the line. It does not seem germane to make any sweeping generalizations about the status of Nantucket women based on these samplers. They were an artistic outlet for young girls and they were also learning devices. The morbid vision sometimes expressed in the verses reflects a time when life *was* chancy for children and for women in childbirth. And, as has often been pointed out, these verses seldom originated with the children. They came from printed sources, teachers, parents, relatives, and friends.

We have checked the dates on these samplers with the *Nantucket Vital Records* and other genealogical records[29] and have often found discrepancies. We tend to accept the dates on the samplers rather than those in the records since they are closer to the people involved.

The samplers of Polly Coffin and Anna Gardner (Plate XXXIII and Figure 72), worked in 1797 and 1798, define the stylistic characteristics of the Nantucket Friends' School.[30] Typical features found in samplers associated with Friends' Schools in Pennsylvania, New Jersey, and Delaware also occur in the Nantucket samplers. These features include small stylized pots of flowers, baskets of fruit, and alphabets featuring wide, angular *M*s and *N*s. Apparently unique to Nantucket are the rows or groups of small rounded trees (Figures 72–74 and Plates XXXIII and XXXIV). Another unusual feature is the use of nervous, wiggly lines for dividers (Figure 73) or tree branches (Figures 73 and 78).

Figures 73 and 74 show samplers by Sally Stubbs. It is unusual to find two "fancy" samplers of the same general subject matter by one young lady. Probably the later sampler, which has neither alphabet nor numbers, was intended more as a decorative picture. The house

Figure 72. Sampler worked by Anna Gardner, aged fourteen, in 1798. The verse reads:

> GRANT me to live and if I die to find
> The dear love'd portion of a peaceful mind
> That health that sweet content that pleasing rest
> Which God alone can give as suits me best
>
> Anna Gardner aged fourteen
> Years September the 12 1798

Anna Gardner, daughter of Micajah and Anna (Glazier) Gardner, was born September 9, 1784. She married Francis Chase June 14, 1803, and died July 26, 1840. Silk on linen, height: $16\frac{1}{2}$ in. (41.9 cm.), width: $16\frac{3}{4}$ in. (42.5 cm.). (*NHA*).

Figure 73. Sampler worked by Sally Stubbs, aged twelve, in 1799. Marked with alphabets and: "Sally Stubbs her sampler mark ed in The Year of our Lord 1799 / When this you do behold You'l See my age is 12 Year old Jan-y the 28 / The Rose is red The grass is green The days are past when I have seen." Sally was born January 28, 1787, the daughter of Samuel and Christina (Worth) Stubbs. She died unmarried July 12, 1832. Silk on linen. Height: 17 in. (43.2 cm.), width: $16\frac{1}{2}$ in. (41.9 cm.). (*Old Dartmouth Historical Society and Whaling Museum*).

Figure 74. Sampler worked by Sally Stubbs in 1802 when she was fifteen. Inscribed: "Sally Stubbs's Sampler mak'd / In the Year of our Lord 1802 / 15 Years old 2 day the / First month . . . This needle work of mine / will tell / That in my youth." Silk on linen, height: $17\frac{3}{4}$ in. (45.1 cm.), width: $17\frac{7}{8}$ in. (45.4 cm.).

in this sampler is more typical of Nantucket architecture, and may actually have represented the five-bay gambrel roof brick house with chimneys at each end at number 5 Orange Street.[31]

Marking Samplers

Usually a young lady's first sampler was a marking sampler done in cross-stitch. If her schooling had progressed beyond this point her next project would most likely have been a "fancy sampler."

Marking or plain-work samplers were specifically designed to teach students how to mark the family linens with initials of the family or individual members of the family, and numbers which were used to identify sets of linens (Figures 75–77). These three marking samplers are the kind of teaching exercises which might have been tackled first by the beginning needleworker learning how to cross-stitch different ways of making letters of the alphabet and numbers. Of the three samplers, that of Hannah Coffin is the most sophisticated and technically competent. Hannah worked eight different alphabets (note the afterthought of the "Z" after the first two). The inscription

Figure 75. Marking sampler worked by Hannah Coffin in 1805 when she was ten, with eight different alphabets and the inscription: "The rule to mark napkins / Hannah Coffin / 12th mo^{th} 23^{d} 1805." The monograms "Z^{C}M R^{O}M S^{C}S M^{C}I" are examples using initials of the Coffin and Olney families. Hannah, the daughter of Shubael and Sarah (Olney) Coffin, was born June 30, 1795. We found no record of marriage or death. Silk on linen, height: $14\frac{3}{4}$ in. (37.5 cm.), width: $17\frac{1}{2}$ in. (44.5 cm.). (*NHA*).

"The rule to mark napkins" and the three-initial monograms clearly demonstrate the purpose of the exercise of making a marking sampler. Sally Starbuck's sampler in Figure 76 was more crudely made than that of Hannah Coffin. The fact that she stretched the thread from one letter to another on the back side is considered poor craftsmanship today, since shadows of these stray lines tend to show through on the front of the sampler. However, standards before the Victorian period apparently varied, since many otherwise carefully worked needlework pieces show this characteristic. Sally's sampler has no border line to contain the lettering. However, her sampler is important in documenting the marking samplers from the Nantucket Friends School.

Figure 76. Marking sampler worked by Sally Starbuck in 1808, with eight alphabets, five of which are identical, a set of numbers, and the following inscription:

Nantucket Friends School 3mo Second 1808
Kimbal Starbuck born first month 22nd 1775
Mary Starbuck born ninth month 22nd 1776
Mary Starbuck born tenth month 3rd 1796
Sally Starbuck born fourth month 11th 1799
Grant I may ever at morning ray
Open with prayer the consecrated day
Sally Starbuck finished this Sampler in the tenth year of her age

Sally (Sarah B.) was the sister of Mary Starbuck (Plate XXXIV) and the daughter of Kimbal and Mary (Coffin) Starbuck. She married Josiah Gorham January 27, 1828. Silk on linen, height: $16\frac{3}{8}$ in. (41.6 cm.), width: $16\frac{3}{8}$ in. (41.6 cm.). (*NHA*).

Susan Hall, the youngest of our sampler workers (Figure 77), used only plain Quaker lettering and the delicate zig-zag border with flowers at the bottom to link her sampler with those of the Friends School. It may be unfin-

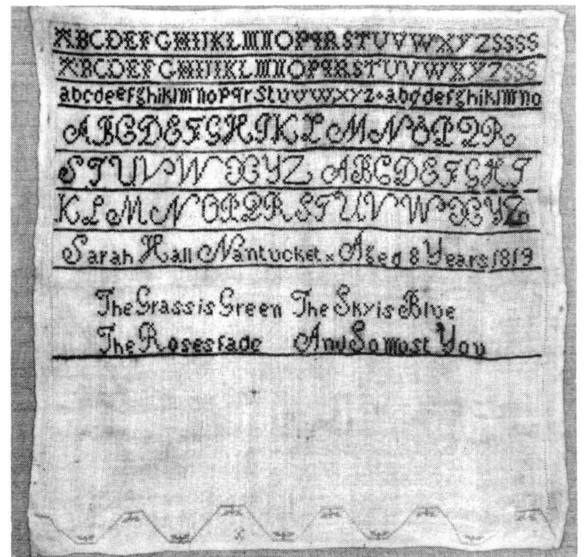

Figure 77. Sampler worked by Susan Hall in 1819 when she was eight years old, with alphabets and the inscription:

> Susan Hall Nantucket. Aged 8 years 1819
> The Grass is Green The Sky is Blue
> The Roses fade And So must You

The *Nantucket Vital Records* show that a Susan Hall, daughter of David and Sarah (Coffin) Hall, married Joseph Millbrook in Nantucket July 29, 1829. However, her birth is listed as July 29, 1806, probably an error. Silk on linen, height: 14 1/8 in. (35.9 cm.), width: 14 1/4 in. (36.2 cm.). (*Private collection*).

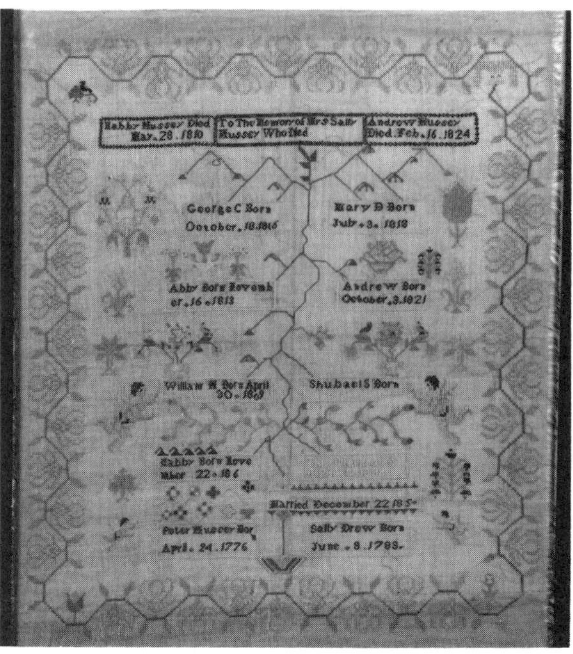

Figure 78. Family-tree sampler. Record of the family of Peter Hussey, born April 24, 1776 and Sally (Drew) Hussey, born June 8, 1783. Probably worked by Abby (Abigal) Hussey, born November 16, 1813 and who married William Dayton September 28, 1836. Included among the names is inscription: "This marked in / 1828 & 1833." Silk on linen, height: 19 1/2 in. (49.5 cm.), width: 17 1/4 in. (43.8 cm.). (*NHA*).

ished because of the empty space below the verse.

Sally Starbuck's sister, Mary, who was three years older, worked a fancy sampler in the same year, 1808 (Plate XXXIV). This sampler has all the Nantucket features: the rows of stylized trees, the birds, the baskets of fruit and flowers floating easily around the verse and inscriptions. Mary's sampler is important because it documents the Nantucket Friends School and the teacher, Lydia Gardner.

The bold scale of floral decorations in the middle portion of Phebe Swain's sampler in Plate XXXV sets it apart from those of the Nantucket Friends School, although the "nervous" branches of her potted plants are characteristic of the School. The sampler in Figure 78, probably worked by Abigail Hussey, is unusual in that it has both genealogical and mourning features. It shows the characteristic nervous branchlike lines and in the lower left displays a single "Nantucket" tree. The last sampler we show, an undated one by Lydia Coffin (Plate XXXVI), is exceptionally finely worked. The fact that the inscription "Lydia Coffin's work" is handwritten in script rather than worked indicates it probably was added at a later date.

Mourning Pictures

Mourning pictures, painted and embroidered, were fashionable in the first quarter of the nineteenth century. These pictures featured one or more great weeping willow trees arching over a tomb, alongside of which were shown a mourner or mourners. The ladies usually had handkerchiefs in their hands. Although the tomb in Plate XXXVII shows no dedication, this does not necessarily mean it ever had one. These pictures were so popular that young ladies sometimes made them with no particular person in mind. Textile specialists usually classify embroideries like this and the one in Plate XXXVIII as "satin-stitch pictures."[32]

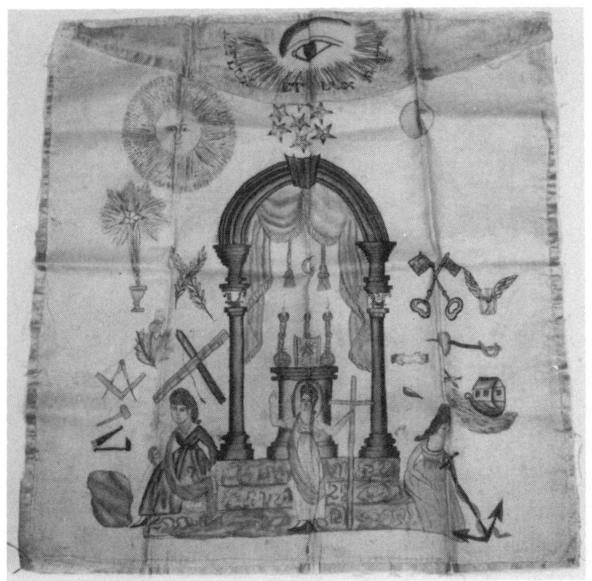

Figure 79. Silk hand-painted Masonic apron, 1800–20. Height: 14½ in. (36.8 cm.), width: 14 in. (35.6 cm.). (*NHA*).

A Masonic Apron

Free Masonry in America produced a distinctive body of decorative artifacts in the last quarter of the eighteenth and the first quarter of the nineteenth centuries, objects adorned with symbols of the fraternal order. The masonic apron was an important item of ceremonial regalia, symbolically relating the Masons to the stonemasons of medieval Europe who wore protective aprons while they worked. The early Masonic aprons were made of animal hides, while those of the nineteenth century were usually cloth, often silk. They were much smaller in size than actual stonemasons' aprons.[33]

A Masonic apron used in the Nantucket Union Lodge in the first quarter of the nineteenth century is illustrated in Figure 79. The apron is a watercolor on silk covered with symbols, both Masonic and traditional, combining Faith, Hope, and Charity with the Masonic symbols of the ark, the arch with drapes, and symbols of the stonemason's trade, the level, the plumb, the square, and the compass. Two other almost identical painted-silk aprons are known. All three aprons were almost certainly painted by the same person. One, belonging to the Museum of Our National Heritage, has been attributed to New England, probably Maine, because it was found in a frame labeled Kittery, Maine.[34] The other apron was included in a 1978 exhibition at the Museum of American Folk Art, New York, titled "Folk Art: The Heart of America."[35]

Although the Nantucket Masonic apron was presented to the Historical Association with a note that it was from China, it seems more likely that it was painted in America, even though Nantucket had extensive commercial contacts with China in the 1790–1860 period. The only Masonic aprons presently known to have been made in China in this period are embroidered.[36]

Other examples of Masonic artifacts are discussed later in Chapters 6 and 7.

Figure 80. Detail of a pieced friendship quilt made for Charles F. Coffin in 1856, with 392 small squares and a large square in the middle with an eagle and the inscription: "Nantucket Agricultural Society, incorporated / in the year one thousand, eight hundred, and fifty six / Lucy S. Mitchell." On the small squares are verses, 258 autograph signatures of the leading men and women of the island, and a few free-hand drawings. A number of the squares have no inscription. Made of cotton throughout, hand stitched, lined with dotted pink fabric. Tape sewn around edges of quilt. Length: 94 in. (238 cm.), width: 77 in. (196 cm.). (*NHA*).

Pictures on Velvet

The vibrantly colored oil on velvet of watermelon slices in Plate XXXIX is a type which today is often called a theorem painting. Actually, the theorem is the cut stencil which the young lady used to make the painting. She may or may not have cut the stencils herself. In 1830, Matthew D. Finn called this "painting in the theorematical style."[37] This particular painting was copied from a lithograph, yet to be identified. There are other paintings of the same subject matter, with the same configuration and number of watermelon slices, the same kind of knife, and the same oblong plate with scalloped edges.[38]

The Agricultural Society Quilt

Quilt making was often a true community effort in the nineteenth century, an activity which provided a social forum while producing a useful and attractive object for the home. The quilt in Figure 80 was no doubt a project that involved a number of women of the community under the direction of Lucy S. Mitchell. After it was finished, 258 Nantucketers signed their names on it. The Nantucket Agricultural Society, which, according to the evidence on the quilt itself, was incorporated in 1856, had its first exhibition in October of that year in the Great Hall of the Nantucket Atheneum, where the quilt was probably exhibited. There were displays of fresh and canned fruit, jellies, "fancy work" embroidery, wild flowers, cakes, bread, and doughnuts. George Gardner received first prize of eight dollars for his collection of vegetables, B. F. Worth was awarded one dollar for his fancy potatoes, W. H. McIntosh was awarded seventy-five cents for his oats and beets, and W. H. H. Smith seventy-five cents for his squash. It was advertised that "articles of needlework in great abundance, objects of virtu, and refreshments of rare excellence, will be constantly exposed for sale."[39]

Figure 81. Quaker dress, brown silk, long sleeves slightly puffed; starched cotton muslin scarf, both late eighteenth or early nineteenth century. The dress has a linen underlining in the bodice, the skirt is lined with cotton. Length of dress: 56 in. (142 cm.), waist: 30 in. (76.2 cm.), circumference of hem: 96½ in. (245 cm.). (*NHA*).

A Quaker Dress

It is difficult to date the brown silk taffeta Quaker woman's dress in Figure 81 any closer than late eighteenth or early nineteenth century. Because of the high quality of the material in the dress and the fine stitching that was used in its making, it was no doubt a "best" dress used for weddings and memorial services and perhaps First Day meetings. Eighteenth-century drawings and paintings and nineteenth-century photographs show such garments. There seems to have been little, if any, change in their design for a hundred years, from the middle of the eighteenth to the middle of the nineteenth century. A cotton band was added to the bottom of the dress at a later date. The white scarf, made of the finest starched cotton muslin, was usually worn with the dress. A matching "Quaker" bonnet would have completed the outfit.

Figure 82. Linen ditty bag owned by William P. Ceely, painted with his name, circa 1830. Height: 38½ in. (142 cm.), width: 19¼ in. (49 cm.). (*NHA*).

W. P. Ceely's Ditty Bag

The classic picture of a sailor in port, leaving or boarding his ship, showed him with a bulging ditty bag casually flung over his shoulder. The bag in Figure 82 was owned by William P. Ceely, born February 13, 1809, the son of Elias and Dinah (Starbuck) Ceely. He married Mary F. Bunker December 16, 1832. William's father, Elias, was captain of the whaleship *Lydia,* out of Nantucket in 1817 and the *Beverly,* out of Boston in 1820.

The Atlantic Silk Company

In the 1830s the idea of developing a homegrown silk industry spread all over New England, including Nantucket. Mulberry trees were planted to feed the silkworms. George Easton planted 1,000 trees near his house on North Water Street and Aaron Mitchell had a grove of 4,000 trees a mile out of town. In the November 14th, 1835 issue of the *Nantucket Inquirer* there was a review of Hendrick's *American Silk Growers' Guide* with the suggestion that silkmaking would be a good industry for the island. The Atlantic Silk Company was incorporated March 31, 1836, with Aaron Mitchell the principal owner.[40] The machinery was installed by Gamaliel Gay of the Rhode Island Silk Company of Providence. In September 1836, the Atlantic Silk Company exhibited its first products, silk vesting and handkerchiefs (Plate XL), at the fair of the New York Mechanics' Institute in New York City. The plant was on Academy Hill at the top of Gay Street (now numbers 10 and 12). Gay Street was originally named Coffin Court; the name was changed in 1836 to honor Gamaliel Gay.

The industry was hardly a success, either in Nantucket or the rest of New England. The mulberry trees did not thrive, and silks produced on the island could not compete outside the local market. The factory was closed about 1844 and the machinery was destroyed in the fire of 1846.

Textiles Since World War II

There has been a remarkable renaissance in weaving and needleworking in Nantucket since the 1950s. Weaving, one of the crafts practiced by the island's early settlers, is a flourishing, vital activity. In addition, a number of needlework specialists have produced embroideries. There is a certain symmetry to be noted in the fact that handmade and handworked textiles, which were so important in seventeenth- and eighteenth-century Nantucket, are being produced again in some quantity at a time when there is a plentiful and relatively inexpensive supply of machine-made goods.

A strong impetus to this renaissance was the foresight of Walter and Mary Anne Beinecke, which led to the restoration of the Jared Coffin house on Broad Street, Nantucket, in 1961. Built as a private home for Jared Coffin in 1845, it was occupied for only a short time. From 1847 the building operated as a hotel, the Ocean House, until it was acquired in 1961 by the Nantucket Historical Trust. It was decided to restore the building, where feasible, to its original state and to furnish it with Nantucket-made crafts, old and new. Under the leadership of Andy Oates (Figure 83), a weaver who studied at Black Mountain College under Anni Albers, a number of local women were taught weaving. This group, the precursor of the Nantucket Looms, wove for the Jared Coffin House bedspreads, curtains, upholstery fabrics for furniture in public rooms, draperies, stair carpets, hall runners, and placemats for the dining room.

Weavers of long association with the Nantucket Looms include Dorothy Backus, Lillian Foster, James Gould, Sam Kasten, and Mary Mauldin. Independent professional weavers on the island include Benjamin Richmond, Gwen Gaillard, Laura Lovett, and Margareta Grandin Nettles. Laura Lovett, a graduate of the Rhode Island School of Design, is both a production weaver of rugs and curtain fabrics, and an artist who makes complex landscape tapestries which employ weaving techniques, batik, and hand needlework. Margareta Nettles, a Swedish designer educated at the State School of Design in Stockholm, came to Nantucket in 1968 as a textile designer. Today she is also a weaver specializing in tapestry-woven rugs (Plate XLI). A sizable group of weavers (full-time, part-time and hobby weavers), perhaps thirty-five in all, work on Nantucket today.

Figure 83. Andy Oates, weaver, at work at his loom, July 1985.

Erica Wilson, graduate of the London Royal School of Needlework, was called in to develop the needle arts. Working with original designs, Miss Wilson taught a group of forty women the art of crewel embroidery. She supervised their making of bed hangings, a coverlet and curtains which she designed for the main bedroom in the Jared Coffin House. Through her publications, Miss Wilson has become well known throughout the United States.

One of the most visible and accessible collections of contemporary needlework on the island is in the church and chapel of St. Paul's Episcopal Church on Fair Street. In the church itself are embroidered rail kneelers, choir cushions, and chair seats, designed by the Nantucket Needlery. Erica Wilson designed for the chapel thirty-two chair seats, embroidered in bright clear colors with Nantucket themes entitled "Song of Creation" (Benedicte), to coordinate with the stained glass windows of the chapel. They were worked in the 1970s by members of the church.

Elizabeth Gilbert, who with Phebe Swain and a number of Nantucket women, made in the 1960s crewel bed hangings and coverlet for a bed in the Hadwen House, continues to be an influential Nantucket needleworker.

6. Ceramics, Glass, and Lighting Devices

Ceramics

Ceramic wares were used in Nantucket from the earliest times for the storage and handling of dairy products, molasses, cider, and other foods. It was not until the middle and latter part of the eighteenth century that ceramic plates were used for dining, and "china" tea and coffee services came into use. As noted elsewhere in this book, woodenware trenchers were commonly used as plates until about 1725, when pewter plates became more common.

Based purely on the inventories, the quantity and quality of ceramics in Nantucket does not appear to have been markedly different from those of Suffolk County, Massachusetts, although by the middle of the eighteenth century there does seem to have been more English delftwares and Chinese ceramics in Nantucket than on the mainland.[1] This could be accounted for by the direct contacts after 1750 with England where almost all of the island's whale oil was marketed. However, the nature of inventory listings, which are usually general and nonspecific, means that we have little precise knowledge of the actual kinds of ceramics used on the island before the Revolution. Archaeological work, correlated with probate inventory and historical studies, *could* give us a better idea of what the early settlers had in their houses at various times in the seventeenth and eighteenth centuries.

After 1790, the overall picture of ceramics in Nantucket becomes clearer, since there are quite a few representative objects with documented histories still on the island.

Ceramics in the Colonial Inventories: Earthenware

Earthenware cups, mugs, pots, basins, plates, and platters were common articles in Nantucket inventories of the 1680–1740 period. For example, Tristram Coffin's 1706 inventory included:

a great Earthen Bason	0–08–06
2 small Earthen Basons	0–01–04
a Jug	0–00–08
2 cups	0–00–08

No colors were mentioned for earthenwares in the inventories until the middle of the eighteenth century, when a very occasional notation of red or brown wares was listed. Although we assume that some of the earthenware pottery was from Charlestown, Massachusetts, the first notation of such pottery was in the inventory of Peter Bunker (1761):

Sundry Charlestown earthen vessels	0–3– 0
2 Brown bowls	0–0–10
Milk Cup / 4d / black Jar 0—4d	0–0– 8
11 Blue and White earthen ware plates	0–4– 0

The "Blue and White earthen ware plates" were probably English delft.

New earthenware forms began to appear in inventories in the 1750s, mostly glazed wares of the type which would today be designated as delft or whiteware. Simeon Bunker's 1753 inventory listed the following:

1 large Earthen punch bowl	0–1–4
1 Do Smaller	0–1–4
1 Do Smaller	0–0–9
1 Do Cracked	0–0–6
1 small Earthen plate	0–0–3
3 brown bowls	0–1–2
1 small Earthen platter	0–1–4
2 white Porringers	0–0–8
3 white Chamber pots	0–1–1
3 blue and white Quart Mugs	0–2–5
2 Do larger	0–2–1

Delftware

English delftware from potteries of London, Bristol, Liverpool, Glasgow, and Wincanton had been exported to the American colonies in quantity since the seventeenth century. English pottery with relatively thick, "warm," opaque tin glazes is known as delft, with a small initial letter. Only Dutch Delftwares are capitalized. (In France and Germany such tin-glazed wares are called faience; in Italy and Spain, majolica.) Delftwares were often mentioned specifically in inventories after 1760, such as that of Joseph Starbuck (1761):

1/2 Dozn. blue & white Delf plates	1–10–0
1/2 Dz. Do yellow & blue	1–10–0
5 odd plates at 4/ each	1– 0–0
1/2 Dozn. Do Delf plates	1– 8–0
1 Delf Wash bason	0– 6–0

The large blue and white shallow English delft bowl in Figure 84 is accompanied by the following notation, which shows a confusion between English delftwares and wares from China, because of the fact that westerners often copied Chinese designs on their ceramics. This confusion existed throughout the eighteenth and nineteenth centuries.[2]

My Chinese Dish

> This dish was given to me by Betsy Cary in 1851. It was in two parts and I mended it. Mrs. Cary told me she bought it from Gorham Macy, and I ascertained the origin of it as far back as having belonged to Robert Folger's parents. Captain Folger built a house on Pearl Street before my rememberance. He had been an Indian Captain of some note and died before I was married.
>
> Eliza W. Mitchell

We were unable to trace the provenance of the delft bowl from this documentation. There are

Figure 84. Blue and white English delft bowl, circa 1750. Diameter: 14 in. (35.6 cm.), height: 3 1/4 in. (8.3 cm.). (*NHA*).

two Betsy Carys in the *Nantucket Vital Records,* both of whom had been Swains: Betsy Swain Cary, who married James Cary in 1799, and Betsy Swain Cary, who married William Baxter Cary in 1830. There were eight different Robert Folgers living in Nantucket in the eighteenth and early nineteenth centuries.

The center of the delft bowl features large-scale freely drawn "Chinese" buds and flowers, surrounded by a border of baroque decorations interspersed with stylized leaves and flowers.

Stoneware

German and English stonewares were widely available in New England throughout the colonial period. The hard, pitted glazes of stoneware are the result of throwing salt into the kiln when it is very hot; sodium from the vaporized salt combines with silica and alumina in the clay to form the "salt glaze." The English stonewares included white and buff wares, while the German wares, often in the form of jugs, tended to be brown or gray in color.

Many of the "jugs" in the early inventories were no doubt stoneware even though they were not so designated. Samuel Stanton's 1745 inventory was more specific, listing "6 Stone Jugs—0–19–6." Jethro Gardner (1737) had "2 stone chamber vessels 8/6," Daniel Chadwick (1750), "2 stone pickle pots—0–15–0," Simeon Bunker (1753), "3 Stone diet bread pans—0–4–0," and in 1750 Daniel Hussey left "2 stone suger pots—0–12–0" and "1 set white Stone Cups—1–4–0."

Joseph Starbuck's 1761 inventory included twelve items of "stone" ware:

1/2 Dozn. brown Stone Chocolate bowls	0–15–0
5 Do. with a white rim around the top	0–15–0
1 Set Stone Tea Dishes	0–11–3
1 Set Do white stone	0–11–3
1 Set flowered Stone Do	0–15–0
1 Small Stone Teapot	0– 3–0
1 Do red earthen	0– 6–0
1 Stone milk pot	0– 3–0
Set broken white Stone Tea dishes	0– 5–6
1 pair Stone glasses	0– 6–0
1 white Stone Quart Mug	0– 9–0
1 red Stone Teapot no cover	0– 3–0

We illustrate in Figure 85 an American stoneware jug with a Nantucket provenance. This large grayish-brown jug, incised with the Masonic symbol of the compass and square enclosing the letter "G," is said to have been used on the whaleship *Ploughboy,* which made five voyages out of Nantucket in the 1821–1843 period.

Figure 85. American stoneware jug, grayish-brown, incised in blue with the number "4" and the Masonic symbol of square and compass enclosing the letter "G." No maker's mark. Height: 16 7/8 in. (42.9 cm.). (*NHA*).

China

The terms "China" and "Cheny" were used throughout the eighteenth century in the Nantucket inventories, but they were used in such ways that it is sometimes difficult to determine whether the pieces referred to were Chinese porcelains or ceramics painted with "Chinese" decorations.

Large quantities of Chinese porcelains were imported into England by the East India Company from the beginning of the eighteenth century[3] and many such wares were transshipped to the American market.[4] "China" wares were frequently mentioned in Nantucket inventories, particularly after 1750. The earlier references are problematic. The "Cheny platter" and "4 flowered Do" in John Swain's 1718 inventory and the "Cheny ware" in Nathaniel Barnard's 1744 inventory could have been English delftware with Chinese-like motifs or possibly Chinese porcelains. However, Thomas Brock's 1750 inventory seems to clearly differentiate between "China" and "Delf":

1 China Bowl 50/ 1 Delf 20/	3–10–0
A set China cups 45/ 6 plates 36/	4–01–0
1 Dozen China plates	15–00–0
1 sett China dishes	3–00–0
1 China bowl & 1 Delf	5–00–0

In the inventories of the third quarter of the eighteenth century there were twenty-five entries of "China," with such descriptions as "1 set China," "1 China bowl," "1 set of China tea cups," "6 small bowls China," "China milk pot," and "a China Mug." In Andrew Myrick's later inventory (1783) there were "4 China salt sellars," "6 China plates," and "a set of Red & White China cups & saucers."

Since at this writing there are no known documented pre-Revolutionary examples of Chinese porcelains with a Nantucket provenance, determination of the kinds and quality of such wares used on the island await archaeological evidence.

Tea Drinking in Nantucket

Tea drinking was introduced into England early in the seventeenth century and by the 1690s tea was being sold in New England.[5] The limited amount of tea available in the western world and its high price limited consumption.[6] It was only after 1750 that tea drinking became commonplace in America.

The earliest evidence of tea drinking in Nantucket seems to be the inventory of Samuel Barker, who died in 1739:

1 Tea pot Cups slop Dishes and Sugar Cup	0–18–0
5 tea Cups & Saucers	0–12–0
1 Earthen Tea pot	0– 2–6

There were two mentions of tea equipment in inventories of the 1740s: Nathaniel Barnard (1744) "1 Tea Cittle—2–10–0" and Samuel Stanton (1745) "1 Tea pot 6/ milk pot 2/6 bowl 2/." It was only after 1750 that teapots, teacups, and saucers became common in the inventories. The first pewter teapot appeared in 1753, and the first silver teapot in 1757.

A Liverpool Pitcher

Liverpool-type creamware pottery pitchers decorated with transfer prints of ships were brought back to Nantucket by a number of mariners in the last decade of the eighteenth and the first quarter of the nineteenth centuries. One of the most interesting and elaborately decorated of these pitchers is the one shown in Plate XLII, with an original spirited whaling scene painted on the obverse side and a transfer print of a symbolic American eagle enclosed in a garland on the reverse. The pitcher, possibly decorated at the Herculaneum Pottery, Liverpool, was brought to Nantucket in the 1790s by Captain James Chase (1738–1819) and is still in the Chase family. During the Revolutionary War, Chase was among the Nantucket men with Commander John Paul Jones in service on the *Bon Homme Richard* and the *Ranger.*[7] After the Revolution, Chase was captain of the *Nancy* (dates unknown) and in 1791–1792 was captain of the whaleship *Harmony* on a cruise to Woolwich Bay on the west coast of Africa.[8]

The whaling scene on the Chase pitcher depicts a right whale being hunted by the crew in the whaleboat in the foreground. The chase was being watched by men lined up along the rail of the ship. The ship on the pitcher may have been a stock design rather than a ship portrait. Robert McCauley, in his book *Liverpool Transfer Designs on Anglo-American Pottery,* noted that the *same* ship transfer design was found on "ten or twelve" different jugs printed in black, sometimes with color added, each of the ships having different names.[9] Apparently, a customer could choose from sample designs a ship which most resembled his own vessel in contour and rigging.

The Chase Liverpool pitcher is, as usual, unmarked, bearing no maker's name. The making of these wares was big business in Chase's time. In 1790, in one area of Liverpool, "Shaw's Brow," there were seventy-four pottery firms employing 437 people.[10]

Nantucket and the China Trade

The American China trade in the post-Revolutionary War era out of Salem, Providence, New York, and other east coast seaports was primarily involved in the importation of goods from China for sale in American markets. Nantucket's involvement in this trade was different. The Nantucket traders, almost all of whom were, and continued to be, whalers, thought of China as a market for products in demand there: the skins of seals and sea-elephants, and, to a much lesser extent, sandalwood and bêche-de-mer. The latter, also called tripang, were dried and smoked sea slugs, or sea cucumbers, a culinary delicacy for the Chinese, from Fiji and other South Seas islands.

In a very real way, Nantucket's China trade was a by-product of whaling. The whalers, alerted by the voyages of Captain Cook, began immediately after the Revolution to hunt seals in the South Atlantic. Combination voyages, with the whalers pursuing the quest for whale oil, whalebone, seal and sea-elephant skins, led them first to the Falkland Islands and later to South Georgia, 500 miles south of Cape Horn, then to the edges of Antarctica and to strange and lonely coasts and islands all over the South Pacific and Indian Oceans. The first cargo to reach Nantucket was a shipment of 13,000 sealskins in 1786, which were sold to New York for $650.[11] When these same sealskins were shipped to Canton on board the brig *Eleanora,* Captain Metcalf, they realized $65,000, five dollars per skin. News of this and similar transactions soon led dozens of whalers from Nantucket and other east coast seaports to the hunt for seals. The number of seals killed in the next three decades ran into the millions. The *Neptune* had 33,340 skins aboard in 1798,[12] the *Minerva* totalled 23,000 skins on an 1802–1804 voyage,[13] and the *Favorite* sold an astonishing 87,080 skins in Canton in January, 1807.[14] The magnificent sea-elephants were hunted both for their skins and for the oil rendered from their fat. The *Hunter,* out of Nantucket in 1791, killed 369 sea-elephants in a nine-day period on Desolation Island (now called Keruelen Island), a remote spot in the South Indian Ocean that fully deserved its name.[15] These commodities were sold in Canton through the Hong merchants for cash, silver or gold coins, and/or the easily negotiable commodities of tea, silks, and nankeens (cotton cloth).

When the *Favorite* returned to Nantucket later in the year 1807, she brought two Chinese merchants from Canton, who were entertained for several months on the island by Paul Gardner, owner of the ship, and Daniel Whitney, the supercargo. The Chinese must have made a spectacular appearance in the staid Quaker town. A young boy noted in a letter "their rich costumes and caps with red buttons upon the top, marking a superior position in their own country." Keziah Coffin's diary (NHA) spoke of one of them in an entry dated January 10, 1808:

> Mrs. Burnell, F. Chase and Nancy Fanning drank tea here & also a Chinaman that came with Mr. Whitney last fall from Canton. He is a merchant there. He is the color of our native whites.

Nantucketers were engaged in sealing until it began to peter out in the 1830s. New York became the principal contraport for the sale of Chinese goods brought back by Nantucket ships, although island-based ships occasionally brought wares back to Philadelphia and Dublin, Ireland. Right up to the time of the Civil War, Nantucket mariners such as Charles Worth and Frederick Sanford were involved in the China trade in Hong Kong and later, Shanghai. It was this continuing presence of Nantucketers in China throughout the first six decades of the nineteenth century that accounts for the considerable number of Chinese artifacts of the period still on the island.

Chinese Export Porcelains

There is no evidence that the Nantucket whalers and sealers became commercially involved in the importation of Chinese porcelains to the island, other than pieces brought back for family and friends. Among the earliest pieces of these wares to be brought to Nantucket were white porcelains decorated with the American eagle. The coffeepot, creamer, cup, and saucer in Figure 86 were not identified with monograms. However, other similar wares belonging to the Nantucket Historical Association are Gardner family pieces with the initial "BPG." It is conventional to date these eagle-decorated pieces circa 1795, but we date the Nantucket examples 1795–1810, the heyday of the early whaler-sealer visits.

The pieces of severely plain export porcelain shown in Figure 87, part of a forty-five piece service, were brought to Nantucket circa 1807 by Captain Thaddeus Bunker for his bride-to-be, Lydia Folger. They were married October 1, 1807. Some of the pieces of the service are in-

Figure 86. Chinese export porcelain coffee pot and cover, sugar bowl with cover, cup and saucer from a service decorated with the American eagle, sepia with touches of red, gold bands, 1795–1810. Height of coffee pot: $9^{3}/_{8}$ in. (23.8 cm.). (*NHA*).

Figure 87. Part of a forty-five piece Chinese export porcelain service, shown on its original brass-bound black leather-covered camphorwood chest, brought to Nantucket circa 1807 by Captain Thaddeus Bunker for Lydia Folger, whom he married October 1, 1807. Some pieces gilded with monogram "LF" in an oval. Height of teapot: 5⁷/₈ in. (14.9 cm.). Brass plaque on chest engraved "T. BUNKER." Dimensions of chest: 1. 42¹/₂ x h. 19³/₄ x d. 21¹/₄ in. (108 x 50.2 x 54.0 cm.). (*NHA*).

scribed with the initials "LF" in an oval. Undoubtedly all the pieces were originally monogramed, but the gilding has worn off many of them. The only other decorations on the pieces are thin gold borders. This service is one of the least decorated of those brought back from China, evidence that the Quaker taste persisted into the nineteenth century for many Nantucketers.

Chinese porcelains decorated with Masonic symbols are among the most attractive of the export wares. The punch bowl in Figure 88, with its brilliant dark blue borders and polychrome Masonic symbols, has two dates on it: 1805 for the year it was purportedly purchased in Canton, and 1875, the year it was presented to the Union Lodge in Nantucket. (The 1805 date may be a commemorative date.) Punch bowls like this one saw plenty of use in the early years of the Lodge. Alcoholic beverages were a part of the Lodge fellowship, in contrast to the more puritanical approach to alcohol later in the nineteenth century when prohibitionist pressures effectively stopped its use in Masonic lodges and other fraternal organizations. Early records of the Union Lodge often mention food and drink:

> October 20, 1773—Voted that Bro. Sec'ty procure a quarter cask of wine for use of this lodge.[16]
>
> November 3, 1777—Voted that the Secretary will do his best endeavors to make some inquiries to swap wine for rum on the best terms he can.[17]
>
> March 2, 1778—Voted that the sum of five pounds be sent by Bro. Jos. Chase for N. Carolina and France as per rect. be taken on lodge risk to be laid out in Brandy.[18]
>
> January 4, 1779—Voted that the stewards doth lay the state of the Lodge for liquors before the Brethern. Voted that the Secretary doth send down to Boston for a quarter cask of good wine, suitable for Lodge use by the first convenient opportunity. [Later the secretary reported that he could not procure any there without giving a large price for same.][19]
>
> November 3, 1781—Voted that we send by Bro. Jas. Ramsdell to get a barrel of good Jamaca Rum as low as he can in New York or Providence, on account and risk as follows: for the Lodge acct. 18 gals.; four Brothers agreeing to take the balance 13¹/₂ gals.[20]
>
> March 2, 1807—A special meeting concerning refreshments was held and voted: First, that we think it expedient to have a refreshment of wine, spirits, crackers and cheese on each regular Lodge night, any former vote to the contrary notwithstanding.[21]
>
> December 8, 1809—Voted that Bro. Benjamin Bunker provide a dinner on St. John's Day, brought into the hall at 5 shillings 6 pence per person, the bill of fare as follows: Plum, apple and plain puddings—baked and boiled; also corned beef, leg of pork, hams,

neat tongues, roast turkeys, ducks, chickens and shoat [young pig], with vegetables and pickles suitable for the above. Table drink beer and cider.[22]

The Union Lodge records noted the gift of four punch bowls:

February 13, 1808—Voted that the Lodge accept of a China Punch Bowl which Bro. Wm. Kelley has made a present of to the Lodge and likewise return him their thanks.[23]

In 1809 Nathan Long presented two punch bowls.[24]

In May, 1875, Secretary Charles P. Swain presented the Lodge with an ancient Chinese punch bowl, made in Canton, and bearing the date 1805.[25] [Figure 88.]

The fine pair of jugs with covers in Plate XLIII, decorated with Masonic symbols, are of a type sometimes called cider jugs, a term we have not found in Nantucket records. The symbols depicted on the jugs include a cluster of seven stars, a severely simple Chinese table on which are unidentified objects, Masonic columns with a face in a sun, a Chinese box with handles, a beehive, square, half-circle and ruler, a compass and square enclosing a carpet, and a man in the moon. The jug with cover in Plate XLIV is a western form, related to the pair of Masonic jugs, but the painted decorations on the jug are in the Chinese taste. On the side shown are four figures in an interior with a screen and a view of a garden beyond, while the opposite side (not shown) depicts two colorfully dressed actors on a golden platform-stage.

Figure 88. Chinese export porcelain punch bowl, decorated with blue borders and polychrome Masonic symbols, circa 1805. One side is inscribed "UNION LODGE / 1805," the other "TO / UNION LODGE / 1875." Height: 5⅞ in. (14.9 cm.), diameter: 13⅜ in. (34.0 cm.). (*Union Lodge, Nantucket*).

The platter and covered vegetable dish in Plate XLV, in the orange Fitzhugh pattern, was brought from China to Nantucket in the 1815–1830 period by Captain Gideon Swain (1786–1841). The celadon washbowl in Plate XLVI is said to have been brought to Nantucket from China in 1830. The bowl has a flanged border decorated with flowers, fruit, and melons. The central medallion of the bowl displays sprigs of flowers, birds, and dragonflies. Surrounding the medallion are four groups of branches with pink and white blossoms and festoon streamers. On the outside of the bowl are orange-colored bamboo branches and leaves. The bowl has no monogram.

The famille-rose porcelain wash bowl in Figure 89 was brought from China to Nantucket, probably in the 1850–1865 period, by Captain George H. Brock. Brock, born May 15, 1826, married Charlotte Coleman in Nantucket May 18, 1847. The flanged top of the bowl clearly designates it as a washbowl rather than a punch bowl, which would have straight, vertical walls without a flange. Stylistically, the washbowl is a type of famille-rose called mandarin.[26] However, it is a late example, a transition piece between the mandarin famille-rose Chinese porcelains of the first half of the nineteenth century and the famille-rose pattern called Rose Medallion, which dates no earlier than the 1850s.[27] This suggests a mid-nineteenth century date for the bowl, circa 1845–1865, dates which fit those of Captain Brock.

Figure 89. Chinese export porcelain *famille-rose* wash bowl, 1845–1865. Diameter: 16 in. (40.6 cm.), height: 5 1/8 in. (13.0 cm.). (*NHA*).

The central medallion of the bowl, surrounded by a double row of Greek-key patterns, shows a Chinese domestic scene with nine figures on a terrace, beyond which is a glimpse of a garden. Three of six melon-shaped reserves around the central medallion depict Chinese interiors with figures, each surrounded by green "C" scrolls, alternating with three reserves with green, leafy tendrils, peonies, colorful butterflies, and birds, enclosed in a double-lined scroll with a leafy green frond at the top. The border of the bowl continues the densely decorated background of the bowl itself, interrupted by six small reserves, each containing two seated figures.

Nineteenth-Century Ceramics: English, French, American

English ceramics dominated American markets in the first half of the nineteenth century. The Jefferson Embargo and the War of 1812 turned out to be only temporary interruptions in the flow of ceramic wares to this country. The Coalport pink luster service in Figure 90, a wedding gift for Lydia Mitchell, who married John W. Barrett October 31, 1816, is evidence that English imports had resumed soon after the end of the War of 1812. The pieces are typical of the products of the Coalport porcelain factory on the River Severn of the 1810–1815 period, both in design and in the fact that the pieces are unmarked.[28] Note the deep saucers, which were designed for the drinking of tea or coffee, a practice which continued to the latter part of the nineteenth century.

The large, plain creamware punch bowl in Figure 91, decorated with black rims on the lip and the foot, a coat of arms and the initials "FF" for Frederick Folger, born in 1794, was very much in the reticent Quaker taste, at a time when most ceramics, English, continental, and Oriental, were covered with decorations.

We end these notes on nineteenth-century

Figure 90. English pink luster teapot and stand, after-dinner cup and saucer (left), tea cup and saucer (right), made by the Coleport Porcelain Co., 1810–1815. Part of a service (now twenty-seven pieces), given as a wedding present to Lydia Mitchell who married John W. Barrett October 31, 1816. No maker's marks. Height of teapot: 6 in. (15.2 cm.). (*NHA*).

Figure 91. English creamware punch bowl, with initials "FF" for Frederick Folger, born August 1, 1794. On the opposite side (not shown) is a coat of arms depicting a yellow and black lion rampant on a field half black and half yellow with black dots. No maker's mark, circa 1830. Height: 6³/8 in. (16.2 cm.), diameter: 17 in. (43.2 cm.). (*NHA*).

Figure 92. American white-glazed pottery mug and pitcher, both inscribed "NANTUCKET," circa 1890. The mug (left) was originally in the Nantucket Hotel on Brant Point. Height: 5³/4 in. (14.6 cm.). (*Courtesy Eva Marie Tausig*). The pitcher (right) was said to have been on the steamship *Nantucket*. Height: 7³/4 in. (19.7 cm.). (*Private collection*).

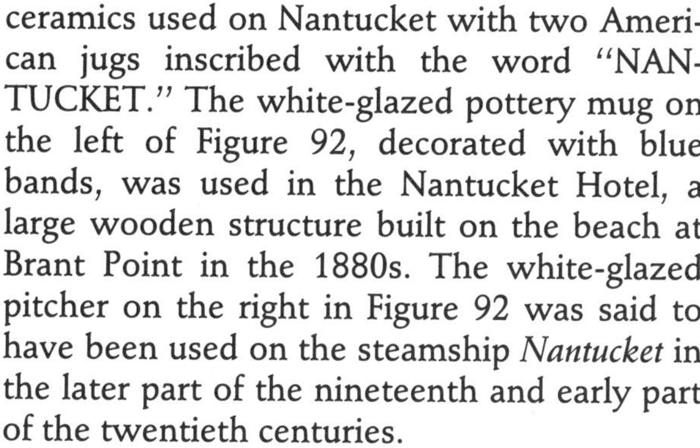

ceramics used on Nantucket with two American jugs inscribed with the word "NANTUCKET." The white-glazed pottery mug on the left of Figure 92, decorated with blue bands, was used in the Nantucket Hotel, a large wooden structure built on the beach at Brant Point in the 1880s. The white-glazed pitcher on the right in Figure 92 was said to have been used on the steamship *Nantucket* in the later part of the nineteenth and early part of the twentieth centuries.

Starting late in the nineteenth century and continuing throughout the twentieth, there has been a flood of souvenir pottery, plates, cups, ashtrays, and so on, mostly made in Europe, picturing the Old Mill, the Oldest House, Stone Alley, the gold-domed church on Orange Street, and other island scenes. Among the earlier of the ceramic souvenir wares were those made for the Coffin family reunion in 1886, commemorating the two hundredth anniversary of the Jethro Coffin house.

Glass in the Colonial Inventories

The table on the following page, summarizing the glass listed in the Nantucket inventories in the first three quarters of the eighteenth century, indicates that bottles were the most common glass form on the island for the period. Approximately 850 bottles of various kinds were recorded. Most bottles were listed as such without any identification. Others were called "large," "small," "French," "square," "junk," and "leaded glass bottles." The inventory of Robert Barnard, who was lost at sea in 1776, had a "Founteney Bottle—1–2–0"; Daniel Hussey's 1751 inventory listed "28 bottles with wine—12–12–0." The bottle and seal from a similar bottle in Figure 6, Chapter 2, with the inscription "T/BROCK/1744," do not appear in Thomas Brock's 1750 inventory. In fact, there were no bottles of any kind in his inventory. Perhaps the bottles were in the still house at the time the inventory was taken.

Glass in Nantucket Inventories of the Colonial Period

Form	*1706–1725*	*1726–1750*	*1751–1776*
Baker		15	27
Beaker		3	32
Bottle	74	251	528
Bowl		1	2
Candlestick			1 pr.
Can			3
Cups and Mugs		19	5
Decanter			18
Glasses		16	56
Glasses, Wine		11	52
Hour Glass	2	1	3
Milk Pot			2
Salt Cellars		1	8
Spectacles	2	4	1
Vinegar Cruet bottle		7	21

The inventories include a total of twenty-seven bottle cases (see Figure 53, Chapter 4). These cases or boxes, usually with spaces for twelve bottles, had hinged lids and handles for easy transport. As noted in Chapter 4, such bottle cases seemed to have been standard equipment in the captain's cabin of whaleships.

The bottle totals include eleven mustard bottles (sometimes called pots), one "sucking bottle," eight snuff bottles, and twenty-eight vinegar cruet bottles.

A "glass" was the next most common form designation in colonial Nantucket. "Glass" included such terms as "scallop glass," "Flowered glass" [with etched flowers], "double flint glass," and "cider glass." Thomas Brock's 1750 inventory listed "Red Glasses—5–15–0," a relatively high value. We have shown wineglasses separately in the table. These include wineglasses with "flowered edge," "large," and a pair of "dram glasses."

Other items of glass in colonial Nantucket *not* included in the table are 145 looking glasses discussed in Chapter 3, and such things in Tabor Morton's 1776 inventory as: "18 squares glass 8×6," and "11 squares glassed in sashes." There was a "Glass Lanthern—2–5–0" in George Macy's 1776 inventory, the only such lantern listed in the colonial period.

Lighting Devices

Except for George Macy's "Glass Lanthern," the only lighting devices listed in the pre-Revolutionary Nantucket inventories in any quantity are candlesticks, mostly iron and brass, plus one pair of glass and one pair of tinplate candlesticks. There were no pewter or silver candlesticks listed in the inventories. Glass lamps did not become commonplace before the 1790s. All of the lighting devices illustrated in this chapter date from the first half of the

Plate XXVII. Coin silver needleholder (left), engraved with initials "SB" for Sarah Barker. There are six Sarah Barkers in the *Nantucket Vital Records*, the earliest of whom was born in 1767. Length: $1^{7}/_{8}$ in. (4.8 cm.). Right: silver chatelaine with silver chain attached to scissors with steel blades in silver case engraved "PF," and round pinholder box with silver frame, the top and bottom of which is covered with canvas worked with silk yarn in Queen's stitch. The engraving on the silver scissors case suggests a date of 1800 to 1810. Neither the needle holder nor the chatelaine has a maker's mark. (*NHA*).

Plate XXVIII. Quilting template, carved from pine, with the inscription "John Webster / Nantucket, to / Miss Diana Gardner / New York / May / 1823." Height: $5^{3}/_{4}$ in. (14.6 cm.), width: $5^{1}/_{2}$ in. (14.0 cm.). (*NHA*).

Plate XXIX. One-piece light blue silk petticoat, said to have been worked by Damaris Gayer for her wedding in 1692. Undulating floral border in very fine running stitch, lined with teal blue and ochre striped woven woolen cloth. The linen top shows signs of fittings for several different waist sizes. Height: 35½ in. (90.2 cm.), width around hem: 99 in. (251.5 cm.). (*Private collection*).

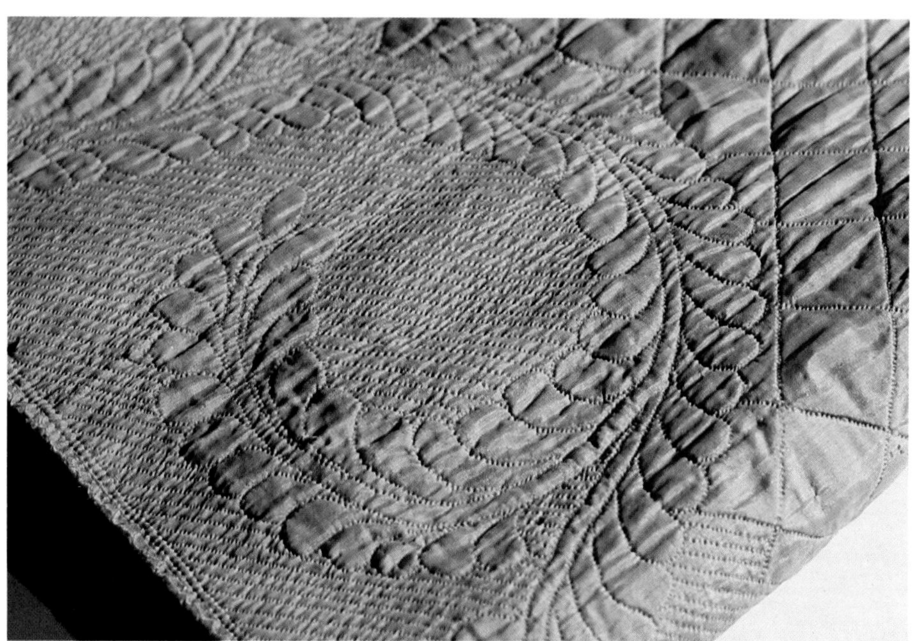

Plate XXX. Detail of one-piece yellow-gold quilted petticoat, probably American, finely quilted on English silk, fine running stitch, late seventeenth or early eighteenth century. Length of petticoat: 36½ in. (92 cm.), waist: 25½ in. (64.8 cm.), width around hem: 100 in. (254 cm.). (*NHA*).

Plate XXXI. Canvas worked picture in crewel and silk of a type called "The Fishing Lady and Boston Commons," wrought in 1765 by Susanna Colesworthy when she was twelve. Susanna was born in Boston in 1752, the daughter of Gilbert and Mary Waldo Colsworthy, and died in Nantucket in 1811. Silk yarns with tent stitch on fine hand-woven canvas, height: 17 1/4 in. (44.5 cm.), width: 20 3/4 in. (52.7 cm.). (*NHA*).

Plate XXXII. Two eighteenth-century pocketbooks. The one on the left is made of black twill-woven worsted fabric, embroidered with crewel yarns in a design of a basket of flowers and two insects that could be bees or butterflies, with a tan twill-woven tape border, 1780–1800. The pocketbook on the right makes use of crewel yarns in Irish stitch and is earlier in date, 1740–1775. Both have engraved silver clasps, the one on the left (not showing) is marked in script "LW" and decorated with feathers and wigglework. Left: 4 3/4 x 5 7/8 in. (12.1 x 14.9 cm.), right: 4 x 4 3/4 in. (10.2 x 12.1 cm.). (*NHA*).

Plate XXXIII. Sampler worked by Polly Coffin in 1797. At the top: letters of the alphabet and "Markt This In aPril 1797." Below is the inscription:

> The Unwearied sun from day to day
> Does his creators power display
> Polly Coffin Born March The 16 1786

Polly was the daughter of Joseph and Elizabeth Coffin. She married Theordore Fish October 5, 1812 in Nantucket. Silk on linen. Height: 14¹/₄ in. (36.2 cm.), width: 13 in. (33 cm.). (*NHA*).

Plate XXXIV. Sampler worked by Mary Starbuck in 1808 when she was in her twelfth year. The verse and inscription reads: "Oh may I now forever fear / To indulge a sinful Thought / Since the great God can see and hear / And write down every thought / Mary Starbuck born / 10mo third 1796 / Finished this Sampler in / the 12th year of her age / 1808 / Friends School kept by Lydia Gardner / Nantucket 2mo 17th 1808." Mary was the daughter of Kimbal and Mary (Coffin) Starbuck. She married Shubael Allen January 5, 1818. Silk on linen, height: 14¹/₂ in. (36.8 cm.), width: 13¹/₂ in. (34.3 cm.). (*NHA*).

Plate XXXV. Sampler worked by Phebe B. Swain in 1818 when she was twelve years old. Inscribed with alphabets, numbers, and: "Phebe B. Swain / Born July 28 in The / year 1805 May 21 1818." Phebe was the daughter of Micajah and Mary (Bunker) Swain. She married Edward G. Coffin January 10, 1828. Height: 10½ in. (26.7 cm.), width: 8 in. (20.3 cm.). (*Private Collection*).

Plate XXXVI. Sampler worked by Lydia Coffin, circa 1795–1815. There are seventy seven Lydia Coffins listed in the *Nantucket Vital Records*, nine of whom were born in the 1782–1796 period, making it difficult to pin down any one person. The verse tells us that a fine sampler is the result of a "Fair Education":

Plain as this Sampler was as plain we find
Unletter'd unadorn'd the Female Mind
No fine Ideas fill the vacant soul
No graceful colouring animates the whole
With close attention, carefully is wrought
Fair Education prints the pleasing thought
Inserts the curious lines in proper Ground
Compleats the work and scatters Roses round

In between the two verses is written in script: "Lydia Coffin's work." Silk on linen, tent and cross stitches, height: 18¼ in. (47 cm.), width: 14 in. (35.6 cm.). (*NHA*).

Plate XXXVII. Satin-stich picture. The tomb has a void oval space in which a dedication written on a paper label usually appears. The features of the lady's face are drawn in. Silk yarns on silk background, 1805–1825. Height: 14¹/₄ in. (36.2 cm.), width: 17¹/₄ in. (43.8 cm.). (*NHA*).

Plate XXXVIII. Satin-stitch picture, circa 1806. The hand-written paper label on the tomb reads:

> To the memory of Jethro Starbuck
> Who died the 13th May 1806
> On smiling Flora's flowering lawn
> Annual by nature's pencil drawn
> The pristine beauties that appear
> Recall the friend—to mem'ry dear

Jethro Starbuck, son of William and Anna (Folger) Starbuck, was born March 29, 1732. He married Anna Upham February 27, 1755. Silk yarns on silk background, height: 16⁵/₈ in. (42.2 cm.), width: 15¹/₄ in. (38.7 cm.). (*NHA*).

Plate XXXIX. Oil on velvet with the use of stencils, sewn on a paper backing with a running stitch, picturing watermelon slices on a feather-edged pearlware (English Staffordshire) plate. On the paper backing, just above the painting, is the inscription: "Painted by Susan Rebecca Pell—1827". Susan Rebecca Pell was named for her mother Susan (Folger) Pell and her grandmother Rebecca (Slocum) Folger, both of Nantucket. Susan Rebecca's mother married Benjamin Pell "of the Manor of Pelham, West Chester County, N. Y." in Nantucket on May 5, 1808. (*NHA*).

Plate XL. Silk handkerchief made by the Atlantic Silk Company, Nantucket, in 1836, 23 1/8 x 24 5/8 in. (58.7 x 62.5 cm.). (*NHA*).

Plate XLI. Tapestry rug made by Margareta Grandin Nettles in 1985, linen warp with wool weft. Length: 11 ft. (3.33 meters), width: 20 ft. 8 in. (6.30 meters). (*Private collection*).

Plate XLII. Liverpool creamware pottery pitcher, painted and transfer-print decorations, 1792–1800. Under the spout is the inscription "JAMES CHASE / NANTUCKET," and "JC / & / MC," for James Chase and his wife Mary (Folger) Chase, who were married in 1760. Height: 11$^{1}/_{2}$ in. (29.2 cm.). (*Courtesy James Franklin Chase*).

Plate XLIII. Pair of Chinese export porcelain jugs with covers, crossed handles, decorated with polychrome Masonic symbols, 1795–1810. Height, left: 11 in. (27.9 cm.), right: 11½ in. (29.2 cm.). (*NHA*).

Plate XLIV. Chinese export porcelain jug with cover, inscribed with the initials "GEM," 1795–1810. Height: 9⅞ in. (25.1 cm.). (*NHA*).

Plate XLV. Chinese export porcelain platter and covered vegetable dish, orange Fitzhugh pattern, brought to Nantucket 1815–1830, by Gidean Swain (1786–1841). Length of platter: $15^{1}/_{4}$ in. (38.7 cm.), length of vegetable dish: 9 in. (22.9 cm.). (*NHA*).

Plate XLVI. Chinese export porcelain celadon bowl, said to have been brought to Nantucket from China in 1830. Diameter: $16^{3}/_{8}$ in. (41.6 cm.), height 5 in. (12.7 cm.). (*The Coffin School, Nantucket, on loan to the NHA*).

Plate XLVII. Tiffany Studios stained glass windows in the sanctuary of St. Paul's Episcopal Church in Nantucket. Left to right: (1) Yellow button and white daisies, "ELIZABETH DAVIS FRENCH / Born Nov 18th—Died Sept 21st 1897." (2) White daisies, blackeyed susans, tiger lilies, and a butterfly, "AARON DAVIS WELD FRENCH / Born Dec 15th 1835—Died Oct 5th 1896." (3) Tiger lilies and cat-o'nine-tails, "HANNAH WELD FRENCH / Born Jan 6th 1801—Died Oct 23rd 1878." (4) Lilies, wild roses, and a bluebird, "JOHN DAVIS WILLIAMS / Born Jan 28th 1770—Died Aug 28th 1848." (5) Wild roses and daffodils, "ANN WELD FRENCH / Born Mar 22nd 1777—Died Aug 30th 1859." Height of each window: 55 in. (140 cm.), width: 34 in. (86.4 cm.).

Plate XLVIII. Whalebone box, mahogany top with turned whale-ivory knob, first half of the nineteenth century. Height over knob: $4^{3}/_{8}$ in. (11.1 cm.), diameter: $8^{1}/_{2}$ in. (21.6 cm.). (*Private collection*).

Plate XLIX. Pair of candlesticks, turned whale-ivory columns made from four separate pieces, whalebone bases, first half of the nineteenth century, height: 9 3/4 in. (24.8 cm.). (*Private collection*).

Plate L. Birdcage, whalebone, whale ivory and mahogany, nineteenth century. Height: 16 1/2 in. (41.9 cm.). (*NHA*).

Plate LI. Free-standing swift or yarn winder, whalebone, whale ivory and baleen, base of ebony and mahogany with whale-ivory parts, nineteenth century. Height: 23 in. (58.4 cm.). (*Private collection*).

nineteenth century. The glass lamps were probably made by either the Boston and Sandwich Glass Company on nearby Cape Cod, or by the New England Glass Company of Boston.

Sandwich glass found a ready market in Nantucket. Many island houses of the 1820–1845 period have clear Sandwich glass doorknobs on interior doors. These knobs are characterized by an X or square-cross design impressed on the backs of the knobs.

Because of the presence of tinsmiths in Nantucket in the nineteenth century (Chapter 8), we assume that the lamps with tinplate (tin-plated sheet iron) parts illustrated were made on the island. According to the Nantucket Historical Association records, the tinplate lantern on the left in Figure 93, with free-blown lantern glass, was the main cabin lantern of the ship *Rebecca Sims,* Captain Barnabas Coffin, on an 1828–1832 voyage. The small tinplate and blown-mold glass lantern on the right in Figure 93 is a portable lamp for trips to the barn or night walks in the unlit parts of town.

The tinplate lantern in Figure 94 was in a "Humane House" on the south shore of the island. These simply furnished huts were for temporary shelter of shipwrecked sailors forced ashore during winter storms. Blankets and a stove kept alive men who made it to shore on days and nights when icy winds howled off the ocean. The first two Humane Houses were built in 1794 by the Massachusetts Humane Society, at Great Point and on the bluff at Coskata.[29] In 1832 Nantucket citizens erected additional shelters:

> Sometime during the winter we completed the building of the Humane Houses—thirteen in number—located around the Island, commencing at Smith's Point in the west, following the south side of the Island to Great Point. We have placed in each house one lantern, with a lamp filled with best quality of sperm oil, ready for lighting, with a sperm candle in the same; fire apparatus; matches, etc.; 1/4 of a cord of dry pine wood; a quantity of chips; a hatchet and some little furniture.[30]

Argand lamps, popular in the 1830s and 1840s, graced the mantels of many of the new

Figure 93. Whale-oil lamps made of tin-plate and blown glass. Left: said to have been the main cabin lantern of the *Rebecca Sims*, captain Barnabas Coffin, circa 1830. Height: 15 1/4 in. (38.7 cm.). Right: small lantern with blown-mold glass, height: 10 3/4 in. (27.3 cm.). (*NHA*).

houses in the town. Plate III, Chapter 2, shows a pair of Argand mantel lamps in the Middle Brick with two burners each. Figure 95 shows a pair of Argand lamps with single burners from the Main Street house of Charles G. Coffin, built in 1834. The lamps in the Middle Brick were made in Boston. Those from the Charles Coffin house may have been made in Boston also, although they are unmarked.

The first patent on these lamps was taken out in England in 1784 by Geneva-born Francois-Pierre Ami Argand (1750–1803).[31] The lamp makes use of the fountain-feed principle, whereby the oil reservoir is separated from the burner by a connecting arm, the reservoir being higher than the burner. Argand lamps generated six to eight times more light than a candle. They were the standard high-quality lighting fixture of the island until replaced by gas lighting in the 1850s.

Figure 95. Pair of Argand lamps, brass patinated to look like gilt and bronze, shades frosted and engraved with ferns and tulip shapes, from Main Street house of Charles G. Coffin, built in 1834. Height: 19¼ in. (48.9 cm.). (*NHA*).

Figure 94. Tin-plate lantern used in "Humane House" on the south shore of the island, circa 1830. Height: 16¼ in. (41.3 cm.). (*NHA*).

Although there are many Sandwich-type pressed glass whale-oil lamps on Nantucket today, we have chosen to illustrate the earlier glass lamps with free-blown fonts and pressed-glass bases. Figure 96 illustrates a pair of lamps, with another lamp of similar design. The fonts of these lamps are cut with simple patterns. In Figure 97 are three unusual types of lamps. In the middle is a miniature lamp with a free-blown font and pressed foot. On the right is a blown-glass font set in a tinplate base. Left is a lamp with free-blown font with a broken base which has been repaired. Each step of the base

Figure 96. Whale-oil lamps, fonts free-blown and cut, bases press-molded, 1820–1830. Height (left): 10⁷/₈ in. (276 cm.), height of pair on right: 9³/₄ in. (24.8 cm.). (*NHA*).

Figure 97. Camphene and whale-oil lamps, all circa 1820–1830. Left, with blown font and broken pressed base repaired with bands of wire, height: 10¹/₄ in. (26 cm.). Middle, miniature lamp, free-blown font, pressed base, height: 4³/₄ in. (12.1 cm.). Right, blown-glass font set in tin-plate base, height: 6³/₈ in. (16.2 cm.). (*NHA*).

is neatly wound with iron wire to effect the repair.

Three-piece candleholders, brass lacquered in imitation of gilt, with glass prisms, were popular mantle decorations in Nantucket and the rest of Victorian America. Many have survived. Those in Figure 98 are decorated with a winged cupid holding a dove, surrounded by grapevines laden with clusters of grapes. The grapevine motif was used widely in the decorative arts of the nineteenth century, ornamenting forms in many media, such as silver, furniture, carpets, and architectural details.

We would expect that Nantucketers would have been more conscious than most of lighting devices. Whale oil, particularly sperm whale oil, when burned in lanterns, lamps, and street lights, produced the clearest, the cleanest, and the whitest of light, and spermaceti candles were universally acclaimed to be the best in the world. Furnishing the sources of these lighting materials had been the island's chief business since the end of the seventeenth century.

Figure 98. Three-piece mantle garniture, brass lacquered in imitation of gilt, marble bases, probably Boston, 1840–1860. Height of candelabrum in center: 17¹/₂ in. (44.5 cm.). (*NHA*).

The Tiffany Windows in St. Paul's Church

One of Nantucket's greatest benefactors was Miss Caroline French (1834–1914), whose father, Jonathan French (1803–1901), was a well-known Boston merchant. In 1897, when Nantucket's 1746 Old Mill came up for sale at auction, Miss French bought the mill and presented it to the Nantucket Historical Association. In 1902 she built the stone St. Paul's Episcopal church building on Fair Street, a beautifully detailed structure which contains first-class stained-glass windows from Tiffany Studios, the world-famous shop of Louis Comfort Tiffany.[32] The large, three-section window on the west wall of the church facing Fair Street (not illustrated), is a typical Tiffany window, with a distant landscape enclosed on both sides by trellised flowers. Above, in the center, is a white-winged dove. This window was dedicated to Miss French's father, in honor of whom the church was built. On the east end of the church, in the curving sanctuary wall facing the congregation, are five modestly sized Tiffany windows (Plate XLVII) which are quite different in concept from the large west wall window. Their simplicity and clarity of color represent a side of Tiffany's work not widely known. It is said that these windows, with their representations of Nantucket wildflowers, were based on designs suggested by Caroline French.

It seems fitting to end this chapter with the beautiful Tiffany windows. They reflect the love of Caroline French for both her family and the island which has captured the hearts of generations of "strangers."

7. Silver

Silver, that most beautiful of metals, played a less important role in colonial Nantucket than it did in Boston and Newport, particularly in the seventeenth and early eighteenth centuries, a time when there were no practicing silversmiths on the island. Nevertheless, a study of the silverwares used and made on the island gives us valuable insights into a side of Nantucket that had little to do with whaling and Quakerism. Whaling, of course, provided the basis of wealth for such possessions. The Quakers, although they tended to be plain in their attire and home furnishings, had no compunction about having and using fine silverwares in their homes. The Quaker household of Thomas Carr,[1] a boatwright who later became involved in whaling, and who died in 1757, had in his inventory, for example, twenty-six silver spoons, two tankards, a spout cup, and the only silver teapot and milk pot recorded in the colonial period inventories of the island.[2]

Silver was not considered an unusual item in the home in eighteenth-century Nantucket. An indication of this is the "Decree for widow's allowance," in which the court granted an insolvent widow (when the assets of the husband's estate did not cover the debts) certain necessities, including a bed and bedding, a table and chair or two, cooking and dining equipment. In addition, if the husband had owned silver spoons, *one* silver spoon was always part of the widow's allowance. Judith Gardner, in her 1764 widow's allowance, received both a spoon and a silver porringer:

> By Jeremiah Gardner Esqr. Judge of Probate for the County of Nantucket in the Province aforesaid—Whereas Ebenezer Gardner late of Sherborn in the County of Nantucket lately died Intestate and his Personal Estate proving Insufficient to pay and Discharge his Just Debts I do by these Present pursuant to the Law of this Province in that Case made and Provided set up and allow the Widow Judith Gardner, widow of the said Deceased the following Necessaries for her necessary support and Susistence apprised as follows in old Tenor viz—[3]

	£ *s d*
a bed Bolster & Pillows	26– 0–0
a Bedsted	5– 0–0
a pair of Blankets	6– 0–0
a Quilt	9– 0–0
a pair of Sheets	8– 0–0
a Trammel	2– 0–0
a Small Iron pot	1–13–6
a Small round Table	3– 0–0
Two Black Chairs	1–10–0
a Candlestick	0– 2–0
Shovel & Tongs	3– 0–0
	65– 5–6

a pair Andirons	4– 0–0
a Spit	2– 0–0
a frying pan	1– 0–0
Two plates	1– 2–0
a Silver porringer	25– 0–9
a Silver Spoon	5– 1–6
a pair Bellows	1–10–0
a platter	0–15–0
a young Cow	40– 0–0
	80– 9–3
	65– 5–6
Total old Tenor	145–14–9
Lawful Money	19– 8–7½

This was, of course, long before the days of welfare and pensions. Destitute widows, often with children, were all too common on the island, particularly in times of great difficulty, as during the Revolutionary War and the War of 1812. The court's gesture was to see that the widow was not deprived of everything, even a piece of silver or two.

The table on the next page summarizes the silverwares in Nantucket inventories of the colonial period. There was no silver listed in the inventories before 1706. (It should be noted that there is an automatic time-lag involved in statistics based on inventories, since they document objects that have been in use for some time.) A few of the inventories listed silver without specifying the form, that is, "silver" or "plate." There were 188 ounces of this miscellaneous silver in the 1725–1750 period and fifty-two ounces in the 1751–1776 period. The table shows the increase in silverwares up to the time of the Revolution. This was due both to the increase in population and the increased wealth of individuals on the island. Sixty percent of the 149 inventories included some silver. The number of inventories in the colonial period *with* silver were:

1706–1725	7
1726–1750	21
1751–1776	60

By far the most common silver form in Nantucket, as in the rest of New England, was a spoon. In the 1706–1725 and 1726–1750 periods there were in the inventories more "large" spoons than "small" or "teaspoons," there being four large spoons for every three teaspoons. Often the early inventories did not differentiate the type of spoon and sometimes large spoons were simply called spoons, while the smaller spoons usually had a teaspoon designation. A large spoon was valued at three or four times a teaspoon and a "new" spoon was valued higher than an "old" spoon. In the third quarter of the eighteenth century, the number of large spoons in the inventories was about equal to the number of teaspoons, but by the end of the eighteenth and the early nineteenth centuries there were more teaspoons.

Cups were listed as such in the inventories until the 1750s, after which time they were given more specific designations, "half pint" or "small" cups and "pint" cups. Today the smaller cups are usually designated as mugs, while pint-sized cups are called cans or canns. A spout cup usually had a thin curved spout at right angles to the handle (or handles). It was used for feeding children or invalids.

A couple of the terms in the table should be defined. A *tag* was a label with chain to identify a wine, gin, or rum bottle. A *girdle buckle* possibly refers to a buckle with strap to hold up a pair of men's pants. In about 1750 men's pants no longer had a laced V in the back. A strap with buckle was put across the V, the forerunner of today's men's belts.[4]

Certain silver forms do not appear at all in the early inventories of Nantucket: candlesticks, coffeepots, salvers, plates, sugar dishes, cake plates, or knives and forks. Although there were no silver forks or silver-handled knives in colonial Nantucket inventories, there *were* knives and forks listed from the second decade of the eighteenth century onward. The inventory of Nathaniel Gardner, taken March

Silver & Gold in Nantucket Inventories of the Colonial Period

Form	*1706–1725*	*1726–1750*	*1751–1776*
Broach			1
Buckle (shoe, knee, girdle)		5	19
Buttons			
gold		5	10
silver		9	59
Chatelaine			1
Cup	4	9	13
Cup (two-handled)			2
Milk pot			1
Necklace (gold)			1
Peg			1
Pepper box		3	9
Porringer	2	10	11
Snuff box		1	
Spoon	36	141	476
Spout cup		3	4
Studs			1
Sugar tongs		1	
Tag			1
Tankard	1	7	13
Teapot			1
Watch	1	1	4

12, 1713, included "case knives 11s," "case of knives—0–10–0," "knife and fork 1/6 ditto 9s," and "a parcel of knives from London—18–12–11." The estate of Nathaniel Coffin, 1723, had "knives & forks 3s"; Nathan Skiff, 1724, had "new knife & fork 3s"; George Coffin, whose inventory is dated December 27, 1728, included "2 Doz knives and forks 10s"; and Nathaniel Gardner, 1729, "knives and forks 20s."

Based on the probate records, there was little jewelry in colonial Nantucket. Hannah Wyer's 1762 will states: "I give unto Edward Wyers Son Timothy my Bible also I Give him my Gold Ring," and "I give unto my Sister Ann Cartwright my new Damask Russel Gown I give her also my Gold Necklace (or Beads)." In George Macy's 1776 inventory there was "a Broach—0–16–0," and Seth Hussey's 1776 inventory listed a "Gold Necklace £10-10."

Jeremiah Dummer and Nantucket

The earliest mention we have found of silverwares or silversmiths (silversmiths were usually called goldsmiths in the seventeenth and eighteenth centuries) in Nantucket court records was in 1697, when the *Book of Records* recorded a sale of land to Stephen Hussey which involved payment of eighty pounds to "Jeremia Dummer of Boston Goldsmith."[5] Dummer received payment in two installments in 1697 and 1698:

Boston July 1st 1697 Then Received from William Bunker by the hand Capt Andrew Belcher forty Pounds money being the first payment, according to the aformentioned Instrument, upon acct. of Stephen Hussey

Jer: Dumer

Boston July 1st 1698. Then Received from Mr. William Bunker by the hands of Captn Andrew Belcher forty Pounds, being the full of the within bond, upon acct of Mr. Stephen Hussey.[6]

Jer: Dumer

Recorded the above Recep
March 7th 1701/2.

Thus, Jeremiah Dummer (1664–1718) of Boston, who was America's first native-born goldsmith whose work has been identified, had active business relationships with Nantucket in the last decade of the seventeenth century. There is one documented piece of Dummer silver that we know of which was made for a Nantucketer, probably during the 1690–1700 period.[7] The tankard in Figure 99, made for John (Jr.) and Experience (Folger) Swain, was reputedly commissioned for their wedding, which took place around 1690. John Swain, Jr. was born September 1, 1664, the first male white child born on the island, the son of the proprietor John Swain discussed in Chapter 2.[8] John Jr. died in 1738 and the inventory of his estate was recorded August 17, 1739. The third line from the bottom of the list of his belongings in that inventory reads (all in one line):

To one Silver Tankard I^{S}E 30£ / do I^{S}M 21£
Silver Spoons 3 at 90s / Silver Cup 8£

The tankard engraved I^{S}E (for John, Jr. and Experience Swain) in Figure 99 was left to their daughter Hannah, wife of Thomas Gardner. The initials on the bottom of the tankard chronicle the owners in the Gardner family until the piece was acquired by Miss Ima Hogg of Houston, Texas in 1954:

THG	1740	Thomas and Hannah (Swain) Gardner
TAG	1784	Thomas and Anna (Worth) Gardner
CAG	1817	Charles and Abigail (Russell) Gardner
ESG	1847	Edmund and Susannah (Hussey) Gardner
EB & MG	1875	Edmund Barnard and Martha (Thompson) Gardner
ECSG	1905	Edmund and Cornelia (Hotchkiss) Sherman Gardner

The tankard itself has tapered, almost vertical sides, a molded base band, and a flat hinged cover with spiral gadrooning on the step and a serrated lip. The ribbed handle curves away from the base to the shield-shaped terminal.

Figure 99. Silver tankard made by Jeremiah Dummer, Boston, circa 1690. Engraved on the bottom: "I^{S}E" for John Swain, Jr. and Experience Swain, plus the initials and dates of subsequent owners. Height: 6½ in. (16.5 cm.), diameter at base: 5 in. (12.7 cm.). (*Bayou Bend Collection, The Museum of Fine Arts, Houston*).

On the lid is a cleft spiral thumbpiece. Dummer stamped his heart-shaped mark, I·D above a fleur de lis, on both the body of the tankard to the left of the handle and on the lid.[9]

At this writing there are eighteen known tankards with Jeremiah Dummer's mark. We suspect the other tankard in John, Jr.'s 1739 inventory, engraved "I^{S}M" for John and Mary Swain, John's father and mother, might also have been made by Dummer. (Its present whereabouts is unknown.) It was listed in his father's 1718 inventory: "A silver Tankard—£12–10–00." The same tankard was also listed in the inventory of the third John Swain, who died in 1744: "1 large Tankard—£61–0–0." The increased value of the tankard gives us a measure of the inflation in the middle of the eighteenth century. Listing the values of the Swain I^{S}M tankard in the inventories of the three John Swains and adding the values of tankards in Daniel Bunker's 1747 inventory and the tankard in John Bunker's 1761 inventory, we can get some idea of the inflation of the time:

1718	£12–10–0
1737	21– 0–0
1744	61– 0–0
1747	72– 0–0
1761	82–10–0

The three trifid spoons in Figure 100 are the earliest pieces of silver flatware we know of with Nantucket associations. The wavy-handled spoon on the left in the illustration, marked "GH" for George Hanners of Boston (1696?–1740?),[10] is engraved "PRISSILLAH SWAIN / BORN 27 7MO 1722." There are four eighteenth-century Priscilla Swains listed in the *Vital Records of Nantucket,* but none of their birth dates fit that on the spoon. However, there was a Priscilla Swain, whose birth date is not known, who married Hezekiah Gardner November 12, 1743, that may be the person whose name is on the spoon.[11] The records of the Nantucket Historical Association indicate that the spoon was purchased in Nantucket at public auction in 1813 by Richard Hosier (1785–1818) and was in his family until given to the Association early in the twentieth century. It was said at the time it was thought to have belonged to Phebe Gardner. The trifid spoon in the middle of Figure 100, made by Samuel Vernon of Newport (1683–1737), is engraved "T^{S}D." The only names in the *Vital Records of Nantucket* of the time that seem to fit the initials are Tristram and Deborah (Coffin) Starbuck, who were married February 10, 1729. The wavy-handled spoon at the right in Figure 100 is engraved on the back "B^{H}A," for Bachalor and Abigail Hussey, and on the front of the handle, "Eunice Coleman 1849." Bachalor Hussey married Abigail Hall in Nantucket October 11, 1704. He "moved with a part of his family of sons to Winter Harbor of Biddeford in the district of Maine and settled at Fletcher's Neck in 1737."[12] The spoon is stamped with the mark "GH" for George Hanners of Boston. The "1704" date was almost certainly engraved on the spoon at a later date, since the maker, George Hanners, was born circa 1696. Post dating was not an uncommon occurrence. The Eunice Coleman whose name is engraved on the front of the spoon could have been a descendant of Bachalor and Abigail Hussey. There were several Eunice Colemans in Nantucket in the nineteenth century, but none seem to have had birth, marriage, or death dates of 1849.

The porringer and cup, or cann, in Figure 101, now in the Whaling Museum of the Old Dartmouth Historical Association in New Bedford, originally belonged to members of the Rotch family, a family who was to dominate the whaling industry in the last half of the eighteenth and the first part of the nineteenth centuries, first from Nantucket and later from New Bedford. Joseph Rotch (pronounced roach), the first of the family, came to Nantucket about

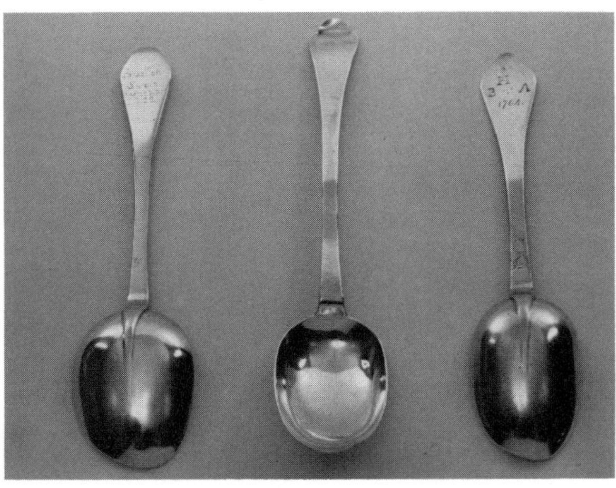

Figure 100. Silver trifid spoons with Nantucket provenances. Left, mark "GH" for George Hanners, Boston, engraved "PRISSILLAH SWAIN / Born 27 7m 1722," length: 7$\frac{1}{4}$ in. (18.4 cm.). Center, mark "SV" for Samuel Vernon, Newport, engraved "F^{S}D," length: 8 in. (20.3 cm.). Right, mark "GH" for George Hanners, engraved on back "B^{H}A" / 1704," on front "Eunice Coleman, 1849," length: 7 in. (17.8 cm.). (*NHA*).

1725 from Salem via Boston and Cape Cod.[13] He was a cordwainer (shoemaker), although there is no record of his practicing that trade in Nantucket. Joseph Rotch married Love Macy, daughter of Thomas and Deborah (Coffin) Macy of Sherborn on February 21, 1773. Joseph Rotch and his wife were Quakers. He was called a mariner in the Nantucket land records from 1735 to 1750, after which time he was listed as a merchant. Between 1735 and 1774, he was involved in thirty-seven land transactions on the island. His son, William, who became the leading whaling merchant of his time, was always listed as a merchant in the land records. From 1757 to 1774, William was involved in sixteen land transactions. Their place of business was the Rotch market, now the Pacific Club, at the foot of Main Street.

The cup in Figure 101, with the initials "I^{R}L" for Joseph and Love Rotch, engraved on the handle and the bottom of the cup, was made by Jacob Hurd, the well-known Boston silversmith, possibly for their wedding in 1733. This beautifully crafted pear-shaped cup with molded foot rim has a simple S-shaped cast handle with only the most reticent of rococo swirls at the top. This cup seems to reflect accurately the Quaker taste of its owners, a taste which admired fine things that were simple and relatively unadorned. The porringer in Figure 101, also made by Jacob Hurd, is engraved "WR" for William, the first child of Joseph and Mary Rotch, who was born October 4, 1734.

Figure 101. Silver made for members of the Rotch family. Left: porringer marked "Hurd" for Jacob Hurd, Boston (1703–58), engraved on the handle "W.R." for William Rotch, born October 4, 1734. Diameter: 5$\frac{1}{2}$ in. (14 cm.). Right: cann marked "Hurd," engraved on handle "I^{R}L" for Joseph and Love (Macy) Rotch, married February 21, 1733. Height: 5$\frac{1}{2}$ in. (14 cm.). (*Whaling Museum of Old Dartmouth Historical Association*).

The First Goldsmith: John Jackson (?–1772)

John Jackson came to Nantucket from Boston in about 1753 to become the island's first practicing goldsmith. Jean Merriman, in her monograph on Jackson, has suggested, in what she calls her "most reasonable case," that Jackson was a New York-trained goldsmith who left New York for Boston in 1731.[14] On August 21, 1753, Jackson married Abigail Fitch in Nantucket. Abigail's mother, Jerusha Matthews, in a deed dated August 2, 1753, gave to "my well respected Friend John Jackson of Boston in the county of Suffolk in the Province aforsaid Goldsmith" eight rods of land in the second Fish Lot between the dwelling house of Seth Hussey and Abishai Folger's barn. The property, which in today's terms is on Orange Street between the Unitarian Church and Main Street, was clearly a dower or wedding present.[15] Jackson's shop was on Straight Wharf near what is now the Pacific Club. In 1766 Jackson built a house further up Orange Street, at the corner of Plumb Lane, where he lived until his death in 1772.

There are today twenty known pieces of Jackson silver: seventeen large spoons, one of which is a marrow spoon, two pepper boxes, and a porringer. Seven of the spoons have rattails, six have double drops, and four have single drops.[16] One spoon also has a foliate scroll on the back of the bowl. A twenty-first possibility is a teapot illustrated in Seymour Wyler's *The Book of Old Silver* said to have been made by "John Jackson, New York, 1736."[17] Its present whereabouts are unknown.

The most unusual of the surviving Jackson spoons is the large spoon in Figure 102 with a single drop and an elaborate foliate scroll on the back of the oval bowl. That Jackson would have had a swage to make such a foliate decoration is somehow unexpected. It would seem to have been a bit fancy for the island Quaker taste.

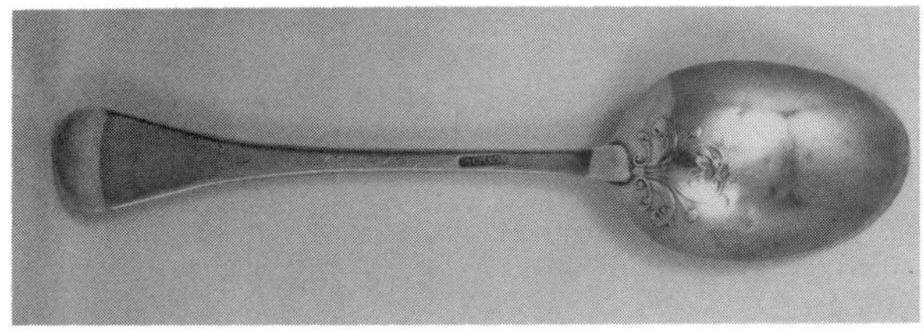

Figure 102. Silver tablespoon with broad drop and foliate scroll, marked "JACKSON," made by John Jackson, 1765–1775. (*The Henry Francis duPont Winterthur Museum*).

The porringer in Figure 103 is engraved "R^C^R" for Richard and Ruth (Bunker) Coffin, who were married November 20, 1718. Richard Coffin was a second cousin of Jerusha Matthews, Abigail Jackson's mother. Richard died in 1768, Ruth in 1779, which suggests that the porringer was made in the fifteen-year period, 1753–1768. The porringer is similar to Boston porringers of the third quarter of the eighteenth century.

Figure 103. Silver porringer, marked "JACKSON," made by John Jackson circa 1765. Engraved "R^C^R" for Richard and Ruth (Bunker) Coffin. Diameter: 5½ in. (14 cm.). (*NHA*).

Figure 104. Silver pepper box, marked "JACKSON," made by John Jackson circa 1761. Engraved "John Way to Anna Joy / 1761." Height: 3⁷/₈ in. (9.8 cm.). (*Museum of Fine Arts, Boston*).

The pepper box in Figure 104 is engraved "John Way to Anna Joy / 1761." Anna Way, who was born in 1737, married Reuben Joy February 10th, 1757. Her father, John Way, gave her the pepper pot in 1761. John Way, a mariner who died in 1772, also owned a pepper pot. His inventory, recorded July 31, 1776, included the following silver:

3 large Silver Spoons	£12– 0–0
6 small tea Spoons	6–10–0
Silver Pepper Box	9– 0–0

John Jackson died February 26, 1772. His will, made in 1766, left everything in his estate to his wife, Abigail.[18] There is no inventory in the probate court records. Abigail was remarried in 1775 to John Woodbury, a widower. Mrs. Merriman suggests she died between 1789 and 1793.[19]

The Joseph Barrett Hoax

The books of Everett U. Crosby (1871–1960) were important contributions to Nantucket history.[20] His *Ninety Five Per Cent Perfect* (1937, 1944, 1953) was the catalyst for the formation of Nantucket's Historic District designation in the 1950s. However, in his *Books and Baskets and Silver of Old-Time Nantucket,* which was published privately in 1940 in an edition of 125, Crosby was the unwitting victim of a hoax. The silver section of this small (nine-by-six-inch), seventy-two page book included a three-page photographic reproduction of a document purporting to be an eighteenth-century account titled "Joseph Barrett Silver Smith / of Nanntockit / here inscribed, yr of Our Lord 1753 / ye Secretes of ye Craft of / Spoon-/ MAKING."[21] The document was a fake. There was no silversmith by the name of Joseph Barrett in eighteenth-century Nantucket.

The three-page document was immediately suspect since it showed spoon-handle forms which did not appear until the middle of the nineteenth century. It included fanciful, made-up names for spoon handles such as "Oar and Locke," "Mous's Tayl," "Hoe," "Spatula," and "Lance." The spelling "Nanntockit" was not used in the eighteenth century. The name for the island and the county has been spelled "Nantucket" in the town records since the latter part of the seventeenth century. Private correspondence occasionally displayed a double *t:* "Nantuckett." There is no Joseph Barrett listed in any of the genealogical records of Nantucket of the eighteenth century. Finally, a mid-eighteenth-century silvermaker usually would have called himself a *goldsmith.* The general opinion is that the Joseph Barrett document was made up out of whole cloth, sometime in the 1930s.

Mr. Crosby obviously recognized the problem with the Joseph Barrett chronicle. When he published an updated version of "Silversmiths of Old-Time Nantucket" in his 1953 edition of *Ninety-Five Per Cent Perfect* he made no mention of Joseph Barrett, even though he retained a section on the Barretts in which he noted the presence of several "S. BARRETT" spoons on the island. He summarized his findings by saying "As stated, we have found at Nantucket no record of any Barretts working there as silversmiths."

The Joseph Barrett material relating to Nantucket was only a small part of a rather widespread fraud that went on for a decade or so. Mr. A. Lenssen, a silver collector who died in the 1940s, was the victim of a small group of swindlers who made and sold to him several hundred pieces of spurious silver supposedly made by famous early American silversmiths. In the case of Joseph Barrett, they invented an eighteenth-century silversmith and fabricated a couple of pieces of silver with his "mark." Donald L. Fennimore, associate curator of metals at the Winterthur Museum, in a personal letter to the authors dated May 4, 1984, summarized the situation:

> I was most interested to learn of Mr. Crosby's inclusion of the J. Barrett document in his book on Nantucket silver, since, as you know, the Lenssen silver collection is presently at Winterthur. That collection has proven to be incredibly interesting for study because it is so well documented. Even though quite large, consisting of almost 1,000 pieces, practically all of it has proven to be spurious. Furthermore, the man who assembled this collection was a meticulous recordkeeper. As a result, we know from whom he bought it, under what conditions the purchases were made, and how much he paid. Visual, tactile, and compositional analyses of the collection have provided an extraordinary insight into duplicity on the part of the perpetrators.
>
> The silver in this collection represents the full spectrum of options available to the fakers in providing spurious objects. There are newly made objects which are literal copies of genuine antiques, newly made adaptations, old objects which have been altered to make them more desirable, objects assembled from bits and pieces of old unmarked objects which have been impressed with the spurious mark of either a real or imaginary silversmith.
>
> J. Barrett is an excellent example of the last of these, since as we know, no such man existed in eighteenth-century Nantucket. The collection includes two objects bearing that mark: a spoon, the style of which would indicate it was made during the first half of the eighteenth century and a chalice which dates to the late nineteenth century. These alone would raise questions, since their existence mandates the maker had been working for between one and two hundred years. When coupled with the admittedly imaginative but simplistic and naive instructions for making spoons, which is dated 1753, but pictures a spoon type that did not come into existence until the 1840s, plus the names of the individuals who were making and supplying these things for Mr. Lenssen, the conclusion is inescapable. The entire collection is the most extensive and best preserved example of duplicity in supplying "antique" American silver in existence.

Samuel Barrett, 1740–1815

Samuel Barrett, a Boston-trained goldsmith, came to Nantucket about 1763.[22] He was born in Boston August 11, 1740. His wife was Sally Manning, born in Boston March 16, 1740. We do not know the date of their wedding but assume it was no later than 1763. The only examples of Barrett's work which have been identified to date are spoons, examples of which are in the Nantucket Historical Association, Winterthur Museum, and, as noted by Crosby, "in the hands of old Nantucket families."[23] That his production was not limited to spoons is suggested by the fact that when his wife, Sally Barrett, died in 1821, her inventory included, in addition to spoons, a silver porringer, a pepper castor, and a pair of sugar tongs. It would seem likely that these pieces were made by her husband, Samuel Barrett.

When Barrett first arrived on the island in May 1763, he was not exactly greeted with open arms. In fact, the selectmen of Nantucket made it clear he was not wanted and ordered him off the island. The notice recorded in the Nantucket court records, signed by the selectmen, is quite explicit:

> Sherborn Is To the Constables of the Town of Sherborn or either of them—Greeting—Information being made to us the Subscribers that one Samuel Barrot [sic] of Boston in the County of Suffolk Goldsmith came from Boston about one week past with a Design to settle and live in this town and as we are not in want of any such tradesman in this town it may be a bad consequence to this town you are therefore required to warn the sd Samuel Barrot that he depart from this town as soon as may be or he will be proceeded against as the law directs in such cases and make return of this and your doings therein unto us or either of us as soon as may be given under our hands & seals at sd Sherborn May ye 19, 1763.[24]

We have found no record as to when Samuel Barrett and his wife actually came to Nantucket to live other than a genealogical record which states he came in 1763.[25] We wonder whether John Jackson, the only goldsmith then on the island, had prodded the selectmen into making their statement quoted above that "we are not in want of any such tradesman in this town." Whatever the case, by 1768 Barrett and Jackson were apparently working in peace in Nantucket. They wrote a joint letter, each in his own handwriting, on the same piece of paper, to John Touzel (1727–1785), a Salem, Massachusetts, silversmith, about a certain troublesome character, John Jones:

> *Nantuckett June 8 1768*
>
> Mr Touzel
>
> Sir In ansur to your leter Respecting the Carecture of John Jones we Cannot say that he was convicted of theft hear but Strongly Suspected of being a Low blackgard man and very burthensum to the Inhabitance of the Island and was ordered of[f] by the authority and when they had got him off would Not bring him again which is all we Say at prasent
>
> Yours to Sarve
> John Jackson
>
> Mr Touzel
>
> Sir I wold farther informe you of Said Jones that he Came to Nantuckett about the first of December 1766 and wose in my Shop Servil times and on the 10 of Said month my Shop wose Broken open and the things which he wonted of me Befor were taken away wich wose Boxes files &c for he Pretended to be a tinker hear and told me that he Sarved in time with a Copper-Smith and Sir I Should Be wary Glad if you wold lett me hear how you make out with this Bad man[26]
>
> Yours to Sarve
> Sam Barrett

The land records note that on August 3, 1774 Samuel Barrett, goldsmith, bought from Stephen Gardner "a Dwelling house in Sherborn aforesaid which the sd Saml Barrett now liveth in also the Piece of Land . . . being the estate of my Father Stephen Gardner" for 100 pounds.[27] Henry Worth states that the house was on Main Street opposite Trader's Lane.[28] Barrett's shop was next door. In 1797 he sold the land on which his shop stood to his son and son-in-law, "Reserving only for myself the Liberty & priveledge of my Goldsmiths Shop to stand and abide on the Front of said Land, so long as my self shall want sd shop to work in."[29]

The land records, all of which list him as a "goldsmith," document Samuel Barrett's activities in the years 1781, 1790 (two transactions), 1791, 1795, 1803 (two transactions), and 1806. Barrett died October 31, 1815. He was seventy-five. There is a quit-claim deed in the *Nantucket County Book of Records* which gave Sally Barrett, widow of "Samuel Barrett late of Nantucket aforsaid Silver and Gold Smith deceased," life rights to the house and estate of her husband.[30] She died in Nantucket in 1821, sometime between March 7, 1821, when she made her will, and June 7, 1821, when her will and inventory were entered into the court records.[31] Her will, which begins with "Be it remembered thet I Sally Barrett of Nantucket and Commonwealth of Massachusetts Widow of Samuel Barrett of Nantucket Silversmith deceased being weak in Body but of sound mind and memory," listed two items of silver: "I give & bequeath unto my daughter Sally Macy wife of Peleg one Silver Porringer to my grand Daughter Rebecca Gardner widow of Hezakiah B. Gardner, one Silver Spoon marked JW to RW." There were seventeen pieces of silver in Sally Barrett's inventory:

1 silver Porringer 8oz 13dwts	9.50
1 do Spoon	1.50
7 Table & 6 Silver T Spoons	12.50
1 pr Sugar Tongs & 1 pepper Castor silver	3.00

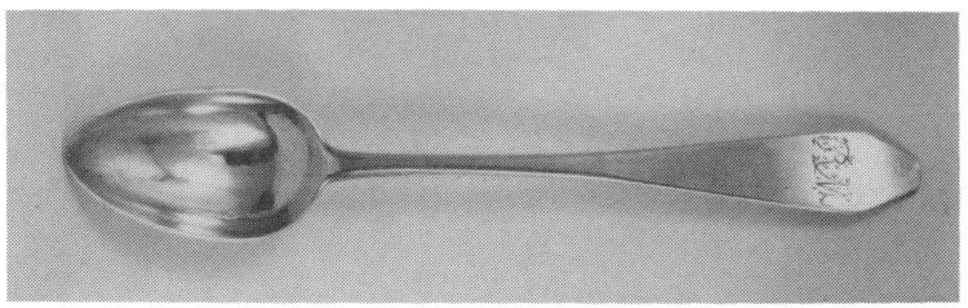

Figure 105. Silver teaspoon with downturned coffin handle, egg-shaped bowl with single drop and shell on back, marked "S. BARRETT" for Samuel Barrett, circa 1800–1810. Engraved "RM." Length: 5½ in. (14 cm.). (*The Henry Francis duPont Winterthur Museum*).

All of this silver could have been made by Samuel Barrett.

The Barrett teaspoon in Figure 105, with a downturned modified coffin handle, has an egg-shaped bowl with shell and single drop. We have not been able to associate the engraved "RM" initials on the handle with a specific name. There were many Macys on the island at the time with such names as Rachel, Rebecca, Reuben, Richard, Ruth. The coffin handle on the spoon suggests an 1800–1810 date.

There seems to have been some confusion in the literature of American silver about Samuel Barrett. For example, Flynt and Fales, in *The Heritage Foundation Collection of Silver,* list Samuel Barrett as working circa 1775–1800 in Providence, Rhode Island and Nantucket, Massachusetts, saying he married 1) Hannah Proctor of Providence January 13, 1791 and 2) Anne Juliet Eddy of Middleboro, Connecticut, December 15, 1829.[32] (Samuel Barrett of Nantucket died in 1815.) We have no knowledge as to whether there was another Samuel Barrett working in Providence (or Hingham or Hull, Massachusetts as suggested) during the time when Samuel Barrett "goldsmith" was working in Nantucket.

Benjamin Bunker, 1751–1842

Benjamin Bunker, Nantucket's first native-born silversmith, was a direct descendant of three of the first white settlers of the island, William Bunker (stepson of Richard Swain), Thomas Macy, and Tristram Coffin. Benjamin was born March 17, 1751, son of William and Mary (Russell) Bunker. He married Rebecca Folger, daughter of George and Sarah (Coleman) Folger, September 2, 1775. William Bunker, Benjamin's father, was a mariner who was lost at sea in May 1768, when Benjamin was seventeen. Jean Merriman, in her monograph on John Jackson, suggests that it is probable that Benjamin was an apprentice of Jackson and as such would have lived in the Jackson house at Orange Street and Plumb Lane during his apprenticeship.[33]

Figure 106. Silver porringer, marked "BB," made by Benjamin Bunker circa 1772–1775. Engraved "E^{C}L" for Edward and Lydia Cary, who were married November 12, 1770. Diameter: 5½ in. (14 cm.). (*Courtesy Robert Cary Caldwell*).

If Benjamin Bunker followed the typical pattern of the time, he would have been apprenticed to Jackson when he was fourteen, in 1765, until he was twenty-one, in 1772. He may have made the porringer in Figure 106 during his first years as an independent silversmith, between 1772 and 1775. Edward and Lydia Cary, whose initials are engraved on the handle of the porringer, were married November 12, 1770. Edward was from Charlestown, Massachusetts, and Lydia, daughter of Christopher and Mary (Coffin) Hussey, was the widow of Hezekiah Barnard, who died in 1768. There are, at this writing, at least four other Bunker porringers known.[34]

Bunker had a lifelong interest in the Masonic Order. Figure 107 shows an ivory mallet and two ivory-tipped rolls, or truncheons, Bunker made for the Nantucket Union Lodge in 1775, and an ivory master's square, made about the same time, attributed to him. The Lodge record book of the period contains the following notation:

> Nantucket Union Lodge No. 5
> Decembr. 15th 5775 1775
> Voted that the Thanks of this Lodge be given to Bro. Benjamin Bunker for the presents Given to the Lodge viz. too Complet Ivory Tipt Rolls and one Ivory mallet.

A year earlier, in 1774, the Lodge records noted:

> March 7, 1774—Voted that the thanks of this Lodge to be given Bros. Jethro Hussey and Benjamin Bunker for their present of a Silver Ladle to the Lodge.

Perhaps Jethro Hussey paid for the silver metal and Bunker made the ladle. Bunker was master of the Lodge in 1805. Thirty years later,

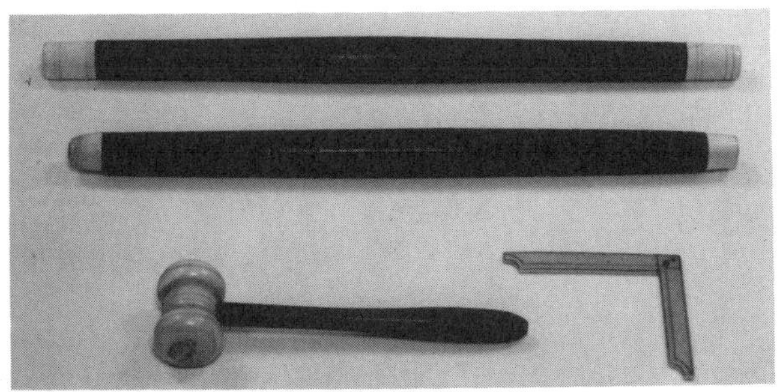

Figure 107. Four whale-ivory and whalebone objects, three of which were made in 1775 by Benjamin Bunker for the Nantucket Union Lodge. Mallet with ivory head and ebony handle, length: 7 in. (17.8 cm.). Two rolls or truncheons, ivory and ebony, lengths: $14\frac{5}{8}$ in. (37.1 cm.) and $13\frac{1}{2}$ in. (34.3 cm.). The Master's whalebone square is attributed to Bunker, $3\frac{1}{2}$ x $3\frac{1}{8}$ in. (8.8 x 7.9 cm.). (*Union Lodge, Nantucket*).

in 1835, he was listed in the Nantucket court records as a trustee of the Lodge.

The first mention we have found in the Nantucket court records of "Benjamin Bunker . . . Goldsmith" was in 1783 when he sold property in the Bocochico section of Wesco (now between Water and Easy Streets) that belonged to his grandfather Caleb Bunker. We believe that Benjamin Bunker's activities as a silversmith were confined to the period 1772 to about 1820. It was not the greatest of times for a silversmith on Nantucket. Although there was great affluence on the island during the years of Bunker's apprenticeship and the first three years or so of his career as an independent craftsman (1765–1775), the Revolutionary War brought the island's prosperity to an abrupt halt. We doubt whether either Benjamin Bunker or Samuel Barrett had much business during the period of the conflict. In fact, the whole forty-year period from 1775 to 1815 was a bad time for the island economically, with only brief times of respite in the 1790s and the first years of the 1800s.

After about 1815 Bunker became primarily a clockmaker. Crosby spoke of a tall clock made in 1809 which was still in the possession of a Bunker family descendant.[35] Bunker's changing career is reflected in the occupations listed with his name in the Nantucket court records. In 1783 he was called a "goldsmith" and in 1809 and 1810 he is named a "silversmith." In 1829 his name is recorded in the court's records without a profession. Two entries in 1835 list him as a "clock and watch maker." In 1839 in two separate entries he is listed first as a "clockmaker," and in the second as "gentleman."

Far more examples of Bunker's silver are known today than that of the other two of Nantucket's early silversmiths. The styles of Bunker's spoons are typical of the time. The six coffin-handle spoons in Figure 108 are charac-

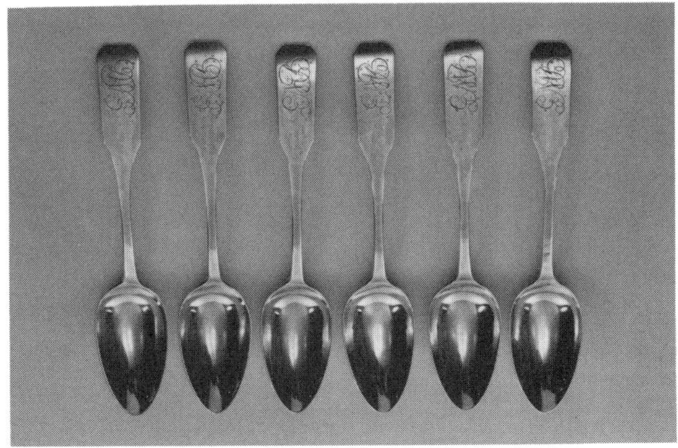

Figure 108. Silver spoons made by Benjamin Bunker, 1800–1810, all with the "BB" mark. Engraved "EMB," length $5\frac{1}{2}$ in. (14 cm.). (*NHA*).

Figure 109. Silver dessert spoon made by Benjamin Bunker circa 1815, stamped "BB" with brackets, engraved "Margaret / Hussey / born 4 mo / 22nd 1815," length: 7⁷/₈ in. (20 cm.). (*Courtesy Robert Cary Caldwell*).

Figure 110. Mark, "BB" with brackets, of Benjamin Bunker, circa 1800–1820. (*Winterthur Library, Decorative Arts Photographic Collection*).

teristic of the 1800–1810 period. The dessert spoon in Figure 109, made for Margaret Hussey, born April 22, 1815, is an example of Bunker's late work. The mark on the spoon, "BB" bracketed by decorative devices (Figure 110), is a mark that appears on a number of Bunker's later pieces. His early spoons are marked with a simple "BB" stamp. There are often two "BB" marks stamped on the same spoon.

The cup or cann in Figure 111, in the collection of Old Deerfield, is the only example of this form made by an eighteenth-century Nantucket silversmith that we have found. The style of the cup would suggest a date of about 1790, although it may have been made a bit earlier.

Figure 111. Silver cann made by Benjamin Bunker, mark "BB," engraved on front in sprigged script "SPE," circa 1790. Height: 5¹/₈ in. (13 cm.). (*Historic Deerfield*).

Figure 112. Masonic silver ceremonial jewels attributed to Paul Revere. Upper left: *Level* for Senior Warden, engraved "Union Lodge N$\frac{m}{5}$ 1773 / 5773," 3 3/8 x 2 5/8 in. (8.6 x 6.7 cm.). Upper right: *Square* for the Master, engraved "Union Lodge N° 5 Nantuckett / 5772" [1772], 3 9/16 x 2 15/16 in. (9.1 x 7.5 cm.). Below: *Plumb* for Junior Warden, engraved "Union Lodge No. 5 Nantucket / 5772" [1772], length 4 1/4 in. (10.8 cm.). (*Courtesy Nantucket Union Lodge*).

Paul Revere and the Union Lodge

The Nantucket Union Lodge Number 5 of Free Masons was founded in 1771, with William Brock, son of Thomas Brock, discussed in Chapter 2, as the first master. One of the first orders of business was to commission a silver seal and silver "jewels" (insignia worn by officers of the Lodge on ceremonial occasions). The seal was made by Paul Revere of Boston. The handwritten receipt reads:

> September 1772
>
> Received of Mr. Joseph Denison one Pound Sixteen shillings and Eight pense in full for Silver Seal & Stock.
>
> Paul Revere[36]

The Revere seal was lost in the fire of 1846. The unmarked silver jewels shown in Figure 112, dated 1772 and 1773, have been attributed to Revere.[37] It was standard practice for Masons to deal in business with fellow Masons and it would have been logical for the Nantucket lodge to order both a silver seal and officer's jewels from Paul Revere, a well-known Mason. However, the jewels, simple pieces of silver cut from a flat sheet, could also have been made in Nantucket. We mentioned earlier Benjamin Bunker's sixty-year relationship with the Nantucket Masons. Samuel Barrett was an early member who, during his lifetime, served more years as master of the Union Lodge than any other, ten years, 1774–1776, 1780–1783 and 1796–1798.

A letter written by Paul Revere in 1797, when he was grand master of Masons in Massachusetts, scolded the Nantucket lodge for their wayward behavior:

> *Boston, August 27, 1797*
>
> Dear Sir
>
> I sent you word some time since by Capt Kelder, our respected Brother, who was a prisoner in Algiers, that except your Lodge sent their Charter, to, And paid their dues to the Massachusetts Grand Lodge, you would not be received by them, or Acknowledged as a regular, constituted, Lodge. He informed me on his return, that you would immediately write the Grand Lodge on the Subject—But nothing having appeared; I have imbraced this opportunity to aquaint you that except you do send your Charter to be indorsed, & that you send a representative too, and pay your dues to the Grand Lodge, you will be represented to every Grand Lodge in the United States as a Lodge, that Acts contrary to the General Regulations.—For they have made it a general Regulation, that any Lodge within the United States, who does not pay their dues to and are Represented in, the Grand Lodge of the State where the lodge is held, shall be viewed as a Clandestin

Lodge & treated as such.—I have thought it my duty to represent you, your Situation, as a Lodge, not doubting you will take such Steps, as true, & Accepted Masons, ought to.

I am Sir with every of affection,
& respect, your Hand Send
Paul Revere[38]

Mr Samuel Barrett

The Union Lodge reacted quickly. The lodge record makes no mention of dues, but it is obvious they wanted to repair their links with the Grand Lodge and Paul Revere:

> September 4, 1797—A letter from Bro. Paul Revere of Boston, dated 27th August, informing us of our situation in the Grand Lodge, as being looked on as a clandestine Lodge by us held, by not acting consistent to the regulations of the Grand Lodge, was read to the Lodge. Voted that the Secretary write Bro. Paul Revere informing him that further order will be taken by the Lodge hereafter. Voted a committee to look into the above letter and to frame an answer for the purpose to be sent forward to the Grand Lodge after the approbation of the Lodge next month. [In October the Lodge approved the letter and voted to inform Paul Revere that it wished to become a part of the Grand Lodge "for a number of reasons."][39]

The master's jewel and the organist's jewel shown in Figure 113 were given to the Nantucket Masons in 1859 by George P. Folger of Boston, where they presumably were made. The jewels, symbols of masons' tools (the plumb, the level, and the square), were worn as chest ornaments hung from a collar. The square is the master's jewel, the level, the senior warden's jewel, and the plumb is worn by the junior warden. Other positions, such as the organist, have their own insignia.

Figure 113. Masonic silver ceremonial jewels presented to the Nantucket Union Lodge in 1859. Left: Master's jewel, unmarked, 4 9/16 x 4 5/8 in. (11.6 x 11.7 cm.). Right: organist's jewel, unmarked, 3 1/4 x 3 1/8 in. (8.9 x 7.9 cm.). (*Courtesy Nantucket Union Lodge*).

The Retailers, 1820 to the 1850s

Everett U. Crosby, in his "Silversmiths of Old-Time Nantucket," a chapter in the 1953 edition of *Ninety Five Per Cent Perfect,* listed seven silversmiths working in Nantucket from 1820 to the 1850s:[40]

William Hadwen
George Cannon
James Easton, 2nd
Frederick C. Sanford
Henry A. Kelley
Edward G. Kelley
James Stanford Kelley

The increase in the number of silversmiths, primarily spoonmakers, working in Nantucket in this period *could* be viewed as a part of the growth in the number of silversmiths all over the eastern part of the United States in the second quarter of the nineteenth century, a growth that was a virtual explosion insofar as the number of makers was concerned. Much of the evidence for this "explosion" has been based on the number of different makers' marks found on coin silver spoons of the time. To the hundreds and hundreds of spoonmakers have been added lists of jewelers and clockmakers, so that there are literally thousands of potential "silversmiths" for the era.

We feel, both for Nantucket, and for the mainland, that this is a false picture, that the great majority of these "makers" were primarily retailers, selling coin-silver spoons and other silver forms, which were *made by a few manufacturers in urban centers and marked only with the names of the local retailers.* We believe that all seven of the Nantucket makers listed above were strictly retailers of silverwares and that none were silversmiths in the accepted sense of the word. None of the seven were listed as silversmiths (or goldsmiths) in any of the town records, none of their advertisements claimed they were silversmiths, none claimed to be spoonmakers, and none of their obituaries characterized any of them as silversmiths. A detailed examination of the seven "silversmiths" in Crosby's list reveals that none of them appears to have made any of the silver spoons, cups, and other simple forms that bear their marks.

James Easton, 2nd, 1807–1903

A key piece of evidence is the account book of James Easton, covering his business activities from 1828 to 1830, and from 1838 to 1855.[41] Easton's account book gives extensive documentation that he was *buying* spoons and other silverwares in Boston and Providence and *selling* them in Nantucket. From 1828 to 1830 he was buying jewelry and other "merchandize" from Jabez Gorham, Providence. There is a seven-year gap in Easton's account book, 1831–1837, during which time he had a partnership with Frederick C. Sanford. From 1838 to 1843 Easton bought most of his silverwares, including many spoons, from Newell Harding, Boston, who was, at the time, the largest spoonmaker in New England. In 1844 he bought silverwares from both Newell Harding and Jabez Gorham & Son, Providence, and from 1845 to 1851 almost all of his purchases were from Gorham. A few silver items were purchased from other suppliers. In 1839 he bought spoons from Boynton & Woodward, Boston, and on February 24, 1845, he bought a "silver cup &c $8.87" from Lows, Ball & Co., Boston. The account for George Starbuck in Easton's records, dated September 27, 1845, notes that he bought a "silver cup wifes 9.50," presumably the same cup Easton had purchased in February from Lows, Ball & Co. The sales of many spoons are listed, and occasionally other silver forms, to customers on the island. Matthew Starbuck bought on May 9, 1846, "1 silver cup 9.00," and on November 18, 1847, "1 doz forks 48.84." Still in the Middle Brick today are fiddle-and-thread-pattern coin-silver forks, a dozen dinner forks and a dozen breakfast forks (Figure 114). The dinner forks are marked "J.GORHAM & SON," and

Figure 114. Silver fiddle-and-thread pattern forks, each one of twelve, purchased by Matthew Starbuck for the Middle Brick circa 1847. Dinner fork (bottom) with mark "J. GORHAM & SON," length 8¼ in. (20.6 cm.). Breakfast fork (top) with marks "J. Easton 2[d]" and "Nantucket," length 7½ in. (19.0 cm.). (*Courtesy Mrs. H. Crowell Freeman*).

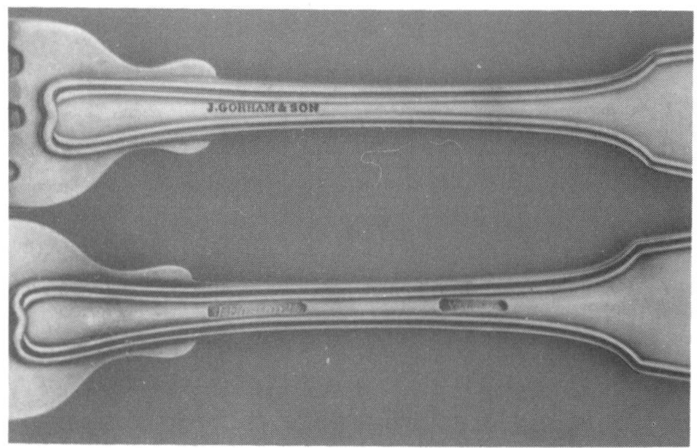

Figure 115. Marks on forks in Figure 114, top: "J. GORHAM & SON," bottom: ".EASTON 2^{d}" and "NANTUCKET."

the breakfast forks are marked "J.Easton 2^{d}" and "Nantucket" (Figure 115). The forks are all similarly engraved with "MCS," for Matthew and Catherine Starbuck. The forks are, except for size, identical in design. They were analyzed at the Winterthur Museum Laboratories and proved to have similar analyses:[42]

	Silver %	Copper %
Fork with Easton mark	86.20	13.34
Fork with Gorham mark	86.26	13.25

The evidence suggests that both sets of forks were made at about the same time, circa 1847, by the same maker, J. Gorham & Son, Providence.

The beautifully crafted spoon in Figure 116 was purchased for a new baby, Lydia Crosby Coffin, daughter of Benjamin F. and Mary (Crosby) Coffin, who was born February 28, 1846. As can be seen from the inscription on the back of the spoon, the child lived only four and a half months. The spoon is documented in the account book of James Easton, 2nd. An undated entry, under the account of Benjamin F. Coffin, notes: "1 dessert spoon 3.25."[43] The high price of the spoon is an indication of its quality at a time when teaspoons were selling at about a dollar. The next entry in the account book "markg spoon .06" was for the engraving on the back of the spoon, "Died July 18, 1846." (The engraving on the front of the spoon would have been done free at the time of purchase.)

James Easton came to Nantucket about 1821 or 1822. To quote his obituary in the *Inquirer and Mirror,* February 21, 1903:

> The honorable James Easton, 2nd, was Nantucket's oldest resident. He was a native of Providence, Rhode Island, and came to Nantucket when a boy as an apprentice to William Hadwen, with whom he learned the trade of watchmaker and jeweler. Soon after he had finished training, he purchased from Mr. Hadwen the entire jewelry business, giving in payment his notes.

An announcement in the *Nantucket Inquirer* March 8, 1828, proclaimed Easton's entry into the jewelry business:

> James Easton, 2nd
> Respectfully informs the publick he has taken the store recently occupied by Mr. William

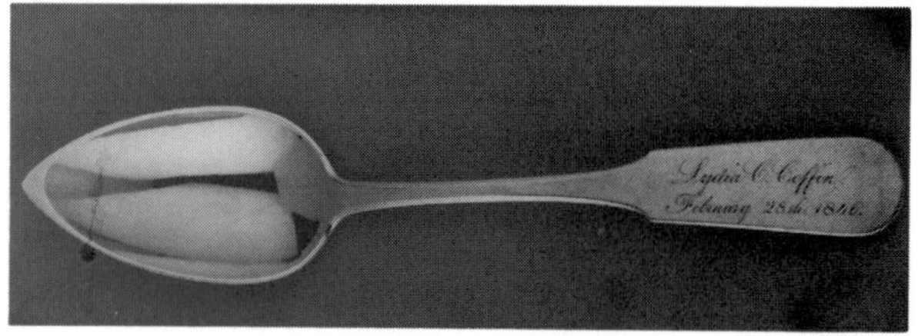

Figure 116. Silver dessert spoon with mark "J. Easton 2d." Engraved on front: "Lydia C. Coffin. / February 28th. 1846." On the back: "Died July 18, 1846." Length: 7 3/4 in. (18.7 cm.). (*Private collection*).

> Hadwen and will keep constantly on hand a complete assortment of Fancy Hardware, Cutlery, Jewelry, etc. Cash paid for Gold and Silver.

Easton's account book gives a detailed record of his sales and services. He sold watches, jewelry, wallets, spectacles, soap, scissors, combs, toothbrushes, looking glasses, curtain rings, accordians, suspenders, and, of course, silverwares, including spoons, forks, silver purse tops, and cups. He also sold in the 1841–1844 period fifty or so miniature frames to Sally Gardner, "Miniature Painter." He repaired watches, clocks, clasps, and other jewelry, locks, spectacles, umbrellas; he riveted a flute for Valentine Hussey for seventeen cents. Easton was an engraver and his accounts list many entries where he "marked" (engraved) spoons, thimbles, napkin rings, and ivory-handled umbrellas with the initials or names of the owners. Easton's account book gives no evidence that he ever made a single silver spoon.

Easton and Sanford

From 1830 to 1837 James Easton and Frederick Sanford operated a jewelry store together. An announcement of the partnership was in the April 10th, 1830, issue of the *Nantucket Inquirer:*

> NOTICE
>
> The undersigned have formed a copartnership in business, under the firm of Easton & Sanford and will occupy the store next east of the Manufacturers and Mechanics Bank, where they will keep constantly for sale a handsome assortment of articles at low prices consisting of Brittania & Japan ware; Fine cutlery; GOLD AND SILVER WATCHES; Gilt and fancy goods; Silver spoons;—Jewelry Watch Trimmings, etc.
>
> They return their thanks for the liberal portion of public patronage heretofore received and solicit continuance of the same. Particular attention will be paid to repairing clocks, watches, and Jewelry.
>
> James Easton 2nd
> Frederick C. Sanford

The ladle in Figure 117, marked "EASTON & SANFORD" on the back of the handle, and, on the front, engraved "Mary Baxter," illustrates the problems of using oral family history to document objects. The ladle had remained in the same family until 1984, when Catherine Defrieze Fitzpatrick, the last family owner, died. In the 1970s Mrs. Fitzpatrick told the authors on two different occasions the history of the ladle, made for Mary Baxter just before her marriage to Francis Colburn, November 4, 1830. She related how Mary's father delivered twenty-five silver dollars to Easton & Sanford on Main Street and that they melted up the coins and made the ladle. There is one major problem with the story. U. S. silver dollars and other silver coins minted from 1792 to January 18, 1837, contained 89.24 percent silver. After 1837, the standard was raised to 90.00 percent. When the ladle was analyzed at the Winterthur Museum laboratory in 1985, it was found to contain 85.99 percent silver in the handle and 80.03 percent in the bowl, both well below the U. S. standard.[44] The ladle could not have been made of only silver dollars. We feel that the Mary Baxter ladle was probably made in Boston, possibly by Newell Harding, and engraved in Nantucket by James Easton.

James Easton and Frederick Sanford dissolved their partnership in 1837. Sanford embarked on a very successful career in the China trade as an agent for the A. A. Low firm of New York. Easton continued in the jewelry business until the 1850s, when he became more involved in whaling, investing in the ships *Gazelle* and *Ocean Rover.*

Figure 117. Silver ladle, down-turned fiddle handle, engraved "Mary Baxter," with mark "Easton & Sanford," circa 1831. Length 13 in. (33 cm.). (*Collection of the authors.*)

William Hadwen, 1791–1862

William Hadwen, born in Newport, Rhode Island, entered into the jewelry business in Providence in 1812 with Jabez Gorham, the founder of the Gorham companies, and three other men. The venture lasted until 1818, when the partnership broke up. Gorham continued the business alone.[45] Hadwen came to Nantucket in 1820 and started a jewelry store. In 1822 he married Eunice, daughter of Joseph Starbuck, and in 1829 entered into the whale-oil and candle manufacturing business with his brother-in-law, Nathaniel Barney, and became a wealthy man. His white-columned Greek Revival mansion on Main Street, opposite the Three Bricks, is now owned by the Nantucket Historical Association and is open to the public. One of his early advertisements in the *Nantucket Inquirer,* January 17, 1822, reads:

> William Hadwen
> Has just received from New York: a handsome assortment of fashionable Ladies' and children's Beaver Bonnets, elegantly trimmed with plumes.

Figure 118. Silver spoons with mark "HADWEN," circa 1820–1825. Tablespoon (bottom) engraved "NC," length 9 in. (22.9 cm.), teaspoon (top) engraved "FSR," length 5⅝ in. (14.3 cm.). (*Courtesy Mr. and Mrs. John A. Lodge*).

In 1823 the following advertisement was repeated many times in the *Nantucket Inquirer:*

WILLIAM HADWEN

> Just received and for sale by subscribers, a very special assortment of gilt and mahogany framed looking glasses.

Hadwen was trained as a jeweler and clock and watch repairer. It should be noted that the five-man firm involving Hadwen and Gorham in Providence dealt only in jewelry, not silver flatware or hollow ware. In fact, when Jabez Gorham himself went into the spoon business in 1831, he went to Boston for his expertise, hiring a well-trained spoonmaker, Henry L. Webster.[46]

Coin-silver spoons with the Hadwen mark (Figure 118) are not seen as often as those of Easton, Easton & Sanford, and the Kelleys. We have found no mention of spoons in his advertisements.

George Cannon, 1767–1835

George Cannon opened a jewelry shop in Nantucket in 1825. An advertisement in the *Nantucket Inquirer,* which appeared, unchanged, regularly from January 1834 to April 1835, spelled out the fact that Cannon was a retail jeweler who imported his goods from the mainland and from England:

WATCHES AND SILVER WARES

> GEORGE CANNON has just received a new assortment of silver ware, consisting of Table and Tea spoons, Sugar Tongs, Salt spoons, Thimbles.
>
> He also offers for sale a great variety of Gold and Silver Watches, viz Plain, Duplex, Lepine, Horizontal and Patent lever—warrented to be good time keepers and well regulated.
>
> He has also a lot of very superior Silver watches, recently imported from England, having been manufactured to order by the most approved workmen; which the public and especially Shipmasters, and persons bound to sea, are invited to call and examine.
>
> The above, together with an extensive stock of jewelry, and other articles in his line, are offered for sale on the most reasonable of terms.

Some of Cannon's engraving was done by James Easton. Easton's account book lists, for example, thirteen entries in 1828 for "marking" spoons and thimbles for George Cannon.

The *Nantucket Inquirer* for May 23, 1835, had the notice of Cannon's death:

DIED

> In this town on Saturday morning last, very suddenly, George Cannon Esq. aged 68—formerly representative from this town in the legislature of Massachusetts.

The Kelleys

Edward G. and Henry A. Kelley, brothers, operated a jewelry store on Main Street from about 1835 to 1842, when the partnership was broken up and replaced by one between

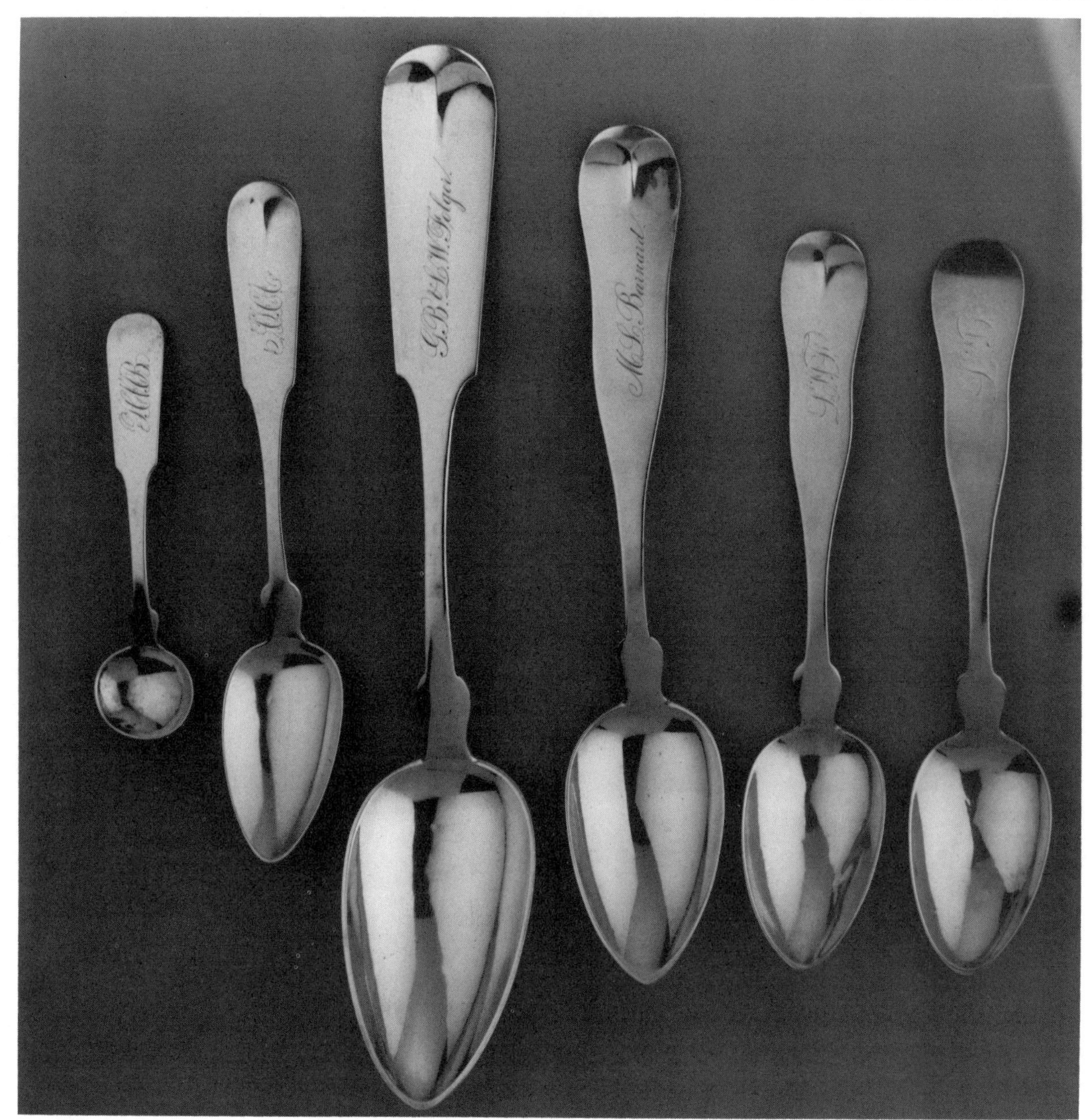

Figure 119. Typical coin-silver spoons sold by James Easton and the Kelleys in the 1840s. Left to right: (1) Salt spoon engraved "HMB" with marks "Pure Coin" and "J. Easton 2d." Length: $3\frac{5}{8}$ in. (9.2 cm.). (2) Teaspoons engraved "AHA" with marks "E & J Kelley" and "Nantucket." Length: $5\frac{3}{4}$ in. (14.6 cm.). (3) Tablespoon engraved "G.B. & L.W. Folger" for George B. and Lydia W. (Swift) Folger, who were married August 8, 1844. Three separate marks: "J. Easton 2d," "Nantucket," and "Pure Coin." Length: $8\frac{7}{8}$ in. (22.6 cm.). (4) Dessert spoon engraved "M. L. Barnard" for Mary Louise Barnard, with marks "J. S. Kelley" and "Nantucket." Length: $7\frac{1}{4}$ in. (18.4 cm.). (5) Teaspoon engraved "LHF," with marks "J. Easton 2d" and "Nantucket." Length: $6\frac{1}{4}$ in. (15.9 cm.). (6) Teaspoon engraved "LTF" (?), with three marks: "J. Easton 2d," "Nantucket," and "Pure Coin." Length: $6\frac{1}{16}$ in. (15.4 cm.). (*Private collection*).

Edward G. and James S. Kelley. James was the half-brother of Edward and Henry. The firm advertised silverwares, watches, clocks, nautical instruments, English and French notepaper, steel pens, and so on. An advertisement in the *Nantucket Inquirer,* August 31, 1846, noted that they had just received a shipment of spoons and cutlery:

> Table cutlery, Spoons &c
> E & J Kelley have just received an assortment of Table Cutlery, Spoons, Brittania Tea & Coffee Pots, Castors, Knives, Scissors &c.

Figure 119 illustrates six spoons, four with the mark "J.Easton 2d," one marked "E&J. Kelley," and one "J.S.Kelley." The three teaspoons, the dessert spoon, and the tablespoon in the illustration have identical "Nantucket" marks, suggesting that the *same* punch was used to make all the impressions. A close examination of the spoons sold by the stores of James Easton and the Kelleys shows great similarities in form. All the spoons closely resemble Gorham spoons of the same period.[47] The marks of the retailer's name and the mark "Nantucket" are placed in the same positions on both the Kelley and the Easton spoons; one on the shoulder, just above the bowl, and the other in the middle of the handle. The stamped marks are about 1¼ inches apart on the teaspoons and 1¾ inches apart on the tablespoons. The marks were placed in exactly the same way on Gorham spoons of the same time. Chemical analyses of the Nantucket spoons are in the same range as those of Gorham.[48] We feel the evidence is conclusive: all the spoons in Figure 119, which are representative of many other spoons retailed by the Kelleys and by James Easton, were made by J. Gorham & Son, Providence, and marked by Gorham with the retailer's name. Only the engraving was done in Nantucket.

The porringer in Figure 120 is stamped with the mark "E & J Kelley" and engraved with the date 1847. A close examination of the porringer bowl reveals telltale spinning marks, indicating that it was shaped on a lathe. In the eighteenth century, porringer bodies were hand raised from flat pieces of silver by means of hammering on stakes and small anvils. Although the use of the spinning lathe was introduced in American silver manufacture in the 1830s, it was not commonly used to make hollow-ware forms until after 1850.[49] It is quite unlikely that the Kelleys would have had such a new and relatively sophisticated piece of machinery as a spinning lathe in Nantucket. The 1847 date on the porringer may have been put on later. The porringer could have been made in Providence by Gorham & Co. in the 1850s.

Figure 120. Coin-silver porringer. Engraved on handle: "I and LBM / 1847;" mark on back of handle: "Pure / Coin / E.&J. Kelley." Diameter: 5⅛ in. (13.0 cm.). (*Courtesy Richard S. Sylvia*).

The practice of retailers buying coin-silver spoons and other simple forms from large makers, with *only* the retailer's mark on the wares, was widespread in the second quarter of the nineteenth century. Newell Harding of Boston and Gorham in Providence, and probably a few other makers, supplied jewelers all over New England with such coin-silver wares. Further study will almost certainly show that New

Figure 121. Six-piece coin-silver tea and coffee service, pieces marked "Jones Ball & Poor / Boston / Pure Coin." Engraved "MCS" for Matthew and Catherine Starbuck, circa 1846. Height of hot-water kettle: 13½ in. (34.3 cm.). (*Private collection*).

York and Philadelphia makers supplied retailers in other areas with retailer-marked wares. The end of the handmade coin-silver spoon era came in the 1850s when the steam-powered drop press revolutionized the silver flatware business. The drop press enabled a few makers to dominate the market and supply attractively designed flatware of a uniform quality at prices often below the old handmade coin-silver products.

A Tea Service and Fireman's Trumpet

Large tea and coffee services became fashionable in the 1840s. Figure 121 shows a six-piece service, made by Jones, Ball & Poor of Boston, that was characteristic of the time, decorated with repoussé chasing. Two of the pieces, the coffeepot and the slop bowl, are slightly different in design. These pieces have no beading around the top and base as do the other four pieces, suggesting they were purchased separately. Probably Matthew Starbuck bought a four-piece tea service, consisting of a hot-water kettle with lamp, teapot, creamer and sugar, and later added the coffeepot and slop bowl. (Today these bowls are usually called waste bowls, but in the nineteenth century they were always called by that inelegant term, slop bowl.) An English tray (not illustrated) accompanies the service.

The silverplated fireman's speaking trumpet in Figure 122 was presented to one of the Nan-

Figure 122. Silver-plated fireman's speaking trumpet, with no maker's mark, circa 1840. Height: 17⁷/₈ in. (45.4 cm.). (*NHA*).

tucket volunteer fire companies circa 1840. There were a dozen such companies on the island at the time.

Souvenir Spoons

The phenomenon of souvenir spoons started in the 1880s. One spoon, the Salem Witch spoon, made in 1890 by the Gorham Manufacturing Company of Providence, Rhode Island, started a collecting fad that became a true craze.[50] Perhaps ten to fifteen thousand different souvenir spoons were made in the United States in the 1890–1905 era, the heyday of their popularity. They celebrated, among other things, towns, cities, locales such as Cape Cod, states, people, expositions, anniversaries of famous events, hotels, railroads and businesses of various kinds, the Statue of Liberty, and Plymouth Rock. The 1893 Chicago Columbian Exposition represented the crest of the souvenir spoon collecting wave. There were several dozen spoons made specifically for that fair.

Souvenir spoons were a natural for Nantucket. The island was well launched into the tourist business by the 1890s, at the very time the fad was at its height. The five spoons in Figure 123, featuring the Old Mill, are the earliest of the Nantucket souvenir spoons. The two on the left, made by N. G. Woods & Sons, Boston, and the two on the right, made by the Durgin Co., Concord, New Hampshire, were both protected by 1891 design patents. The middle spoon, made by the Alvin Company of New York circa 1892, is the most elaborate, picturing the Old Mill, the Unitarian Church, Sankaty Light, and, in the bowl, an embossed picture of the Oldest House. All five of these spoons are conventional in form, while the three spoons in Figure 124 are less so, being really small pieces of sculpture. Their handles depict, respectively, a lobster and starfish, an oar with a fish hanging from it, and a fishing pole with the day's catch. Figure 125 shows a different kind of souvenir spoon, made by engraving or embossing regular flatware patterns. The two spoons on the left, with engraved bowls, could have been engraved in Nantucket. Figure 126 shows three twentieth-century Nantucket souvenir spoons with pierced handles. Like many twentieth-century souvenir spoons, they are light in weight and are thinner in gauge than those made in the nineteenth century.

Nantucket souvenir spoons of the post-1890 era, like the silverwares retailed on the island

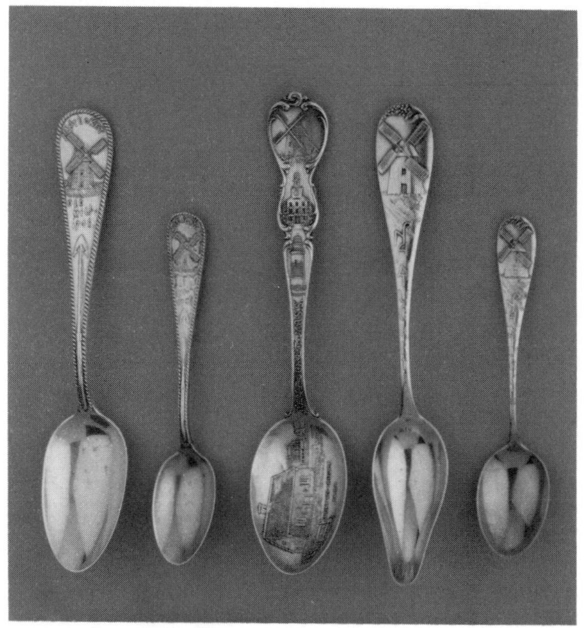

Figure 123. Sterling Nantucket souvenir spoons with the Old Mill depicted on heads of handles. Left to right: (1) teaspoon with beaded border on handle with harpoons, inscription "NANTUCKET / OLD / MILL / 1746." On back: "STERLING PATENTED. N. G. WOOD & SONS" (Boston). The spoon received a design patent at the U.S. Patent Office No. 20,515, December 29, 1891. Length: 5 13/16 in. (14.8 cm.). (2) Coffee spoon with similar motif, marked "N. G. WOOD & SONS" with same inscription on back. Length: 4 3/8 in. (11.1 cm.). (3) Large teaspoon with windmill, Unitarian Church, and lighthouse plus "NANTUCKET, MASS." embossed on handle, bowl embossed with oldest house and "COFFYN-HOUSE / 1686." Made by the Alvin Company of New York, N.Y., with their trademark and "STERLING" on back. Length: 5 15/16 in. (15.1 cm.). (4) Grapefruit spoon, "NANTUCKET" on handle, made by Durgin, Concord, N. H. On back: Durgin trademark plus "STERLING PAT.D APR 21 91, E.V. HALLETT." Hallett was the retailer. Length: 5 7/8 in. (14.9 cm.). (5) Coffee spoon with similar design and same marks on back, gilt bowl. Length: 4 3/16 in. (10.6 cm.). (*Private collection*).

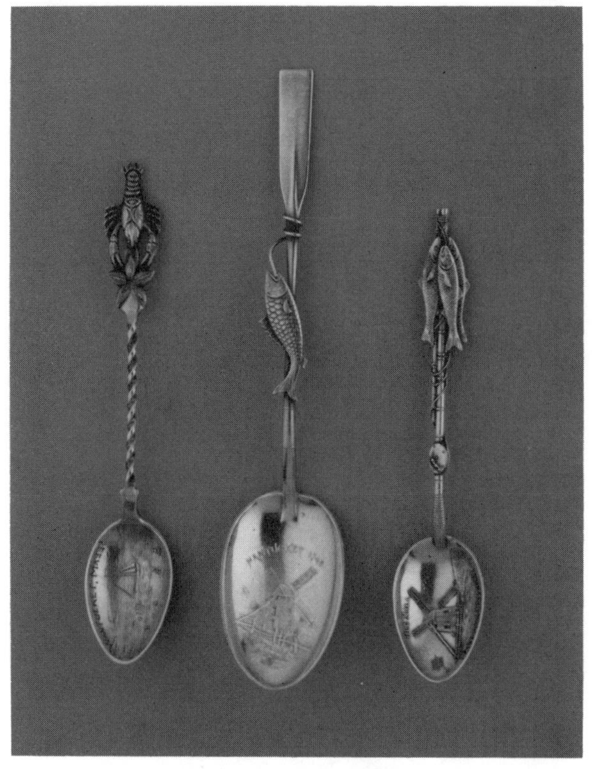

Figure 124. Sterling Nantucket souvenir spoons. Left to right: (1) Lobster above starfish on twisted handle. Bowl embossed with beach scene in foreground, lighthouse on right, steamboat on left, engraved "Nantucket, Mass." marked on back "STERLING," no maker's mark. Length: 4 3/8 in. (11.1 cm.). (2) Handle in form of an oar with cast codfish applied on silver line. Bowl embossed with windmill, "NANTUCKET 1746." Mark on back "CB&H STERLING." Made by Codding Bros. & Heilborn, North Attleboro, Massachusetts. Length: 5 3/8 in. (13.7 cm.). (3) Cast handle in form of fishing pole with reel and three fish. Bowl embossed with windmill and "OLD MILL / NANTUCKET, MASS. 1746." On back, trademark of pennant with "W" and "STERLING," made by Watson Company, Attleboro, Massachusetts. Length: 4 1/8 in. (10.5 cm.). (*Private collection*).

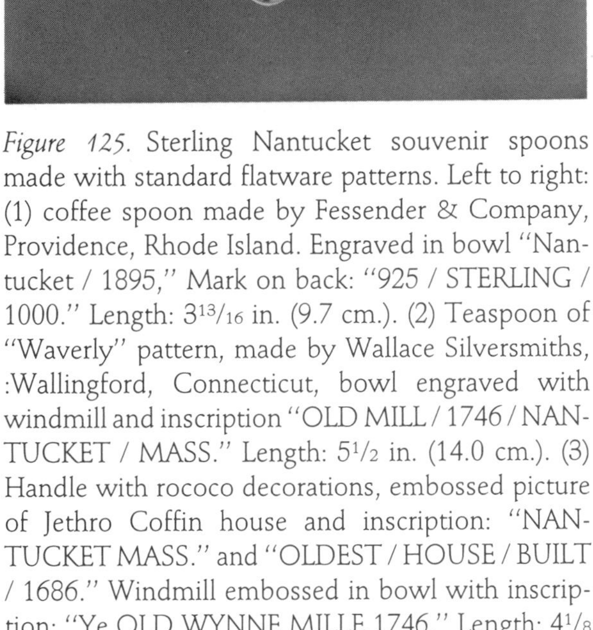

Figure 125. Sterling Nantucket souvenir spoons made with standard flatware patterns. Left to right: (1) coffee spoon made by Fessender & Company, Providence, Rhode Island. Engraved in bowl "Nantucket / 1895," Mark on back: "925 / STERLING / 1000." Length: $3\frac{13}{16}$ in. (9.7 cm.). (2) Teaspoon of "Waverly" pattern, made by Wallace Silversmiths, :Wallingford, Connecticut, bowl engraved with windmill and inscription "OLD MILL / 1746 / NANTUCKET / MASS." Length: $5\frac{1}{2}$ in. (14.0 cm.). (3) Handle with rococo decorations, embossed picture of Jethro Coffin house and inscription: "NANTUCKET MASS." and "OLDEST / HOUSE / BUILT / 1686." Windmill embossed in bowl with inscription: "Ye OLD WYNNE MILLE 1746." Length: $4\frac{1}{8}$ in. (10.6 cm.). (*Private collection*).

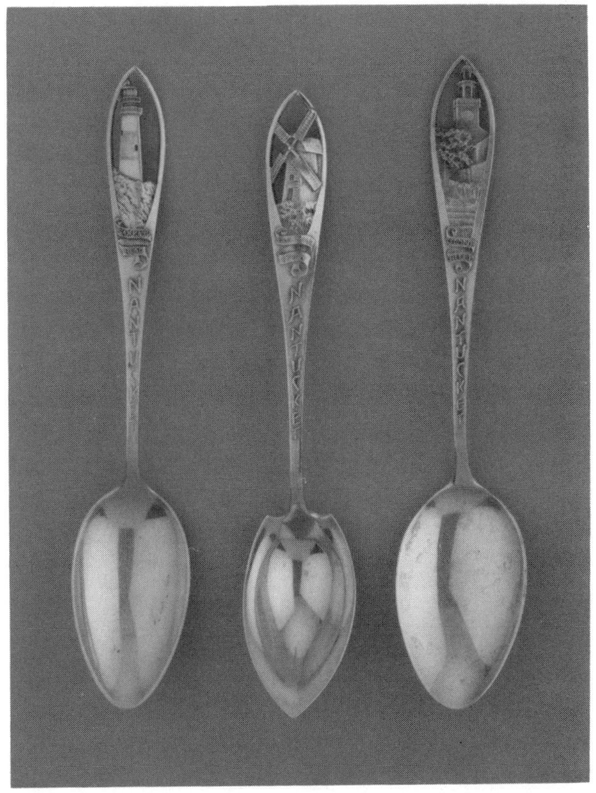

Figure 126. Twentieth-century sterling Nantucket souvenir spoons with pierced handles, all made by Charles M. Robbins, Attleboro, Massachusetts. Left to right: (1) lighthouse on handle with inscription "SANKATY / HEAD / NANTUCKET." Trademark on back plus "STERLING," 1900–1926. Length: $5\frac{5}{8}$ in. (14.3 cm.). (2) Orange spoon, Old Mill on both front and back, with inscription "OLD MILL / 1746 / NANTUCKET." Trademark on back plus "STERLING," 1900–1926. Length: $5\frac{7}{16}$ in. (13.8 cm.). (3) Stone Alley with inscription "STONE / ALLEY / NANTUCKET." Trademark on back indicates spoon was made after 1926, plus "STERLING." Length: $5\frac{9}{16}$ in. (14.1 cm.). (*Private collection*).

in the 1820s to the 1850s, were made on the mainland, but the former are far rarer today in Nantucket and are almost never found in old homes on the island. This is to be expected. The earlier silverwares were acquired for local usage, while souvenir spoons were bought by tourists and summer residents. One is more likely to find a Nantucket souvenir spoon in Chicago or Pittsburgh than on the island.

The symbols used on souvenir spoons, their iconography, tell us something about how tourists on Nantucket, and the merchants who catered to them, perceived the island in the 1890s: a quaint, quiet old town with the pleasures of the sea—bathing, boating, sailing, and fishing. There was little to remind visitors of the whaling days; there were men on the island who had been on whaleships, but they were just a part of the fading past. How different from today! The archetypical symbol of the island since World War II has been the whale. Depictions of whales are on basket tops, tie-pins, dish towels, placemats, beer mugs, sweaters, trousers, T-shirts, neckties, and, for a brief time, the town street signs.

The story of Nantucket silver—the eighteenth-century goldsmiths, usually working alone, making mostly spoons, the marketing of silverwares in the nineteenth century from the large manufacturers in urban areas, the souvenir spoons—mirrors, in a small way, the story of American silver. Silver has always had a special kind of importance and appeal to a relatively limited number of people. This is as true today as it was in the eighteenth century.

8. Iron, Pewter, Brass and Copper, Tin

Iron

From the seventeenth to well into the nineteenth century, Nantucket kitchens would have had an assortment of iron pots, often with three legs (Figure 127), kettles (Figure 128), and skillets, cranes, pot hooks, gridirons, and trammels. Much of the cooking was done in cast-iron vessels. In the seventeenth century some of the cast-iron utensils, the iron pots, kettles and skillets (some skillets were called "spiders," which were pans or pots with legs and long handles), were made on the mainland at the Saugus Iron Works. But by the eighteenth century most would have come from the middle-Atlantic colonies or from England. Cast-iron objects were not fabricated locally, since the island never had iron-making facilities. All the rest of the ironwork in the kitchen would have been forged by an island blacksmith. We described in Chapter 2 the kinds of ironwork made by Nathaniel Starbuck (1668–1753), the earliest Nantucket blacksmith we have found. His account book has entries beginning in 1683, when he was fifteen years old.[1]

In addition to cooking vessels, there were many other objects made of iron in an early house. Fireplaces were equipped with andirons (called handirons or firedogs; see Figure 129), tongs, shovels, and occasionally firebacks. (There were five iron firebacks or "back irons" in the pre-Revolutionary inventories.) There were iron candlesticks, smoothing irons (sometimes designated as "iron goose" and/or "box iron and heaters"), iron spoons and iron basins.

There does not seem to have been any substantial change in the amounts and kinds of ironwork in the average Nantucket inventory from the beginning of the eighteenth century to the time of the Revolution, indicating a con-

Figure 127. Three iron pots with handles, probably nineteenth century. The middle has lost its legs. Left: small pot with lid, diameter 4 in. (10.2 cm.), height over handle 6¼ in. (15.9 cm.); center: diameter 11½ in. (29.2 cm.); right: diameter 9 in. (22.9 cm.), height over handle 9¾ in. (24.8 cm.). (*NHA*).

Figure 128. Iron kettle with lid, nineteenth century, height over handle 13½ in. (34.3 cm.). (*NHA*).

tinuity of life-styles. Based on this, one might expect to see the number of blacksmiths to be a function of the number of people on the island, that is, to show an increase approximately proportional to the population. This was not so. The population of Nantucket increased about fourfold from the 1720s to the time of the Revolution, while the number of blacksmiths increased at least sevenfold. The third quarter of the eighteenth century, particularly in the 1760s, saw a great increase in the number of blacksmiths. In 1768 alone there were ten new blacksmiths listed in the Nantucket land records. It was a boom time.

Blacksmiths in Colonial Nantucket

1663–1700	1
1701–1710	2
1711–1720	2
1721–1730	3
1731–1740	6
1741–1750	8
1751–1760	11
1761–1770	22
1771–1776	11

This listing is based on the first mention in the records, which means that the total number of blacksmiths at any one time would include both the number for the period plus some of those listed in earlier years. Thus, in the 1761–1770 period there would have been thirty-five to forty, or more, blacksmiths active on the island, a remarkable number. These numbers can only be accounted for by the great increase in whaling in the third quarter of the eighteenth century, necessitating large quantities of ship fittings and whaling gear.

The expansion of whaling activity did not show up as an increase in the amount of whaling tools in inventories. The number of harpoons, lances, whale spades (and anchors) was not much different in the third quarter of the eighteenth century than it was in the first quarter. In fact, only twenty-one inventories

Figure 129. Pair of iron andirons, late eighteenth or early nineteenth century, height 11⅜ in. (28.9 cm.). (*NHA*).

listed whaling tools in the pre-Revolutionary period. The reason is simple. Whaling tools were considered part of the equipment of whaling vessels. This is confirmed by the 1747 inventory of Daniel Bunker in the item:

> 2 whale boats Craft and Irons belonging to sd Sloop 194–13–0

Since most vessels had a number of owners, the iron whaling tools would never have appeared in individual inventories. As noted earlier, from 1750 to 1775 the number of Nantucket whaleships doubled and the tonnage tripled, creating a great demand for blacksmithing products.

By the nineteenth century, factory-like shops on the mainland supplied whaling tools to many ports, including Nantucket. The iron-forging activities of the 1760s may have represented an all-time peak for the island. Never again was there such a flurry of blacksmithing.

Pewter

Pewter, in the form of plates, platters, and basins, was used in Nantucket throughout the colonial period. However, based on the inventories, the quantity of pewter in most of the houses was never as great as in the average house of Boston and surrounding towns of the same time.[2] Even by the second quarter of the eighteenth century there were only eight pewter forms listed in the Nantucket inventories: cups, spoons, dishes, plates, platters, "basons," porringers, and tankards.[3] The inventories suggest that during the first fifty or sixty years of the white man's occupation, most food in island homes was served and eaten from wooden trenchers and plates. It was only after the middle of the eighteenth century that the level of wealth had increased to the point where it became common for the islanders to have pewter plates and platters.

The table on page 152 is a summary of the pewter in pre-Revolutionary inventories in Nantucket. The picture presented by the table is somewhat confused by the fact that Nantucket inventory-takers often lumped together all the pewter in a house, not bothering to itemize individual items. In 1725, Joseph Coffin's inventory, which indicated he had a well-furnished house, listed all his pewter in three different places in the inventory:

> 32 lb 3/4 of puter at 2/6 is 81/19
> 24 lb 3/4 of puter at 2/9 is 68/
> 13 lb puter at 2/6 is 32/6

Occasionally the quality or age of pewter in the inventories was indicated by such descriptions as: "old puter," "old puter poorest sars [sic]," "sundry midling sort puter," "new pewter," "good pewter," "hard pewter," "common pewter." A few of the inventories gave specific data on the pewter. The inventory of Joseph Starbuck (1761) listed pewter items as carefully as if they were silver:

one Tee pot of pewter	0–18–0
one Quart cup	0– 9–0
one pint pot pewter	0– 9–0
3 New porringers at 12/6 each	1–17–6
3 Do old Porringers at 7/ each	1– 1–0
11 pewter Spoons at 12/ 3 Do teespoons at 1/	0–13–0
1/2 Doz^n plates pewter Markt RM	3– 5–0
1/2 Doz^n Do Markt IRS	2– 1–0
3 Do IRS old	1– 0–0
1 pewter platter Markt RDM	1–19–0
1 Do RMP	2– 6–9
1 platter small no Mark	1– 9–0
5 Basons	6– 0–0
2 platters Markt IRS	3– 0–0
1 Do Markt I	1– 7–6
9 lb old pewter	3– 7–6
12 small pewter tea spoons new	0–15–0
1 new tea pot	1–15–0

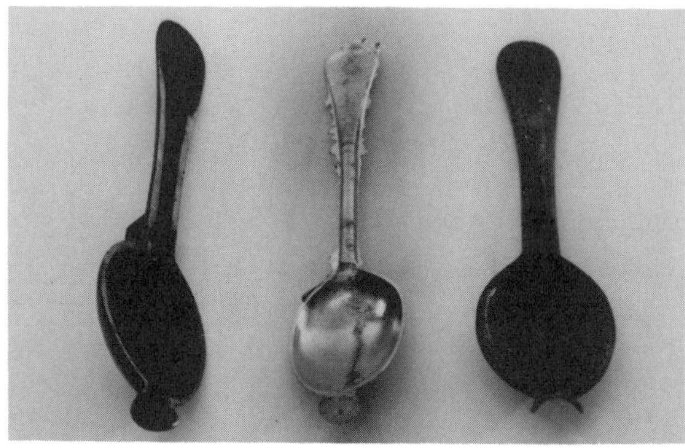

Figure 130. Two piece spoon-mold, with rough unfinished cast-pewter rat-tail spoon in the middle. The outside of one part of the mold is engraved "Walter Folger, Jun.," on the other "Nantucket / 1790." Length of mold: 8 in. (20.3 cm.). (*NHA*).

The first mention of a pewter teapot in a Nantucket inventory was in 1753 (Simeon Bunker); there was a total of twenty-two pewter teapots in the 1750–1776 inventories. The first and only silver teapot in the pre-Revolutionary inventories was that of Thomas Carr (1757). Although a pottery teapot appeared in an inventory as early as 1739 (Samuel Barker), tea drinking on the island does not seem to have become fashionable until the 1750s.

The scarcity of pewter spoons in the inventories before 1750 could either mean they were seldom used or, more likely, that they were lumped together in the inventories with other miscellaneous items. The fact that there were only three spoon molds in the inventories of the whole colonial period suggests that wooden spoons were used for a long time. Figure 130 illustrates a spoon mold engraved with Walter Folger, Jr.'s name and dated 1790. The mold was for the making of a rattailed spoon, indicating the survival of an out-of-date form in the 1790s.

The mention in John Swain's 1718 inventory of both wide- and narrow-brimmed platters ("3 broad brimmed platters / 3 narrow

Figure 131. Left: pewter hot water plate marked "S. ELLIS / LONDON," for Samuel Ellis, working 1721–1773, diameter 9½ in. (24.1 cm.). Right: pewter plate, engraved with the initials "MC," with four marks of Richard King, Gracious Street, London, working 1745–1798, diameter 9⅜ in. (23.8 cm.). (*NHA*).

brimmed platters—1–16–0") indicates that the old broad-brimmed platters typical of the seventeenth century were still in use in the eighteenth century. Figure 131 shows an English narrow-brimmed eighteenth-century plate with a long Nantucket history. It is marked "MC," but the name of the original owner has been lost.

The English double volute baluster measure in Figure 132 was a type of pewter measure made in a series of seven graduated sizes, from a gallon down to a one-half gill. They were made from about 1720 to well into the nineteenth century.[3] William S. Whippy apparently acquired the measure during a Pacific voyage, when he was captain of the Nantucket whaleship *James Loper* (1846–1851).

We end this brief survey of pewter in Nan-

Figure 133. Pair of pewter teapots, one of which is marked "Dixon & Smith," England, circa 1840. Height: $6^{5}/_{8}$ in. (16.8 cm.), length: $12^{1}/_{2}$ in. (31.6 cm.). (*Courtesy Mrs. H. Crowell Freeman*).

Figure 132. Double volute baluster measure, a pint-sized pitcher with lid, scratched on the bottom with "WSW 49" for William S. Whippy, whaling captain on a whaling voyage in the Pacific (1846–1851), English, circa 1845. Height: 6 in. (15.3 cm.). (*Private collection*).

Figure 134. Pewter tea caddy, mother-of-pearl finial on lid, marked "James Dixon & Sons," England, circa 1840. Height: 5 in. (12.7 cm.), length: $4^{3}/_{4}$ in (12.1 cm.), depth: $3^{1}/_{2}$ in. (8.9 cm.). (*Courtesy of Mrs. H. Crowell Freeman*).

Pewter in the Inventories of Colonial Nantucket

Form	*1706–1725*	*1726–1750*	*1751–1776*
Basin	3	20	54
Chamber pot			2
Cup (pint and quart)		3	14
Dish		34	29
Inkstand			1
Milk pot			1
Plate	25	30	313
Platter	14	11	86
Porringer	4	11	41
Pot			6
Server			1
Soop [sic] plate			20
Spoon		4	120
Tankard	1	2	2
Teapot			22
Miscellaneous pewter by weight (est.)	90 lb.	370 lb.	610 lb.

tucket with objects from the Middle Brick, part of the Starbuck pewter shown on the sideboard in Plate VI, Chapter 2. The pair of Dixon & Smith teapots in Figure 133 was acquired by Matthew Starbuck in the 1840s. After decades of use they ended up in the basement of the Middle Brick where they were used for "watering the furnace." The present owner rescued them and restored them to the dining room. The little tea caddy in Figure 134 has a beautifully carved mother-of-pearl finial. The flask in Figure 135, engraved with Matthew Starbuck's name and the date 1852, fits the image of his man-about-town life-style so well described in Joseph Farnham's account of him quoted in Chapter 2.

Figure 135. Pewter flask with lid that doubles as a cup. Engraved "Matthew Starbuck / 1852." Mark on screw-lid "G & J.W. Hawksley." Height: 5 in. (12.7 cm.). (*Courtesy Mrs. H. Crowell Freeman*).

Brass and Copper

There were brass objects in Nantucket in the first detailed inventory in the probate records,

Brass and Copper in the Inventories of Colonial Nantucket

Form	*1680–1700*	*1701–1725*	*1726–1750*	*1751–1776*	*Total*
Andirons (pr.)		1		1	2
Buttons (pr.)				22	22
Candlesticks		9	15	27	61
Chafing Dish		1	1	1	3
Cock (a tap)		1		1	2
Coffee Pot				4	4
Egg Slice			1	1	2
Fender				1	1
Flower Box		1			1
Funnel			1	1	2
Ink Cap			1		1
Kettle	2	17	31	51	102
Ladle		3	6	16	25
Lock				1	1
Mortar & Pestle			3		3
Pepper Box			2	2	4
Pot		3	1	1	5
Sauce Pan		1	1	3	5
Scales		1	1		2
Shovel & Tongs		1		1	2
Skillet	1	5	29	31	66
Skimmer		2	5	11	18
Snuffer		2		1	3
Weights			3		3

that of Nathaniel Weir (Wyer), whose estate was probated March 3, 1681:

> an Iron pot two old brass Kettles on[e] Scillet, on[e] frying pan on[e] Iron Cettel a gridiron a tramell—1–6–0 [Note the vagaries of seventeenth-century spelling.]

Although the terms skillet and frying pan are used interchangeably today, in the seventeenth and eighteenth centuries they had more specific meanings. A skillet was a cooking utensil, usually made of brass or copper, with three or four legs and a long handle, that was used for boiling liquids, stewing meats, and so forth. It functioned as a saucepan or stewing pan. A frying pan was a shallow pan with a long handle, usually made of iron, in which food was fried.

Most of the objects in the brass and copper category in the pre-Revolutionary inventories were made of brass, an alloy of copper and zinc. There were a few copper pots and pans. We group bell-metal objects (mostly skillets) with those made of brass, although technically bell metal is a bronze, an alloy of copper and tin.

The table on this page summarizes the brass and copper objects in the colonial inventories of Nantucket, with kettles, skillets, candlesticks, ladles, and skimmers being the most

Figure 136. Brass warming pan, engraved with a peacock, late eighteenth or early nineteenth century. Diameter: 10½ in. (26.7 cm.), overall length: 45⅝ in. (115.9 cm.). (*NHA*).

commonplace. One surprising fact is the scarcity of brass andirons; there were only two pairs in total. Over half (59 percent) of the inventories contained brass or copper objects of some kind.

There were two brasiers (workers in brass) listed in the court records of pre-Revolutionary Nantucket, Daniel Coffin (1739) and William Coffin (1774). We were not able to determine which of the two Daniel Coffins or the six William Coffins in the *Vital Records of Nantucket* were the ones involved in brass work.

The brass bed warmer in Figure 136, possibly an eighteenth-century example, is engraved with a strutting peacock. The wooden handle of the bed warmer (not shown) is a fascinating example of the thrifty re-use of materials. The handle is a stile from a broken four-back chair of the type shown in Figure 16, Chapter 3. The handle still retains the stub-ends of the four tenons of the slats that made up the back of the chair.

The Brass Foundry

In 1821 a brass foundry was set up on South Beach at the corner of Commercial Wharf (now named Swain's Wharf) and Washington Street. Very little is known about the history of the foundry and no business records have been located. It was started by Benjamin Field (1774–1841), originally from Providence, and a Macy, possibly Peleg Macy (1760–1838). After Benjamin Field's death in 1841, his son, also named Benjamin, took over. When the Commonwealth of Massachusetts made its survey of the "Industrial Resources of Nantucket" in 1845, the brass foundry was listed as having a value of $6,000, an invested capital of $4,000, with four persons employed.[4] The foundry operated up to the time of the Civil War. Whether or not it was active afterwards has not been determined. The deep recession on the island starting in the 1860s makes it doubtful that much work came out of the brass foundry after 1861. The foundry was one of the relatively few businesses not affected by the great fire of 1846, being just south of the fire zone.

In 1875, soon after the death of the second Benjamin Field, the foundry and its equipment were offered for sale. There were two notices in the August 21, 1875, *Inquirer & Mirror:*

> We call attention to the advertisement of Mr. A. M. Myrick offering for sale the well-known brass foundry of the late Benj. Field. A fine opportunity is here offered any young and enterprising man to establish himself in business, as the building with all the fixtures, can probably be purchased for a tithe of their real value.

The for-sale notice read:

> The Brass Foundry and land under and adjoining together with a large lot of valuable tools, moulds, patterns, and everything necessary for carrying on the casting, gas-fitting

and foundry business being the property occupied by the late Benjamin Field.

A. M. Myrick

They couldn't give it away. The brass foundry never operated again.

The most important of the surviving products of the Nantucket brass foundry are the two cast-bronze school bells now in the Peter Foulger Museum. The bell in Figure 137, marked "MACY FIELD NANTUCKET," is decorated with rococo flourishes and swags, stars, and hearts. It was made for the new white-columned Greek Revival schoolhouse of the Coffin School, built on Winter Street in 1852.

The pair of miniature brass andirons in Figure 138 probably date from the early period of the foundry, the 1820s or 1830s. The brass foundry no doubt made regular-sized andirons but at the time of this writing none have been identified. The brass door fittings in Figure 139 are said to have been made in the foundry, but they are unmarked, as are the andirons. The brass steelyard in Figure 140, stamped "*E. FIELD*," was used for weighing. The object to be weighed is put on the hook of the short arm and the weight is found by moving the weight on the long arm to the point of balance. The Edward Field name on the steelyard was a younger brother of Benjamin Field. Edward was born in Providence in 1801 and came to

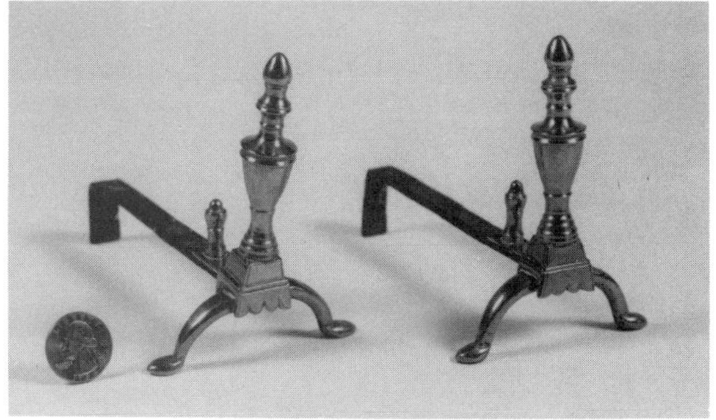

Figure 138. Pair of miniature brass andirons, said to have been made in the Nantucket brass foundry, circa 1821–1840, shown with a U. S. twenty-five cent piece for scale. Height: 4¾ in. (10.8 cm.). (*NHA*).

Figure 137. Bronze bell and bracket, made for the Coffin School, circa 1852. Bell inscribed "MACY FIELD NANTUCKET." Height: 15⅜ in. (39.1 cm.), diameter: 16 in. (40.6 cm.). (*NHA*).

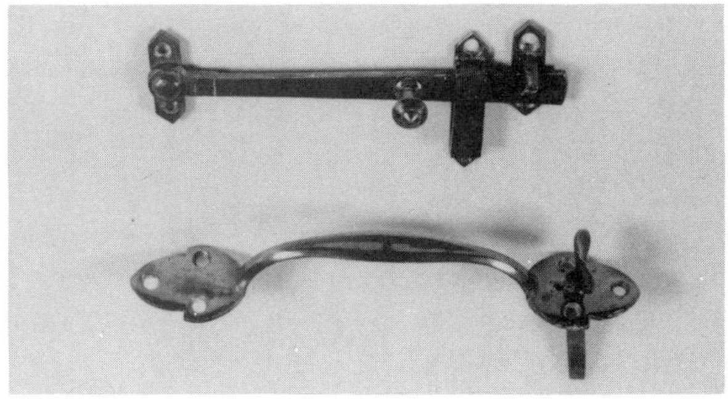

Figure 139. Brass door fittings, said to have been made in the Nantucket brass foundry, 1821–1861. Length of lower latch handle: 7⅝ in. (19.4 cm.). (*NHA*).

Figure 140. Brass steelyard, scale on right graduated to the figure 50, stamped "*E. FIELD*," 1821–1861, length: 27¼ in. (69.2 cm.). (*NHA*).

Nantucket in the 1820s, where he worked in the brass foundry.

Tin

Painted tinwares have long been collected, but plain, undecorated articles made of tin have never been of much interest to the collector or the curator. It is partly a matter of appearances. Tinware, made from sheet iron (or later, steel) with a thin coating of tin, is bright as silver when new, but it does not weather well. It rusts easily and tarnishes to a brownish-black color which many find unattractive. Most tin is unmarked, making identification difficult. These points, plus the fact that tin has never been highly valued, means that comparatively little eighteenth- and early nineteenth-century tinware has survived.

There were only a relatively few pieces of tinware mentioned in the inventories of the colonial period in Nantucket, and we have not found any record of a tinsmith working there before the Revolution. Apparently it was not until the nineteenth century that the island had its own tinsmiths. Thirty-eight percent of the 149 inventories of colonial Nantucket included one or more items of tinware. Most inventories noted only one piece, a tin pan or tin cup. Eight inventories listed tin funnels, six had tin coffeepots, and four had tin colanders. Altogether, there were only one or two of each of the following types of tinware: lamps, ladles, pepper boxes, candlesticks, candle boxes, stoves, porringers, and kettles.

The two inventories of the time that contained the most tinwares were those of Joseph Starbuck, who died in 1761, and Tabor Morton, who died in 1776. Starbuck's inventory listed:

tin pint cup	0– 5–0
1 coffee pot of tin	0–18–0
1 large new saspan tin	0– 7–6
1 tin pepper box new	0– 4–6
1 tin twilight	0– 7–6

Figure 141. Tin-plate percolator, pewter finial, circa 1830–1870, height: 8¼ in. (21.0 cm.). (*NHA*).

Figure 142. Tin-plate spout cup and lid, with asphaltic finish, nineteenth century, height: $8^1/_2$ in. (21.6 cm.). (*Private collection*).

We have not identified the "tin twilight." Perhaps it was a tin punched-hole lantern. The inventory of Tabor Morton contained the more usual tin items:

a Tin pail	0–15–0
a Tin pan	0–18–0
a Tin Funnel	0– 3–0
a small do	0– 3–6
a Tin Sauce pan	0– 2–6
a Tin Tea Canister	0– 9–0

Figure 141 shows a percolator-type coffeepot, made in Nantucket in the middle of the nineteenth century. The water or oil can in Figure 142 has a black rust-inhibiting asphaltic coating.

James Austin, 1809–1892

The 1845 survey of the "Industrial Resources of Nantucket" indicated considerable activity in the making of tinwares:[5]

Factories	Value	Invested Capital	Persons Employed
7	$4000	$2000	12

Two of the twelve tinsmiths working in 1845 were James Austin and Peleg Mitchell. We focus on James Austin for two quite different reasons: first, because of the availability of some of his business records and because pieces of his tinware have been identified (Figure 143 and Figure 59, Chapter 4, the latter being a tinplate horse made for his sons in the 1840s); and second, because James Austin was one of the last of the Nantucket Quakers.

James Austin was born September 12, 1809, and was apprenticed to learn the trade of tin and sheet-metal working in 1823, the year his father died. For more than sixty years, he had

Figure 143. Tin-plate wares made by James Austin and Peleg Mitchell, circa 1830–1870. Left: tin-plate coffee pot, pewter finial on lid, said to have been made by James Austin for his wedding in 1833, height 10 in. (25.4 cm.). Center: spout lamp set in drip pan, height over handle $7^3/_8$ in. (18.7 cm.). Right: tin-plate box with asphaltic finish, said to have been made by Peleg Mitchell, height $4^3/_8$ in. (11.1 cm.), width $6^1/_4$ in. (15.9 cm.), depth $3^1/_2$ in. (8.9 cm.). (*Maria Mitchell Association*).

a shop on the south side of Main Street between Union and Orange. The only interruption was when his shop was destroyed in the 1846 fire. Austin had a partnership with Peleg Mitchell in the 1840s and 1850s; we do not know exactly how long the partnership lasted.

A sampling of James Austin's bills of sale of the 1866–1874 period gives some idea of the kinds of work he did:

1866	coffeepot	.66
	1 cake turner	.20
	1 tin plate for round box	.25
	1 gal. cannister	1.10
	2 lamps	.50
	Repairing hand dish	.15
	mop pail	1.65
1869	stove pipe	.08
	1 sheet iron pan	.25
	1 tea cannister	.38
	1 mop pail	1.33
1871	1 wine needle	.08
1873	1 flour scoop	.40
	Bottom to watering pot	.25
	1 coffee pot	1.38
	mending cover	.10
1874	mending tin ware	.10
	stove pipe for Alice	.92
	mending kettle cover	.06

We noted in the Introduction the decline of Quakerism on the island in the nineteenth century. James Austin was one of the few who stayed with the Meeting. He was true to his Quaker faith to the very end. Mary Starbuck, in her book *My House and I,* tells a story of Austin's attendance at the midweek Meeting of the Friends at the Fair Street Meeting House:

> James Austin for instance would leave his little shop on Main Street open with nobody in charge, and go to his place on the Elder's Bench in the Meeting House with unfailing regularity and sit the hour through as placidly as if he hadn't a care in the world. Mrs. Barnes waiting one day in the shop for his return, ventured to expostulate with him on his carelessness, saying that one might help himself to money or small articles and make off with the spoils in his absence without fear of detection. James looked at her gravely and asked, "Is thee honest?"
>
> "Indeed I trust so," she replied.
>
> "Other people are like thee," observed James simply.[6]

Mary Starbuck chronicled Nantucket's last Quaker Meeting in the nineteenth century. (We noted in the Introduction the reestablishment of an informal Friends Meeting on the island in the 1930s.) James Austin and a woman identified only as Huldah were the last of the vanishing sect:

> James and Huldah were the members of that Meeting who held the last service in the old Meeting House, literally a service of "waiting." James asked Huldah to come up from her usual place and sit with him, on the woman's side of the Elder's Bench, but she didn't feel that she was "worthy"; so as the Spirit moved neither of them to speak they "waited in silence before the Lord" for the customary hour, and then there was a quiet handshake, a gentle farewell, and they parted, as it happened, not to meet again on earth.
>
> It was a chilly, stormy day, and James, an old man, took a cold which rapidly developed into a serious illness and in a short time Huldah was the only surviving member of that Meeting. She died not long afterwards, and hers was the last Quaker funeral on Nantucket.[7]

James died February 9, 1892, in his eighty-third year. His obituary in the *Inquirer & Mirror,* briefly reviewing his life, ends with the sentence:

> During the hour of services all business houses were closed as a mark of respect and esteem to his memory.

9. Scrimshaw

The literature of scrimshaw has, to date, emphasized engraved and carved decorations, particularly engraved whales' teeth. Most books on scrimshaw, both those describing old sailor-work and "how-to" books for the craftsperson, have treated scrimshaw as a collectible, describing the many kinds of forms, giving the collector, the dealer, and the craftsperson a basis for identification and comparison.[1]

We take a different tack. We emphasize the chronological development of scrimshaw, how it was used, how it was perceived, and how, after a century and a quarter from about 1690 to 1815, when it was primarily used functionally, it developed pictorially in the nineteenth century. This approach of treating scrimshaw as part of the material culture will, we hope, give a basis for a more rational and systematic study of the whole subject.

What is Scrimshaw?

The common perception of scrimshaw as whales' teeth with engraved pictures is far too limiting. Any usable definition must take into account those myriad undecorated objects made through the eighteenth and nineteenth centuries of whale ivory and whalebone and whaling-related materials. Most definitions of scrimshaw stress its decorative nature. *Webster's New Collegiate Dictionary:* "any of various carved or engraved articles made esp. by American whalers usu. from whalebone or whale ivory."[2]

We use the term scrimshaw in a broad sense, first as a noun, to include objects, decorated and undecorated, made from whalebone, baleen, and/or the ivory of whales' teeth and walrus tusks; and second, as a verb, to denote the making of such objects. A piece of scrimshaw, which may combine whalebone or whale or walrus ivory with such materials as wood, metal, or shell, should have a nautical association, being made on board ship or in an area where such materials were directly available from whalemen. The nautical or maritime connection is important, ruling out objects made of whalebone and whale ivory that have nothing to do with mariners or the sea. Thus, such things as medieval walrus-ivory religious carvings, eighteenth-century Dutch cutlery with baleen handles, whale-ivory netsukes, corset stays, and commercial ivory buttons are not classified as scrimshaw. The word scrimshaw is, according to the *Oxford English Dictionary,* "of obscure origin; the name *Scrimshaw,* if not actually the source, may have influenced the form of the word." The word has a number of variations in spelling such as scrimshon, scrimshant, scrimshont, scrimshander. The earliest known reference to the word appears to be in the log of the brig *Orion,* out of Rochester, Massachusetts. The entry for March 14, 1821 reads:

> First and middle part these 24 hours calm. Latter part light breezes and pleasant weather. All hands employed scrimshonting. So ends this day—no Whales and hard times.[3]

The earliest reference in the *Oxford English Dictionary* is from *Moby Dick or The Whale*), 1851.

A number of authors have speculated on the possible origin of the word scrimshaw. It has been suggested that it was related to the Low Dutch word *scrimshoning,* meaning those kinds of passing-the-time labor such as whittling; that it was a bastardization of a Nantucket Indian word, to denote the carving of a pipe or arrowhead; or that it came from eighteenth- or nineteenth-century American slang.[4] We are uncomfortable with all of these explanations, agreeing with the *Oxford English Dictionary* that the word is "of obscure origin."

The principal materials of scrimshaw, whale ivory, whalebone, and walrus ivory, should be described. Whale ivory, a sperm whale tooth, is a hard, dense, fine-grained material whose outer parts are white with a large darker center part. Walrus ivory, the tusk of a walrus, has a consistency similar to whale ivory, but has a center of compact crystals. Elephant ivory is softer than whale ivory. A cross section of elephant ivory has a wood-grain effect and the end grain has a hatchlike structure. American and British scrimshawers worked with whale ivory and whalebone, less often with walrus tusks, and only occasionally with elephant ivory.

The fact that the word whalebone had two different meanings has caused confusion. Baleen, the traditional brownish-black "whalebone" of commerce, used for stays and corset ribs, was, in a prechemical age, a natural plastic material, flexible and strong. Eighteenth-century Nantucketers used strands of baleen fibers in their bedsteads to support the mattress. The inventory of Samuel Barker, who died in 1740, listed: "whale sinew bed cord—0/5/0." Baleen is a flexible, hornlike substance that grows in the mouth of the right whale and other related whales. On the other hand, the white bone of the skeleton of a whale, although long used for scrimshaw, was not widely used in utilitarian objects before the middle of the nineteenth century, when it began to be employed for crochet hooks, knitting needles, bodkins, shoehook handles, and for bristle holders of brushes. Skeletal bone is a relatively hard, dense form of connective tissue, hardened by inorganic matter, chiefly calcium carbonate. The bone of a whale skeleton, like that of other mammals, is porous, with stringy cavities (appearing as surface streaks) that distinguish it from the harder, more uniform surface of ivory. Other materials used by scrimshawers include tortoiseshell, seashells, tropical woods, coconuts, pewter, and silver.

We divide scrimshaw into two categories: (1) functional or utilitarian scrimshaw, and (2) decorated scrimshaw. (We use the term *decorated* scrimshaw to designate specifically scrimshaw that has been carved in a decorative manner or has images engraved *on* it. Any scrimshaw, decorated or undecorated, can be decorat*ive.*) There are, of course, a number of pieces of scrimshaw which fit into both the functional and decorated categories, that is, functional scrimshaw that has been decorated or carved, or vice versa. At the two ends of the definitional spectrum there is no problem. Engraved whales' teeth are clearly in the decorated category, while plain whalebone clothespins are certainly functional. Busks with engraved decorations *did* have a function, but surely the decorations *on* them are more important. Cane heads may be beautifully carved, but most canes were primarily functional walking sticks. We do not want to labor these distinctions. We feel the division of scrimshaw into the two basic categories is valid and sufficient, even though there are objects that could fit in both categories.

Functional and decorated scrimshaw were made in overlapping time periods:

Functional scrimshaw	1690–1900
Decorated scrimshaw	1815–1900

Although these dates are somewhat arbitrary, they have a rational basis. The 1690 date corresponds to the beginning of whaling on Nantucket. Offshore whaling was practiced by white men before this time on both Long Island and Cape Cod, but we know of no relevant artifacts of the time, although we do show whalebone articles made by Indians that predate the coming of the white settlers. The 1900 date was chosen as the approximate end of traditional nautical-associated scrimshaw, particularly on Nantucket. The return of the last whaleship, the *Eunice Adams,* in 1870 marked the end of island whaling. However, Nantucketers continued to ship out of other ports, particularly New Bedford, and they continued to make scrimshaw.

Twentieth-century scrimshaw tends to be of two types: survival work by old-time whalemen in the first quarter of this century, and modern scrimshaw, sometimes in the style of the nineteenth century, and sometimes in a contemporary manner. The best of contemporary scrimshawers, such as William Gilkerson, Nancy Chase, and Robert Spring, are far more technically competent than the average sailor of the nineteenth century would have been and probably should not be compared with them. This is not to denigrate the work of the past. At its best, the pictorial scrimshaw of the nineteenth century has a charm and associational interest quite different from the studio productions of today.

The date 1815 for the beginning of decorated scrimshaw is based on a study, "Early Dated Scrimshaw," published by one of the authors in 1972, listing all known pieces of scrimshaw *dated* before 1825.[5] This list, which has been kept up to date, includes only one engraved whale's tooth dated in the eighteenth century, plus two of the 1800–1815 era. The eighteenth-century example, a tooth engraved with a map of Boston harbor dated 1790, now in the Mystic Seaport Museum,[6] seems more related to the engraved map-powderhorns of the French and Indian War than to later scrimshawed whales' teeth. It is clear that scrimshaw engraved with pictures of ships, port scenes, ladies, and children is a product of the nineteenth century, after 1815. There is a reasonable explanation for this. It was not until after the end of the War of 1812, in 1815, that really long voyages to the Pacific and Indian Oceans, averaging three and four years, became common. There was more leisure time aboard ship for such activities as scrimshawing on those long voyages, and the emphasis on sperm whaling meant there were more teeth available for engraving. The sperm whale had the large ivory teeth used by scrimshawers, while the other whale commonly hunted in the South Pacific, the right whale, had only baleen in its mouth.

Scrimshaw was made everywhere, on board ship and ashore. It was not limited to the ships of any one port, nor to any one country, although most was made aboard American and British ships. (Eskimo scrimshaw does not concern us here, although examples (Chapter 12) were brought back to the island by whalemen.) Only a tiny minority of scrimshaw in museums and private collections can be attributed to a specific maker. Probably no more than one piece of authentic scrimshaw out of a hundred is dated.

This chapter can give only a sampling of scrimshaw forms, emphasizing pieces with

Nantucket provenances. Examples of scrimshaw are illustrated in other chapters in this book: furniture and boxes inlaid with whalebone and whale ivory in Chapter 4, whale-ivory needleholders in Chapter 5, and ivory Masonic emblems in Chapter 7. At the end of this chapter we include a note on that melancholy aspect of the antiques business—fakes.

Figure 144. Indian whalebone adzes or spades, excavated in Nantucket in 1970. Late Woodland culture, 1500–1650. Lengths: right, 10 in. (25.4 cm.); left, 9½ in. (24.2 cm.). (*Courtesy Paul C. Morris*).

Functional Scrimshaw

Objects made of whalebone existed on Nantucket long before the coming of the white man. Archaeological digs have uncovered whalebone at several sites.[7] One site had blackfish remains and a gorget made from a whale's vertebra, associated with charcoal with a carbon-14 date of 940 A.D. The presence of whalebone in these sites does not necessarily mean that the Nantucket Indians were active whalers in prehistoric times. Stranded whales washed ashore on a fairly regular basis. Based on twentieth-century records, drift, or stranded whales, wash ashore on Nantucket at the average rate of one per year. There is no evidence that Indians were involved in offshore whaling from Nantucket until after 1690, and then only as members of the white men's crews.[8] Almost all drift whales were right whales or smaller whales such as blackfish. The appearance of a stranded sperm whale on Nantucket was a rare occurrence.[9] The fact that most of the stranded whales were toothless baleen whales would account for the absence of whales' teeth in the island's archaeological sites so far examined.

The two Indian whalebone artifacts in Figure 144, designated as adzes or spades, have tapered, sharpened, axlike ends which show signs of considerable use. These objects were part of a cache found on the western end of Nantucket in 1970 when a trench was being dug for the sewer line of a new house.[10] The cache, which was uncovered at a depth of about twenty-six inches, contained the two paddle-shaped tools shown, directly below which were found two stone celts (stone axes) about six inches in length. Nearby were several other Indian artifacts, including two small triangular stone points and a grooved hammerstone. It has been suggested that the cache dates from the Late Woodland Culture, 500–1650.

The earliest documented example of whalebone used functionally by white men in coastal Massachusetts is the whale vertebra chopping block in Figure 145, found in an archaeological dig on Grand Island in Wellfleet harbor on Cape Cod.[11] Offshore whaling was practiced on Cape Cod in the 1680s, and Cape Codder Ichabod Paddock is credited by Obed Macy with being Nantucket's teacher of whaling. From 1690 onward, skeletal whalebone would have been available as a material of construction both on Nantucket and in other coastal areas. On Nantucket it was the practice to cut up the whales on the south shore of the island and cart the blubber to tryworks in Sherborn

Figure 145. Chopping block made from a whalebone vertebra, excavated at Great Island, Wellfleet, Cape Cod in 1969–1970. Circa 1690–1740. Block measures approximately 15 x 14 x $7\frac{3}{8}$ in. (38.1 x 35.6 x 18.7 cm.). (*National Park Service photograph by Dorinda Partch, Cape Cod National Seashore*).

for rendering the whale oil. Macy describes the procedure:

> The process called *saving* the whales after they had been killed and towed ashore, was to use a *crab,* an instrument similar to a capstain, to heave and turn the blubber off as fast as it was cut. The blubber was then put into their carts and carried to their try-houses, which, at that early period, were placed near to their dwelling-houses where the oil was boiled out and fitted for market.[12]

Evidence of this practice is in several early Nantucket account books, including those of Netowa and of Nathaniel Starbuck, which list accounts for carting blubber or "whale fat" from the south shore to the town.[13] After the blubber and the baleen were removed, the whale carcasses were left on the beach to decompose, eventually leaving only the skeleton. The south shore of the island must have been periodically cluttered with pieces of white whalebone skeletal remains during the offshore whaling period, which lasted from 1690 to the middle of the eighteenth century.

The original building at Wellfleet where the whale-vertebra cutting block was found was probably a tavern, as evidenced by local history and by the large number of wineglass fragments found at the site.[14] It has been suggested that the building could also have been an offshore whaling station.[15] The dating of the site, based on pottery shards and pipestem bore diameters, has been fixed at circa 1690–1740, which corresponds with the beginnings of whaling on Nantucket.

Whalebone vertebrae were often used to make low three-legged stools of the type

Figure 146. Stool made from whale vertebra, oak legs. An 1830 United States one-cent coin is nailed to the bottom of the right leg. Height: $17\frac{3}{4}$ in. (45.1 cm.), diameter: $10\frac{1}{4}$ in. (26.0 cm.). (*NHA*).

shown in Figure 146. This particular stool may be a nineteenth-century example. A large 1830 United States one-cent coin was nailed to the bottom of one of the legs to act as a leveling shim. Whale-vertebra stools of the milking-stool type were made throughout the eighteenth and nineteenth centuries.

The fact that whalebone was resistant to rot made it an attractive alternative to scarce wood on Nantucket. It was reported to have been used for surveying markers.[16] Figure 147 shows a whalebone post for a split-rail fence that dates from the eighteenth century. Our guess is that, because of its availability, more use was made of whalebone as a material of construction in the eighteenth century than at any time since.

Whaling practices began to change in the middle of the eighteenth century. As whales became scarce off the shores of New England and Long Island, longer voyages became necessary. These longer voyages required larger sailing vessels with facilities to cut up the whale alongside the ship, with tryworks installed on the deck that enabled the whalemen to immediately render the oil, and with space below deck to store the casks.[17] Meeting this demand of longer voyages forced the technological changes that revolutionized the industry and paved the way for the three- and four-year voyages to the Pacific in the nineteenth century. But this new procedure also meant that the whale carcasses were dumped at sea, with perhaps only the panbone lower jaw of the sperm whale being recovered. It also meant there was less skeletal bone on Nantucket.

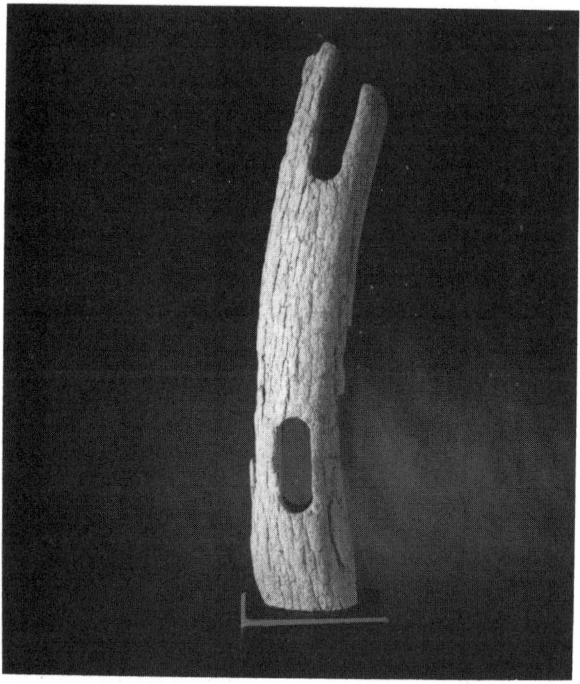

Figure 147. Fragment of a whalebone fencepost found on Nantucket. Height: 21½ in (54.6 cm.). (*NHA*).

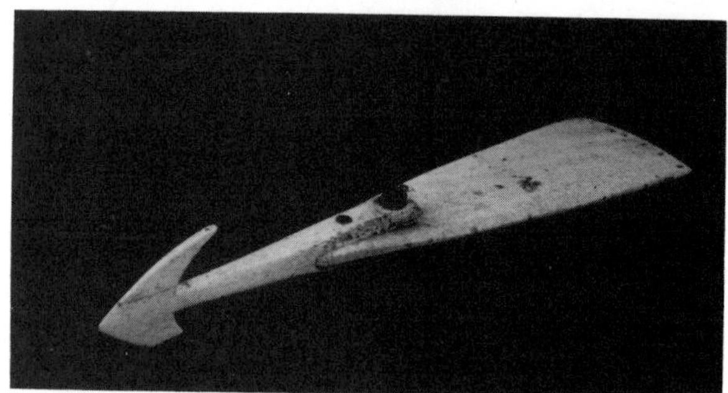

Figure 148. Whalebone weathervane wind direction indicator. Length: 19⅝ in. (49.8 cm.). (*NHA*).

The objects we have discussed so far were purely functional artifacts. They were not designed as works of art. On the other hand, whalebone was used in certain utilitarian objects in aesthetically satisfying ways that tell us the maker had an "eye," that he was consciously making a work of art. The weather vane in Figure 148 has a strong logical sculptural form.

The following sections discuss the more conventional varieties of functional scrimshaw: household furnishings, swifts, measuring sticks, tools, and utensils. Some of these pieces were purely utilitarian in their time, and are so judged today, but other, more decorative objects tend to be judged today only as works of art, a point of view that might have seemed strange to their makers.

Household Furnishings

We have already seen in Chapter 4 examples of the sailor-made inlaid furniture of the nineteenth century which, incidentally, could logically have been included in this chapter.

The whalebone chair arms in Figure 149 are frustrating. Although we are grateful that at least the arms of the chair have survived, they only make us want all the more to have the whole chair. The chaste whalebone box with mahogany top and ivory knob in Plate XLVIII is a good example of Nantucket scrimshaw. The present-day collector might prefer such a box to have scrimshawed pictures engraved on it, but the box, as it is, is quite characteristic of the plain Quaker-influenced Nantucket taste. On the other hand, the rather regal whalebone and whale-ivory candlesticks in Plate XLIX represent a rare and more sophisticated form. Although there have been numerous fake whalebone candlesticks on the market in recent years, few genuine period candlesticks are to be found, and even those are of indifferent design. In quite another vein, bird cages of whalebone and mahogany (Plate L) were a favorite with sailors, housing their parrots and other brilliantly colored tropical birds.

Swifts

The swift or yarn-winder has been pronounced the ultimate scrimshaw form, the most difficult to make. It was a utilitarian object, a reel of adjustable diameter, opening and closing like an umbrella, upon which a skein of

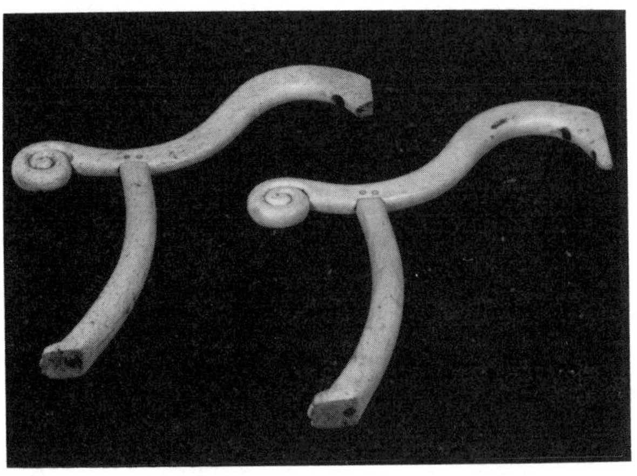

Figure 149. Whalebone chair arms, circa 1830, height: 19 in. (48.3 cm.) (*NHA*).

yarn was placed in order to be wound off into balls for the knitter. The *Oxford English Dictionary* traces the word swift back to the sixteenth century. There were three swifts in the colonial inventories of Nantucket: Paul Starbuck's 1759 inventory included "Case and Swift—0–0–10"; Nason Mederos (1769) had "a Swift—0–5–0"; and Tabor Morton (1776) owned "a Swift 2/6." We do not know whether these swifts were made of whalebone or wood. However, the fact that Paul Starbuck's inventory listed a "Case and Swift" suggests a boxed whalebone swift. Whalebone swifts are sometimes found with their original boxes, but the authors have never seen an early wooden swift with box, or "case."

Most scrimshaw swifts, made of whalebone and whale or walrus ivory, had adjustable clamps so that they could be mounted on the edge of a table. The much less common freestanding swifts were often mounted on boxes, such as the one on the front jacket cover, or on ornamental bases (Plate LI). Although scrimshaw swifts are definitely useful objects, they are now more appreciated in sculptural terms, often being displayed as pure sculpture. The best of the scrimshaw swifts are quite satisfactory works of art, even though their makers may not have been thinking in such terms.

Canes

Although most scrimshaw canes are purely functional objects decorated with bits of whalebone and/or ivory, occasionally an inspired maker crafted something that we can accept as a work of art. Canes with ivory knobs have been known in America since the seventeenth century,[18] although we have found only one such cane in the colonial-period inventories of Nantucket: the inventory of James Codode, an Indian who died April 5, 1748, included "ivory headed cane 20s."

The "crooked" cane in Figure 150, with a Nantucket provenance, may date from the latter part of the eighteenth century. It was a popular form, reminding us of the childhood rhyme which begins "There was a crooked man." The themes of the three handles in Figure 151 run the gamut from the profane to the divine. The cane on the left with the lady's leg simulates the lady's striped stocking with strips of baleen. The delicately carved baleen shoe carefully depicts the shoelace and holes. On the right is a stylized hand holding a Bible, perhaps a Quaker artifact. In the middle is an ivory-headed depiction of a sailor's Turk's-head knot.

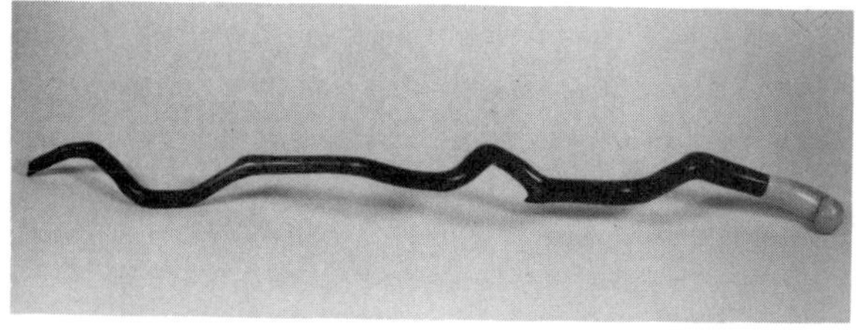

Figure 150. Crooked cane with whale-ivory handle. Engraved on cane just below the handle are the initials "PFC." Total length: 34¼ in. (87.6 cm.). (*Private collection*).

Figure 151. Details of three whalebone and whale-ivory canes, with baleen and tortoise shell parts. (*Private collection*).

Canes with fists were a common scrimshaw motif in the nineteenth century and occasionally the fist gripped a coiled snake, but seldom did a scrimshawer make a cane head as powerful as the one in Plate LII. This beautifully carved cane would have made a fitting walking stick for Captain Ahab! Certain subtleties in the design indicate how carefully and thoughtfully the details of the cane were planned and executed. There is a delicately carved cord bracelet around the wrist, below which are tiny round baleen inlays which line up with the diamond-shaped inlays below. A turned piece of mahogany with silver straps separates the ivory fist from the whalebone shaft. The top of the shaft is octagonal in shape and the bottom is round. The flat surfaces of the top of the shaft, with diamond-shaped baleen inlays, blend imperceptibly into the round part of the shaft near the middle of the cane.

Measuring Sticks

Yard-long scrimshaw measuring sticks very probably date from the eighteenth century, although the earliest ones still extant that can be dated are from the first quarter of the nine-

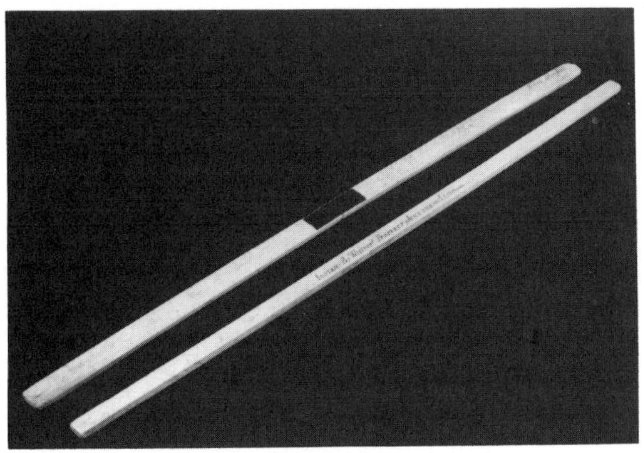

Figure 152. Yard-long whalebone measuring sticks. Top stick, with nineteenth-century riveted copper patch, inscribed "1 nail" and "Eliza Russell." Lower inscribed "Josiah B. Whippy's Property. June.the.18.AD.1819." (*Author's collection*).

Figure 154. Detail of inscription on Josiah B. Whippy's measuring stick.

teenth century. They were used principally for measuring cloth, with marks for half, quarter, and eighth of a yard. (Dealers sometimes call these whale-oil measuring sticks, but measuring the oil through the bung-hole of a forty-five inch diameter whaleship cask with a yard-long stick is clearly impractical.) One stick that can be dated with some confidence to the 1809–1818 period has on it the archaic designation for a sixteenth of a yard, "1 nail" (Figures 152 and 153.) The stick was made for Eliza Russell, wife of Captain Daniel Russell. He commanded the Nantucket whaleship *Essex* on four voyages between 1809 and 1818. It was on the next voyage of the *Essex,* in 1819, with George Pollard as master, that the famous incident occurred when the ship was sunk by an enraged whale.[19] It was the sinking of the *Essex* that formed the basis of the climax of Herman Melville's *Moby Dick.*

The other measuring stick in Figure 152 was made by Josiah B. Whippy in 1819 (see detail in Figure 154). The Whippy measuring stick can be completely documented from the log, or journal, of the whaleship *Francis,* Timothy Fitzgerald, master, which left Nantucket November 10, 1818, returning November 28, 1821. On June 18, 1819, the date inscribed on the measuring stick, Josiah Whippy, the twenty-eight-year-old first mate of the *Francis,* who kept the log, was whaling about two hundred miles north of Callao off the coast of Peru. The log entry for the day makes no mention of the measuring stick:

Figure 153. Details of the two ends of the whalebone measuring stick in Figure 152 made for Eliza Russell.

Figure 155. Comparison of Josiah B. Whippy's name on the measuring stick and in the log of the ship *Francis.*

Friday June the 18th	Commenced with strong trades and thick weather—middle part much the same—Latter part
Latitude aboard 9′ = 23.″	moderate breezes and overcast saw several humpbacks

The signature on the stick is strikingly similar to that in the log entry for October 22, 1819 (Figure 155). In both, he used the old-fashioned I when spelling his first name, even though the J in June is written in the modern manner. Even the doodle after the date on the measuring stick is duplicated in the log entry for September 18, 1819 (Figure 156).

It seems logical to suppose that the measuring stick was made from bone taken from the whale landed on May 15, 1819—the first whale of the voyage. This would account for the slight warping of the measuring stick since the whalebone, little more than three weeks old, was unseasoned when it was engraved.

Figure 156. The doodle on the measuring stick is matched by one in the log of the *Francis* kept by Whippy.

Tools and Utensils

A favorite use of whalebone and whale ivory was for tools and tool handles. Food choppers were sometimes made entirely of whalebone, such as the one in Figure 157, or were metal choppers with ivory or bone handles. The whalebone serving mallet in Figure 157 was used by a sailmaker to wind marline around the standing rigging to protect it from wear and weather. The serving mallet is engraved "G C Coffin." There was a Nantucket mariner, George Cobb Coffin, son of Jethro and Mary Coffin, who was born March 29, 1818. He married Salina Eldridge of Chatham, Cape Cod, on August 3, 1847.

Careful craftsmanship was used in the making of such objects as coconut dippers and rolling pins (Figure 158). The combination of carved or turned ivory and exotic tropical woods produced handsome and useful objects that were no doubt full of nostalgia for retired

Figure 157. Top: whalebone food chopper, length 6 in. (15.3 cm.); below: whalebone serving mallet, enscribed "G C Coffin," length 9 1/4 in. (23.5 cm.). (*NHA*).

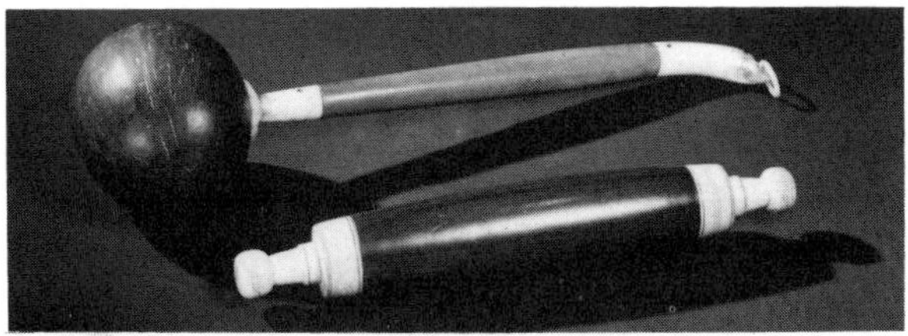

Figure 158. Coconut shell dipper, handle of light-colored tropical wood, whale-ivory fittings, length: 17 1/2 in. (44.5 cm.). Rolling pin, mahogany, turned whale-ivory handles, length: 13 in. (33.0 cm.). (*Private collection*).

Nantucket sailors remembering dreamlike South Sea islands. The dipper handle in Figure 158 is carved with a favorite motif, the American bald eagle with a ring in its mouth, all carved from one piece of whale ivory.

Whalebone clothespins (Figure 159) were used on Nantucket for a very long time, from the eighteenth to well into the twentieth century. Clothespins were usually made in sets. The pairs shown in Figure 159 are all parts of larger sets of four, six, and eight. Edouard Stackpole, Nantucket historian, tells of his mother still using whalebone clothespins when he was a young boy in Nantucket. Clothespins are prime examples of functional scrimshaw.

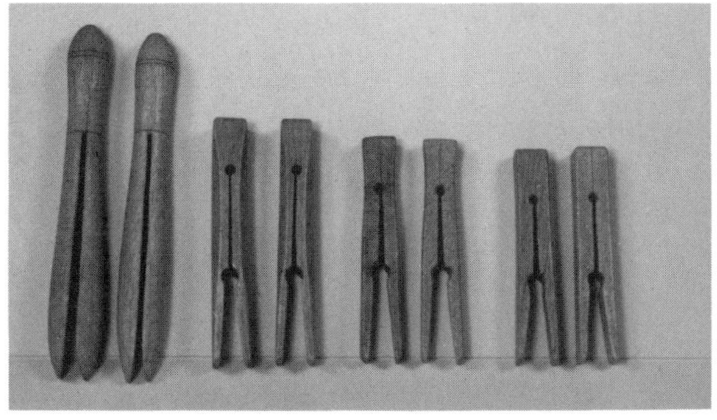

Figure 159. Whalebone clothespins. Lengths of pairs, left to right: 6 3/8, 4 1/2, 4, 3 7/8 in. (16.2, 11.4, 10.2, 9.8 cm.). (*Private collection*).

The Pequod *as Scrimshaw*

Functional and utilitarian scrimshaw was an integral part of Nantucket life. The islanders used whale ivory and whalebone for practical purposes, for fence posts, tools, and for measuring sticks. These functional objects were almost always well designed, sometimes quite decorative, contrasting the gleaming white ivory and bone surfaces with the browns of mahogany and other woods used in furniture and tool making. Decorated scrimshaw, which will be discussed in the next section, was different. Scrimshaw was decoratively carved, pictures were engraved *on* objects, decorating them for aesthetic purposes only.

This dichotomy, these two ways of looking at scrimshaw, is very much in evidence in Herman Melville's *Moby Dick.* An often-quoted passage speaks primarily of decorated scrimshaw:

> Throughout the Pacific, and also in Nantucket, and New Bedford, and Sag Harbor, you will come across lively sketches of whales and whaling-scenes, graven by the fishermen themselves on Sperm Whale-teeth, or ladies' busks wrought out of the Right Whale-bone, and other like skrimshander articles, as the whalemen call the numerous little ingenious contrivances they elaborately carve out of the rough material, in their hours of ocean leisure. Some of them have little boxes of dentistical-looking implements, specially intended for the skrimshandering business. But, in general, they toil with their jack-knives alone; and, with that almost omnipotent tool of the sailor, they will turn you out anything you please, in the way of a mariner's fancy.[20]

On the other hand, the descriptions in *Moby Dick* of undecorated objects made of whalebone and whale ivory, objects that we classify as functional scrimshaw, are used for symbolic reasons, reasons that have little to do with the just-mentioned "lively sketches" on whales' teeth and busks. The "ivory Pequod,"[21] the "rare old" whaleship commanded by Captain Ahab, is itself presented metaphorically by Melville as functional (symbolically functional) scrimshaw:

> Peleg, during the term of his chief-mateship, had built upon her original grotesqueness, and inlaid it, all over, with a quaintness both of material and device, unmatched by anything except it be Thorkill-Hake's carved buckler or bedstead. She was apparelled like any barbaric Ethiopian emperor, his neck heavy with pendants of polished ivory. She was a thing of trophies. A cannibal of a craft, tricking herself forth in the chased bones of her enemies. All round, her unpanelled, open bulwarks were garnished like one continuous jaw, with the long sharp teeth of the Sperm Whale, inserted there for pins, to fasten her old hempen thews and tendons to. Those thews ran not through base blocks of landwood, but deftly travelled over sheaves of sea-ivory. Scorning a turnstile wheel at her reverend helm, she sported there a tiller; and that tiller was in one mass, curiously carved from the long narrow lower jaw of her hereditary foe. The helmsman who steered by that tiller in a tempest, felt like the Tartar, when he holds back his fiery steed by clutching its jaw. A noble craft, but somehow most melancholy! All noble things are touched with that.[22]

The *Pequod* was laden with whalebone and whale ivory as were many things on it. On deck, before departure, was "a strange sort of tent or rather wigwam . . . consisting of the long, huge slabs of limber black bone taken from the middle and highest part of the jaws of the Right Whale."[23] There was the "ivory-inlaid table"[24] in Captain Ahab's cabin, his "ivory stool,"[25] and, of course, Ahab's "barbaric white leg,"[26] the leg that "had at sea been fashioned from the polished bone of a Sperm Whale's jaw,"[27] the whalebone leg that replaced the one lost in his first encounter with Moby Dick. Then there was Captain Ahab's counterpart, the English captain of the *Samuel Enderby* out of London, whose whalebone arm substituted for one lost in *his* battle with the White Whale:

> With his ivory arm frankly thrust forth in welcome, the other captain advanced, and Ahab, putting out his ivory leg, and crossing the ivory arm (like two sword-fish blades) cried out in his walrus way, "aye, aye, hearty! let us shake bones together!—an arm and a leg!—an arm that never can shrink, d'ye see; and a leg that never can run. Where did'st thou see the White Whale?—how long ago?"[28]

We counted at least thirty references in *Moby Dick* relating to the use of whale ivory and whalebone in and on the *Pequod.* Only four of the references deal with engraved or decorated scrimshaw. Melville treats decorated scrimshaw as part of the scholarly background information on whales that permeates the book. He did not give such scrimshaw an emotional content and did not use it symbolically. It did not fit his purpose. On the other hand, the functional scrimshaw, the whale-ivory pins, the whalebone blocks, the "glittering fiddle-bows of whale ivory"[29] used by the Long Island Negroes, Ahab's "ivory" leg, the English captain's whalebone arm, are highly charged, emotive metaphors, part of the symbolism of Ahab's fanatical and suicidal search for Moby Dick, the White Whale.

Decorated Scrimshaw

Although the idea of engraved pictures *on* whales' teeth, ladies' busks, and pieces of panbone primarily started about 1815, it was not until the 1820s that the craze for pictorial scrimshaw became widespread. The heyday for such scrimshaw was in the 1825–1870 period, although pictorial scrimshaw continued to be made in the twentieth century. Decorated scrimshaw has an undetermined origin. It does not seem to come from the previously mentioned decorated powder horns of the mid–eighteenth century, nor does it seem to derive from South Seas art. Polished sperm whale teeth, tambua, have been known in such areas as the Fijis since the eighteenth century, but Fijian tambua were not usually engraved.[30]

The whole explosion of do-it-yourself art in America and Britain in the first part of the nineteenth century led naturally to putting pictures on such things as whales' teeth and busks. It was a time when many everyday things were decorated: walls of rooms, furniture, tools, and machinery. Decorated scrimshaw was related to many other popular art forms in its procedures and its predilection for copying professional or high art.

There was, as mentioned earlier, more time for such activities as scrimshawing in the mid-nineteenth century than in the pre-1815 era. This can be demonstrated by comparing statistics on whaling from Starbuck's *History of the American Whale Fishery*. The average length of a Nantucket whaling voyage in the five-year period 1800–1804 was about 13.7 months.[31] The voyages were primarily to the South Atlantic. In the second quarter of the nineteenth century, Nantucket whalers were almost entirely in the Pacific Ocean. The average length of a whaling voyage in the 1840–1844 period was 43.4 months, more than three times the length of the average voyage in the first part of the nineteenth century. It seems clear that there would have been proportionally more free time for such activities as making scrimshaw on the long Pacific voyages of the second quarter of the nineteenth century than there would have been for the earlier, much shorter voyages.

The fact that more free time was available to the average sailor on a mid-nineteenth-century whaling cruise has led to the simplistic idea that scrimshaw was the result of boredom, that whalemen had nothing better to do. However, such an idea leaves out an important element in the creation of any work of art, the pleasure principle. The true joy of making one's own work of art, however crude and however humble it may be, should never be underestimated.

Originality was never a primary aim of the scrimshawer. The three engraved teeth in Figure 160 demonstrate some of the typical approaches to the craft. The tooth on the left shows a meticulously rendered tropical bird. A close examination of the work on the tooth reveals telltale holes that indicate how the picture was made. A common practice was to paste a picture from a magazine or a book onto the tooth and to punch dozens of tiny holes through the design into the tooth with a pin or a sharp awl. The artisan then connected the dots on the tooth with lines cut with a sharp knife. The lines were filled with India ink or with carbon black made by collecting soot from a candle or lamp onto a plate. The excess ink or carbon black was rubbed off, leaving the darkened design on the white tooth. This is the kind of artwork that allowed even a novice to do a creditable job; in this case, to scrimshaw a tropical bird on the surface of a whale tooth. It is only when we turn this particular tooth over and examine the crudely drawn "Java House" on the back of the tooth that we realize it was decorated by an untrained craftsman (Figure 161). The front and back of the tooth were scrimshawed by the same man, one side being a mechanical copy, the other being a freehand drawing of an observed scene. The large tooth in the middle of Figure 160 is another matter. Here the scrimshawer has drawn freehand, without the use of guide holes, a ship over which flies an American eagle. The eagle is stylized and a bit crude, but the ship is drawn with considerable verve and realism. This tooth illustrates a general principle of scrimshaw, in that sailing vessels on which the scrimshawers lived and worked are depicted accurately. We should expect this. After years at sea the sailor would know every spar and every line and every sail of his ship, how they functioned and how they looked. Time and

Figure 160. Scrimshawed whale's teeth, second quarter of the nineteenth century. Heights, left to right: 6, 7, 5¹/₈ in. (15.2, 17.8, 13.0 cm.). (*Private collection*).

Figure 161. Reverse side of tooth at the left in Figure 247, inscribed "Java House."

again we see relatively crude scrimshawed pictures with carefully drawn, believable ships. The tooth on the right, a Victorian depiction of Anne Boleyn, was obviously copied from a magazine or book. The tooth retains evidence of pinholes in the design to indicate how it was made.

Scrimshaw reflected the often-turbulent times in which the scrimshawers were living. The first years of the nineteenth century were full of strife and uncertainty for American mariners. The possibility of being "pressed" into the service of the British navy was a hazard in British ports, and the threat of capture by British ships during the War of 1812, were added to the ever-present dangers of whaling. An intense patriotism developed in many Americans, particularly in those American seamen wandering the oceans of the earth. This patriotism was often expressed in scrimshaw. The female figure of Liberty was a favorite theme. The pair of teeth in Plate LIII, scrimshawed in color, depict resolute, beautifully costumed figures of Liberty, with American flags in their hands and shields with stars and stripes at their feet. The slim, gracefully curved pair of teeth in Plate LIV are filled with symbols of the Republic, eagles, shields, and banners with slogans. The slogans on the teeth, "VIRTUE LIBERTY AND INDEPENDENCE" and "FREE TRADE AND SAILORS RIGHTS" were references to those forces of harassment by the British that led to the War of 1812. The currency of these slogans in the first two decades of the nineteenth century (they also appeared on Liverpool creamwares[32]) suggests that these teeth were engraved in the 1810–1825 period.

The pair of large teeth in Plate LV, with engravings of children in lush, colorful tropical landscapes, are based on the tale *Paul and Virginia,* one of the most popular stories of the nineteenth century. The publication, written originally in French as *Paul et Virginie,* by Jacques Henri Bernardin de Saint-Pierre (1737–1814), is the story of two children growing up in a tropical paradise on the Ile de France (now Mauritius) in the Indian Ocean, and how their simple childhood affections for each other grew into love which was intensified when Virginia returned to France. She drowned offshore the island when her returning ship was wrecked, and Paul died of a broken heart. The sentimental story of the joys and sorrows of two children growing up in a peaceful utopia was greatly influenced by Jean-Jacques Rousseau, who, incidentally, was a close friend of Bernardin de Saint-Pierre.

The tooth in Figure 162 is a most unusual example of sailor-made scrimshaw. On it is pictured John Adams (born Alexander Smith), the last survivor of the famed *Bounty* mutiny. The story of the *Bounty* and Pitcairn Island was well known to whalemen in the South Seas. The island was a regular stopping place for supplies, even though access was difficult and dangerous. The engraving of John Adams was copied from an engraving in Captain F. W. Beechey's *Narrative of a Voyage to the Pacific,* published in 1831. The engraving itself was made from a drawing made by Captain Beechey in 1825. The practice of copying printed engravings was no doubt widespread, but only a relatively few original engravings have been identified.[33] The scrimshawer of the John Adams tooth used a Fiji Island tambua (or tabua) for his engraving. The tambua is a sperm whale's tooth which

Figure 162. Top: South Seas "tambua" whale's tooth, engraved with portrait of John Adams and the inscription "John Adams / Patriarch of Pitcairn's Island." Height: $6\frac{1}{8}$ in. (15.6 cm.). (*Private collection*). Bottom: illustration from Captain F. W. Beechey's *Narrative of a Voyage to the Pacific,* 1831.

was originally used as a ceremonial object or fetish. Holes were drilled in the tip of the tooth and the base, through which was attached a cord of sennit (coconut fiber). The tambua teeth were colored a deep reddish hue with candlenuts and turmeric powder. By constant handling they became brilliantly polished. The John Adams tooth was probably quite old when it was acquired by the scrimshawer since two holes in the base of the tooth had worn through, necessitating the drilling of a third hole. The outside of the tooth has bleached somewhat from light exposure, but the inside retains some of the dark reddish tambua-stain color.

The Susan*'s Teeth*

The best-known pieces of decorated scrimshaw are a group of engraved whales' teeth bearing views of a three-masted whaleship identified as the *Susan* of Nantucket. Most of the teeth are signed Frederick or Fred^{K} Myrick and dated 1829. The ship *Susan,* built in 1826, Captain Frederick Swain, left Nantucket September 6, 1826, and, after cruising the Pacific whaling grounds for more than two and a half years, returned to Nantucket June 9, 1829. At this writing (1986), the consensus seems to be that there are at least twenty known *Susan*'s teeth.[34] *Susan*'s teeth and teeth attributed to Frederick Myrick which have been sold at public auction in the last half-dozen years have outstripped all other pieces of scrimshaw in price, even though the auction prices have varied considerably.

We have collected scrimshaw for twenty-five years and have had a continued scholarly interest in the subject. Before writing this chapter we reviewed the rather extensive literature on scrimshaw and reexamined the principal museum collections and interviewed museum directors and curators, collectors, modern scrimshawers, dealers, and auctioneers. One of the results of this informal, though extensive, survey was the rather widespread off-the-record skepticism about the *Susan*'s teeth. To say the least, these artifacts are controversial, and we feel it would be irresponsible on our part if we did not bring the discussion into the open. The problem is whether all known *Susan*'s teeth are genuine period scrimshaw.

Two of the *Susan*'s teeth have impeccable provenances, having been in the Peabody Museum of Salem since about 1830, not long after the ship *Susan* returned to Nantucket. The "Catalog of the Museum," published in 1831, whose title page reads "The / East-India Marine Society / of / Salem," lists on a page numbered 177 at the top (and 23 at the bottom) the following items:

> 4282, Tooth of a Sperm Whale, curiously carved, [*Capt. James Cheever*]
> 4283, Another, carved by the same hand, *George Peirce.*

These two teeth, with their original East-India Marine Society numbers 4282 and 4283, are still in the Peabody Museum of Salem. Because of the fact these two *Susan*'s teeth are so well documented, we have chosen to illustrate the front and back views of one of them (Figures 163 and 164). The two sides of the tooth illustrate aspects of nineteenth-century whaling practices. In the water are men in whaleboats pursuing and harpooning whales. The front view shows the cutting-in operation with the blanket piece being cut from the whale, while the reverse side shows the rendering of the blubber in the tryworks, with a plume of smoke being whipped from the ship by the wind. The engraving on the tooth is neat, economical, and accurate. The sea is depicted by four parallel rippling lines. All the main features of the ship and its rigging are clearly shown. This tooth gives us an authoritative,

Figure 163. Scrimshawed whale's tooth, inscribed on obverse "The Susan on the Coast of Japan / Death to the living long life to the killers / Success to sailor's wives & Greasy luck to whalers." The eagle holds a banner inscribed "E. PLURIBUS / UNUM." Given to the East-India Society of Salem (NO. 4283) by George Pierce in about 1830. Length: 5$\frac{7}{8}$ in. (14.9 cm.). (*Peabody Museum of Salem*).

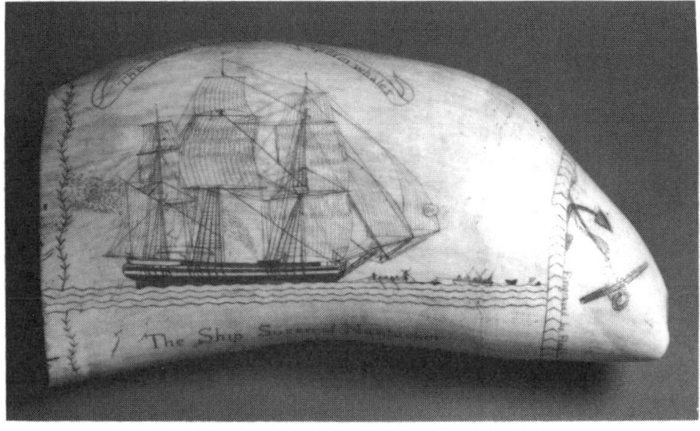

Figure 164. Reverse of tooth in Figure 163, inscribed (above) "The Susan boiling & killing sperm whales" and (below) "The ship Susan of Nantucket / Frederick Swain Master Jany 22nd 1829." At the tip: "Engraved by Fred^{k} Myrick."

contemporary picture of whaling, by a competent and knowledgeable observer. This, plus the fact the tooth entered America's oldest maritime museum soon after the return of the ship on which it was scrimshawed, underlines its importance as a landmark object of American scrimshaw.

Photographs of the Salem *Susan*'s teeth were featured in Marius Barbeau's 1952 publication, "All Hands Aboard Scrimshawing."[35] Barbeau's article focused attention on the *Susan*'s teeth, but the publication that made them famous was Everett U. Crosby's *Susan's Teeth and Much About Scrimshaw,* published privately in Nantucket in 1955. Crosby's book itself has become a much-sought item, having fetched at auction prices as high as $2400. In his book Crosby listed seven *Susan*'s teeth, four from private collections including his own, one from the Nantucket Historical Association, and two from the Peabody Museum of Salem. Crosby also referred to the publication of photographs of *Susan*'s teeth in the books of Clifford Ashley and George Dow.

In 1925 George Francis Dow's *Whale Ships and Whaling* included what may have been the first publication of a *Susan*'s tooth, picturing one belonging to the Peabody Museum.[36] Clifford Ashley's *The Yankee Whaler* (1926) included a photograph showing five teeth, one of which was a *Susan*'s tooth, with the caption: "Scrimshaw whales' teeth. The upper right tooth is the earliest dated piece of scrimshaw on record. In the author's collection."[37] (We know now that there are at least nineteen pieces of scrimshaw with dates earlier than those on the *Susan*'s teeth.)

We take a neutral position on the problem as to whether all of the twenty or more known *Susan*'s teeth are genuine period artifacts. Scrimshaw has never been subjected to the kind of rigorous systematic scientific scrutiny that many museum objects have undergone in recent years, and we feel that until the *Susan*'s teeth have been so studied, individually and as a group, no real answer to the problem will be available.

Busks

The decorated busk, which must have been a rather formidable object for a woman to cope with, was a favorite form of scrimshaw. The busk, which is a strip of whalebone, wood, or other rigid material, passed down through the front of a woman's corset to stiffen it, had been used since medieval times. A seventeenth-century definition reads: "A busk is a strong piece of Wood, or Whalebone thrust down the middle of the Stomacher."[38] Edward H. Pinto, in his book *Treen or Small Woodenware Throughout the Ages,* illustrates several English busks with eighteenth-century dates and explains their usage:

> Most busks were purely utilitarian and not intended for view, but the fashions of 1670–80 and of 1785–90 both decreed a form of bustle or crinoline for women. To accentuate the fullness at the hips, the corsage [the body of the dress] was long and wasp waisted, descending to a deep "V" in front and this created a fashion for long busks. In rustic circles, these busks were adorned with carving and presented as love tokens for insertion in the corsage. I have only seen one carved busk of the seventeenth century and, apart from one dated 1749, all the others which I have examined date between 1777 and 1799. The fashions appear to have been short-lived, which is not surprising considering how uncomfortable wearers must have found busks 14 to 15 in. long, of unwielding wood or whalebone.[39]

No busks are mentioned in Nantucket inventories of the colonial period. Photographs of two eighteenth-century busks in American collections have been published. The earlier, a slim one-inch wide whalebone busk in the Kendall Whaling Museum, is inscribed on the obverse "AS 1766" and decorated with drawings of a sloop, a sperm whale, and a six-man whaling crew in a whaleboat, and on the reverse with the name "Alden Sears."[40] The other is a baleen busk with geometric chip carving dated 1792, illustrated in Flayderman's *Scrimshaw and Scrimshanders.*[41] The latter busk is similar to those illustrated in Pinto's book on treenwares, suggesting an English origin for the piece.[42]

The five busks in Figure 165 display the same range of skills and subject matter as the scrimshawed whales' teeth illustrated earlier. Two of the busks, Number 2 and Number 5, appear to have been freehand copies of printed illustrations, while the compositions of the other three seem to have been designed for the busks, with perhaps reference to pictures in books and magazines. The busk on the left (1) has geometric decorations that made use of the ruler and a compass. Number 2 is topped with an American eagle and American flag; below are rural scenes, scenes that would have been particularly dear to a farm boy three years away from home in the South Pacific. The center busk (3) displays delightfully naive drawings of a lady (see detail in Figure 166) and an elegantly dressed gentleman. The scrimshawer, like some primitive portrait painters, was completely unable to cope with the draw-

Figure 165. Scrimshawed whalebone busks. (1) Geometric decorations with touches of red, length: 13¼ in. (34.3 cm.). (2) Free-hand drawings including American eagle and flag, height: 11¼ in. (28.6 cm.). (3) Primitive drawings, touches of red on ship flags and lady's clothing, length: 13⅛ in. (33.3 cm.). (4) Primitive drawings, inscribed "WHC/1832," length: 12¾ in. (32.4 cm.). (5) Latin American motifs, length: 13⅛ in. (33.3 cm.). (*Private collection*).

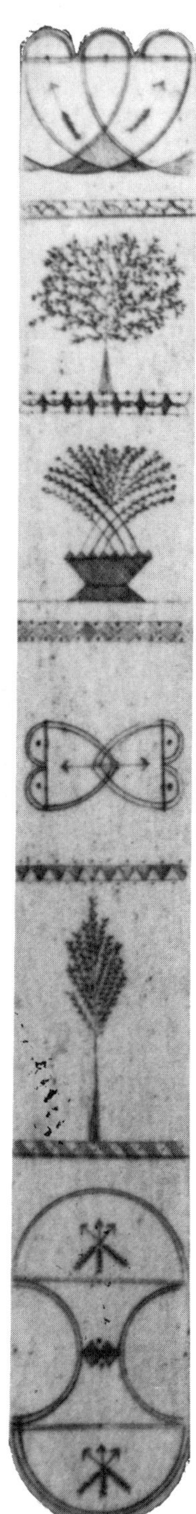

1832

Figure 166. Detail of center busk (No. 3) in Figure 165.

Figure 167. Detail of busk far right (No. 5) in Figure 165.

ing of hands. However, his ship, in the middle of the two figures, is drawn, as usual, with believable accuracy. The second busk from the right (4) is sketchy and primitive. This busk celebrates a wedding that has already taken place, or one planned. At the top is a bust of a lady enclosed in a heart shape, above a swag and a sketch of a cottage with smoke from its chimney, and the inscription "WHC / 1832." Centered are a woman and a man, arm in arm. Below is a ringing bell, the wedding bell. The busk on the far right (5) is more carefully drawn, more detailed. The motifs recall Latin America, perhaps Chile or Peru, which were regular stopping places for whalers. A detail of the majestic ship, with touches of red in its American flag, is shown in Figure 167. There is no evidence of pin-pricks on any of the busks, which suggests copying was not purely mechanical.

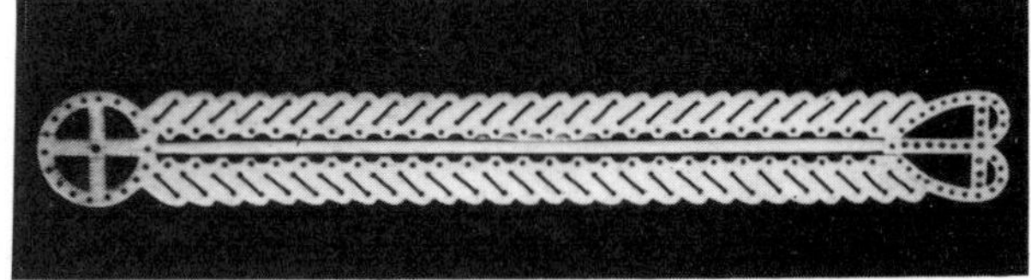

Figure 168. Pierced whalebone busk inlaid with dots of silver. Length: 13⅞ in. (35.2 cm.). (*NHA*).

One of the most spectacular of the whalebone busks is the pierced and carved busk in Figure 168. The repeated pattern of the cut-out spaces is reinforced by the pattern of the inlays of small dots of silver. The heart at the top is balanced by the circle with a cross at the bottom.

The best of the nineteenth-century busks, like the best of the jagging wheels, show little sign of use. Although in theory they were designed to be used, in practice they seemed to have functioned primarily as sentimental keepsakes. Some of the most loving work, and, to us, some of the most interesting work of the scrimshawers, was poured onto these bits of whalebone.

Jagging Wheels

Heretofore the decorated scrimshaw we have considered, teeth and busks, have been objects with engraved pictures on them. We now look at a different aspect of decorated scrimshaw, jagging wheels, utensils that were conceived in sculptural terms. Although an occasional jagging wheel has engraving on it, the best of these wheels are really small pieces of sculpture.

The jagging wheel, or pie crimper, is a tool for ornamenting pastry, having a wheel with teeth that is set in a handle. In the eighteenth century and earlier it was primarily designated a jagging iron. Whether or not the term jagging

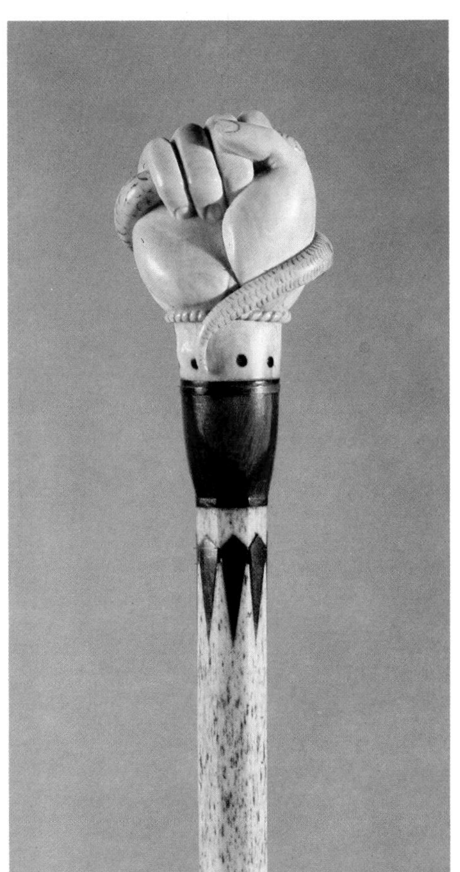
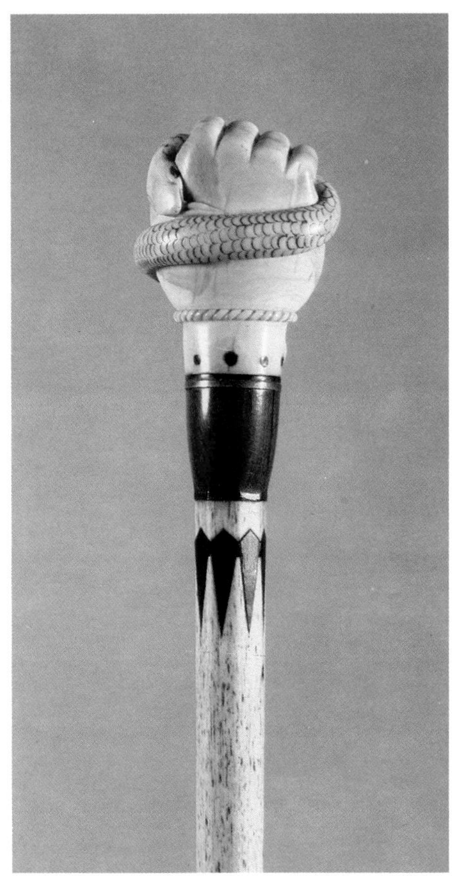

Plate LII. Detail front and back views of whalebone and whale-ivory cane, with baleen, mahogany, and silver parts. (*Private collection*).

Plate LIII. Pair of scrimshawed whale's teeth with depictions of Liberty. Height: 6½ in. (16.5 cm.). (*NHA*).

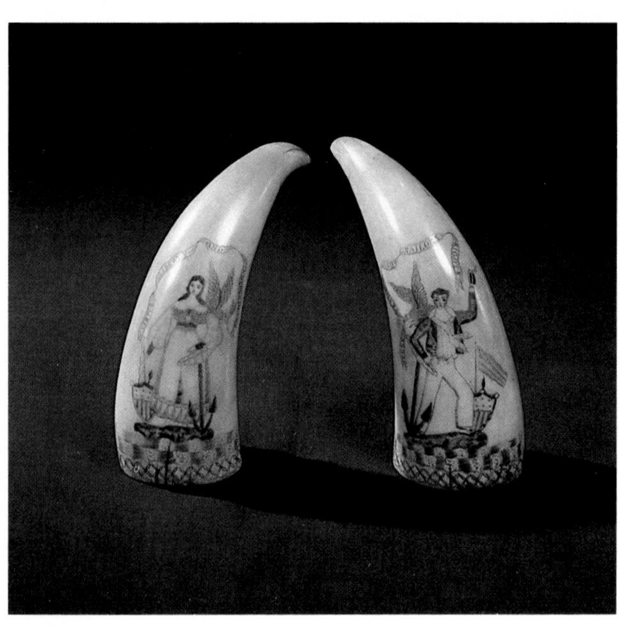

Plate LIV. Pair of scrimshawed whale's teeth. Left: lady whose dress has great balloon sleeves. In her right hand is an emblem-shield with stars and stripes, her left hand holds an anchor. On her shoulder is an eagle with banner reading: "VIRTUE LIBERTY AND INDEPENDENCE." Right: sailor holding anchor with right hand and his cap in left. By his left leg is an American flag with fifteen stars and shield with stars and stripes. On his right shoulder is an eagle with banner reading "FREE TRADE AND SAILORS RIGHTS." Height: 4⅞ in. (11.6 cm) (*Private collection*).

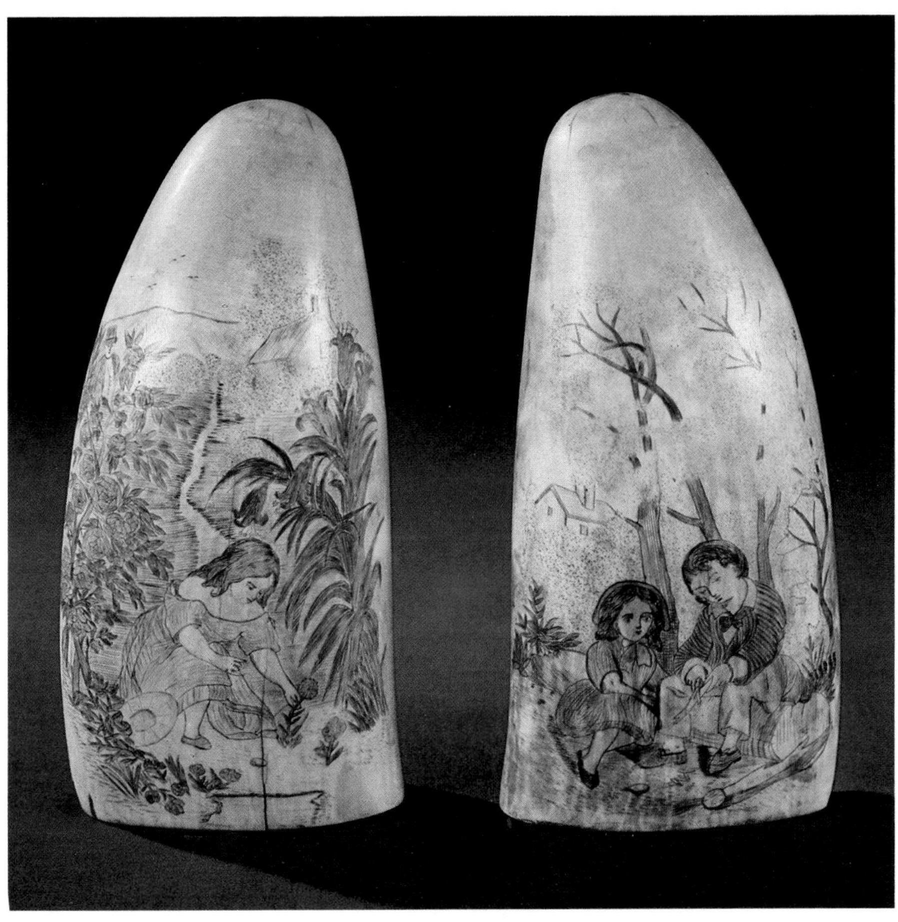

Plate LV. Pair of whale's teeth, scrimshawed in color, with pictures depicting Paul and Virginia, fictional children growing up on Ile de France (now Mauritius). Height, left: 6$^{1}/_{2}$ in. (16.5 cm.), right: 6$^{3}/_{4}$ in. (17.1 cm.). (*NHA*).

Plate LVI. Round basket, oak staves and rim, carved, half-round oak handle, cherry bottom with two lathe-turned grooves, bevelled on bottom edge. On the bottom is a mark of a label, now lost. Possibly made by Elijah Alley, circa 1875. Diameter: 8 5/8 in. (21.9 cm.), height: 3 3/4 in. (7.0 cm.). (*Private collection*).

Plate LVII. Open basket with large loop handles, mahogany bottom, oak staves, rim and handles, last half of the nineteenth century. Diameter: 12 1/2 in. (31.8 cm.), height over handles: 7 7/8 in. (20.0 cm.). (*Private collection*).

Plate LVIII. Bird carvings, painted wood on driftwood bases, by Patricia Gardner. Left to right: (1) Piping plover (1967), length: 5½ in. (14.0 cm.), height: 2½ in. (6.4 cm.). (2) Yellowlegs (1964), length: 11 in. (27.9 cm.), height: 5¼ in. (13.3cm.). (3) Black-bellied plover (1965), length: 9¼ in. (23.5 cm.), height: 3¼ in. (8.3 cm.). (4) Golden plover (1967), length: 7½ in. (19.1 cm.). (*Private collection*).

Plate LIX. Cock weather vane, painted white (with the date 1822 restored), originally on the Lancasterian School on Fair Street. Length: 30 in. (76.2 cm.), height: $19^{1}/_{2}$ in. (49.5 cm.), depth: $4^{1}/_{4}$ in. (10.8 cm.). (*NHA*).

Plate LX. Copper fire-house weather vane that was on a tall pole outside Engine House No. 8 on Center Street, Nantucket, late nineteenth century. Length: 46½ in. (118.1 cm.), height: 24 in. (61.0 cm.). (*NHA*).

Plate LXI. Sailor-boy whirligig, pine, carved and painted, made by Charles F. Ray, circa 1890. Height of figure: 15 in. (38.1 cm.). (*NHA*).

Plate LXII. Sailor-boy whirligig, painted and carved pine, tin–plate hat, attributed to William H. Chase, circa 1900–1920. Height of figure: 18 in. (45.7 cm.). (*NHA*).

Plate LXIII. Painted wood carving of a lion's head, made by James Walter Folger in 1883. Signed on back: "Jas. Walter Folger / Nantucket / Mass. 1883." Height: 19 1/2 in. (49.5 cm.), width: 17 1/2 in. (44.5 cm.), depth: 10 1/2 in. (26.7 cm.). (*Collection of the authors*).

Plate LXIV. Coat of arms of the Gardner family, inscribed: "Drawn by Eunice Gardner / Nantucket June ye 7th 1796." Height: 14 in. (35.6 cm.), width: 10 in. (25.4 cm.). (*NHA*).

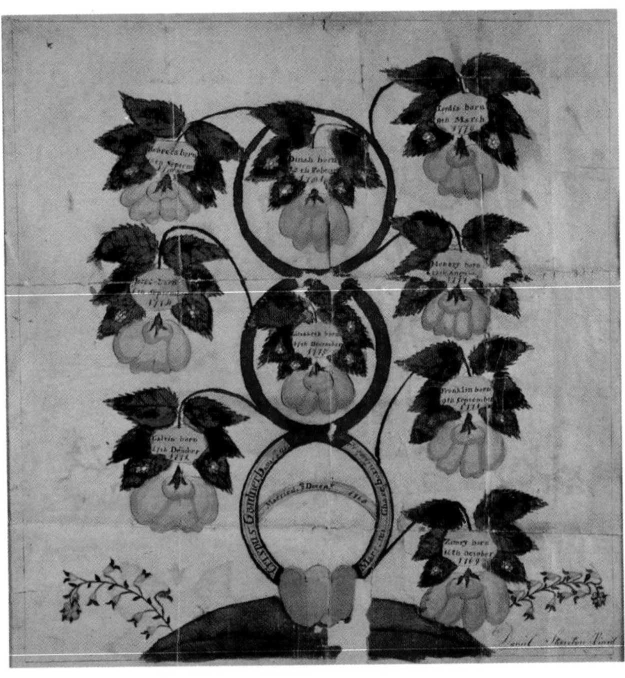

Plate LXV. Gardner family tree, from Crispus Gardner and Margaret Chase, married December 4, 1766; latest date: 1779. Signed: "Daniel Stanton, Pinxit." Height: $13^{1}/_{8}$ in. (33.3 cm.), width: $12^{1}/_{2}$ in. (31.8 cm.) (*Courtesy Robert Cary Caldwell*).

Plate LXVI. Sea chest of Albert W. Starbuck, with a watercolor drawing of the ship *Agnes,* a merchantman out of New York, circa 1831. Height: 13 1/2 in. (34.3 cm.), depth: 13 1/2 in. (38.4 cm.), length: 29 3/4 in. (75.6 cm.). (*NHA*).

Plate LXVIII. A watercolor from the journal of the *Edward Cary* titled "A View of / Tharataka Beach / Bay of Islands," February 1855. Height: 7 1/2 in. (19.1 cm.), width: 12 in. (30.5 cm.). (*NHA—L73*).

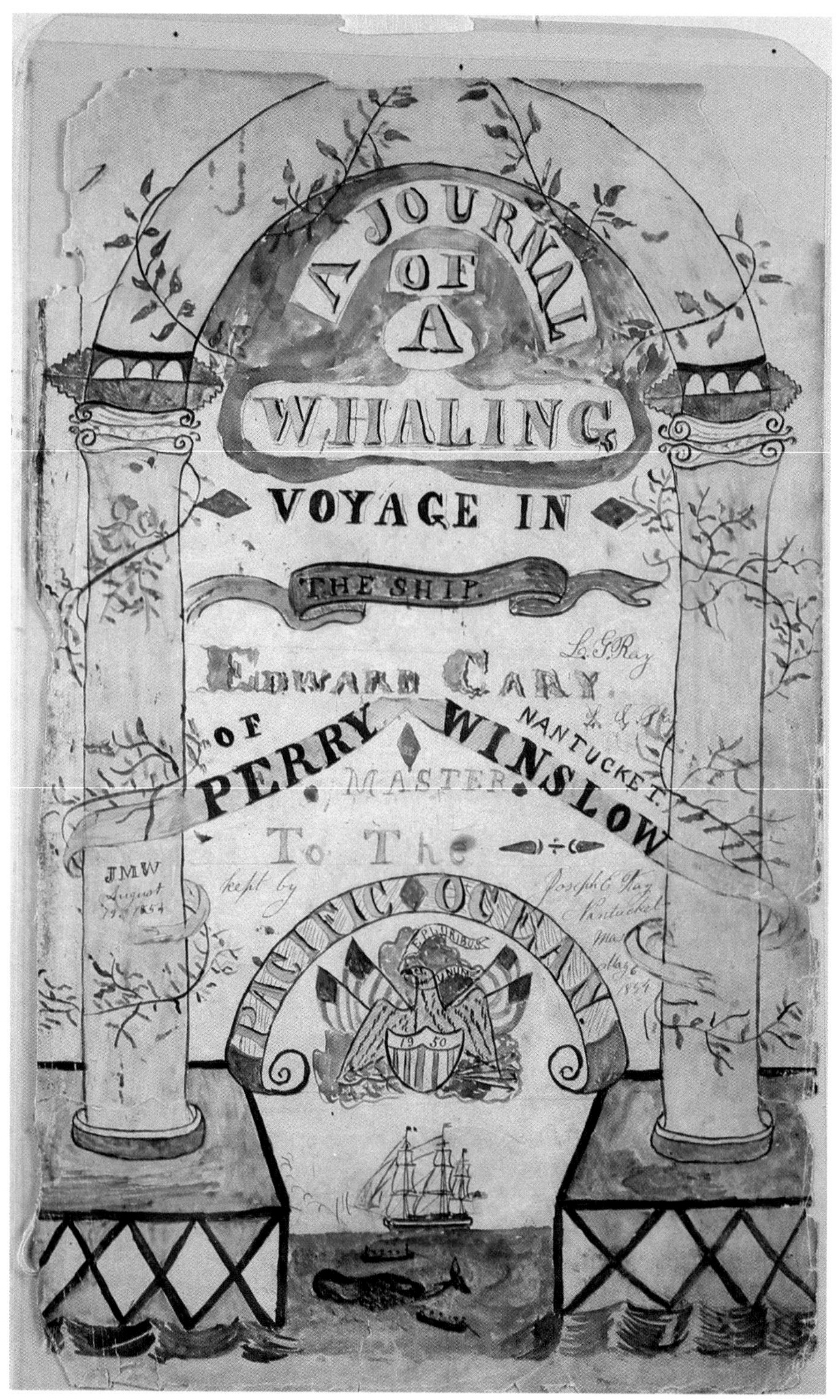

Plate LXVII. Title page of a whaling journal: "A JOURNAL / OF / A/ WHALING / VOYAGE IN / THE SHIP / EDWARD CARY / OF Nantucket / PERRY WINSLOW / MASTER / TO The / PACIFIC OCEAN." In script: "L. B. Ray," "kept by Joseph E. Ray / Nantucket / May 6 / 1854"; "JMW / August / 19th 1854." Height: 12 in. (30.5 cm.), width: $7\frac{1}{2}$ in. (19.1 cm.). (*NHA–L73*).

Plate LXIX. Tea caddy, wood, painted in red and black, three Chinese figures on front, water lilies on sides, inside are two pewter compartments to hold tea, circa 1804. Owned originally by Captain James Cary, master and half owner of Ship *Rose*. Height: $10\frac{1}{2}$ in. (26.7 cm.), depth: $9\frac{1}{2}$ in. (24.1 cm.), length: $12\frac{1}{2}$ in. (31.6 cm.). (*Courtesy Robert Cary Caldwell*).

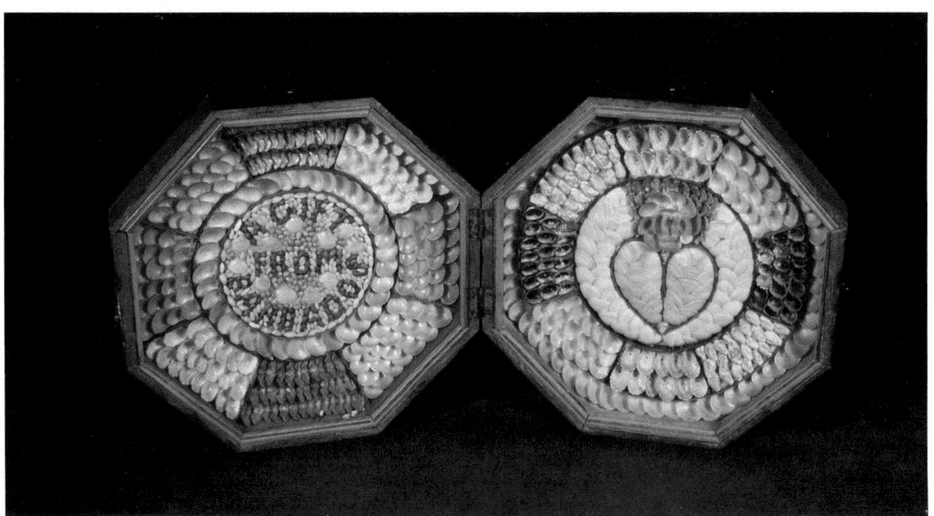

Plate LXX. Sailor's valentine with an inscription in brown shells: "A GIFT / FROM / BARBADOS." Size of each octagonal case: 9 x 9 in. (22.7 x 22.7 cm.). (*Collection of the authors*).

Plate LXXI. Portrait of Emma Cartwright painted in China by Hinqua, circa 1860, above the daguerreotype from which it was copied. On the back of the portrait is a label with the inscription: "HINQUA / Portrait & Chart / Painter / Hongkong." The portrait: 16 x 13 in. (40.6 x 30.0 cm.). The daguerreotype: 3½ x 2½ in. (8.9 x 6.4 cm.). (*Courtesy Mrs. John P. Elder*).

Plate LXXII. Reverse painting on glass portrait of Mary Coffin Nichols, circa 1849. Height: 19⅝ in. (49.8 cm.), width: 13¾ in. (34.9 cm.). (*NHA*).

Plate LXXIII. Shadow-box lithograph picture of Napoleon III and his bride, Eugenie-Marie de Mentijo of Spain, tinsel on figures and in background, in its original gilt rococo Victorian frame. Brought to Nantucket, possibly from England, circa 1860, by an ancestor of Catherine Defrieze Fitzpatrick. Height of frame: 23¼ in. (59.1 cm.), width: 20 in. (50.8 cm.). (*Collection of the authors*).

Plate LXXIV. Model of an Indonesian prau, made entirely of cloves, brought to Nantucket in 1855 by Captain Richard Mitchell in the ship *Milton*. Length: 20 1/2 in. (52.1 cm.). (*NHA*).

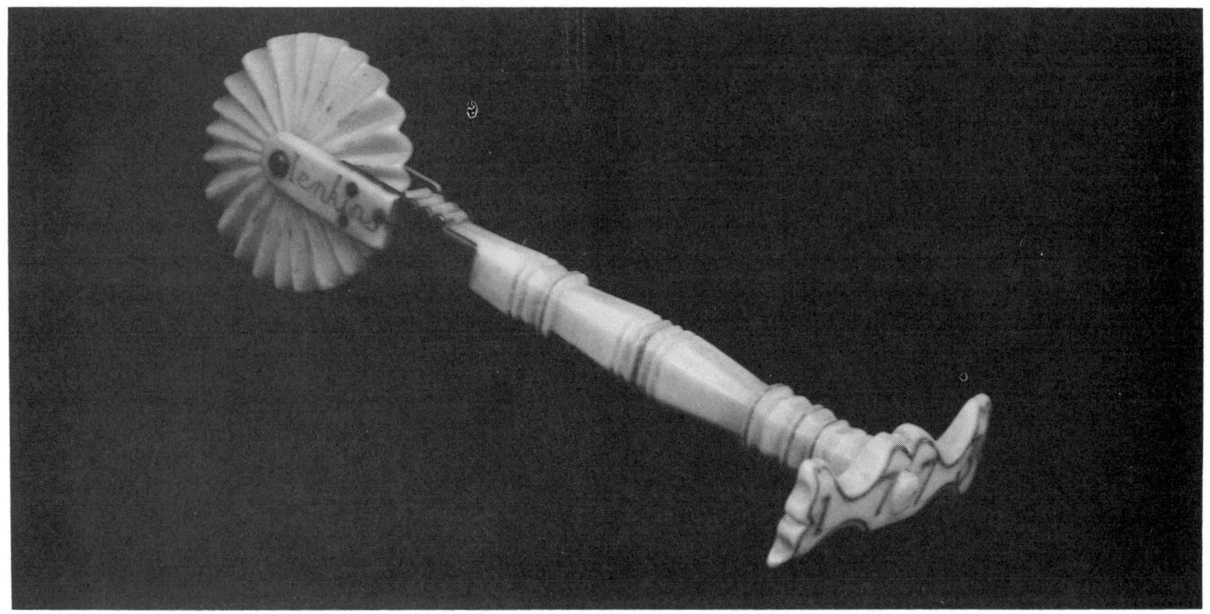

Figure 169. Walrus-ivory jagging wheel given by Captain Charles Jenkins of Nantucket to his five-year old daughter Judith in 1773. Engraved: "Judith / Jenkins / 1773." (*Museum of Art, Rhode Island School of Design*).

iron included wheels made of wood or whalebone is not known. There are jagging "irons" listed in twelve Nantucket inventories of the colonial period. Samuel Barker's 1740 inventory listed "1 Jagging iron—0–4–0," and William Bunker's 1772 inventory included a "Jagging iron—0–10–." Two of the inventories had variant spellings: "Janing iron" and "Jag iron."

The walrus-ivory jagging wheel in Figure 169, dated 1773, is the oldest known dated piece of Nantucket scrimshaw. It was given to the Museum of Art of the Rhode Island School of Design in 1914 by Miss Eliza A. Peckham. The museum's original inventory card, which calls it a "Pie-pinker," notes:

> This wheel was brought to Miss Peckham's grandmother, Judith Jenkins, when she was five years old, in 1773, by Judith Jenkins' father, a sea captain of Nantucket.

The information on the 1914 Rhode Island School of Design inventory card checks precisely with Nantucket records. The *Nantucket Vital Records* lists Judith Jenkins, daughter of Charles and Margaret (Swain) Jenkins, as being born July 17, 1768, which indicates she would have been five years old in 1773. Her father, Charles Jenkins, who was born May 19, 1743, was listed in the land court records as a "mariner" in 1771.

The Jenkins jagging wheel looks as if it had had a piece broken off. There appears to have been a finial, or perhaps an ivory fork, on the end nearest the viewer in Figure 169, the rounded stub of which is still visible.

The group of eight jagging wheels in Figure 170 shows a variety of subject matters, techniques, and materials. These wheels feature a snake, a dog, a tropical bird, and a horse, plus baroque, openwork compositions. The mate-

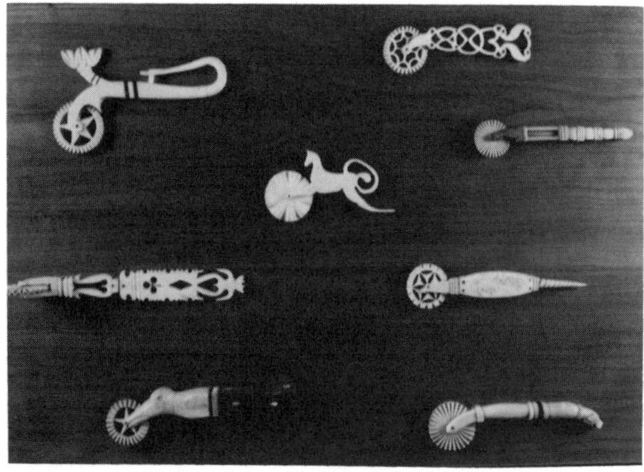

Figure 170. Jagging wheels or pie crimpers. Clockwise from upper right: (1) carved handle with tortoise shell between layers of ivory, length 6 1/8 in. (15.6 cm.); (2) ivory and whalebone with brass fittings, length 6 3/4 in. (17.1 cm.); (3) ivory and whalebone, handle inset with mahogany, length 7 5/8 in. (19.4 cm.); (4) ivory with baleen collar, length 7 3/8 in. (18.7 cm.); (5) ivory, fitted with baleen, ebony handle, length 7 5/8 in. (19.4 cm.); (6) carved ivory, length 9 1/2 in. (24.1 cm.); (7) carved ivory with baleen fittings, length 7 in. (17.8 cm.). Center: carved ivory, length 5 1/4 in. (13.3 cm.). (*Private collection*).

Figure 171. Jagging wheel in center of Figure 170.

rials include whale ivory, whalebone, baleen, tortoiseshell, brass, and mahogany. The hand of an inspired whittler is evident in these wheels. The center jagging wheel of the group (Figure 171) is a tiny piece of sculpture fashioned with great verve. The paper-thin fluted ivory wheel is a tour de force of craftsmanship.

The fancier jagging wheels were clearly valued more as works of art than as tools. Late in the nineteenth century jagging wheels became almost completely ornamental. The multiple-wheel jagging wheels (with up to seven wheels) were not designed for ornamenting pies.[43] They were made for show.

Reproductions and Fakes

Curators of two museums having collections of scrimshaw informed us that more than 90 percent of the "scrimshaw" brought to them for inspection and valuation by the general public in recent years have been fakes or reproductions. Such material can be classified in three categories:

1. Outright fakes, objects meant to fool the unwary.
2. Copies of old scrimshaw, made without any attempt at faking. Modern scrimshaw.
3. Plastic teeth.

1. *Outright fakes.* Some are very good indeed. When old "period" plain polished teeth are scrimshawed by an expert and great care is used to remove the "burr" left by the knife inscribing the surface, very convincing fakes can be made. Such fakes often have the names of specific vessels and dates on them. Experts who have handled a lot of scrimshaw over a long period of time are seldom fooled, but there will always be questionable pieces. Our advice is that if there is any doubt about a piece, have nothing to do with it. There are

many other forms of fake scrimshaw besides teeth: fake doll beds, fake candlesticks, fake pie crimpers, fake furniture, and on and on. Many fakes, however, are fairly obvious. They look new! We discussed in Chapter 4 the practice of "beautifying" old wood boxes and other objects by inlaying them with whalebone and whale ivory.

2. *Copies of old teeth; modern scrimshaw.* Hobbyists and others have for years copied old teeth for fun. Such scrimshawed teeth only become fakes when they are presented as the real thing, that is, as period scrimshaw. To these must be added the considerable volume of contemporary scrimshaw made in the last quarter century by professional scrimshawers, a business that has reached almost the level of a cottage industry. Most modern scrimshaw is signed by makers who are proud of their work. Nevertheless, such modern scrimshaw *has* been sold as nineteenth-century, sailor-made work.

3. *Plastic teeth.* In recent years plastic "polymer ivory" teeth have been widely marketed. Many of these teeth are reproductions of scrimshawed teeth from well-known public collections such as the Mystic Seaport Museum, the Peabody Museum of Salem, and the Nantucket Historical Association. These plastic reproductions are clearly marked. The problem is that some of these reproductions have had their mold marks removed or obliterated and have been sold as real scrimshaw, fooling some novices. In addition to the American plastic teeth, there has been a flood of plastic "scrimshawed" teeth, walrus tusks, panbone, and so forth, from England, with real and fictitious vessels and dates, which are *not marked as reproductions.* Richard Malley has suggested ways of identifying plastic "scrimshaw":

> Under long-wave ultra-violet light, real bone and ivory appear bright white, while polymer pieces so tested do not react. Another nondestructive test involves the use of moderate power (about 30x) magnification. Tiny, perfectly round air bubbles, a result of the liquid molding process, can be seen on the surface, especially near the ends of the piece.[44]

These brief notes on fakes and reproductions are primarily cautionary. Every field of arts and antiques has the problem. Objects of value have been reproduced and faked since Roman times. *Caveat emptor.*

10. Baskets

The Nantucket basket, the wooden-bottomed, finely made rattan basket, long designated a lightship basket, and the post–World War II lady's pocketbook-basket are well known on and off the island. They are living evidence of this oldest of crafts, but they are only part of the history of island basketry. A great variety of baskets were used by the white settlers in the seventeenth and eighteenth centuries, and, long before the coming of the white man, the island Indians made and used baskets for the storage and transport of foodstuffs.

The basket, most simply defined as a woven container, dates far back in the history of mankind:

> Basket-making has been called the mother of pottery; as evidence may be gathered from the early ceramic art of the more remote antiquity of the former craft. The potter used a basket mould long before the invention of his wheel, for such pieces of pottery show that the clay had been moulded around a basket structure.[1]

A 1674 account by Daniel Gookin describes contemporary Massachusetts Indian baskets:

> From the tree where the bark grows they make several sorts of baskets, great and small. Some will hold four bushels, or more: and so downward, to a pint. In their baskets they put their provisions. Some of their baskets are made of rushes, some of bents: others of maize husks: others, of a kind of wild hemp: and some, of barks of trees: many of them very neat and artificial, with the portraitures of birds, beasts, fishes, and flowers upon them in colours.[2]

Although no Nantucket Indian baskets of the seventeenth or eighteenth centuries are known to have survived, two seventeenth-century coastal New England Algonkin baskets are known.[3] One of these baskets was shown at the exhibition "New England Begins: The Seventeenth Century" at the Museum of Fine Arts, Boston, in 1982. It was a small 4½-inch Narragansett basket from Rhode Island, circa 1675. The vertical warp of the basket was made from the inner bark of basswood, the horizontal weft of twisted corn husks, interwoven with red wool, producing a pattern of two bands of zigzags with striped borders.[4]

In the eighteenth century, a time when Nantucket probate inventories were specific and detailed, there was only one mention of baskets in the ten inventories of the island Indians.[5] The inventory of Benjamin Tashimays, whose estate was probated November 29, 1770, listed: "To Baskets—0–0–8½."[6] That the ten inventories, covering the period 1727 to 1770, would contain only one mention of baskets seems odd when we consider that the inventories of the English Nantucketers of the same period included eighty-three baskets. However, we do have evidence that Indians were making baskets in the pre-Revolutionary War period. The account book of the Starbuck "store," which had extensive dealings with Indians in the seventeenth and eighteenth centuries, includes records of Indians selling baskets over a seventy-one year period:[7]

1686: Solomon: "by feathers, baskets and all 23¼ lb. of feathers—00/40/00."
1687: Wimond: "credit by—of a basket—00/05/03."
1691: Old Squa: "by 5 baskets 00/05/00."
1731: Beriah: "basket 3/9."
1757: Job: "By 2 new baskets 5/0."

There are a number of nineteenth-century Indian baskets still extant on the island. Several of these baskets are associated with Abram Quary, the last male Nantucket Indian, who died in 1854.[8] The best visual evidence we have of Abram Quary is the painting of him in the Nantucket Atheneum (Figure 172), done in 1851 by Herminia Borchard Dassel, a German-born genre and portrait painter who came to America in 1849. The matter-of-fact depiction of Quary in his small house, with a view of the harbor and the town through the window, gives us a glimpse of some of his possessions, which include three baskets and a handwoven straw hat. On the floor by Quary's feet is an old basket, with a broken spot, filled with newly gathered herbs. This coarsely woven splint basket, slightly smaller than a clothes basket, is of an undetermined origin. The basket on the table, woven with contrasting brown and straw-colored horizontal stripes, is similar to other nineteenth-century Algonkin baskets of the kind often decorated with "potato"-stamped designs. The most unusual basket in the painting is the square bottle–shaped basket with handle on the mantel at the left. Although it is difficult to discern from the painting, it appears that the basket may have been woven around a bottle, the top of which is hinted at in the picture.

Dassel, an itinerant artist, while she was on Nantucket in 1851, also painted a smaller bust portrait of Quary and two portraits of Maria Mitchell, who by that time was recognized as America's leading woman astronomer.[9]

Baskets in Colonial Inventories

We counted a total of eighty-four baskets in the pre–Revolutionary War inventories of Nantucket (eighty-three in the English inventories and one in the Indian inventories). The table on page 195 lists these baskets using the names as recorded in the inventories. Baskets were listed in thirty-five inventories, about one-fourth of the total. Most had values of one to twelve shillings, with an overall average value of 5½ shillings. Five were valued at one pound sterling or more. Thomas Brock (1750) had a "clothes basket £1." Benjamin Worth (1750) had "one nuns basket—1–0–0," and "Ditto one with a cover—1–5–0." Thomas Carr (1757) had a "Baby Basket—0–30–0," and Seth Hussey's 1776 inventory included "One Western Island Basket—0–30–0." The higher value of these baskets suggests that all five were large baskets. The baby basket could have been a crib or cradle with hood, perhaps of a type related to the famous wicker cradle belonging to the Pilgrim Society of Plymouth, Massachusetts, that was supposed to have rocked Peregrine White (1620–1704) after her birth on board the *Mayflower* in Provincetown Harbor.[10] We have not identified the term "nuns basket," only guessing it might be a large oblong willow basket with a handle in the middle. A clothes basket would probably

have been a large oblong basket, possibly with small handles at each end. The "Western Island Basket" refers to a basket from the Azores, a place regularly visited by whalers fishing the South Atlantic. The most common basket in the inventories of eighteenth-century Nantucket was a "stick" basket, probably a rough type of splint basket woven around "sticks" or twigs, usually round, resulting in a fairly stiff, sturdy basket.[11]

The variety of baskets in the early inventories suggests that many were imported to the island, either from the mainland or from England. Basket making had been a recognized trade in England since medieval times and there had been a "Basketmakers' Company Craft Gild" in London since the year 1569.[12] There was no one called a basket maker in either the land court or probate records of Nantucket in the seventeenth and eighteenth centuries.

The Lightship Basket

The origin of the classic Nantucket basket, a type known since the latter part of the nineteenth century as a lightship basket because of the fact that some were made on board the *South Shoal Lightship,* is obscure. The lightship basket was a tightly woven rattan (cane) basket, usually with white oak staves or ribs, an oak rim around the top, an oak handle, and a wooden bottom. An old rhyme emphasized the oak parts of the lightship basket:

I'm made out of oak
I'm strong and I'm stout
Don't lose me or burn me
And I'll never wear out

Figure 172. Herminia Bochard Dassel, "Abram Quary, the Last Indian on Nantucket Island" (1851), oil on canvas, 33 x 30 in. (83.8 x 76.2 cm.). (*Nantucket Atheneum*).

(In the 1920s Mitchy Ray revised the verse by changing the first line to read: "I was made on Nantucket.")

This type of basket dates from at least the middle of the nineteenth century and probably earlier. The descriptions of baskets in the eighteenth-century inventories are not explicit enough to tell whether the lightship basket–type dates that far back. All we know is that it was a well-established form by 1856 when molds were first brought onto the *South Shoal Lightship,* and that by 1866 considerable numbers were being made on board the lightship. Based purely on appearances, there are some very dark, aged-looking, unsophisticated baskets that *seem* to be much older than such dated baskets as the 1868 basket made by R. Folger in Figure 173 and the basket in Figure 174 made by Captain James Wyer in 1877. This, of course, is a subjective judgment, but it seems reasonable to think the form dates back at least to the 1820s or 1830s or possibly earlier. It was only in the last quarter of the nineteenth century, after the baskets had been made on lightships for some time, that they were dubbed lightship baskets. In the 1860s they were called rattan baskets.

That the lightship would become a center of Nantucket basket making in the last half of the nineteenth century was due in great measure to the lonely life aboard a vessel which went nowhere, anchored twenty-four miles off Sankaty Head, with two bright beacon-lights and a bell which rang every two minutes during a fog that could last for days. Gustav Kobbé, who wrote in 1891 about the lightship, the full name of which was *No. 1 Nantucket, New South Shoal,* a 275-ton schooner, 103 feet long, noted:

> Another old whaling captain told me that the loneliest thing he had ever seen at sea was a polar bear floating on a piece of ice in the Arctic Ocean; the next loneliest object to that had been the South Shoal Lightship.[13]

Figure 173. Basket made by R. Folger, stencilled on the inside of the maple bottom: "R. FOLGER/ MAKER/NANTUCKET/MASS." On the bottom, printed in ink, is the inscription "DAWES/1868." Oak staves, rim and handle. Diameter: 8 in. (20.3 cm.), height: 5³/₈ in. (13.7 cm.). (*Heritage Plantation of Sandwich*).

The job of the men aboard the lightship was both dangerous and filled with monotony. By 1891 the lightship had, in storms, broken loose from its moorings twenty-seven times, once drifting ashore at Montauk on Long Island. A greater danger was that of being run down and sunk by another vessel. This happened on May 15, 1934, at 11:05 A.M. The White Star Liner *Olympia* appeared suddenly out of the fog heading straight for the *South Shoal Lightship*, cutting her in two, killing seven of the eleven men on board.

The monotony involved the long hours between chores. There was a library of books on board but apparently the men were not readers. Basket making quickly became a favorite time-occupier. The men spent eight months out of the year on the vessel and were entirely out of touch with the mainland from December to May. Twice during the spring and summer the men had two two-month leaves at home in Nantucket.

Everett Crosby, in his *Books and Baskets Signs and Silver of Old-Time Nantucket* (1940) noted that: "James Wood, Sr., states he was on the South Shoal boat from August, 1866, to July, 1867, while Ben Morris was captain, and that most of the men aboard were making baskets and clothes pins."[14] Crosby also stated: "In November, 1866, Captain Charles B. Ray informed the *Inquirer and Mirror* that he had completed his 200th rattan (lightship) basket, 140 of which he had sold up to that time."[15] (The latter statement could be misleading since Ray, who had been a whaleship master (the *Russell*, 1841–1845, the *Susan,* 1846–1851), did not

Figure 174. Basket made in 1877 by Captain James Wyer, a retired whaling master, at his house at 8 Pleasant Street, and exchanged with his step-daughter, Mary Starbuck, for a blueberry pie. Diameter: 10 in. (25.4 cm.), height: 6¹/₄ in. (15.9 cm.). (*Presented to the Nantucket Historical Association by Mary Starbuck*).

serve on the *South Shoal Lightship.* His baskets were made in Nantucket, not on the lightship.)

Kobbé discussed basket making aboard the *South Shoal Lightship* in 1891:

> A number of stores in Nantucket sell what are known as lightship-baskets. They come in "nests," a nest consisting of five or eight baskets of various sizes fitting one into the other. These baskets are made only on the South Shoal Lightship. Their manufacture has been attempted ashore, but has never paid. This is because there is a very narrow margin of profit in them for the purpose of whiling away the weary winter hours. In summer the crew occupies its sparetime "scrimshawing," an old whaling term for doing ingenuous mechanical work, but having aboard the South Shoal the special meaning of preparing the strips of wood and rattan for the manufacture of the baskets in winter. The bottoms are turned ashore. The blocks over which the baskets are made have been aboard the ship since she was first anchored off the New South Shoal in 1856. The sides of the basket are of white oak or hickory, filled in with ratan, and they are round or oval, of graceful lines and great durability, the sizes to a nest ranging from a pint to a peck and a half.[16]

Kobbé's statement that baskets were only made aboard the lightship is erroneous. Many baskets were made ashore, some by people with no connection with the lightship.[17] Neither R. Folger nor Captain James Wyer, whose baskets are shown in Figures 173 and 174, was ever involved with the lightship.

Although baskets were made for family and friends, the summer people were a prime market. An advertisement in the *Inquirer & Mirror,* July 5, 1889, announced their availability:

> LIGHTSHIP BASKETS
>
> of superior workmanship made on board/ South Shoal Lightship by
>
> THOMAS BARRALLY
>
> For sale at residence, Mt. Vernon St.

Figure 175 shows lightship baskets for sale in the shop of Jacob Abajian's *Oriental Bazaar,* which was located on the east side of Center Street between Main and India, as it was in 1897. The "bric-a-brac" included Oriental carpets, antique furniture and silver, knickknacks for the mantel, and beside the lady at the left in the photograph, lightship baskets, including a nest of five, each with two small flattened loop handles. Abajian came to Nantucket in 1883 and maintained a shop on Center Street until the 1930s. He died in 1937.

Construction

The construction of lightship baskets varied little from their beginnings. We feel a brief description of how they were made[18] plus a discussion of some of the fine points of construction will be helpful in establishing a basis for connoisseurship.

The foundation building block of the basket is the bottom. The round bottoms were turned on a wood lathe, from pine, maple, cherry, and occasionally mahogany. Oval bottoms were cut with a jigsaw. Usually the bottoms were left plain, but sometimes concentric circles were scored in round bottoms, and, once in a while, a maker formed a more elaborate turned bottom with grooves. A slot was cut around the edge of the bottom to receive the ribs or staves of the basket. The slot was about one-quarter inch deep, cut by a small handsaw or a chisel on the lathe. Most of the bottom edges were left plain, although once in a while the edge was shaped.

The bottom was then fastened with a screw onto a mold made in the form of the basket. A round bottom would have a hole in the center and an oval basket would have two symmetrically placed holes through which screws were placed. The staves or ribs of the basket were made by splitting a wedge of oak or hick-

Figure 175. The shop of Jacob Abajian on Center Street, Nantucket, as it was in 1897. On the left are lightship baskets for sale. (*Photograph NHA*).

ory into thin (perhaps 1/16 inch) strips, the length and width of which depended on the size of the basket. The staves were tapered, so that they were smaller at the bottom, and usually beveled. The staves, after being softened in water, were then placed in the slot of the bottom and bent to fit the mold and held in place by a cord. When dry, they assumed the shape of the basket mold. Then a thin strip of rattan, or cane, also softened in water, was woven in and out around the staves until the weaving was completed. Figure 176 shows Clinton Mitchell "Mitchy" Ray making an oval basket in the 1930s. The hollow mold belonged originally to his grandfather, the previously mentioned Captain Charles B. Ray. In the photograph Ray is shown completing the weaving of the cane on the oak staves.

The top of the basket was finished off with a rim made of two hoops of half-round oak strips which were riveted to the top of the staves to form the rim. The rim was finished by wrapping it with cane, with the slot at the top, where the cane-ends separate the two parts of the rim, being covered by a strip of cane. Rims were wrapped with either one continuous piece of cane or with double criss-crossed strips. Occasionally a basket is found with a rim that apparently never had been wrapped with cane.

Handles were an important element in the design of a basket. Much attention was given

Figure 176. Clinton Mitchell "Mitchy" Ray, in the 1940s, working on a basket using a mold originally belonging to his grandfather, Captain Charles B. Ray. (*Photograph courtesy Edouard Stackpole*).

to handle design in the nineteenth century, compared to the often featureless, flat handles of many recent baskets. Nineteenth-century handles were often slim, with individual makers developing their own style of handle. The bail handles were fastened onto the basket in two ways. Some of the older baskets simply extended sturdy staves above the tops of the baskets and the handles were held on the inside of the staves by means of rivets or pins. The other method was to rivet brass "ears" onto staves on opposite sides of the basket and to insert the ears into slots in the handle, holding it in place by means of riveted metal pins.[19] These two types of fasteners were used in overlapping time periods. It is thought that the wooden ears were used on the earliest baskets and continued to be used until the beginning of the twentieth century. The brass ears appear on baskets dated in the 1860s and their use continues today.

Flattened *loop* handles were often so delicately made that they were easily broken. Plate LVII shows a basket with boldly sculptured loop handles that complement the rim of this sturdy, neatly woven basket.

The cane used in weaving lightship baskets is rattan, obtained from a tough and flexible climbing palm found in Asia, which comes in long lengths and has sharp barbs. The outer layer is pulled off and discarded, and the outer bark is split into strands for use in chair caning and basket making. The inside pith of the rattan is milled into many thicknesses and is widely used in present-day pocketbook-baskets for staves and rims since it is softer and easier to work than the oak traditionally used for these parts.

Lightship baskets are said to have come out of the cooperage tradition. As pointed out earlier in the book, there was a very large concentration of coopers in colonial Nantucket making whale-oil casks and other woodenware containers—a total of 189 coopers recorded in the pre–Revolutionary War era. The construction of a lightship basket is related to that of a wooden cask in that it has a flat wooden bottom and staves acting as ribs for the rattan basketwork. The cask has a groove around the bottom of the staves to receive the flat barrelhead; the groove or channel is "plowed out" by a circular plane called a croze, while the bottom of a basket has a slot sawed into its edge to receive the bent staves. The rim of the basket is related to the hoops of a cask. Certainly the Nantucket lightship basket, as made in the 1860–1940 period, is more closely related to the products of the cooper than to the usual Indian basket.

Mitchy Ray, his father, Charles F. Ray, and

his grandfather, Charles B. Ray, all basketmakers, *did* come from a family of coopers. Charles B.'s grandfather, Alexander Ray (1734–1822), was a cooper, as were four of Alexander's brothers, William, Samuel, John, and Enoch. All five were listed as coopers in pre–Revolutionary War Nantucket court records.

Although the Rays are mentioned in a well-known piece of doggerel, "The Rays and Russells coopers are," a study of the occupations in colonial Nantucket (page 221) shows that there were far more coopers with names *other* than Ray and Russell. There were a total of six Rays and five Russells listed as coopers, while there were twenty-seven Coffins, twenty Gardners, thirteen Folgers, twelve Swains, ten Bunkers, ten Colemans, nine Barnards, and seven Worths listed as coopers in the seventeenth and first three-quarters of the eighteenth century.

There is no evidence that the baskets made by members of the Shaker sect in the first half of the nineteenth century had any influence on Nantucket basket making, but Shaker baskets *were* known on the island. Henry J. Dufrees' account book[20] includes the following entry:

> March 11, 1842—gave Gorham Macy 7 Shaker bushel Baskets to sell on my account a/4 4.67

Figures 177–181 and Plates LVI and LVII illustrate a sampling of Nantucket lightship baskets made in the last half of the nineteenth and the first part of the twentieth centuries.[21] The nest of baskets in Figure 177 may or may not have been made on the *South Shoal Lightship*, but it is typical of the baskets made there. The covered basket in Figure 178, a lady's "work-basket," inscribed on the bottom "M F HAMMOND / 1891," is a type made by a number of makers. Oblong baskets, like the one in Figure 179, were also covered by fitting them with two simple wooden lids hinged on a fixed piece across the middle of the basket beneath the handle.

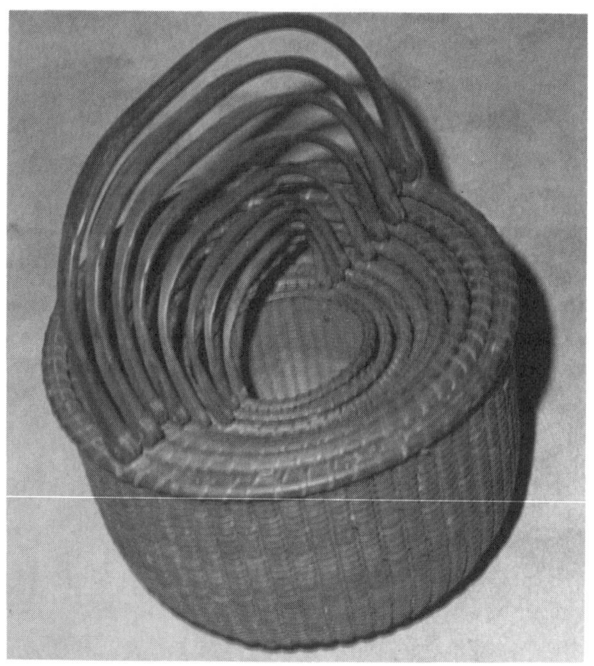

Figure 177. Nest of eight baskets, oak staves, rims and handles, late nineteenth century. Diameter of largest basket: 13 in. (30.0 cm.), height: 8¾ in. (21.0 cm.). (*Heritage Plantation of Sandwich*).

The basket on the right in Figure 180, the bottom of which is shown in Figure 181 with its large-scale brand "HADWICK" (for CHADWICK), has an unusual provenance. It was made in the town jail in 1885 by William H. Chadwick, the cashier of the Pacific National Bank in Nantucket, who had been caught with his hand in the till. It was found that Chadwick, a highly respected businessman, had falsified bank statements and borrowed heavily, to the tune of $50,000 (the equivalent of a million dollars or more today), to build a "mansion," later called Chadwick's Folly, in Squam with a spectacular view of the Atlantic. The family legend is that he made the little basket while in jail awaiting trial. The case never went to court; he was never convicted.[22] In 1914

Figure 178. Lady's work basket, hinged cover with sycamore finial, oak staves, rim and handle, maple bottom. Brass hinge and brass straps on handle. Written in script on bottom: "M F HAMMOND / 1891." Diameter: 9 in. (22.3 cm.), height over finial: 7 1/2 in. (19.1 cm.). (*Heritage Plantation of Sandwich*).

Figure 180. Three small baskets, circa 1860–90. Left: oak staves, rim and handle, cherry bottom with two turned grooves and three scored circles. Inscribed on bottom: "May H. Congdon / from / Aunt Mary's house / Nantucket / Mass." Diameter: 7 3/4 in. (19.7 cm.), height: 4 5/8 in. (11.7 cm.). Center: oak staves, rim and handle, mahogany bottom with two turned grooves and four scored circles, block initials "FF" on bottom. Diameter: 6 3/4 in. (17.1 cm.), height: 4 3/4 in. (12.1 cm.). Right: oak staves, rim and handle, birch bottom with two turned grooves and four scored circles, made in 1885 by William H. Chadwick. Brand mark on bottom shown in Figure 12. Diameter: 5 7/8 in. (14.9 cm.), height: 4 3/8 in. (11.1 cm.). (*Private collection*).

Chadwick's son, William Emerson Chadwick, gave the basket to his niece, Marjorie Burgess, saying "Pa made this while he was in the jail," with the admonition to say nothing about the whole affair.

Quality Judgements

Although all of the baskets illustrated in this chapter are well made, we feel that at least two

Figure 179. Oblong basket made by William Dayton Appleton, circa 1900. Pine bottom, oak staves, rim and handle. Old lable on bottom with inscription "Wm. D. Appleton/Nantucket, Mass." Length: 11 1/2 in. (29.2 cm.), width: 7 in. (17.8 cm.), height: 5 1/8 in. (13.0 cm.). (*Private collection*).

Figure 181. Brand mark on bottom of the Chadwick basket on the right in Figure 273. The Chadwick brand was too wide for the bottom, only registering "HADWICK."

are lightship baskets at their very best: the round baskets in Plates LVI and LVII. We are not speaking here of either rarity of form, material of construction, or maker, but of that mysterious matter of quality. Quality judgments are sometimes thought to be subjective, but when such judgments are made by a knowing and loving "eye," there is surprising agreement among experienced observers. We suggest the following points be considered when developing criteria for judging a lightship basket:

The weaving should be neat and even. This is perhaps the most obvious quality and, by the way, one that is achieved fairly often. The other qualities which separate a great basket from a good one are more subtle. Form is the most subjective and elusive of these qualities. The "look" of the basket, which is a function of the mold form and the relationship of the basket form to the handle, must be exactly right. The basket bottoms were discussed earlier. The best baskets often have bottoms with turned rings and a beveled edge on the outside. The staves must be straight, directed in line to the center of the bottom. During the weaving, the tension tends to draw the staves in the direction of the pull of the cane, causing the staves to shift out of alignment. The rim treatment is particularly important to a fine basket. It should be neat and not too big for the size of the basket. The rims of some of the earlier baskets are remarkably slim; that of the basket in Plate LVI is only five-sixteenths of an inch in diameter. Compare this with the bulky rattan rims often used in the post–World War II era. The best baskets have beautifully shaped and carved handles, often with gentle oval curves that seem to be exactly right for the basket, or, in the case of baskets with loop handles such as the basket in Plate LVII, with handles that are both functional and handsome. The last quality to be considered in a basket is color. Color is, of course, a quality that changes with time and is independent of the maker. An even rich brown color is desirable.

The Makers

Some baskets bear the name of the maker, usually on the bottom in script, or on a paper label, or by a brand. Many paper labels have been partially or completely lost from baskets. An additional problem is that some names on baskets are those of owners rather than makers. The following very incomplete list includes a number of the well-known basket makers of the 1854–1940 period, the heyday of the Nantucket lightship basket. The names on the list with asterisks indicate Nantucket men who served on the *South Shoal Lightship* in the 1856–1905 period. After 1905 there were no Nantucketers on the lightship.[23] Although fourteen of the thirty-five names in the list of basketmakers (40 percent) served on the *South Shoal* it does not mean that baskets made by these men were made aboard the lightship.

Probably far more "lightship" baskets were made ashore than on the lightship.

Lightship Basket Makers 1860–1940

Elijah Alley
William Dayton Appleton*
A. D. W. Atkins
William Barnard
Thomas Barrally*
Francis H. Brown
Lincoln Ceely
Frederick Chadwick
William H. Chadwick
Oliver C. Coffin*
John Cook
Charles G. Coggeshall
Joseph Fisher*
R. Folger
David Hall*
Davis Hall*
M. F. Hammond
William Hadwen Hoosier
Albert Hussey*
Capt. Thomas James*
Capt. George F. Joy
Uriah Manter
Capt. Henry Plaskett
Capt. Charles B. Ray
Charles F. Ray
Clinton Mitchell "Mitchy" Ray
Capt. David E. Ray*
Sylvester B. Raymond*
Capt. Andrew J. Sandsbury*
William P. Sandsbury*
George Swain*
Ferdinand Sylvaro
Charles Sylvia*
A. D. Williams
Capt. James Wyer

The last baskets were apparently made on the *South Shoal Lightship* in the 1890s, but after that time they continued to be made on shore by men who had been on the lightship and by other island residents. Men like William D. Appleton and A. D. Williams made baskets in the first quarter of this century, but by the Depression years of the 1930s the making of lightship baskets had gone into decline and there was talk of it being a "dying" craft. Mitchy Ray made open-top baskets, as did Ferdinand Sylvaro and such hobbyists as Harry Gordon and Bunt Mackay.

*Served on the *South Shoal Lightship* in the 1854–1905 period.

Post–World War II Pocketbook-Baskets

It was the "invention" of the pocketbook-basket in the 1940s which gave basket making on the island new life by making it an article of fashion, a woman's handbag, something quite different from the utilitarian objects baskets had been in the past. The pocketbook-basket had a lid with cane-covered leather-thong hinges, and a flat plaque on the top that was usually decorated with a carved whale, whaleship half-model, seagull, and so on, of ivory, whalebone, or wood. The top of the basket became an important decorative element, as important as the basket itself. Other embellishments included handle-pins with heads of ivory carved in the form of scallop shells, ivory clasps, ivory hinges, and ivory scrimshawed plaques. Thus the trim and often prim Nantucket lightship basket of the nineteenth century was transformed into a highly decorative object which had, and still has, an immense appeal. The post–World War II pocketbook-basket has become one of the status symbols of the island. The making and decorating of pocketbook-baskets, by islanders and off-islanders, has become a thriving cottage industry, a fact that would probably have astonished those lonely men who made baskets on board the *South Shoal Lightship*.

The first pocketbook-baskets were made by

Figure 182. Pocketbook-basket made by Jose Reyes in 1948, rattan staves and rim, ebony plaque on lid on which are mounted five ivory whales: blue, finback, right, humpback and sperm, all carved by Charles F. Sayle. Ivory buttons on handle pins, ivory inset on inside of oak bail handle, ivory peg fastener. Basket height: 7 1/2 in. (19.1 cm.), width: 6 3/4 in. (17.1 cm.), depth: 5 3/4 in. (14.6 cm.). Length of ivory whales: 1 1/8 in. (2.9 cm.). (*Courtesy Mr. and Mrs. Charles F. Sayle*).

José Reyes in about 1948. The first of these was small, a basket made of cane with rattan staves and rattan rim and a woven top.[24] Soon he made larger, more usefully sized baskets with wooden plaques on top. The wooden plaque was made like a lightship basket bottom, with a deep slot around the edge into which were placed rattan staves for the cane-woven top. It was the suggestion of Mickey Sayle to place one of Charlie Sayle's carved whales on the plain plaque-top that gave the pocketbook-baskets their real appeal. The basket in Figure 182, the second Reyes basket to be so embellished, has five miniature carved whales mounted on its ebony plaque.[25] The handle on this basket is a replacement, the original basket having had a leather shoulder strap.

Reyes baskets had rattan staves, rims, and weavers. The use of these materials came from Reyes' background in the Philippines. This rep-

Figure 183. Pocketbook-basket made by Stanley M. Roop in 1964, oak staves, rattan rim, rosewood plaque on lid on which is mounted a whale-ivory half model of a whaleship hull carved by Charles F. Sayle, who also carved the scallop-shell handle pins. The peg fastener is a nineteenth-century ivory bodkin. On the bottom is the inscription: "Nantucket, Mass. / 1964 / Stanley M. Roop." Basket height: 7 in. (17.8 cm.), width: 8 3/4 in. (22.2 cm.), depth: 6 1/4 in. (15.9 cm.). Length of ivory half model: 2 13/16 in. (7.1 cm.). (*Private collection*).

resented a new element in Nantucket basket-making, taking it away from the coopering tradition of using oak staves and oak rims. Because of this, some old-time Nantucketers criticized Reyes' baskets, saying they were not lightship baskets. However, Reyes never designated his baskets as lightship baskets, calling them "Friendship baskets."[26] On the other hand, Stephen Gibbs and Sherman Boyer in the 1950s made pocketbook-baskets using oak staves in the lightship-basket tradition, as did Stanley Roop, who bought Boyer's molds and continued the tradition in the 1960s (Figure 183). Other pocketbook-basket makers in the 1950s and 1960s included Mr. and Mrs. Eugene Benoit, Bee Booth and Helen van Netta, Edward N. Burchell, Charles Donnellis, John and Frances Elder, Norman Giffen, Susan Chase Ottison, William J. Reis, William Sevrens, and Paul Whitten. By the 1970s the number of basket makers, on and off the island, had multiplied, and at the present time there are perhaps two or three dozen people making baskets for sale and many dozens (including the authors) who have made a basket or two for the fun of it.

Basket making, the most ancient of the crafts, is thriving in present-day Nantucket.

Baskets in the Nantucket Inventories of the Colonial Period

TYPE	*1706–1725*	*1726–1750*	*1751–1776*	*TOTAL*
Baby Basket		1	1	2
Basket	2	10	16	28
Clothes Basket		1	2	3
Great Straw Basket			6	6
Half Bushel Basket		1	1	2
Long Basket			1	1
Nun's Basket		1	2	3
Nun's Basket with Cover		1		1
"Sive" Basket			1	1
Stick Basket	2	19	9	30
Western Island Basket			1	1
Wicker Basket			3	3
Willow Basket			2	2
4-Handle Basket			1	1
Totals	4	34	46	84

11. Carvings and Drawings

Art was a relatively scarce commodity in colonial Nantucket. In Chapter 1 we noted three portraits of eighteenth-century Nantucketers. However, we found no portraits listed in the probate inventories of the time. Two inventories mention "pictures": Thomas Brock (1750) had "7 pictures at 20/" and David Bashard (1776), an innkeeper and trader, owned "23 pictures—23/." Five inventories included maps: Daniel Hussey (1750/1) owned a "Map of diverse Streets—0–5–0" [Nantucket?] and "2 Maps of City of London—1–0–0"; Benjamin Swain (1757), "Map of America—0–1–4"; Nason Mederas (1769), "Map of Canada River—0–15–0"; John Way (1776), "Map of Europe—1–2–6"; George Macy (1776), "Map of Boston Massacre—0–7–6," the latter being a print of Paul Revere's famous drawing of the 1770 confrontation which foreshadowed the coming Revolutionary War.

This chapter endeavors to give a representative sampling of the everyday, popular arts of Nantucket, carvings and drawings. Except for one 1746 gravestone, all the objects illustrated date from the 1790s to the twentieth century.

Gravestones

In the eighteenth century, the Quakers of Nantucket did not mark their graves. Hundreds and hundreds of Friends were buried in the gently rolling plot of land off upper Main Street, between Quaker and Madaket Roads, known today as the Quaker Burying Ground, without gravestones of any kind. Only in later years, well into the twentieth century, in the west corner of the Burying Ground, were a few Quaker graves marked by low, plain gravestones. Because of the heavy concentration of Quakers in Nantucket in the eighteenth century, there were far fewer early gravestones on the island than there would have been in a similar-size non-Quaker community on the mainland.

A few eighteenth-century gravestones are found in the Old North Burying Ground on New Lane. All are in characteristic eighteenth-century styles, with restrained, often simplified decorations. Figure 184 pictures the gravestone of Margret Hussey, who died December 14, 1746. She was born Margret Wilson and married Obed Hussey November 19, 1730. The gravestone, with its conventional winged death's-head on the cap and stylized border, is typical of the work of the brothers Nathaniel Lamson (1693–1755) and Caleb Lamson (1697–1769), sons of the pioneer stone carver of Charlestown, Massachusetts, Joseph Lamson (1658–1722). The characteristic Lamson touches include the shape of the skull, the in-

Figure 184. Gravestone in the Old North Burying Ground of Margret Hussey, who died December 14, 1746, is attributed to Caleb and Nathaniel Lamson of Charlestown, Massachusetts.

verted V-shape of the nose, the carving of the border, the two lines framing the inscription, and the style of the lettering.[1] It was said that the Lamson brothers, in the period 1722–1767, had an almost complete monopoly of the making of gravestones in Middlesex County. They also furnished stones for locations all over New England.[2] There appear to be no records of any gravestones being carved in Nantucket in the eighteenth century. The Boston area would have been a logical source for most of the island stones.

In the New North Burying Ground, across the lane from the Old North Burying Ground, there are a number of interesting nineteenth-century stones. The 1859 gravestone of Joseph Henry Sheffield, shown in Figure 185, has a clean, rational, almost abstract design, so chaste that it is hardly in tune with the decorative exuberance we usually associate with the mid-Victorian years. It reflects an earlier neoclassical style that lingered on in American design throughout the Victorian era. The hand, with finger pointed heavenward, is repeated in other nearby tombstones in the New North Burying Ground. A few yards away is the 1867 gate to the William Whippy family plot (Figure

Figure 185. Gravestone of Joseph Henry Sheffield in the New North Burying Ground. Sheffield was nineteen years old when he died July 6, 1859.

Figure 186. Cast-iron gate in the cemetery plot of Captain William Whippy in the New North Burying Ground, inscribed "1867 / WILLIAM WHIPPY."

186). The gate with anchor is no doubt a standard foundry casting, made especially for mariners. William Whippy was a member of a Nantucket seafaring family that included many ship masters in the eighteenth and nineteenth centuries.

Decoys

The idea of using an artificial bird to catch a live bird was the invention of the American Indian.[3] We do not know specifically what kinds of decoys Nantucket Indians used, but they were probably crude constructions of bundled cattails and reeds and stuffed bird skins. Birds were shot both for food and for their feathers. The Indians were the chief source of supply of bird feathers for bedding, which had such inordinately high values in colonial Nantucket. Mary Starbuck's account book has many entries of Indians supplying feathers for the English community.[4] For example, Soloman (Solhoman) in 1685–1686 often bought powder and shot and sold feathers. The Indians would probably have been shooting such year-round resident birds as black ducks and wood ducks for their desirable small feathers, and no doubt many birds were shot during the great fall migrations.

Mary Starbuck, in her book *My House and I* (1929), remembered the excitement generated by the passing of incalculable numbers of golden plover on the way south to Patagonia from the Arctic:

> The plover were due the last week in August, and about the twenty-seventh or twenty-eighth an easterly storm usually heralded their approach; the birds would stop overnight on their way south. Sometimes portions of the commons near the ponds were burned over that birds might be lured to linger and search for food in the bare spaces. Certain insects were said to swarm in the warm earth.
>
> There would come an evening when Stepfather would hurry home earlier than usual from the 'Cap'ns' Room,' where he always spent at least two hours before supper. He would rush in as excited as a boy, his blue eyes shining, and his voice vibrating with eagerness as he called out, 'They're going over! Put up my lunch! We're off in the morning at four o'clock!' I would drop whatever I was doing, and so would any one else who happened to be there, except Mother, who sat unmoved and tolerant. And we would follow Stepfather out into the dooryard and stand listening while the grape leaves flapped in the east wind, and the Macy elms across the street swished with a sound of boisterous surf . . .
>
> And then out of the inky blackness overhead there would come a faint little peeping note.
>
> 'There! Hear 'em!'
>
> The sound came nearer, a little soft, staccato whistle, then louder, a bit shriller but the

notes dropping still softly, though more quickly, and then the upper air was filled with the nervous, plaintive notes of the plover until the whole atmosphere seemed to become of an unbearable density with the mysterious crying of the invisible birds, driven by instinct into the blackness, fearfully, pathetically leaving the known for the unknown.

It was poignant and exciting beyond words! Gradually the air cleared and only a faint and lonely, more plaintive peeping was heard at intervals, until at last there sounded in our ears but the surfing of the trees and the riotous flapping of the grape leaves in the wind.[5]

[We are indebted to Donal C. O'Brien, Jr. for the following notes on Nantucket shorebird decoys.]

Nantucket, because of its position as the United States' easternmost island, was a natural stopping-off place for the long-range migrants, notably plover and curlew. These birds were the strongest flying of the shorebirds and did not need to hug the coast as much as yellowlegs and other shorebirds did. The plover and the curlew took off from their northern nesting grounds in the Arctic and boldly set off across the Atlantic. The first stopping place for many of them was undoubtedly the island of Nantucket and, in August, driven towards land by a rainstorm, they would come down on the commons, moors, hummocks, pastures, and beaches, no doubt exhausted from the first leg of their long journey south, to rest and dry out and feed and, unfortunately, in the nineteenth century, to be slaughtered by the tens of thousands.

The major shooting grounds on the island were near the "Chord of the Bay" on Coatue, the narrow strip that tapers down from Great Point and forms the northern side of Nantucket's inner harbor; the "Middle Ground" near Altar Rock between Pocomo, Wauwinet, Squam, Quidnet, and Polpis; the large pasture area between Miacomet, Hummock, and Long Ponds (the most famous being "Ram Pasture," where even today the plover pits can be seen as depressions in the land); Muskeget Island and the flats (now washed away) between Muskeget and Tuckernuck.

It was on the Middle Ground and the inland pastures around the ponds that most of the plover shooting was done. The curlew, yellowlegs, willet, and the smaller sandpipers were primarily shot in the lagoons and bays and sandy points, although some curlew were taken on the inland stands. There were actually two flyways over the island, only a few miles apart. The north shore flyway was a land flyway and was used by the smaller birds that came down along Cape Cod, the land migrants. The south shore flyway came east of Nantucket and was the way of the plover and the curlew.

A favorite shooting area was Hummock Pond, a freshwater pond which runs north and south and which is separated from the Atlantic by only yards of sand. Hummock Pond is the geological remains of a run-off river from the last glacier, which receded from Nantucket some ten thousand years ago. In August each year a horse-drawn scoop would make a channel to the sea, allowing much of the water from the pond to empty into the ocean. The purpose was to expose the "flats" of the pond and attract the shorebirds to the wide variety of crustaceans and vegetation. Decoys were placed on the shore and in the shallow water in natural-looking arrangements, while the hunters waited in nearby camouflaged blinds. The pond never fully drained and southwest winds would soon close the breach, allowing the pond to fill up again. Ponds were also drained for the seining of eels and freshwater fish and, in the twentieth century, for the purpose of mosquito control.

The "best" of the Nantucket shorebird decoys had rather specific characteristics. First, many were hollow ("light as a blown egg"). Few areas seemed to have produced hollow shorebirds and no area produced as many as Nantucket. Nantucketers probably made their shorebirds hollow because of the distances which the decoys had to be carried—down Coatue, over the moors of Ram Pasture, deep into the Middle Ground, or over the marshes of Pocomo Meadows. Although large settings were uncommon, the twelve or twenty-four decoys that were generally used were far lighter when "scooped out" and made "holler." Second, the decoys frequently had stylish and crisp wing and tail carvings. Third, many of them had whalebone bills most frequently made out of baleen. Finally, the early Nantucket decoys were mostly Eskimo curlews and golden plover. The latter were made in both spring and fall plumage.

Figure 187. Pair of hollow Eskimo curlew decoys, baleen bills, shoe-button eyes, circa 1850–1865. Length: 10 in. (25.4 cm.), height: 6¼ in. (15.9 cm.). (*Courtesy Mr. and Mrs. Donal C. O'Brien, Jr.*).

Few Nantucket decoys can be attributed to a specific maker. Nineteenth- and twentieth-century Nantucketers who have been associated with decoy making include: James Allen, Allen Backus, James Backus, Emerson Chadwick, Ned Chase, Charles Fred Coffin, Edward Fisher, Franklin Folger, Franklin Folger, Jr., Wallace Gardner, Arthur Harris, Gilbert Mantor, Arthur McCleave, Alec Pitman, Mitchell "Mitchy" Ray, Albert Silva, Reuben Small, Herbert Smith, David Webster, Putty Winslow, James Worth, and "Captain" Wyer.

Figures 187–189 show examples of nineteenth-century Nantucket decoys which elevate the craft to its highest level. Even though such objects may have functioned perfectly well as decoys, they exist now as sculpture. Carved with verve and imagination, these birds reflect the loving and knowledgeable hands of their makers.

The life-size Canada goose decoy in Figure 190 was made by Wallace Gardner (1859–1937) in the 1915–1925 period. Gardner also

Figure 188. Left: hollow golden plover decoy, fall plumage, baleen bill, shoe-button eyes, circa 1850. Length: 9¾ in. (24.8 cm.), height: 5½ in. (14.0 cm.). Right: hollow Hudsonian curlew or whimbrel decoy, tack eyes, wooden bill, made by Charles Fred Coffin circa 1875. Length: 11⅞ in. (30.2 cm.), height: 7½ in. (19.1 cm.), length of bill: 4 in. (10.2 cm.). (*Courtesy Mr. and Mrs. Donal C. O'Brien, Jr.*).

Figure 189. Pair of golden plover decoys, spring plumage, possibly made by a member of the Folger family, circa 1850. Bird at top has applied carved wings. Lower: 8 x 5 in. (20.3 x 12.7 cm.), upper: 8½ x 4⅞ in. (21.6 cm. x 12.4 cm.). (*Courtesy of Mr. and Mrs. Donal C. O'Brien, Jr.*).

Figure 190. Canada goose decoy, made by Wallace Gardner, 1915–1925. Height: 11 in. (27.9 cm.), length: 22 in. (55.9 cm.). (*Courtesy Patricia Gardner*).

made larger barrel-stave decoys called "loomers" because they "loomed" larger than life to attract high-flying geese.

The contemporary bird carvings of Patricia "Pat" Gardner are part of the Nantucket decoy tradition, although they are made as works of art, as sculpture, not as decoys. Miss Gardner, whose grandfather was Wallace Gardner, was trained as a sculptor in the modeling tradition. After graduating from Skidmore College with a degree in fine arts, she worked for several years as a cartographer for the Army Map Service, Corps of Engineers, in Rhode Island. When Miss Gardner returned to Nantucket in 1960, she became interested in the decoys her grandfather and other islanders had made. Working with Earl S. Ray, she learned the use of woodworking tools and learned to carve. Using old working decoys as models, Miss Gardner evolved her own version of Nantucket shorebirds, sensitively and thoughtfully carved, painted in the seeming casual manner of her models, and mounted on driftwood bases. Plate LVIII shows four of Patricia Gardner's birds made in the 1960s.

Ship Carvings

The earliest wood carvings seen by many Nantucketers could have been carved billetheads and figureheads of ships visiting the island. We have no records of figureheads on eighteenth-century Nantucket-based vessels, but we assume that the Quaker shipowners and captains would have frowned on such ornamentation.[6] The most famous whaleship of the nineteenth century, the *Essex,* did not have a figurehead.[7]

The handsome figurehead of the *Eunice H. Adams* (Figure 191), now in the collection of the Mystic Seaport Museum, and the painted sternboard of the same vessel, now in the New Bedford Whaling Museum (Figure 192), are probably the best-documented carvings of any Nantucket-related whaler.[8] The 118-ton, eighty-two-foot schooner was built in Bristol, Rhode Island. She was named for the wife of

Figure 191. Bust figurehead, painted white pine, from the schooner (later brig) *Eunice H. Adams*, built Bristol, Rhode Island, 1845. Height: 17¾ in. (45.1 cm.). (*Mystic Seaport Museum*).

Freeman H. Adams, one of the owners, who, with his brother Zenas L. Adams, operated a boating business on what is now Steamboat Wharf in Nantucket. For twenty years the *Eunice H. Adams* worked as a cargo vessel, first between Nantucket and Baltimore. In 1865 the vessel was converted to a whaler and in successive years sailed on two five-month Atlantic cruises. In 1867 she was converted to a brig and made two more whaling voyages out of Nantucket. Her return on June 20, 1870, marked the end of Nantucket whaling.[9] She was sold to New Bedford where she made five voyages in the 1872–1882 period.[10] Then her home port became Martha's Vineyard, where she made four voyages out of Edgartown between 1885 and 1894.[11] Her return on September 11, 1894, marked the end of whaling from the Vineyard. Thus, the *Eunice H. Adams* was the last whaleship to return to both the two neighboring islands, Nantucket and Martha's Vineyard.

The lady of the figurehead seems clearly to be the same lady of the sternboard. However, although the vessel was named for Mr. Adams' wife, Eunice Hopkins (Nickerson) Adams, a 1902 newspaper account stated that the figurehead was modeled after Mrs. Adams' sister.[12] Freeman Adams and his wife's family were closely associated, jointly owning several ves-

Figure 192. Sternboard from the *Eunice H. Adams*, painted pine carving, 17½ x 91½ in. (44.5 x 231 cm.). (*Whaling Museum of Old Dartmouth Historical Society*).

sels. The carver of the figurehead and the sternboard is unknown.

Weather Vanes and Whirligigs

Weather vanes were standard fixtures on many high buildings in Nantucket. Although they had the practical function of showing wind direction, they also functioned as sculpture, often with a great sense of exuberance. These swinging objects in the sky clearly gave people pleasure, as they continue to do today.

The jaunty cock weather vane in Plate LIX, dated 1822, was originally on the Lancasterian School on Fair Street.[13] In 1826 the building was sold to the trustees of the Coffin School, and the vane was kept on the ridgepole until the school was moved to the new classical red-brick Greek Revival building on Winter Street in 1852. The large firehouse weather vane in Plate LX, in the form of a fireman's speaking trumpet with the number eight, was for many years a familiar sight on a high pole on Center Street, just off Main Street, in front of Engine House Number 8. The copper codfish weather vane in Figure 193 was originally painted white. After being on the Nantucket Hotel on Brant Point until the early part of this century, it was atop a fisherman's house in Madaket.

Figure 193. Codfish weathervane, copper, for two decades atop the Nantucket Hotel on Brant Point, circa 1884. Length: 29½ in. (74.9 cm.). (*NHA*).

Those objects we now call whirligigs, carved figures with two paddles which rotate in a breeze with a whirling motion, were designated as weather vanes in Nantucket in the nineteenth and early twentieth centuries, being called "Sailor-Boy" and "Happy Jack" weather vanes. The earliest makers of these "weather vanes" of which we presently know are Charles F. Ray (father of Mitchy Ray), born 1826, and William H. Chase (1850–1931). Charles F. Ray, who also made decoys, made the whirligig in Plate LXI. The figure is carved in the round, with straight legs and trousers that flare at the bottom. The arms and the feet are carved separately and are movable. The face is painted. The whirligig in Plate LXII, which is attributed to William H. Chase, is a flat figure, cut with a jigsaw and painted. The arms are dowels with the suggestion of hands holding the paddles. The flat figure, with cutout bowed legs and feet pointed out, has become the prototype form of Nantucket whirligigs made by Lincoln Ceely and others in the twentieth century.

William H. Chase (Figure 194) was an island craftsman who received recognition for carving a group of small wooden boats which were shown at the Philadelphia Centennial Exposition in 1876 and which were afterwards acquired by the Smithsonian Institution. Chase was a boatwright by profession; it is said he was the last of the Nantucket boat builders.

James Walter Folger, 1851–1918

James Walter Folger, the wood carver and painter,[14] was the great-grandson of Walter Folger, maker of the famed astronomical clock. After leaving Nantucket High School in 1869,

Figure 194. Photograph of William H. Chase and his son Billy, by Henry B. Wyer, taken in 1919 for a postcard which had the title: "The Carver of 'Sailor Boys' and his son, Nantucket Island." (*NHA*).

James Walter served a period as an apprentice in a wood-carving shop in Cambridge and soon obtained a job as a carver in Boston. He returned to Nantucket about 1874, remaining on the island until his final illness in 1917.

One of Folger's early commissions was the huge frame he carved for the 1869 Wyer map of Nantucket surrounded by photographs of the island which was shown in the 1876 Centennial Exposition in Philadelphia. In the 1880s Folger carved a series of animal heads which were exhibited in the store window of Pitman and Ellis's Pharmacy on Main Street (Plate LXIII). About the same time Folger began carving wooden relief pictures, which are the basis for his reputation as a master carver. These pictures, the largest of which were no more than ten by fourteen inches, were carved in low relief, about five eighths of an inch deep, and then painted. An account of these pictures in the *Inquirer & Mirror,* April 23, 1904, noted:

> It takes Mr. Folger several months to make one of these panels, even in winter, when his money-making work of carved bread boards and furniture pieces is not so plentiful. Every slip of the tools spoils the panel, and there is no correcting a fault as in a painting. The color seems to give these painted panels durability which carved wood usually does not have. Mr. Folger has had only one complaint of cracking of the wood in over sixty panels.

The 1904 newspaper account also says that

Folger's workshop was in the back room of a joiner's store, with the sign "Wood Carver." A 1912 photograph of the white-bearded Folger shows him working in a tiny studio in the attic of his house.[15]

The subject matter of Folger's painted relief carvings included "The Olde Swain House in Podpis," "The Island's Oldest House," "Stone Alley," the town pump in Sconset, and the wreck of an old beached whaleboat. Figure 195 illustrates a painted relief titled "A Building in 1704 on Washington Str." This imaginary view of the past illustrates one of the problems of the Colonial Revival discussed in Chapter 2. James Walter Folger was a highly competent artist, but he clearly was not knowledgeable about the contents of an early eighteenth-century Nantucket house. On the mantel in the

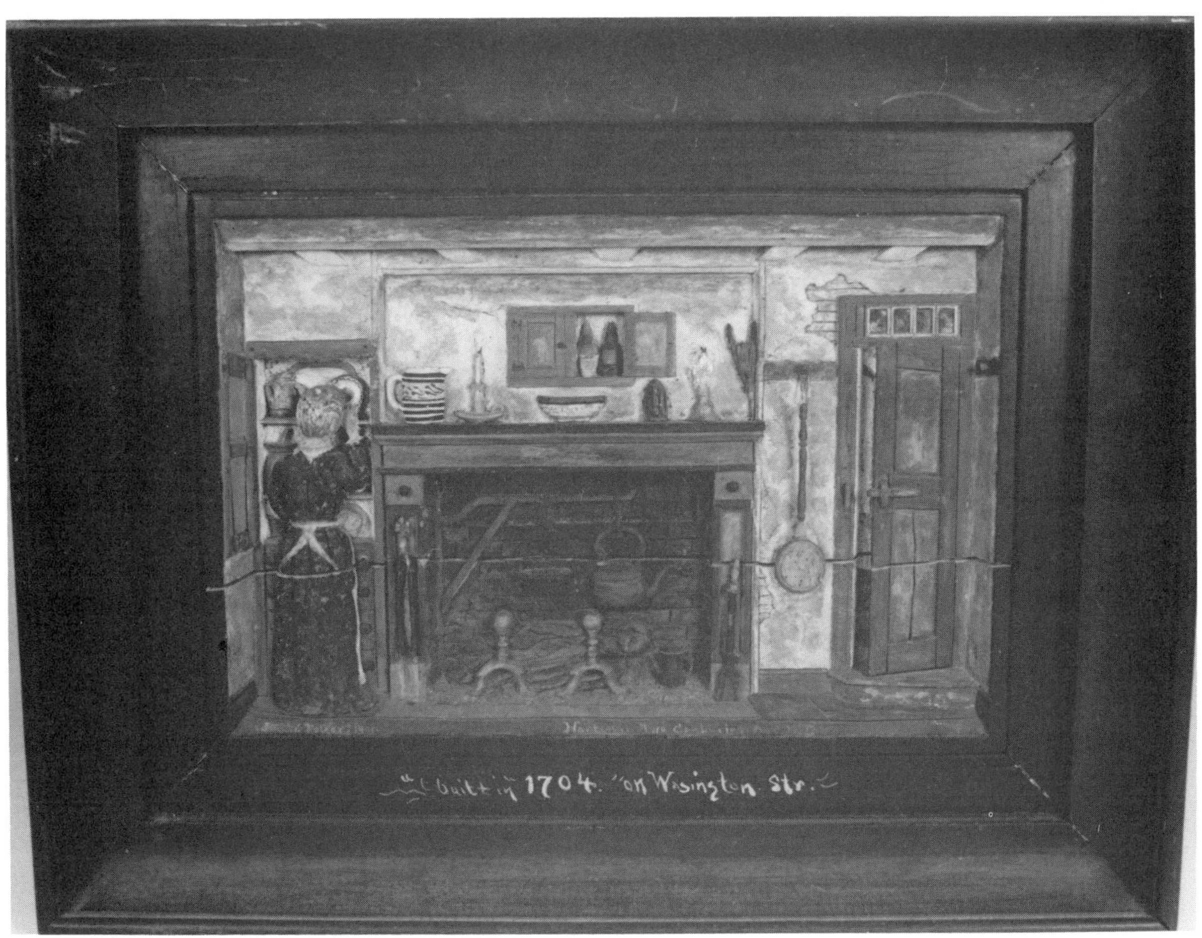

Figure 195. Painted carved relief by James Walter Folger, 1901. Painted in script on the frame: "A Building in 1704 on Washington Str." On the back is the inscription "Jas. Walter Folger / Feb. 1901 / Wood Carver / Painted in / Water / Color." Overall height of frame: 14⅞ in. (37.8 cm.), width: 19⅝ in. (49.8 cm.). (*NHA*).

"1704" picture are nineteenth-century objects, a mocha jug, a glass Sandwich-type lamp; in the fireplace are nineteenth-century ball-top andirons, and the lady to the left in the picture wears a nineteenth-century dress and apron.

George Arthur Grant, 1857–1942

The large carved and painted whaling scene mounted on the outside of the Nantucket Whaling Museum was made by one of the last of the Nantucket whalers, George Arthur Grant. Grant was born on the island of Upulu, the Samoan group of the Navigator Islands, when his parents, Nancy and Captain Charles Grant, were on a South Pacific whaling cruise. George himself became a whaler in the 1870s and 1880s, retiring from the sea about 1889. He served nineteen years at the Surfside Life-saving Station and, in 1930, became the first custodian of Nantucket's newly opened Whaling Museum, serving until 1942, the year of his death.

Grant made a number of small whale carvings, but his major work was the ten-foot painted relief carving of a whaling scene now mounted on the side of the Whaling Museum (Figure 196). The figures of the relief are stiff and the carving is highly stylized, but the over-

Figure 196. Painted wood relief carving on the side of the Nantucket Whaling Museum, made by George Arthur Grant, circa 1930. Approximate size: 68 x 120 in. (173 x 305 cm.).

all effect is one of great charm. Even though the relief has a toylike look, one can believe that it was carved by a man who had experienced such a scene many times.

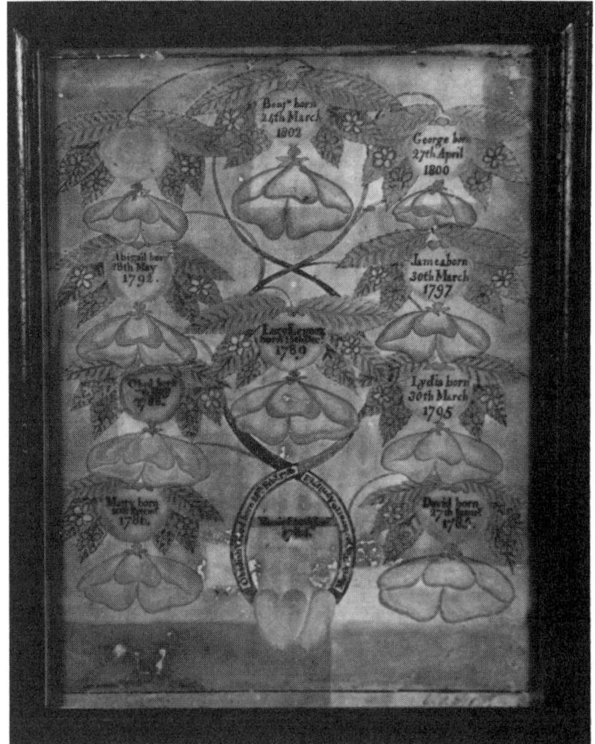

Figure 197. Wood family tree, from Obadiah Wood and Martha Tupper, married January 29, 1784; latest date: 1802. Signed: "Edw.d D. Burke, Pinxit." Height: 10½ in. (26.7 cm.), width: 8¼ in. (21.0 cm.). (*Private collection*).

Drawings

The most common types of drawings that have survived from the last quarter of the eighteenth century are those depicting family coats of arms and family trees. The English tradition of displaying the family coat of arms in the home carried over into New England. The Nantucket Historical Association has two similar coats of arms of the Nantucket Gardner family, both painted in the 1790s. The more sophisticated of the two (not illustrated) is attributed by the authors to John Coles (1748–1809), a well-known Boston heraldry painter. Coles was possibly the teacher of Eunice Gardner, who painted the Gardner family coat of arms in Plate LXIV. The coat of arms by Eunice Gardner is tentative in its drawing and less accomplished than that of John Coles, but we illustrate it because of its strong Nantucket connection. On the back of the picture is a handwritten note:

> Colored with home made paints from cranberry and blueberry juices / yellow ochre and Indigo.

We have not identified Eunice Gardner. There were sixteen Eunice Gardners in eighteenth-century Nantucket who could have drawn the family coat of arms.

Plate LXV and Figure 197 illustrate quite decorative Nantucket family trees of the latter part of the eighteenth and early nineteenth centuries. The Gardner family tree in Plate LXV was painted by Daniel Stanton, circa 1779, in the middle of the War of Independence. Edward Burke, in his Wood family tree (Figure 197), was more flamboyant in his approach, decorating his "tree" with leaves and great, spreading flowers.

Sailors' Drawings

The sea chest of Albert W. Starbuck (Plate LXVI) is lined with newspapers from Boston, New Bedford, and Nantucket, bearing dates 1825, 1829, and 1831. On the inside of the lid is a splendid watercolor drawing of the ship *Agnes* of New York, a merchantman aboard

Figure 198. Drawing from the Journal of the ship *Edward* (1849), Shubael Clark, master, out of New Bedford for the California Gold Rush, kept by the mate, Francis Barrett of Nantucket. Left: "New-year's calls—The first call," right: "The last call." Height: 8 1/8 in. (20.6 cm.), width: 13 1/4 in. (33.7 cm.). (*NHA–L77*).

Figure 199. Drawing, pencil on paper, circa 1875: "North Water street,/ Nantucket, / Mass., the great fire, July '46," plus the verse:

My childhood's home I seem to see again,
Far down the vista of the bygone years,
A great white house with many a weather stain,
The birthplace of so many smiles and tears.
A. M.

Height: 9 in. (22.9 cm.), width: 11 in. (27.9 cm.). (*Collection of the authors*).

which Albert Starbuck sailed. Starbuck was born in Nantucket October 3, 1811. He married Mary Ann Joy October 21, 1832.

The artwork in most whaling logs and journals was limited to whale-stamp pictures of whales and passing ships, or drawings of the same. The contours of islands were often sketched in logs for the very practical purpose of identification on future voyages. There are occasional drawings of ships and views of ports. The colorful drawings in the 1854–1858

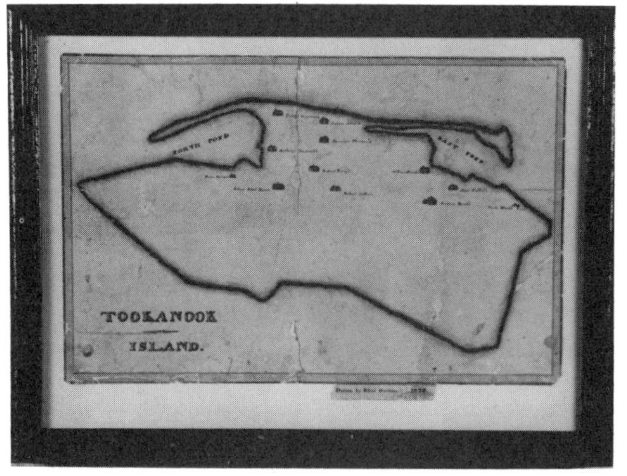

Figure 200. Map of "Tookanook Island" drawn by eleven-year-old Eliza Gardner in 1829. Houses identified: "Peter Norton's, Anthony Chadwick's, Daniel Dunham's, James Alley's, Ebenezer Dunham's, Robert King's, Robert Coffin's, William Brock's, Abel Coffin's, Uncle Black's cave," plus the "Salem School House." The houses have red roofs, the island is outlined in blue. Signed at the bottom: "Drawn by Eliza Gardner 1829." Height: 8 3/4 in. (22.2 cm.), width: 13 in. (33.0 cm.). (*NHA*).

journal of the *Edward Cary,* Perry Winslow, master, kept by Joseph E. Ray, boatsteerer, are quite exceptional (Plates LXVII and LXVIII). The journal contains a dozen watercolors, plus numerous sketches, which give us a firsthand view of places visited by the ship. These are the work of an untrained hand, but they have freshness and vitality.

Figure 198 is a humorous sketch from the journal of the ship *Edward,* Captain Shubael Clark, on an 1849–1850 voyage from New Bedford to San Francisco during the Gold Rush. The journal, kept by the mate, Francis Barrett of Nantucket, is a gossipy account of the eight-and-a-half-month voyage, interspersed with many lines of doggerel and humorous drawings. The drawing in Figure 198 shows two well-dressed men with top hats making their polite and proper first New Year's call to a young lady, and then a sketch of the two at the end of the day, quite tipsy.

The drawing of the large gambrel-roof house which burned in the 1846 fire is one of the relatively few pictorial remnants we have of buildings lost in that devastating fire (Figure 199). Finally, we illustrate the delightful map of "Tookanook" (Tuckernuck) Island, drawn by Eliza Gardner, aged eleven (Figure 200). Eliza made tiny individual drawings of each house on the island, with the owner's name, plus a drawing of the "Salem School House." It is fascinating to remember that there was a school on Tuckernuck for the children of these few families.

12. Souvenirs from Far-Away Places

Even by present-day standards of international travel, Nantucketers of the eighteenth and nineteenth centuries experienced a remarkable variety of distant ports and exotic places. During their lifetimes many mariners logged hundreds of thousands of miles aboard ships, regularly visiting such locations as Cape Verde, the Azores, and the Falklands in the Atlantic Ocean; Trinidad, Belem, Rio de Janeiro, Valparaiso, and Callao in Latin America; spots all over the vast Pacific, from the dream islands of Tahiti and Hawaii to Fiji and the Marquesas; Canton, Macao, and Hong Kong in China; Sydney and Melbourne in Australia; and those lonely islands in the Indian Ocean and islands at the edge of Antarctica; Capetown and Walvis Bay in southern Africa; and London and Liverpool and Dublin and the French ports across the English Channel.

Throughout this book we have noted the wanderings of Nantucket seafarers and some of the objects they brought back to the island, but in this chapter we emphasize, quite informally, the bringing back of souvenirs, a phenomenon which has gone on since the beginnings of civilization. Roman tourists returned home with souvenirs from Greece and the Near East, and Englishmen of the eighteenth century crammed their great country houses with souvenirs from the Grand Tour.

We illustrate a sampling of some of the unusual, amusing, sometimes important, sometimes trivial things that Nantucket mariners brought back to waiting wives, children, sweethearts, and friends, and some of the tales evoked by the objects.

From France

We mentioned earlier (Chapter 4) the Nantucket whalers and their families who lived in France, in and around Dunkirk and Le Havre, from about 1785 to the early years of the nineteenth century. The wax life-size doll in Figure 201 was brought home to Nantucket from Paris in 1796 by Captain Jonathan Coffin, who stated he had purchased it at a nunnery in that city, and that it was a life-size model of the dauphin of France. Born March 27, 1785, the younger son of Louis XVI became dauphin on the death of his elder brother in 1789, on the eve of the French Revolution. Imprisoned in the Temple, he was put in the care of a shoemaker named Simon after the execution of his parents by the guillotine in 1793. There were stories of his being spirited away and a doll being substituted for him while he was in

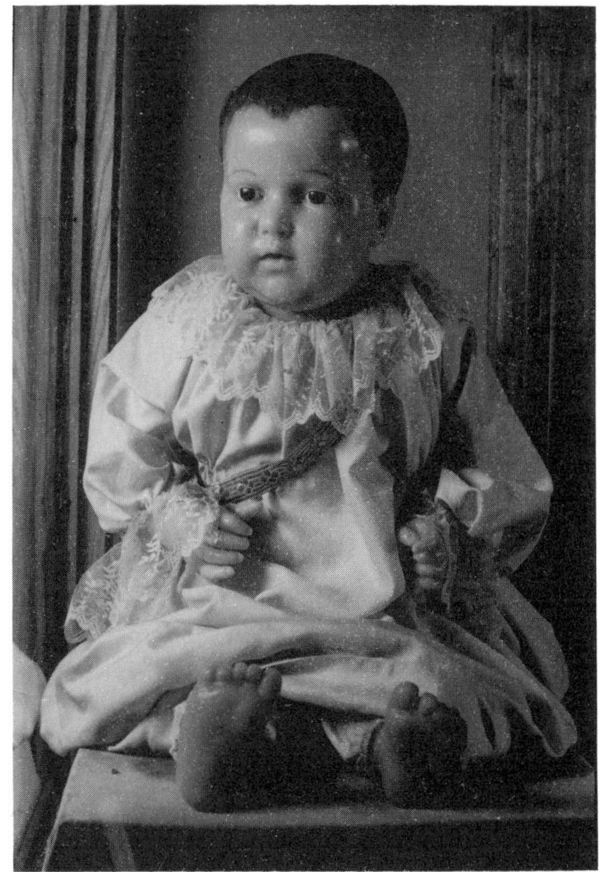

Figure 201. Wax doll, said to have represented the Dauphin of France, acquired by Captain Jonathan Coffin in Paris in 1796. Height of doll in sitting position: 17 1/2 in. (43.8 cm.). (*NHA*).

prison. Royalists in exile proclaimed him as Louis XVII, king of France. He was supposed to have died June 8, 1795, but rumors persisted that he had been spirited away. Some forty claimants, including one American, presented themselves as candidates for the legitimate succession to the French throne, most of them after the restoration of the monarchy in 1815. To this day the fate of the dauphin is unknown.

The small wooden box, at the left in Figure 202, with a tiny watercolor on its lid, and a silver plaque engraved "Sarah Barker," was purchased in Paris in 1793 by Gideon Gardner. Inside the box is a faded note:

> "This snuff box GG had Made in Paris & *his* hair put in for the figure. I presented it to his mother & she was very choice of it & shewed it to all friends over 50 years."

The octagonal box to the right of Figure 202 was brought to Nantucket from France in 1802 by an ancestor of Susan E. Brock.

The calligraphic school exercise piece in Figure 203 was made by Reuben Gardner Folger when he was thirteen and attending M. Cavalier's school in Balbec, France, which is on the road to Paris, twenty miles from Le Havre. There is a note with the picture stating the frame was made in Nantucket:

> "The frame was made from locust wood, a part of a tree brought here by John Vait, in France, the said Reuben Gardner having married Vait's daughter Elizabeth, and brought her to Nantucket at the time."

Figure 202. Two French snuff boxes, circa 1790–1800. Left: ebony box with a tiny gold-framed watercolor on the lid, and a silver plaque engraved "Sarah Barker," 2 1/4 x 3 1/2 x 1 in. (5.7 x 8.9 x 2.5 cm.). Right: gilt-metal octagonal box, painting on lid of figures in a rural scene, 2 3/4 x 4 × 1 in. (7.0 x 10.2 x 2.5 cm.). (*NHA*).

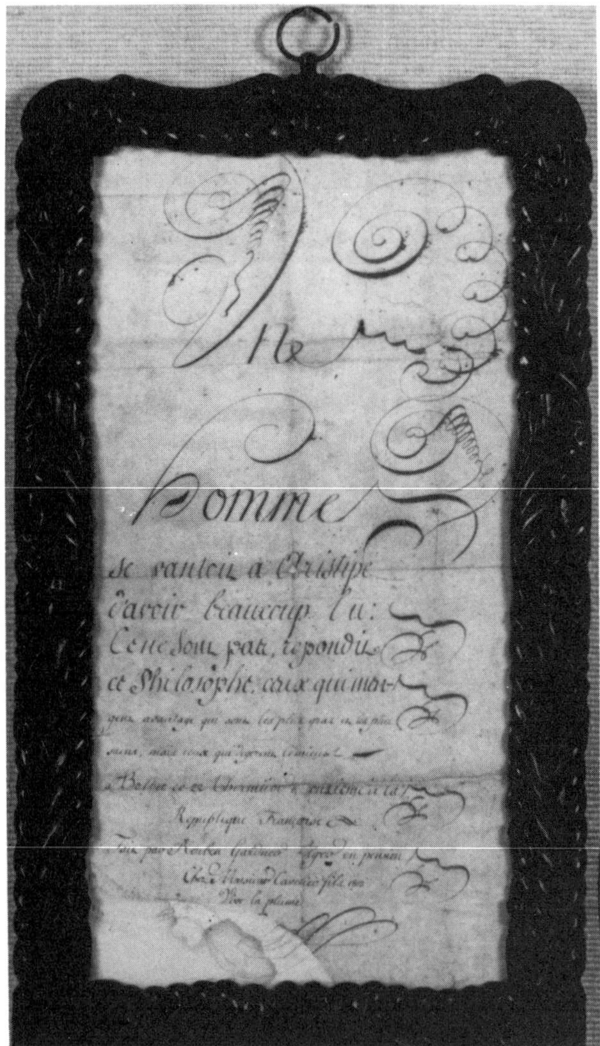

L'Homme

se vantoit a Aristipe

d'avoir beaucoup lu:

Ce ne sont pas, repondit

ce Philosophe, ceux qui man-

Figure 203. Framed manuscript document, written by a Nantucket Gardner when he was in a French school. The translation accompanying the document reads: "A man, boasted to Aristipies of having much to read. 'Tis not those, answered the Philosopher, who eat to the best advantage that are the fleshiest or the healthiest, but those who digest the best.

Written by Reuben Gardner Folger aged 13 years, at the school of M. Cavalier in Balbec, France on a quarter day in the year 1803. 'Long live the pen.' " Height: 16½ in. (41.9 cm.), width: 10 in. (25.4 cm.). (*NHA*).

From China

The seventy-year period, 1790–1860, saw continuing contacts between Nantucket and China. Seafarers to China usually brought souvenirs home. Some of the Chinese souvenirs were art objects of high quality. In Chapter 6 we illustrated some of the fine export porcelains brought to the island. The ivory-covered wood box in Figure 204 is of this level of quality. The ivory carving of the box is the fine lace-like work for which the Chinese have long been known. The box housed the cards and counters for the game of Boston, a game at cards, allied to whist, named after the siege of Boston in the American War of Independence, to which the technical terms of the game refer.

The colorful Chinese tea caddy in Plate LXIX was acquired by Captain James Cary, master of the ship *Rose,* when he visited Canton in April 1804 with a load of sealskins.[1] On his next voy-

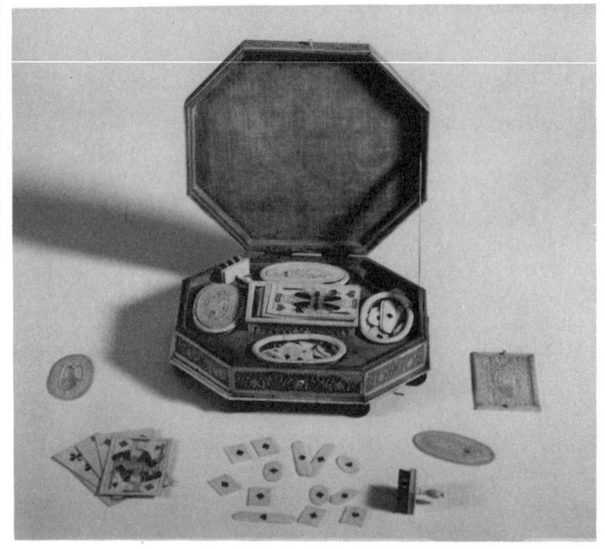

Figure 204. Chinese wooden box, covered with carved ivory panels, housing the cards and counters for the game of Boston. Circa 1790–1830. Dimensions: 9½ x 8 x 2½ in. (24.1 x 20.3 x 6.4 cm.). (*NHA*).

age to China in 1812 Captain Cary died in Canton. He was buried on the island of Wampoa, twelve miles downriver from Canton. His funeral was under the care of brother Masons from his own and other American ships. When the *Rose,* under the command of First Mate R. Gardner, was returning home, the War of 1812 had begun and the ship was captured by a British frigate off the Cape of Good Hope.

A Tea Caddy from the Bounty

In 1851 the Nantucket whaleship *Peruvian* visited a favorite stopping place for whalers, Pitcairn Island, that tiny island in the mid-South Pacific where Fletcher Christian and his co-mutineers had gone to hide after they set Captain Bligh afloat in a small boat to wend his way across 4,000 miles of the Pacific. Pitcairn was an island of high romance, even for hardened and experienced mariners. There were two separate logs kept of the 1848–1852 voyage of the *Peruvian,* one by Francis Barrett of Nantucket, first mate of the ship, and the other by Captain George B. Folger. Francis Barrett's log chronicles the Pitcairn visit in 1851:

> Monday, March 31st
> "at 5¹/2 saw Pitcairn's Island, 2 points forward the weather beam heading W, distant about 20 miles"
> Tuesday, April 1st
> "at sunset the island was off the weather beam, very little nearer than this morning."
> Wednesday, April 2nd
> "at 5 passed leeward of the island about 8 miles; at sunset made out the sail of a hermaphrodite brig, saw her luff too to leeward of the island . . . Latter part, at 6¹/2 a canoe came off; at 7¹/2 tacked in; at 8 the bow boat went on shore ship laying off and on. Saw blackfish lowered the waist boat, but got none."
> Thursday, April 3rd
> "at 6 the boat came off with limes, oranges and pumpkins"
> Friday, April 4th
> "bow and waist boats went ashore with all hands that did not go before."
> Sat. April 5th
> "at sunset the boats came on board, brought some limes, oranges and pumpkins; a boat came off from the shore for some few things; at 7 she left us with 3 cheers each, for the shore".[2]

Captain Folger's journal entry for Saturday, April 5th reads:

> "at 5 P M the boats came off. at 6 finished trading and shore boat left."[3]

It is clear from the two accounts that the crew members of the *Peruvian* had a cordial and interesting visit with Pitcairners. It was only natural that Captain Folger was able to acquire a nice box from the descendants of the *Bounty* mutineers.

The box (Figure 205), which he brought back

Figure 205. English tea caddy, mahogany with inlay on top, brass handles, bracket feet. Acquired on Pitcairn Island by Captain George B. Folger of the ship *Peruvian* in 1851. Height: 6³/4 in. (17.1 cm.), width: 12 in. (30.5 cm.), depth: 6⁵/8 in. (16.8 cm.). (*NHA*).

to Nantucket in 1852, has a checkered history, with an unexpected twist. A faded handwritten note in the box reads:

> "Box made on Pitcairn Island in 1853 and given as a Christmas present in 1875 from E. W. & P. W. Ewer to Anna Barrett."

The note contains two errors. The 1853 date is incorrect, since the *Peruvian,* which brought the box back to Nantucket, visited Pitcairn in 1851 and returned to Nantucket in 1852. The second error is more significant: the box was not *made* on Pitcairn Island. The box is an *English* mahogany tea caddy, with bracket feet, inlay on the top, and English cast-brass handles on the two ends. The box is a relatively sophisticated piece of cabinetmaking, the work of a competent English joiner. The style is typical of the 1780–1785 period.

Nineteenth-century Pitcairn-made boxes, baskets, and coconut shell vases are known, but the work on them is uniformly crude and rough. There were clearly no craftsmen with the tools and the training to make such a tea caddy on Pitcairn Island in the 1850s.

There seems to be a logical conclusion. The box, originally a tea caddy, must have come from Captain Bligh's cabin on the *Bounty.* Soon after Fletcher Christian, the eight other mutineers from the *Bounty,* and the eighteen Tahitians landed on Pitcairn, they stripped the ship of everything movable, the contents of the officers' and crews' quarters, supplies, sails, and masts. Then the ship was burned, destroying the visible evidence of the mutiny. They were safe. The fate of the *Bounty* was not known to the outside world for eighteen years, until 1808, when the whaleship *Topaz,* Captain Mayhew Folger of Nantucket, visited Pitcairn Island and heard the whole story of the mutiny and its aftermath.

We do not know whether Captain George B. Folger of the *Peruvian* knew of the origin of the tea caddy. It could have been given to the captain in a moment of special (perhaps drunken) generosity, and/or for perhaps a sufficient sum of money. Sometime between 1852, when the *Peruvian* returned to Nantucket, and late in the nineteenth century, when the note was written about the gift of the box to Anna Barrett in 1875, the nature of its origin was lost. Oral history is never completely reliable.

Nevertheless, it is a fascinating and tantalizing thought that the tea caddy from Captain Bligh's cabin of the *Bounty* may have ended up in the Peter Foulger Museum in Nantucket.

Sailors' Valentines

Sailors' valentines, made of one or two octagonal glazed wood cases framing a variety of seashells in symmetrical patterns, were a favorite souvenir brought home by mariners. At one time it was thought that these objects were made by sailors aboard ship, but a 1961 study by Judith Coolidge Hughes found that most of them were made on Barbados, easternmost of the British West Indies, a regular stopping place for returning American whalers. Hughes noted that "of the hundred thousand species of shells in the world only about thirty-five appear in the valentines—and these are all native to the West Indies." Some of the valentines, such as the one in Plate LXX, proclaim their origin with a motto "A GIFT FROM BARBADOS." All the valentines date from the early 1800s to about 1880, with many made in the 1830–1860 period. They are all assembled in the same manner with the same wood (cedrela, or Spanish cedar) and the same shells, in similar designs.[4]

Although Hughes believed that *all* sailors' valentines came from Barbados, there were others made elsewhere. The Nantucket Whaling Museum owns a rather crude valentine made with shells from South Sea islands, almost certainly made by a seafarer. The work is not as neat as those from Barbados and may be a one-of-a-kind example. In 1985, a sailor's valentine was sold at auction in London with the motto "A GIFT FROM TRINIDAD," which tells us that Trinidad was also a source of the valentines.

Portraits

Artists in Canton and Hong Kong carried on a thriving business painting portraits of ship captains and their ships and Chinese domestic scenes as well as scenes of Macao, Hong Kong, and Canton. They also painted portraits of wives and children from photographs. Plate LXXI shows a portrait of Emma Cartwright painted in Hong Kong by Hinqua in about 1860 and the daguerreotype from which it was copied. Emma, who was born in 1855, had died before 1860, when her father, Captain William Joy Cartwright (1819–1864), master of the *Hanqua,* took the daguerreotype to China to have the portrait painted. The appealing portrait of Emma depicts her in a prim, velvet-trimmed dress, with ribbons in her hair. There are today on the island quite a few portraits of nineteenth-century Nantucketers which were painted in China from photographs.

Occasionally, when a wife accompanied a captain on a sea voyage, her portrait was painted in the port being visited. The odd but charming reverse painting on glass in Plate LXXII of Mary Coffin Nichols was made in about 1849 in a South American port, possibly Valparaiso, Chile, a port frequently visited by Nantucket whalers. Mary Coffin Nichols was the wife of Captain James Nichols. She accompanied her husband on two whaling voyages aboard the ships *Lion* and *Noble,* during which time three of her four children were born, including a set of twins born off the coast of Chile. On her first voyage Mary Nichols circumnavigated the world.

The tinsel-decorated lithographic portraits of Emperor Napoleon III and his beautiful wife Eugenie-Marie de Mentijo of Spain in Plate LXXIII are examples of what have sometimes been labeled Victorian bad taste. Although there is a clear element of camp in this "tourist souvenir" picture, it reminds us of the great popularity the couple had after their much-publicized marriage in Notre Dame Cathedral in 1853, when Eugenie wore a gown which reputedly cost $50,000. Its skirt was padded with five layers of handmade lace and was held in place with a diamond-studded belt. The belt was matched by earrings hung with diamonds. To top things off, the emperor-groom gave his bride a fifty-one-carat diamond pendant, still known today as "The Eugenie" after a half-dozen changes in ownership. Napoleon III died in exile in Kent, England, in 1873. Eugenie died in England in 1920.

Native Arts of the South Seas

In the post–World War II era, museums of the Western world have paid increasing attention to the native arts of the islands of the South Seas, staging major exhibitions of their work. Most of these artifacts disappeared from islands of the South Pacific in the nineteenth century. "Heathen idols," hated by the missionaries, were destroyed by the thousands; highly decorated war clubs and war canoes were discarded. Although there are today excellent collections of native arts in such places as Hawaii and New Zealand, there are many South Sea islands which have few artifacts from their past. The director of the National Museum of Fiji in Suva told the author, "We have almost nothing earlier than 1880. If you want to see early Fijian materials you must go to American whaling museums and ethnological museums in Europe."

Nineteenth-century American mariners

were fascinated with things from the South Seas. The Peabody Museum in Salem has one of the great collections of artifacts from the Pacific Basin, and the Nantucket Historical Association has a splendid group of objects from the area. Nantucket whalers began to bring native arts back from the South Seas early in the nineteenth century. Nantucket ships such as the *Criterion,* Captain Peter Chase, made extended visits to the Fiji Islands in search of sandalwood as early as 1806.[5] The "Museum" in the Nantucket Atheneum was the public depository in the nineteenth century for South Sea islands artifacts brought back to Nantucket Island. Fortunately, those things which are the nucleus of the Nantucket Historical Association's present collection were rescued from the Atheneum before the building burned in the 1846 fire.

Figure 206. Group of artifacts in South Seas Room of the Nantucket Whaling Museum. In the center are two models of war canoes from New Zealand, the larger one having a length of 9 ft. 8 in. (2.95 meters). The four paddles bracketing the small canoe came from the Austral Island located south of Tahiti; the two long, flaring spears with needle points above are from Nive, a mid-Pacific island south of Pago Pago, and on the left, just above the bow of the large canoe, is a paddle from Fiji.

Figures 206–208 show artifacts from the South Pacific and the Pacific Northwest in the Nantucket Whaling Museum.[6] The importance of the nine-foot, eight-inch Maori war canoe from New Zealand was emphasized by the great Maori Exhibition in the Metropolitan Museum of Art in 1984. The quality of the Nantucket canoe in Figure 206 is comparable to the one shown in the Metropolitan Museum.

The spectacular circular piece of tapa in Figure 207 is only one of many examples brought back to Nantucket. There was at least one house in town, on Union Street, where tapa cloth was used for wallpaper.

The ship model in Figure 207 is, as noted in the caption, the oldest whaleship model in the United States. The hull was made in 1765 by William Meader when he was fourteen years old, perhaps guided by his elders. Meader was born in Nantucket May 12, 1751, and died there May 4, 1829. He became a sea captain and a Nantucket street was named for him. The model was owned at one time by Clarence Stanhope, a descendant of the Meader family on his mother's side. After he died in 1924, his daughter, Clara Stanhope of Newport, sold it to Duncan Hazard of Newport. In November 1940, it was sold at the New York auction house of Parke Bernet. In 1941 the old rigging of the model, which was of a much later period than the hull, was entirely replaced by Charles F. Sayle and Nikita Carpenko in the manner of the 1750–1800 period.

The Indonesian prau (or proa) in Plate

Figure 207. Center: Samoan tapa cloth, diameter 54 in. (137 cm.). Surrounding the tapa are Fijian war clubs. The hull of the ship model on the sea chest was made by William Meader in 1765, the earliest known American whaleship model. Length of model: 21 1/2 in. (54.6 cm.). (*NHA*).

LXXIV, with its depiction of oarsmen, and an elevated covered deck amidship with banners on the topside, was made entirely of cloves, the aromatic dried flower buds of an East Indian evergreen tree. The model was held together by threads. There does not seem to be a single clove missing. If it had been held together by glue it probably would never have survived.

Figure 208. South Pacific and Pacific Northwest war clubs, spears and paddles in the South Seas Room. On the left, a group of ten war clubs from Fiji and Tanga. Left center, a group of five spade-shaped war clubs from the Cook Island. In the center are two decorated, pointed paddles made by Indians in the Pacific Northwest. Right: (1) massive war club from Cook Island, (2) and (3) Tonga, and (4) and (5) Samoa.

An Eskimo Walrus Tusk

Nantucket whalemen, whaling in the Arctic on ships out of New Bedford on the east coast and San Francisco on the west coast, brought back a number of fine examples of Eskimo scrimshaw to the island. The Eskimos, with their highly developed visual sensibilities, faithfully chronicled their hunting activities. Figure 209, a scrimshawed walrus tusk, shows them hunting walrus, and, in the center of the tusk, the cutting-in operation. The walrus supplied the Eskimo with food and clothing and the tusks were adorned as works of art.

The souvenirs brought to Nantucket by its much-traveled mariners were no doubt welcomed by families and friends, but these things must have meant much more to the men who brought them back. Such objects, sprinkled casually through a Nantucket house, would have had an effect on decor, contributing to that "difference" noted at the beginning of the book. For the men who brought them home, these objects would have been charged with secret memories of different and distant places and people and times.

Figure 209. Eskimo scrimshawed walrus tusk, decorated with red and black dyes. Eastern Canada (?), circa 1890–1900. Length: 24½ in. (62.2 cm.). (*NHA*).

OCCUPATIONS IN COLONIAL NANTUCKET

NOTES

SELECTED BIBLIOGRAPHY

GLOSSARY

INDEX

OCCUPATIONS IN COLONIAL NANTUCKET

The following list of occupations (and, occasionally, social categories) was developed primarily from the Book of Records of the Registry of Deeds, County of Nantucket, Massachusetts. When real estate changed hands in the seventeenth and eighteenth centuries, it was usual to record the occupations of both the buyer (lessee) and the seller (lessor). A few entries were obtained from Nantucket Probate Court records and from account books.

Since the focus of this book is on the arts and crafts of the island, we first list the actual individuals of three categories: joiners, chairmakers, and weavers. This is followed by a tabulation of the other occupations in alphabetical order. The table involves some duplications. We noted in Chapter 2 that Thomas Brock (1698?–1750) was called a "Mariner" in 1730, a "Distiller" in 1738, a "Merchant" in 1746, and a gentleman, "Thomas Brock, Esqr." in 1750. However, the great majority of men and women were listed with the same occupations throughout their lives.

Some of the occupations in the tabulation, such as cordwainer and fellmonger, are obsolete today and are defined in the glossary, as are such designations as spinster, which had a different primary meaning in the eighteenth century than it does today.

The tabulation of the occupations and social categories highlights the changes that took place in the economic life of eighteenth-century Nantucket, and underlines the spectacular growth of whaling, particularly in the third quarter of the eighteenth century. At a time when the population of the island was increasing rapidly (the *Vital Records of Nantucket* lists the population in 1765 as 3320, and as 4,412 in 1776, an increase of 33 percent), the number of yeomen was actually decreasing, there being fifty-four in the period 1726–1750 and forty from 1751 to 1776. During the same time the number of mariners jumped more than two and a half times, from seventy-nine in the period 1726–1750 to 210 in the period 1751–1776. The statistics for the support activities of coopering, boatbuilding, sailmaking, and blacksmithing show an even more dramatic increase in the same time period:

	1726–1750	*1751–1776*
Coopers	39	146
Boatbuilders and Boatwrights	0	62
Sailmakers	1	6
Blacksmiths	16	36

Clearly, the third quarter of the eighteenth

century was a boom time in Nantucket, and it was entirely due to whaling. The War of Independence brought an abrupt end to the prosperity. It was forty years before Nantucket really recovered, after the War of 1812.

Joiners

	Name	*Birth & Death*	*Date of first mention in the records*	*Reference**	
	Nathaniel Starbuck	1668–1753	1707	Acct. Book No. 128 NHA	
	Richard Macy	1689–1779	1710	Acct. Book No. 422 NHA	
	Richard Evans	?	1735	v.4	p. 34
	John Descow	?	1736	v.4	p.139
	Benjamin Folger	1716–1778	1747	v.5	p.119
	Jonathan Ramsdell	? –1799	1749/50	v.5	p.171
	Benjamin Fosdick	1713–1801	1757	v.6	p. 95
	John Barnard	1720–1802	1761	v.6	p.336
	John Ramsdell	? –1782	1764	v.7	p. 72
**	Ebenezer Calef	1739–1807	1768	v.7	p.259
	Nathaniel Bunker	1743–1834	1769	v.7	p.332
***	Richard Gardner	1729–1811	1771	v.7	p.455
	William Gardner	? –1787	1772	v.8	p.163
	Stephen Kidder	working 1758	1773	v.8	p.383
****	Ichabod Aldrich	1733–1821	1773	v.8	p.257
	John Fosdick	?	1776	v.9	p.310

* Reference in land records, account books, etc.
** Also called house joiner
*** Also a chairmaker and turner
**** Also listed as a "shiprite"

Chairmakers

	Name	Birth & Death	Date of first mention in the records	Reference*	
	Caleb Stretton	1708–1786	1747	v.5	p.108
	Charles Chase	1731–1815	1758	v.6	p. 66
**	Richard Gardner	1729–1811	1761	v.6	p.260
	Robert Clasby	1731–1812	1761	v.6	p.284
	Christopher Swain	? –1807	1762	v.6	p.428
	Stephen Barnard	1723–1813	1763	v.6	p.517
	Samuel Whippy, Jun[r]	1741–1795	1771	v.7	p.462
	Francis Clark	1748– ?	1772	v.8	p.158
	Jonathan Paddock	1729–1780	1773	v.8	p.397
	Benjamin Paddock	1734–1815	1773	v.8	p.397
	Silas Paddock	1739–1795	1773	v.8	p.397
	Ebenezer Barnard	1747– ?	1775	v.9	p.176

* Land records, Registry of Deeds office
** Also called a turner and joiner

Weavers

Name	Date of first mention in the records	Reference in Land Records, etc.	
Peter Folger	1663	v.6	p. 66
Benieman Austin	1681	Back of Registry of Deeds Book No. 1	
Tobiah Coleman	1686	v.2	p. 33
Nathaniel Paddock	1708	v.3	p. 6
Stephen Pease	1709	v.3	p. 17
Jeremy Netowa	1711	Acct. Book No. 110 NHA	
John Trott, Jun[r]	1720	v.3	p.148
Nathan Pease	1721	v.4	p. 2
Shubal Pinkham	1721	v.4	p. 2
Esop	1722	v.4	p. 6
Africa	1722	v.4	p. 18
Samuel Long	1724	v.4	p.28/9
William Clasby	1726	v.4	p. 49
Eleazer Arthur	1738	v.4	p.175
Nathan Macy	1740	v.5	p. 4
Gideon Folger	1740	v.5	p. 8
Francis Blackhouse	1741	v.5	p. 10
Peter Swain	1742	v.5	p. 21

Name	*Date of first mention in the records*	*Reference in Land Records, etc.*
Eliphas Folger	1743	v.5 p. 35
John Swain	1743	v.5 p. 38
Ebenezer Ellis (comber)	1745	v.5 p. 66
James Whippy, Senr:	1747	v.5 p.127
Joseph Marshall	1749	v.5 p.164
Daniel Long	1750	v.5 p.169
Silvanus Starbuck	1750	v.5 p.185
Edmond Heath	1750	v.5 p.184
Benjamin Pinkham	1752	v.5 p.203
Peleg Coleman	1753	v.5 p.224
Enoch Coleman	1753	v.5 p.283
Joseph Chase	1755	v.5 p.288
Richard Swain	1755	Inventory–1755 p.242
Benjamin Trott	1755	Inventory–1755 p.225
Silvanus Worth	1758	v.6 p. 64
William Clasby, Junr:	1758	v.6 p. 68
Jonathan Folger	1758	v.6 p. 93
Zachariah Bunker	1758	Inventory–1758 p.302
Joseph Worth, Junr:	1758	v.6 p. 98
Thomas Macy	1759	Inventory–1759 p.380
William Clasby, Senr:	1761	v.6 p.284
John Clasby	1761	v.6 p.284
Charles Clasby	1761	v.6 p.284
Isaac Chase	1761	v.6 p.292
Stephen Paddock	1764	v.7 p. 18
Nason Meador	1765	v.7 p. 40
Clark Clasby	1768	v.7 p.247
Jedidiah Folger	1769	v.7 p.308
Uriah Folger	1770	v.7 p.401
Silvanus Bunker	1771	v.7 p.414
James Marshall	1773	v.8 p.375
William Pinkham	1773	v.8 p.403
Nathan Waldron	1774	v.9 p. 95
Jabez Waldron	1774	v.9 p. 95

Occupations and Social Categories

Occupation	*1660–1700*	*1701–1725*	*1726–1750*	*1751–1776*	*Total*
Barber	0	0	0	2	2
Blacksmith	0	5	16	36	57
Blockmaker	0	1	1	5	7
Boatbuilder	0	0	0	36	36
Boatwright	0	0	0	26	26
Brasier	0	0	1	1	2
Bricklayer	0	0	1	1	2
Brickmaker	0	0	0	1	1
Butcher	0	0	0	2	2
Carpenter	0	15	22	22	59
Chairmaker	0	0	1	11	12
Clothier	0	1	0	0	1
Collector	0	0	0	1	1
Cooper	0	4	39	146	189
Cordwainer	0	6	20	62	86
Distiller	0	0	1	0	1
Farmer	0	7	8	12	27
Fellmonger	0	0	1	1	2
Feltmaker	0	0	1	1	2
Fisherman	0	0	3	6	9
Fuller	0	1	0	0	1
Gentleman-Esquire	1	11	6	16	34
Gentlewoman	0	0	1	0	1
Glasier	0	0	1	7	8
Goldsmith	0	0	0	3	3
Governor	0	0	0	1	1
Hangman	0	0	0	1	1
Hatter	0	0	1	3	4
Husbandman	1	5	1	0	7
Indian	4	15	22	27	68
Innholder	0	1	1	5	7
Joiner	0	2	4	10	16
Judge of Probate	1	2	2	1	6
Laborer	0	6	16	6	28
Lot Layer	0	0	0	2	2
Mariner	0	15	79	210	304
Mason	0	1	2	1	4
Merchant	2	1	4	45	52
Miller	0	0	1	3	4
Negro Man	0	2	0	4	6
Painter	0	0	0	2	2
Physician	0	1	0	2	3
Registrar of Deeds	1	2	1	1	5
Rigger	0	0	0	1	1
Ropemaker	0	0	0	4	4
Saddler	0	0	1	0	1

Sailmaker	0	0	1	6	7
Schoolteacher	0	1	1	6	8
Sheriff	0	0	0	2	2
Shipwright	0	0	3	14	17
Tailor	0	4	5	17	26
Tanner	0	0	1	4	5
Trader	1	1	1	4	7
Victualler	0	0	0	1	1
Weaver	3	9	14	26	52
Whaleboatwright	0	0	0	3	3
Whalefisherman	0	0	7	11	18
Wheelwright	0	0	0	1	1
Yeoman	2	29	54	40	125

NOTES

1. *Introduction*

1. R. A. Douglas-Lithgow, *Nantucket, A History* (New York: G.P. Putnam's Sons, 1914).
   R. F. Mooney and Andre R. Sigourney, *The Nantucket Way* (Garden City, N. Y.: Doubleday & Co., 1980).
   Lydia S. Hinchman, *Early Settlers of Nantucket* (Philadelphia: W. A. Henry Press, 1926).
   Will Gardner, *The Coffin Saga* (Cambridge, Mass.: NHA, 1949).
   Will Gardner, *The Clock That Talks and What It Tells* (Boston: NHA, 1954).
   Will Gardner, *Three Bricks and Three Brothers* (Cambridge, Mass.: Riverside Press, 1945).
   Edward K. Godfrey, *The Island of Nantucket* (Boston: Lee & Shephard, 1882).
   Emil Frederick Guba, *Nantucket Odyssey* (Waltham, Mass.: 1951).
   Joseph E. C. Farnham, *Brief Historical Data and Memories of My Boyhood Days in Nantucket* (Providence: Snow & Farnham Co., 1915).
   Edward Byers, *The "Nation of Nantucket": Society and Politics in an Early New England Center.* (Doctoral dissertation, Brandeis University, 1983).
   Proceedings of the Nantucket Historical Association, 1895 to date.
2. Obed Macy, *The History of Nantucket* (Boston: Hilliard Gray, and Co., 1835. Reprinted by Macy's, Ellenwood, KS, 1985)
3. Alexander Starbuck, *The History of Nantucket* (Boston: C. E. Goodspeed & Co., 1924. Reprinted by Charles E. Tuttle, Rutland, Vt., 1969).
4. Robert A. diCurcio, *Art on Nantucket* (Nantucket: NHA, 1982).
5. Macy, *The History of Nantucket,* p. iv.
6. Crèvecoeur's name was Michel-Guillaume St. Jean de Crèvecoeur. He wrote under the pseudonyms of J. Hector Saint John, Saint John de Crèvecoeur, and Agricola.
7. J. Hector St. John, *Letters from an American Farmer* (London: printed for T. Davies, 1782), p. 118. Pages 114 through 212 are devoted to Nantucket.
8. Ibid., p. 119.
9. Franklin's letter was quoted in Everett U. Crosby, *Nantucket In Print* (Nantucket: privately printed, 1946), p. 94.
10. Proceedings of NHA, 1941, p. 30.
11. See Edouard A. Stackpole, *The Sea Hunters* (Philadelphia: J.B. Lippincott, 1953), a history of Yankee whaling, and Starbuck's *History of the American Whale Fishery from its Earliest Inception to the Year 1876.* (New York: Argosy-Antiquarian Ltd., 1964). (Washington: Government Printing Office, 1878).
12. Alexander Starbuck, *The History of Nantucket:* (Boston: C.E. Goodspeed & Co., 1924), pp. 32–33.
13. James F. Shepherd and Gary M. Walton, *Shipping, Maritime Trade, and the Economic Development of Colonial North America* (Cambridge, England: University Press, 1972), pp. 211–230; Richard C. Kugler, *The Whale Oil Trade 1750–1775* (New Bedford: Old Dartmouth Historical Society, 1980), p. 3.
14. Kugler, *The Whale Oil Trade 1750–1775,* p. 9.
15. Henry Chandlee Forman, *Early Nantucket and its Whale Houses* (New York: Hastings House, 1966), pp. 81–89.

16. Starbuck, *The History of Nantucket,* note, p. 54.
17. Kugler, *The Whale Oil Trade 1750–1775,* p. 6.
18. The *Oak* never returned to Nantucket. It was sold at Panama in 1872, sending home 60 bbl. sperm oil and 450 bbl. whale oil. The last whaler to return to Nantucket was the brig *Eunice H. Adams,* Zenas Coleman, master, leaving Nantucket March 31, 1869, returning June 14, 1870.
19. Edouard A. Stackpole, "Peter Folger Ewer—The Man Who Created the 'Camels,' " *Historic Nantucket,* July, 1985, pp. 19–30.
20. Helen L. Winslow, "Nantucket Forty-niners," *Historic Nantucket,* January 1956, p. 6.
21. *Nantucket Vital Records,* Vol. I, p. 3.
22. *Nantucket County Book of Records:* No. 62, p. 22; No. 62, p. 358; and No. 93, p. 527.
23. Clay Lancaster, *The Architecture of Historic Nantucket* (New York: McGraw-Hill, 1972), p. xiii.
24. Obed Macy, *The History of Nantucket,* p. 13.
25. Starbuck, *The History of Nantucket,* pp. 16–17.
26. Ibid., pp. 14–18, 516; Macy, *History of Nantucket,* pp. 13–17.
27. Macy, *The History of Nantucket,* p. 39.
28. Starbuck, *The History of Nantucket,* p. 516 (footnote).
29. Ibid., pp. 530–531.
30. Ibid., p. 520.
31. Will Gardner, *Three Bricks and Three Brothers* (Cambridge: Riverside Press, 1945), p. 109.
32. Starbuck, *The History of Nantucket,* p. 520.
33. See Arthur J. Worrall, *Quakers in the Colonial Northeast* (Hanover, N.H.: University Press of New England, 1980), particularly pp. 9–15.
34. John C. Miller, *The First Frontier: Life in Colonial America* (New York: Dell Publishing Co., 1966), pp. 74–75.
35. Worrall, *Quakers in the Colonial Northeast,* pp. 13–14.
36. Ibid., p. 78.
37. Ibid., p. 50.
38. Robert J. Leach, "The First Two Quaker Meeting-Houses on Nantucket," *Proceedings of the NHA,* 1950, pp. 24–33. Arthur Worrall, *Quakers in the Colonial Northeast,* p. 74, tells of the visit of the English Friend, Mary Weston, to Nantucket during her 1750–1752 American visit, when she spoke to 1,500 people on the island, corroborating Leach's 1,500 figure for the capacity of the Friends Meetinghouse at that time.
39. See: Henry Barnard Worth, *Quakerism on Nantucket Since 1800* (Nantucket: NHA, 1896), for an account of the decline of Quakerism on the island.
40. Katherine Seeler, "Phebe Folger's Watercolors," *Historic Nantucket,* October 1966, pp. 12–18.
41. Clay Lancaster, *Architecture of Historic Nantucket,* Chapter V, "The Typical Nantucket House."
42. Frederick B. Tolles, " 'Of the Best Sort but Plain': The Quaker Esthetic," *American Quarterly,* Winter 1959, pp. 491–492.
43. Ibid., p. 497.
44. Ibid., p. 499.
45. Robert diCurcio, *Art On Nantucket,* p. 26, Figs. 28 and 29. We use the term Pollard *Painter* instead of the more common Pollard *Limner.* Jonathan Fairbanks makes a clear distinction between the terms:

    > A limner was a painter of miniatures, a specialist who painted on a small scale in watercolor on velum or card. In fairly recent times the term "limner" has been indiscriminately applied to all early American painters. Printed texts of the period maintain a clear distinction between limners and oil painters, although the term may have been popularly misused even in the seventeenth century. To continue the error in terminology today may confuse the search for names of artists who made the earliest large-scale portraits in America. *New England Begins: The Seventeenth Century* (Boston: MFA, 1982), p. 414.

2. *At Home in Nantucket: Life-Styles, 1700–1900*

1. Abbott Lowell Cummings, Ed., *Rural Household Inventories* (Boston: The Society for the Preservation of New England Antiquities, 1964), p. 84, in which the inventory of Joshua Gardner, a farmer who lived in rural Suffolk County, Massachusetts, south of Boston, and who died in 1700, gives us a very graphic idea of what was in the parlor of a relatively modest mainland home of the time: "A feather bed, bolster & pillows, Curtains and vallains with ye bedstead & furniture and a trundle bed and bedstead with the Covering thereunto belonging," two tables, a chest of drawers, twelve chairs ("6 Leathered Chairs. 6 other chairs & 6 Cushions"), a small trunk, a desk, and a "framed Stool." On the wall was hanging a looking glass.
2. Ibid., pp. 83–149.
3. Emerson lectured at the Nantucket Atheneum in November, 1844, and in May, 1847 gave a series of six lectures on "Representative Men."
4. *Probate Records of Nantucket County,* Book A, No. 1, p. 8. This inventory has long been a puzzle to historians. One might assume that the Tristram Coffin whose inventory was recorded October 17, 1706, was that of Tristram Coffin, Jr., who died in 1704. But this just cannot be. There is no evidence that Tristram, Jr. ever lived in Nantucket, but there is considerable evidence that he lived in Newbury, Massachusetts, where he died February 4, 1704, aged 72, leaving 177 descendants. (Louis Coffin, Ed., *The Coffin Family* (NHA, 1962), p. 69.) His grave is in the first parish yard of Newbury. (Ibid., p. 70.) He was a merchant and filled many public positions in Newbury. His wife was Judith Somerby, widow of Henry S. Somerby. The wife of the Tristram in the 1706 Nantucket probate records was named Hannah.

   There *is* a Tristram Coffin in the genealogical records who seems to fit the bill: Tristram, grandson of Peter Coffin, the eldest son of the first Tristram. His wife was Hannah, which checks with the court records. However, the genealogical records list his death as December 13, 1730 (Ibid., p. 121), which is almost certainly wrong, since *that* date is the date of Hannah's death (*Vital Records of Nantucket,* Vol. 5, p. 483, under listing of Hannah Pinkham), and she had remarried Jonathan Pinkham *after* Tristram's death. We do not know the exact date of Tristram Coffin's death. It was obviously before September 27, 1706 at which time Hannah, his widow, was appointed administrator of Tristram's estate. (Nantucket County *Probate Records,* Book A, No. 1, p. 1.)
5. Elizabeth A. Little, *The Indian Contribution To Along-Shore Whaling At Nantucket* (NHA, 1981), pp. 44–49. Clifford W. Ashley, *The Yankee Whaler* (Boston: Houghton Mifflin Co., 1926), p. 129.
6. *Probate Records of Nantucket County,* Book A, No. 1, p. 5.
7. Alexander Starbuck, *The History of Nantucket* (Boston: C. E. Goodspeed & Co., 1924. Reprinted by Charles E. Tuttle, Rutland, Vt., 1969), map opposite p. 56.
8. Helen Winslow Chase, *Jethro Coffin House Chronology 1686–1986* (Nantucket: NHA, 1986.) A comprehensive report on the restoration of the Jethro Coffin house is being prepared (1986) by Morgan W. Phillips, architectural conservator, Society for the Preservation of New England Antiquities.
9. Cummings, *Rural Household Inventories,* p. 62.
10. Ibid., p. 61.
11. Susan J. Montgomery, ed., *Unearthing New England's Past: The Ceramic Evidence* (Lexington, Mass.: Museum of Our American Heritage, 1984), p. 51.
12. Ibid., p. 47.
13. NHA Account Book AB128. We found no inventory for Nathaniel Starbuck, Jr. in the records of the Nantucket Probate Court.
14. Starbuck, *The History of Nantucket,* p. 531.
15. *Pollard Papers,* The Nantucket Atheneum, Vol. 3, p. 418. John Swain's inventory is recorded in the *Probate Records of Nantucket County,* Book A, no. 1, pp. 48–49.
16. Starbuck, *The History of Nantucket,* p. 33.

17. Ibid., map opposite p. 56.
18. Henry Barnard Worth, *Nantucket Lands and Land Owners,* NHA, Vol. II, Bulletin No. 5 (1906), p. 225.
19. Worth states on p. 225: "The safe judgment would be that the Swain house was built between 1684 and 1694, with a preference for the first part of the decade." In 1687 John Swain gave to the town his "house Lott at Kachkesset" and other parcels of property, which seems to indicate that he may have moved to Polpis in that year, according to Starbuck, p. 96.
20. Robert F. Trent, *New England Begins: The Seventeenth Century* (Boston: Museum of Fine Arts, 1982), Vol. 2, p. 288.
21. Little, *The Indian Contribution to Along-Shore Whaling at Nantucket,* p. 28.
22. Communication from Mrs. John D. Little (August 12, 1985).
23. Obed Macy, *The History of Nantucket* (Boston: Hilliard Gray and Co., 1835. Reprinted by Macy's, Ellenwood, Kans., 1985), p. 42.
24. *Nantucket County Book of Records,* Vol. 5, p. 184.
25. *Probate Records of Nantucket County,* Book A, No. 1, p. 92.
26. Ibid., p. 206.
27. Ibid., No. 2, 1737–1762, p. 31.
28. Ibid., p. 122.
29. Elizabeth A. Little, *Probate Records of Nantucket Indians* (Nantucket: NHA, 1980), pp. 35–63.
30. *Nantucket County Book of Records,* Book 2, p. 41.
31. Grindal Rawson and Samuel Danforth, "Account of an Indian Visitation, A.D. 1698," *Collections of the Massachusetts Historical Society* (Boston: 1809, reprinted 1857), p. 132. "At Nantucket, we find five congregations. The preachers unto which Job Muckermuck, who succeeds John Gibs deceased; John Asherman, a person well reputed of; Quequenah, Netowah a man greatly esteemed by the English for his sobriety . . . These are their constant teachers."
32. *Probate Records of Nantucket County,* Book A, No. 1, p. 129.
33. Jeremy Netowa's name does not appear in Account Book No. 110, but we believe the evidence is quite strong in favor of it being a record of his activities, primarily his accounts as a weaver. The dates are right and the internal evidence fits. Netowa was the only Indian weaver working during the entire 1711–1728 period covered by the account book. His wife, Abigail, a spinster, is referred to in the account book. The section of records with Indians is in the back of the account book, suggesting more intimate and informal dealings. (Mrs. John D. Little, the leading authority on Nantucket Indians, agrees with our reasoning concerning Account Book No. 110.)
34. *Probate Records of Nantucket County,* Book A, No. 1, p. 137.
35. Macy, *The History of Nantucket,* p. 65: "From the best information that can be obtained, ten persons have been hanged on the island, since it was settled by the English. They were all native Indians, and the crime of each was murder. The first execution, of which we have any particular account, took place in 1704, the last in 1769. . . . Their names were as follows: Finch, 1704; Sabo, Jo Nobby, 1736; Heppy Comfort, 1745; Henry Jude, 1750; Tom Ichabod, Joel Elisa, Simon Hews, Nathan Quibby, 1769."
36. Starbuck, *The History of Nantucket,* p. 101.
37. Macy, *The History of Nantucket,* p. 58.
38. Ibid., p. 45.
39. Elizabeth A. Little and Marie Sussek, *The Indians Who Died of the Sickness* (Nantucket: NHA, 1979), p. 8.
40. Macy, *History of Nantucket,* p. 120.
41. Harry B. Turner, *Nantucket Argument Settlers,* (Nantucket: *Inquirer & Mirror,* 1959), p. 40.
42. Macy, *History of Nantucket,* p. 47.
43. *Probate Records of Nantucket County,* Book A, No. 1, pp. 145–147.
44. *Nantucket County Book of Records,* Vol. III, p. 130A.
45. Arthur J. Worrall, *Quakers in the Colonial Northeast* (Hanover, N.H.: University Press of New England, 1980), p. 161.
46. Thomas E. Drake, "Elihu Coleman, Quaker Antislavery Pioneer of Nantucket," *Byways in Quaker History: A Collection of Historical Essays by Colleagues and Friends of William I. Hull* (Wallingford, Pennsylvania: Pendle Hill, 1944), p. 121.

47. Ibid., pp. 121–122.
48. NHA Collection 52 - Box 6, Folder 6A, "Nantucket Friends Records: Births, Deaths, Received, Disowned, Restored, 1711–1838."
49. *Nantucket County Book of Records,* Vol. 5, p. 225.
50. Ibid., Vol. 7, p. 459.
51. *Probate Records of Nantucket County,* Book A, No. 1, p. 26.
52. Henry Barnard Worth, *Nantucket Lands and Landowners, NHA* Vol. II, No. 5 (1906), pp. 246–7.
53. James Deetz, *In Small Things Forgotten* (Garden City, New York: Anchor Press/Doubleday, 1977), p. 10.
54. Family records, courtesy Mrs. John P. Elder. Thomas Brock's inventory is recorded in the *Probate Records of Nantucket County,* No. 2, 1737–62, pp. 187–90.
55. *Nantucket County Book of Records,* Vol. 4, p. 82A.
56. Ibid., Vol. 4, p. 170A.
57. Ibid., Vol. 5, p. 94.
58. Ibid., Vol. 5, p. 170.
59. Starbuck, *The History of Nantucket,* p. 358.
60. Richard C. Kugler, *The Whale Oil Trade 1750–1775* (New Bedford: Old Dartmouth Historical Society, 1980), p. 6.
61. Ibid., p. 9.
62. *Vital Records of Nantucket,* Vol. I, p. 125.
63. Ibid., Vol. III, p. 120.
64. Textile definitions from: Florence M. Montgomery, *Textiles in America 1650–1870* (New York: W. W. Norton & Co., 1984).
65. See: NHA Account Books AB61, AB99, AB103, AB158.
66. NHA Account Book AB158.
67. Martha Gandy Fales, *Early American Silver for the Cautious Collector* (New York: Funk & Wagnalls, 1970), p. 3.
68. *Nantucket County Book of Records,* No. 20, p. 378.
69. Starbuck, *The History of Nantucket,* pp. 295–302.
70. *Nantucket County Book of Records,* No. 20, pp. 376–9 and 388–9.
71. *Probate Records of Nantucket County,* No. VII, 1823–1825, pp. 6–7.
72. Everett U. Crosby, *Ninety Five Per Cent Perfect* (Nantucket: privately printed, 1953), pp. 16–23.
73. We have been informed by Clay Lancaster (letter, January 22, 1985) that such designations are "late nineteenth century. The early builders called them a house, house-and-a-half, and double." See Ernest Allen Connaly, "The Cape Cod House: An Introductory Study," *Journal of the Society of Architectural Historians,* Vol. XIX, No. 2, May 1960, p. 53.
74. Peter F. Coffin's will, dated December 22, 1821, was entered into the Nantucket Probate Court records July 31, 1823, pp. 368–369.
75. *Probate Records of Nantucket County,* 1822, p. 246.
76. Clay Lancaster, *The Architecture of Historic Nantucket* (New York: McGraw-Hill, 1972), pp. 108–111.
77. For more information on Joseph Starbuck, see: Will Gardner, *Three Bricks and Three Brothers,* (Cambridge, Mass.: Riverside Press, 1945).
78. Ibid., pp. 39–40.
79. Ibid., pp. 39–40.
80. Ibid., p. 68.
81. Webster defines "caparison" as: "1a: an ornamental covering for a horse; b: decorative trappings and harness."
82. Joseph E. C. Farnham, *Brief Historical Data and Memories of My Boyhood Days in Nantucket* (Providence: Snow & Farnham Co., 1915), p. 92.
83. Obituary in Nantucket Atheneum.
84. Information from Mrs. H. Crowell Freeman.
85. Richard H. Cook (born Nantucket 1847), *Historic Notes of the Island of Nantucket and Tourist's Guide* (Nantucket, July 1871).
86. We are grateful to Mrs. W. S. Archibald, Jr. for information on the Underwood cottage.

3. *Furniture in the Home*

1. Joseph K. Ott, "Rhode Island Furniture Exports 1783–1800," *Rhode Island History,* Vol. 36, No. 1, February 1977, p. 6.
2. Ibid., p. 9.
3. NHA Account Book, AB422.
4. Alexander Starbuck, *The History of Nantucket* (Boston: C. E. Goodspeed & Co., 1924. Reprinted by Charles E. Tuttle, Rutland, Vt., 1969), p. 520.

5. Wallace Nutting, *Furniture Treasury,* (New York: The Macmillan Co., 1928), Nos. 1981–2003.
6. Brock Jobe and Myrna Kaye, *New England Furniture: The Colonial Era* (Boston: Houghton Mifflin, 1984), p. 360. The term "round" chair, regularly used in Nantucket inventories, was also used on the mainland. See the Roxbury, Massachusetts inventory of Ebenezer Pierpont (1768), recorded in Abbott Lowell Cummings, *Rural Household Inventories* (Boston: The Society for the Preservation of New England Antiquities, 1964), p. 219.
7. The only record of the *Beaver*'s 1773 cargo notes: "Freight of 112 chests Tea on the Beaver, for Boston." Francis S. Drake, *Tea Leaves: Being a Collection of Letters and Documents Relating to the Shipment of Tea to the American Colonies in the Year 1773* (Boston: A. O. Crane, 1884), p. 257.
8. Thomas H. Ormsbee, *The Story of American Furniture* (New York: The Macmillan Co., 1946), Fig. 84, p. 195.
9. Charles Santore, *The Windsor Style in America* (Philadelphia: Running Press, 1981), fig. 82.
10. Ibid., fig. 68, p. 82.
11. Ibid., p. 91.
12. Nancy A. Goyne, "American Windsor Chairs: A Style Survey," *Antiques,* April 1969, fig. 11, p. 542.
13. *Vital Records of Nantucket,* Vol. 5, p. 632.
14. The table in Plate XIII belonged to Grace Brown Gardner, and is illustrated in the frontispiece of Kenneth Duprey's *Old Houses on Nantucket* (New York: Architectural Book Publishing Co., 1959).
15. This fact was pointed out by Paul Madden.
16. A cricket is a small, low wooden footstool.
17. Information on the Yale desk courtesy of Gerald W. R. Ward.
18. Duprey, *Old Houses on Nantucket,* p. 189.
19. Benjamin Goldberg, *The Mirror of Man* (Charlottesville, Va.: University of Virginia Press, 1985), p. 172.
20. Helen Comstock, *The Looking Glass in America, 1700–1825* (New York: Viking Press, 1968), Fig. 65, p. 103.
21. Most of the information on Walter Folger, Jr. and his astronomical clock is from: Will Gardner, *The Clock That Talks and What It Tells* (Cambridge, Mass.: The Riverside Press, 1954).
22. Ibid., pp. 35–38.
23. Ibid., p. 81.
24. Ibid., p. 33.
25. William O. Stevens, *Nantucket, The Far Away Island,* (New York: Dodd, Mead & Co., 1936), p. 91.
26. Meredith Brenizer, "Notes From the Historical Association," *Inquirer and Mirror,* Feb. 21, 1985, p. 4–13.

4. *Mariners' Things, Boxes, Toys, Woodenware*

1. Nancy Grant Adams, *My Seafaring Family,* unpublished manuscript (circa 1965), p. 18.
2. Ibid., p. 18.
3. Clifford Ashley, *The Yankee Whaler* (Boston: Houghton Mifflin Co., 1926), p. 327.
4. Wallace Nutting, *Furniture Treasury* (New York: Macmillan Co., 1954), fig. 3487.
5. Alexander Starbuck, *History of the American Whale Fishery* (New York: Argosy-Antiquarian Ltd., 1964), pp. 500–501. Captain Archer, born in Nantucket in 1810, had, like many local whalemen, to go off-island to find a command in the 1850s, in this case to New Bedford.
6. Ibid., p. 410; and Reginald B. Hegarty, *Addendum to "Starbuck" and "Whaling Masters"* (New Bedford: New Bedford Free Library, 1964), p. 62.
7. See Chapter 9 for descriptions of whalebone, whale ivory, and such scrimshaw terms as busk.
8. Henry J. Cadbury, "The Dunkirk Colony in 1797," *Proceedings of the NHA,* 1945, p. 44.
9. Information on the pinky *Eagle* from Charles F. Sayle, August 1985.
10. Charles G. Davis, *Shipping & Craft in Silhouette* (Salem, Mass.: Marine Research Society, 1929), p. 34.
11. Silvio A. Bedini, *Early American Scientific Instruments and Their Makers* (Washington: Smithsonian Institution, 1964), pp. 85–93.
12. Ibid., p. 87.

13. *Vital Records of Nantucket,* Vol. IV, p. 154.
14. *Memorial to William E. Gardner,* a scrapbook in the Nantucket Atheneum Library, pp. 221 and 253.
15. Ibid., p. 4. The *James T. Stewart* is not listed in Alexander Starbuck's *History of the American Whale Fishery.*
16. We wish to thank Roderick S. and Marjorie K. Webster, curators, History of Astronomy Collection, The Adler Planetarium, Chicago, Illinois, for the information on Alexander Cairns.
17. We wish to thank Robert Ray and Jane Ray Richmond for information on the Nantucket Ray family.
18. Information on Thomas Pool courtesy of Mr. and Mrs. Webster.
19. *Probate Records of Nantucket County,* Book A, No. 1, p. 53.
20. *Probate Records of Nantucket County,* No. 2, 1737-1762, pp. 37–39.
21. Mary Earle Gould, *Early American Wooden Ware* (Rutland, Vt.: Charles E. Tuttle Co., 1962), p. 57.
22. Ibid., pp. 188–192.

5. *Textiles*

1. Alexander Starbuck, *The History of Nantucket,* (Boston: C. E. Goodspeed & Co., 1924. Reprinted by Charles E. Tuttle Co., Rutland, Vt., 1969), p. 96.
2. Ibid., p. 96.
3. Abbott Lowell Cummings, *Rural Household Inventories* (Boston: The Society for the Preservation of New England Antiquities, 1964), p. 267.
4. The first edition of Samuel Johnson's *Dictionary of the English Language* was published in 1755. We used the sixth edition, London, 1785.
5. David S. Landes, *The Unbound Prometheus; Technological Change & Industrial Development in Western Europe from 1750 to the Present* (London: Cambridge University Press, 1969), p. 57: "Much of the difficulty was due to the difference in labour requirements for spinning and weaving: it took at least five wheels to supply one loom, a proportion ordinarily at variance with the composition of the population." Kay Wilson, *A History of Textiles* (Boulder, Colo.: Westview Press, 1979), p. 241: "It has been said that it took at least four spinners to keep one weaver in yarn."
6. Cherryderry is a striped or checkered cloth of mixed silk and cotton, imported from India.
7. There is a D. Thomas listed in: D. Pennington and M. Taylor, *American Spinning Wheels* (Sabbathday Lake, Maine: The Shaker Press, 1975), p. 99.
8. Marion L. Channing, *The Textile Tools of Colonial Homes* (Privately printed, Marion, Mass., 1971), p. 27.
9. Patsy and Myron Orlofsky, *Quilts in America* (New York: McGraw-Hill, 1974), p. 155.
10. E. Norman Flayderman, *Scrimshaw and Scrimshanders, Whales and Whalemen* (Privately printed, 1972), p. 223.
11. Mary Thomas, *Mary Thomas's Knitting Book* (New York: Dover Publications, 1972), p. 18.
12. Ibid., p. 20.
13. Ibid., p. 22.
14. Ibid., p. 21.
15. Patricia L. Fiske, Ed., *Imported and Domestic Textiles in 18th Century America* (Washington, D. C.: The Textile Museum, 1975), pp. 161–165.
16. Such quilted petticoats were made with two layers of fabric quilted together with a filling which was often woolen cloth.
17. Averil Colby, *Quilting* (New York: Charles Scribner's Sons, 1979), p. 116.
18. According to the *Vital Records of Nantucket,* Nathaniel Coffin, son of James, married Damaris Gayer, daughter of William and Dorcas (Starbuck) Gayer, on August 17, 1692, instead of 1697, as mentioned in the handwritten note.
19. Eliza (Starbuck) Coffin, born February 10, 1811, married Henry Coffin in 1833. She was still living when her husband died in 1900, which suggests that the later note on the petticoat was written about that time (1900).
20. The NHA petticoat has been examined by Susan Burrows Swan of the Winterthur Museum and by Patsy Orlofsky and her associates at the

Textile Conservation Institute, South Salem, New York.

21. *Pollard Papers,* The Nantucket Atheneum, Vol. V, p. 475.
22. Ms. Barbara Nathan brought this fact to our attention.
23. *Pollard Papers,* p. 475.
24. *Vital Records of Nantucket,* Vol. V, p. 217.
25. *Pollard Papers,* p. 475.
26. Susan Burrows Swan, *Plain & Fancy, American Women and Their Needlework, 1700–1850* (New York: Holt, Rinehart & Winston, 1977), p. 228.
27. Ibid., p. 51.
28. *Vital Records of Nantucket,* Vol. II, p. 113.
29. *Pollard Papers* and *Barney Papers,* Nantucket Atheneum Library.
30. We are grateful for the help of Susan Burrows Swan in analyzing these samplers. She pointed out the recurrence of rows of trees in many of the samplers and the sometime use of a "nervous" wavy line.
31. Kenneth Duprey, *Old Houses on Nantucket* (New York: Architectural Book Publishing Co., 1959), p. 152.
32. Unpublished brochure for Winterthur Museum docents, courtesy of Susan Burrows Swan.
33. See Barbara Franco, *Bespangled, Painted & Embroidered Decorated Masonic Aprons in America* (Lexington, Mass.: Museum of Our American Heritage, 1980).
34. Ibid., p. 58 and color plate IV, p. 12.
35. Elaine Eff, "Folk Art: The Heart of America," *The Clarion,* Summer 1978.
36. Franco, *Bespangled Painted & Embroidered Decorated Masonic Aprons in America,* figure 74, p. 108.
37. Matthew D. Finn, *Theoremetrical System of Painting* (New York, 1830), demonstrated "painting in the theoremetrical style" using cut-out "theorems."
38. Virginia Clark called our attention to a similar pastel on paper titled "Sliced Watermellon" by J. Bower, a nineteenth-century artist illustrated in Paul F. Rovetti, *Nineteenth-Century Folk Painting: Our Spirited National Heritage* (Storrs, Conn: William Benton Museum of Art, 1973), fig. 133.
39. *Historic Nantucket,* April 1957, p. 14.
40. Myron S. Dudley, "Silk Industry in Nantucket," *Historic Nantucket,* October 1963, pp. 19–22; *Proceedings of the Nantucket Historical Association,* 1898, p. 12.

6. *Ceramics, Glass, and Lighting Devices*

1. Abbott Lowell Cummings, *Rural Household Inventories* (Boston: The Society for the Preservation of New England Antiquities, 1964), pp. 83–262.
2. Geoffrey A. Godden, *British Pottery, An Illustrated Guide* (London: Barrie & Jenkins, 1974), p. 49. Fig. 51 illustrates a related piece dated 1754.
3. Geoffrey A. Godden, *Oriental Market Porcelain* (London: Granada Publishers, Ltd., 1979), pp. 21–53.
4. Ibid., pp. 281–300.
5. Rodris Roth, *Tea Drinking in 18th-Century America: Its Etiquette and Equipage* (Washington: Smithsonian Institution, 1961), p. 64.
6. Ibid., p. 65.
7. Alexander Starbuck, *The History of Nantucket* (Boston: C. E. Goodspeed & Co., 1924. Reprinted by C. E. Tuttle Co., Rutland, Vt., 1969), p. 257.
8. The information on James Chase was contributed by Helen Winslow Chase.
9. Robert H. McCauley, *Liverpool Transfer Designs on Anglo-American Pottery* (Portland, Maine: The Southworth-Anthoenson Press, 1942), p. 40.
10. Ibid., p. 6.
11. Edouard A. Stackpole, *The Sea Hunters* (Philadelphia: J. B. Lippincott, 1953), p. 188.
12. Ibid., p. 192.
13. Ibid., p. 218.
14. Ibid., p. 234.
15. Ibid., p. 201.
16. *Union Lodge, F. & A.M. / Nantucket, Mass. / 1771—History—1941* (privately printed in Nantucket in an edition of 370 copies, 1941), p. 34.
17. Ibid., p. 36.
18. Ibid., p. 37.
19. Ibid., p. 37.
20. Ibid., p. 38.
21. Ibid., p. 45.

22. Ibid., p. 47.
23. Ibid., p. 46.
24. Ibid., p. 67.
25. Ibid., p. 79.
26. John Quentin Feller, "Canton *famille-rose* porcelain / Part II: Mandarin," *The Magazine Antiques,* February 1984, pp. 444–453. See Fig. 10, p. 453.
27. John Quentin Feller, "Canton *famille-rose* porcelain / Part I: Rose Medallion," *The Magazine Antiques,* October 1983, pp. 748–758.
28. Geoffrey A. Godden, *An Illustrated Encyclopedia of British Pottery and Porcelain* (New York: Bonanza Books, 1966), p. 96, fig. 164.
29. Edouard A. Stackpole, *Life Saving Nantucket* (Nantucket: Nantucket Life Saving Museum, 1972), p. 31.
30. Ibid., p. 38.
31. Jerry O. Powell, "Argand Lamps," *Winterthur Newsletter,* Winter 1986, pp. 8–9.
32. Other stained-glass windows in St. Paul's were made by the Willet Studios and the Connick Studios.

7. *Silver*

1. Although we have found no records as to whether Thomas Carr was a member of the Society of Friends, his wife Mary was called a Quaker when his will was probated:

> Nantucket In Sherborn, March ye 4:1757. At a Probate Court held this day George Hussey & Mary Carr Executors to the Last Will of Thomas Carr, appeared in Court and they being of those People called Quakers gave their Solemn affirmation (upon the Penalty of Purgery) that the foregoing Inventory contained all the Estate of their Testator that was Come to their Knowledge and if they knew of any more they will add it to their Inventory
>
> Jerh. Gardner
>
> Fredrick Folger Regr. Judge

2. *Probate Records of Nantucket County,* Vol. 2, 1737–1762, pp. 276–278.
3. Ibid., Vol. 3, p. 42.
4. Communication from Susan Burrows Swan.
5. *Nantucket County Book of Records,* Vol. 3, p. 10A.
6. Ibid., Vol. 3, p. 41.
7. Martha Gandy Fales' *Early American Silver* (New York: E. P. Dutton & Co., 1973) illustrates in figure 10 a two-handled cup with a Nantucket association made by Jeremiah Dummer owned by the Winterthur Museum. It is engraved on the bottom "Benjamin Coffin to R. G." The "R. G." is suggested to be Ruth Gardner who married James Coffin in 1692. There *was* a Ruth Gardner who married James Coffin, Jr. on March 19, 1692, but the only two Benjamin Coffins in Nantucket before 1718 were both born in 1683. It seems unlikely either of these nine-year-old boys would have given a silver cup wedding present circa 1692. There are two possibilities: (1) the inscription on the cup is later, perhaps after 1730–1740, or, (2) some Benjamin Coffin not part of the Nantucket Coffin family gave the cup to some unknown "R. G." In either case we question the early Nantucket provenance of the piece.
8. Neither the date of Experience Folger's birth nor of her marriage to John Swain, Jr. is known, but since their son, also named John, married Mary Swett January 6, 1712, it suggests that John III might have been born in the first part of the 1690s, which could give a date of circa 1690 as the marriage date of his parents.
9. We wish to thank Michael K. Brown, associate curator, Bayou Bend Collection, Museum of Fine Arts, Houston, for supplying information on the Swain tankard.
10. *Vital Records of Nantucket,* Vol. 4, p. 444.
11. Ibid., Vol. 4, p. 62.
12. Henry N. Flynt & Martha Gandy Fales, *The Heritage Foundation Collection of Silver* (Old Deerfield, Mass.: The Heritage Foundation, 1968), p. 241.
13. See John M. Bullard, *Joseph Rotch in Nantucket and Dartmouth* (New Bedford: Old Dartmouth Historical Society, 1931).
14. Jean R. Merriman, *The Mystery of John Jackson, 18th Century Silversmith, One Man or Two?* (Nantucket: Poets Corner Press, 1976), p. 34.
15. Ibid., p. 14.

16. Ibid., p. 21.
17. Seymour B. Wyler, *The Book of Old Silver* (New York: Crown Publishers, 1937), after p. 84.
18. *Probate Records of Nantucket County,* Vol. 3, p. 174.
19. Merriman, *The Mystery of John Jackson, 18th Century Silversmith, One Man or Two?,* p. 19.
20. Everett U. Crosby's books, all privately printed, included:

Ninety Five Per Cent Perfect (1937, 1944, 1953)
Books and Baskets Signs and Silver of Old-Time Nantucket (1940)
The Spoon Primer (1941)
Eastman Johnson at Nantucket (1944)
Nantucket in Print (1946)
Susan's Teeth (1955)

21. Crosby, *Books and Baskets Signs and Silver of Old-Time Nantucket,* p. 30.
22. *Pollard Papers,* The Nantucket Atheneum, Vol. 1, p. 136.
23. Crosby, *Ninety Five Per Cent Perfect,* p. 204.
24. *Nantucket County Court Records,* 1721–1785, p. 211.
25. *Pollard Papers,* Vol. 1, p. 136.
26. Essex Institute, Salem, Mass., "English / Touzell / Hathorne Papers," Box 4, Folder 1.
27. *Nantucket County Book of Records,* Vol. 9, p. 83.
28. Henry Barnard Worth, *Nantucket Lands and Land Owners,* NHA Vol. II, No. 5 (1906), p. 278.
29. *Nantucket County Book of Records,* Vol. 15, p. 88.
30. Ibid., Vol. 23, p. 459.
31. *Probate Records of Nantucket County,* No. 6, 1815–1824, p. 222 (will), pp. 347–348 (inventory).
32. Flynt & Fales, *The Heritage Foundation Collection of Silver,* p. 153.
33. Merriman, *The Mystery of John Jackson, 18th Century Silversmith, One Man or Two?,* p. 18.
34. Other Bunker porringers are owned by the NHA, the Bayou Bend Collection of the Museum of Fine Arts, Houston, and two by a dealer.
35. Crosby, *Ninety Five Per Cent Perfect,* p. 190.
36. The Paul Revere receipt is on loan from the Nantucket Union Lodge to the library of the Grand Lodge of Masons in Boston.
37. In the 1950s the "jewels" were sent to the Masonic Grand Lodge in Boston at which time they were attributed to Revere. It is not known who actually made the attribution.
38. Text of Revere letter courtesy Nantucket Union Lodge.
39. *Union Lodge, F. & A. M. / Nantucket, Mass. / 1771—History—1941,* p. 41.
40. Crosby, *Ninety Five Per Cent Perfect,* p. 186.
41. *NHA Account Book,* AB221: "The / Property / Of / Jas. Easton 2nd / July 20, 1828," 161 pages.
42. The analytic data in this chapter is from the Winterthur Museum Analytical Laboratory, Request No. 1682, Jan. 31, 1985. The conclusions based on the analytical data are the authors alone.
43. *NHA Account Book,* AB221, p. 42.
44. Charles H. Carpenter, Jr., *Gorham Silver 1831–1981* (New York: Dodd, Mead & Co., 1982), p. 36.
45. Ibid., p. 23.
46. Ibid., p. 28.
47. Ibid., p. 33, figs. 22 and 23.
48. Ibid., p. 36.
49. Charles H. Carpenter, Jr. with Mary Grace Carpenter, *Tiffany Silver* (New York: Dodd, Mead & Co., 1978), pp. 224 and 234–236.
50. See Carpenter, *Gorham Silver 1831–1981,* Chapter 10, "Souvenir Spoons."

8. *Iron, Pewter, Brass and Copper, Tin*

1. *NHA Account Book,* AB128.
2. See George Francis Dow, "Pewter in the Early Days," *Every Day Life in the Massachusetts Bay Colony* (New York: Arno Press, 1977), pp. 84–90; also Abbott Lowell Cummings, Ed., *Rural Household Inventories* (Boston: The Society for the Preservation of New England Antiquities, 1964).
3. W. Gill Wylie, *Measure for Measure* (Privately printed, 1952), p. 15.
4. Emil F. Guba, *Nantucket Odyssey* (Waltham, Mass.: published by the author, 1951), p. 319.

5. Ibid.
6. Mary Eliza Starbuck, *My House and I* (Boston and New York: Houghton Mifflin Co., 1929), pp. 259–260.
7. Ibid., pp. 258–259.

9. *Scrimshaw*

1. Clifford W. Ashley, *The Yankee Whaler* (Boston: Houghton Mifflin Co., 1926).
   Marius Barbeau, "All Hands Aboard Scrimshawing," *American Neptune* 12 (1952), pp. 99–122.
   Clare Barnes, *John F. Kennedy: Scrimshaw Collector* (Boston: Little Brown & Co., 1969).
   Joseph F. Caron, *Scrimshaw and Its Importance as an American Folk Art,* Doctoral Dissertation, Illinois State University, 1976.
   Everett U. Crosby, *Susan's Teeth and Much About Scrimshaw* (Nantucket, Mass.: Everett U. Crosby, 1955).
   Walter K. Earle, *Scrimshaw: Folk Art of the Whalers* (Cold Spring Harbor, New York: Whaling Museum Society, 1957).
   E. Norman Flayderman, *Scrimshaw and Scrimshanders, Whales and Whalemen* (Privately printed, 1972).
   William Gilkerson, *The Scrimshander,* rev. ed. (San Francisco: Troubador Press, 1978).
   Richard C. Malley, *Graven by the Fishermen Themselves Scrimshaw at Mystic Seaport Museum* (Mystic, Conn.: Mystic Seaport Museum, Inc., 1983).
   Charles R. Meyer, *Whaling and the Art of Scrimshaw* (New York: Henry Z. Walck Inc., 1976).
   Edouard A. Stackpole, *Scrimshaw at Mystic Seaport* (Mystic, Conn.: Marine Historical Association, 1958).
   Helen L. Winslow, *The Folk Art of the American Whaleman* (Nantucket: NHA, 1955).
2. For other definitions of scrimshaw see: Flayderman, *Scrimshaw and Scrimshanders, Whaling and Whales,* p. 4, and Malley, *Scrimshaw at Mystic Seaport,* p. 15.
3. Malley, *Scrimshaw at Mystic Seaport,* p. 16.
4. Flayderman, *Scrimshaw and Scrimshanders, Whaling and Whales,* p. 4.
5. Charles H. Carpenter, Jr., "Early Dated Scrimshaw," *The Magazine Antiques,* September 1972, pp. 414–419.
6. Ibid., p. 415.
7. Elizabeth A. Little and J. Clinton Andrews, *Drift Whales at Nantucket: The Kindness of Mashup* (NHA, 1982), p. 25.
8. Ibid., pp. 18–19.
9. Obed Macy, *The History of Nantucket* (Boston: Hilliard Gray & Co., 1835. Reprinted by Macy's, Ellenwood, Kans., 1985), p. 35.
10. William S. Fowler, "Metal Cutouts of the Northeast," *Bulletin of the Massachusetts Archaeological Society,* Vol. 34, April-July 1973, p. 28.
11. Erik Ekholm, James Deetz, "Preliminary Report: Excavation at C-9, Wellfleet, Massachusetts." Cape Cod National Seashore, National Park Service, U. S. Dept. of Interior; Alan T. Synenki and Sheila Chales, *Archaeological Collections Management of the Great Island Tavern Site* (Boston: U.S. Dept. of Interior, 1984).
12. Obed Macy, *The History of Nantucket,* p. 31.
13. *NHA Account Books,* 110 and 128.
14. Ekholm and Deetz, "Preliminary Report: Excavation at C-9, Wellfleet, Massachusetts," p. 4.
15. Ibid., p. 5.
16. Personal communication from Nelson O. Dunham (circa 1975).
17. Richard C. Kugler, *The Whale Oil Trade 1750–1775* (New Bedford, Mass.: Old Dartmouth Historical Society, 1980), p. 4.
18. Robert F. Trent, *New England Begins: The Seventeenth Century* (Boston: MFA, 1982) II, p. 350.
19. Owen Chase, *Narrative of the Most Extraordinary and Distressing Shipwreck of the Whale Ship Essex of Nantucket* (New York: W. B. Gilley, 1821).
20. Herman Melville, *Moby Dick or The Whale* (New York: Modern Library, 1944), p. 393.
21. Ibid., p. 438.
22. Ibid., pp. 101–102.
23. Ibid., p. 102.

24. Ibid., p. 214.
25. Ibid., pp. 179 and 185.
26. Ibid., p. 178.
27. Ibid., p. 178.
28. Ibid., p. 629.
29. Ibid., p. 708.
30. Edward Dodd, *Polynesian Art* (New York: Dodd, Mead & Co., 1967), p. 139: "The whale tooth itself without carving, though nicely polished, was a prized pendant in Fiji and in the Hiva Islands."
31. The statistics in Starbuck's *History of the American Whale Fishery* for the 1800–1804 period are incomplete and spotty. Although arrival dates are usually given, it was necessary to estimate the time of the year of departure for a number of voyages. Thus the 13.7 months figure for the 1800–1804 period is much less precise than the 43.4 months figure for the 1840–1844 period, where definite departure and arrival dates have been recorded.
32. Robert H. McCauley, *Liverpool Transfer Designs on Anglo-American Pottery* (Portland, Maine: The Southworth-Anthoeson Press, 1942), pp. 27 and 71.
33. Flayderman, *Scrimshaw and Scrimshanders,* pp. 76–79, Malley, *Scrimshaw at Mystic Seaport,* pp. 72–73 and 80. Sotheby's New York, auction catalog No. 4881, *Barbara Johnson Whaling Collection: Part II* (1982), No. 114.
34. Malley, *Scrimshaw at Mystic Seaport,* p. 134: "Depending on whom you ask the number of "*Susan*'s teeth" ranges from perhaps twelve to twenty-one." Others have appeared since Malley's book was written.
35. *The American Neptune,* April 1952, frontispiece and Plate 4.
36. George Francis Dow, *Whale Ships and Whaling* (Salem, Mass.: Marine Research Society, 1925), fig. 198, p. 421.
37. Ashley, *The Yankee Whaler,* p. 303.
38. *The Compact Edition of the Oxford English Dictionary,* (Oxford University Press, 1971), p. 302.
39. Edward H. Pinto, *Treen or Small Woodenware Throughout the Ages* (London: B. T. Batsford Ltd., 1949), p. 69.
40. Carpenter, "Early Dated Scrimshaw," p. 414, fig. 1.
41. Flayderman, *Scrimshaw and Scrimshanders,* p. 165.
42. Pinto, *Treen or Small Woodenware Throughout The Ages,* Figs. 85 and 86.
43. Flayderman, *Scrimshaw and Scrimshanders,* p. 175.
44. Malley, *Scrimshaw at Mystic Seaport,* pp. 136–7.

10. *Baskets*

1. H. H. Hobart, *Basketwork Through the Ages* (London: Oxford University Press, 1936), p. 8.
2. Daniel Gookin, *Historical Collections of the Indians in New England,* Massachusetts Historical Society, Collection for the year 1792, Vol. 1, Boston, 1806, in *The North American Basket 1790–1976,* Craft Center, Worcester, Mass., p. 3.
3. Robert F. Trent, *New England Begins: The Seventeenth Century* (Boston: MFA, 1982), Vol. I, p. 77.
4. Ibid., Vol. I, figure 68.
5. Elizabeth A. Little, "Probate Records of Nantucket Indians," (NHA, 1982), p. 12.
6. Ibid., p. 62.
7. Ibid., p. 13.
8. Katherine and Edgar Seeler, *Nantucket Lightship Baskets* (Nantucket: The Deermouse Press, 1972), pp. 18–19, illustrates two baskets attributed to Abram Quary.
9. Charlotte Striefer Rubenstein, *American Women Artists* (Boston: Avon Books, 1982), p. 54.
10. Trent, *New England Begins: The Seventeenth Century,* Vol. II, pp. 330–331, No. 341.
11. Dorothy Wright, *The Complete Guide to Basket Weaving* (New York: Drake Publishers Inc., 1972), pp. 42 and 136; Gloria Roth Teleki, *The Baskets of Rural America* (New York: E. P. Dutton & Co., Inc., 1975), pp. 14–15.
12. Hobart, *Basketwork Through the Ages,* p. 112.
13. Gustav Kobbé, "Life on the South Shoal Lightship," *The Century Magazine,* August 1891, p. 537.

14. Everett U. Crosby, *Books and Baskets, Signs and Silver of Old-Time Nantucket* (Privately printed, 1940), p. 68.
15. Ibid., p. 68. We were unable to confirm Crosby's statement in the files of the *Inquirer & Mirror* at the Nantucket Atheneum.
16. Kobbé, "Life on the South Shoal Lightship," pp. 544–545.
17. For example, Joseph E. C. Farnham, in his book *Brief Historical Data and Memories of My Boyhood Days in Nantucket* (Providence: Snow & Farnham Co., 1915), tells of making a basket in the 1860s in his father's shop where baskets were also being made by Captain George F. Joy and Charles G. Coggeshall (p. 125).
18. For description and diagrams on the making of a pocketbook-basket, see: Charles H. Carpenter, Jr., "A Cabinetmaker's Baskets in the Nantucket Tradition," *Fine Woodworking,* Nov./Dec. 1985, pp. 84–87.
19. We were told by Bill Sevrens, who learned basketmaking in the 1920s from Mitchy Ray, that old-time Nantucket basketmakers used the term "bail" instead of ear, a bail being the metal strip or end of a wooden stave that holds the handle. This creates confusion since basket handles were sometimes called bails.
20. *NHA Account Book,* AB 290.
21. For additional photographs of baskets see: Katherine and Edgar Seeler, *Nantucket Lightship Baskets.*
22. Robert F. Mooney and André R. Sigourney, *The Nantucket Way* (Garden City, N. Y.: Doubleday & Co., 1980), p. 177.
23. The names of the sixty-six Nantucketers who served on the *South Shoal Lightship* were listed in the *Inquirer & Mirror* May 16, 1931. (Also Vol. 9, Grace Brown Gardner's *Scrapbook,* NHA).
24. The Reyes basket is now in the Peter Foulger Museum.
25. Others who supplied carvings for basket tops included Nancy Chase, Aletha Macy, and Paul Morris.
26. Reyes' baskets were described in a sixteen-page brochure printed for Reyes to publicize his business: *The Friendship Baskets and Their Maker José Formosa Reyes* (Nantucket, 1960).

11. *Carvings and Drawings*

1. See Harriette Merrifield Forbes, *Gravestones of Early New England* (New York: Da Capo Press, 1967), p. 39, the gravestone of George Payson, Dorchester, 1734.
2. Ibid., p. 46.
3. Adele Earnest, *The Art of the Decoy: American Bird Carvings* (New York: Bramhall House, 1965), p. 33.
4. *NHA Account Book,* AB 475.
5. Mary Eliza Starbuck, *My House and I* (Boston and New York: Houghton Mifflin Co., 1929), pp. 144–146.
6. Georgia W. Hamilton, *Silent Pilots / Figureheads in Mystic Seaport Museum* (Mystic, Conn., 1984), p. 17 notes: "There is an account of a mock funeral in 1785 for the figurehead from the New Bedford whaleship *Rebecca.* The figure, which was a carving of a woman, was thought by the owners to be inappropriate."
7. Description of the *Essex* in a bill of sale of one-sixteenth ownership of the ship to Captain Daniel Russel, dated Sept. 19, 1811.
8. Hamilton, *Silent Pilots / Figureheads in Mystic Seaport Museum,* pp. 31–34, and *New Bedford and Old Dartmouth, A Bicentennial Exhibition,* 1975–1976 (New Bedford: Old Dartmouth Historical Society, 1975), p. 99.
9. Alexander Starbuck, *History of the American Whale Fishery* (Washington: Government Printing Office), pp. 606, 612, 620, 632.
10. Ibid., pp. 642, 648, 654, and Reginald B. Hegarty, *Returns of Whaling Vessels Sailing From American Ports* (New Bedford: The Old Dartmouth Historical Society, 1959), pp. 3, 7, 10.
11. Hegarty, *Return of Whaling Vessels Sailing From American Ports,* pp. 16, 18, 21, 29.
12. Hamilton, *Silent Pilots / Figureheads in Mystic Seaport Museum,* p. 33.
13. Joseph Lancaster (1778–1838) established in England a monitorial form of school instruction

which influenced educational procedures in the United States.

14. Robert A. diCurcio, *Art on Nantucket,* (Nantucket: NHA, 1982), pp. 91–99.
15. Ibid., fig. 112, p. 93.

12. *Souvenirs from Far-Away Places*

1. Edouard A. Stackpole, *The Sea-Hunter* (Philadelphia and New York: J. B. Lippincott Co., 1953), p. 341.
2. NHA Research Center, ship's log L208.
3. NHA Research Center, ship's log L191.
4. Judith Coolidge Hughes, "Sailors' Valentines," *The Magazine Antiques,* February 1961, p. 187.
5. Everard Im Thurn and Leonard C. Wharton, editors, *The Journal of William Lockerby,* (London: The Hakluyt Society, 1965), p. liii.
6. The South Seas artifacts in Plate LXXIV and Figures 206–208 were identified by Peter Fetchko, director, The Peabody Museum of Salem.

SELECTED BIBLIOGRAPHY

In writing this book, we made use of research materials of the Nantucket Historical Association, the Nantucket Atheneum Library, the Nantucket County Probate and Land Court records, the New Canaan, Connecticut library, and the library of the Winterthur Museum in Delaware. In addition, the authors have a sizable personal library of Nantucket and whaling history and the decorative arts. To list *all* of the sources we consulted would be tedious and of little use to either the general reader or the specialist. We felt it would be more productive to annotate those sources we found to be of particular value. For references to specific statements in the text, please consult the endnotes.

Ashley, Clifford, *The Yankee Whaler* (Boston: Houghton Mifflin Co., 1926).
Many photographs of whaling gear, scrimshaw, and Ashley paintings.

Bedini, Silvio A., *Early American Scientific Instruments and Their Makers* (Washington: Smithsonian Institution, 1964).
Important study with much data on makers.

Channing, Marion L., *The Textile Tools of Colonial Homes* (Privately printed, Marion, Mass., 1971).
Textile tools, their names, and their uses.

Crosby, Everett U., *Nantucket in Print* (Privately printed, Nantucket, 1946).
A rich miscellany of rare and odd out-of-print Nantucket publications. Lists of Nantucket publications and maps.

Cummings, Abbott Lowell, ed., *Rural Household Inventories* (Boston: The Society for the Preservation of New England Antiquities, 1964).
Excellent introduction plus 109 inventories of rural Suffolk County, Massachusetts, between 1675 and 1775.

diCurcio, Robert A., *Art on Nantucket* (Nantucket: NHA, 1982).
Survey of the work of Nantucket artists and off-island artists who worked there.

Dow, George Francis, *Every Day Life in the Massachusetts Bay Colony* (New York: Arno Press, 1977).
Fascinating, well-researched account.

Dunbar, Michael, *Windsor Chairmaking* (New York: Hastings House, 1976).
The craftsman's point of view.

Duprey, Kenneth, *Old Houses on Nantucket* (New York: Architectural Book Publishing Co., 1959).
Photographs of the interiors of Nantucket houses as they were in the 1950s.

Earnest, Adele, *The Art of the Decoy: American Bird Carvings* (New York: Bramhall House, 1965).
Pioneer work, by a knowledgeable and gifted writer.

Fales, Martha Gandy, *Early American Silver for the Cautious Collector* (New York: Funk & Wagnalls, 1970).
Excellent survey, scholarly and readable.

Fales, Martha Gandy and Flynt, Henry N., *The Heritage Foundation Collection of Silver* (Old Deerfield, Mass.: The Heritage Foundation, 1968).
Survey of New England silversmiths and their work.

Farnham, Joseph E. C., *Brief Historical Data and Memories of My Boyhood Days in Nantucket* (Providence: Snow & Farnham Co., 1915).
A well-written memory of life in mid-nineteenth-century Nantucket, full of interesting details.

Flayderman, E. Norman, *Scrimshaw and Scrimshanders Whales and Whalemen* (Privately printed, 1972).
Survey of scrimshaw types with notes on whaling. Many illustrations.

Forman, Henry Chandlee, *Early Nantucket and its Whale Houses,* (New York: Hastings House, 1966).
Emphasis is on the early whale houses of Sconset.

Gardner, Will, *The Clock That Talks and What It Tells* (Boston: NHA, 1954).
Biography of Walter Folger and description of his famous clock.

Gardner, Will, *Three Bricks and Three Brothers* (Cambridge, Mass.: Riverside Press, 1945).
The story of Joseph Starbuck and his three sons and the identical brick houses he built for them on Main Street, Nantucket.

Godden, Geoffrey A., *An Illustrated Encyclopedia of British Pottery and Porcelain* (New York: Bonanza Books, 1966).

———*British Pottery, An Illustrated Guide* (London: Barrie & Jenkins, 1974).

———*Oriental Market Porcelain* (London: Granada Publishers, Ltd., 1979).
Geoffrey Godden's books on ceramics made and used in Britain cover a wide range of objects with great thoroughness.

Goyne, Nancy A., "American Windsor Chairs: A Style Survey," *The Magazine Antiques,* April 1969.
Nancy Goyne Evans, the leading authority on American Windsor chairs, is preparing for publication the definitive work on Windsors.

Hegarty, Reginald B., *Addendum to "Starbuck" and "Whaling Masters"* (New Bedford: New Bedford Free Library, 1964).
Brings Alexander Starbuck's *History of the American Whale Fishery* up to date, with added voyages and corrections.

Hobart, H. H., *Basketwork Through the Ages* (London: Oxford University Press, 1936).
Survey, with emphasis on early baskets of many cultures.

Gould, Mary Earle, *Early American Wooden Ware* (Rutland, Vermont: Charles E. Tuttle Co., 1962).
Reprint of the only general study of American woodenwares. Primarily descriptive.

Jobe, Brock and Kaye, Myrna, *New England Furniture: The Colonial Era* (Boston: Houghton Mifflin, 1984).
Scholarly survey of the Society for the Preservation of New England Antiquities' holdings.

Kirk, John T., *American Furniture and the British Tradition* (New York: Alfred A. Knopf, 1982).
Valuable for its study of the British origin of American furniture forms.

Kugler, Richard, *The Whale Oil Trade 1750–1775* (New Bedford: Old Dartmouth Historical Society, 1980).
A fine overview of the 1750–1775 period of great growth for the American whaling industry.

Lancaster, Clay, *The Architecture of Historic Nantucket* (New York: McGraw-Hill, 1972).
A broad and erudite survey of Nantucket's architecture.

Little, Elizabeth A., *Nantucket Algonquin Studies* (NHA, 1979–1981).
Dr. Little's extensive writings on the Nantucket Indians are presently available at the Research Center of the Nantucket Historical Association.

Macy, Obed, *The History of Nantucket* (Boston: Hilliard Gray and Co., 1835). Reprinted (1985) by Macy's, Ellenwood, Kans.
This great classic, written in the style of the King James version of the Bible, has charmed and informed people from Herman Melville to today's students. It is the basic book for any study of Nantucket and whaling history.

Malley, Richard C., *Graven by the fisherman themselves Scrimshaw at Mystic Seaport Museum* (Mystic, Conn.: Mystic Seaport Museum, Inc., 1983).
Survey of scrimshaw types based on the collection of Mystic Seaport Museum.

McCauley, Robert H., *Liverpool Transfer Designs on Anglo-American Pottery* (Portland, Maine: The Southworth-Anthoenson Press, 1942).
Excellent survey of Liverpool wares at the end of the eighteenth and beginning of the nineteenth centuries.

Melville, Herman, *Moby Dick or the Whale* (New York: Modern Library, Rockwell Kent Illustrations. 1944).

Montgomery, Florence M., *Textiles in America 1650–1870* (New York: W. W. Norton & Co., 1984).
Informative survey of textile usages and the definitive dictionary of textile terms.

New England Begins: The Seventeenth Century (Boston: Museum of Fine Arts, 1982). Three volumes.
A rich, detailed account of the material culture of New England's first century.

Nutting, Wallace, *Furniture Treasury* (New York: The Macmillan Co., 1928). Two volumes.
"Nutting," with its 5,000 illustrations, has been the bible of American furniture for generations of dealers, collectors, and writers. Although it is considered quite out of date, we found ourselves continually consulting it. Ian Quimby of Winterthur has suggested the need for an up-to-date, annotated edition of the book.

Pinto, Edward H., *Treen or Small Woodenware Throughout the Ages* (London: B. T. Batsford Ltd., 1949).
Valuable information on such things as seventeenth- and eighteenth-century busks.

Proceedings of the Nantucket Historical Association, 1896 to date.
A vast storehouse of Nantucketiana.

Roth, Rodris, *Tea Drinking in 18th-Century America: Its Etiquette and Equipage* (Washington: Smithsonian Institution, 1961).
A gracefully written, scholarly account of the beginnings of tea drinking in America.

St. John, J. Hector (Crèvecoeur), *Letters from an American Farmer* (London, 1782).
Pages 114–212 are devoted to Nantucket. An idyllic but basically accurate account.

Santore, Charles, *The Windsor Style in America* (Philadelphia: Running Press, 1981).
General review of American Windsors, with drawings of chair details.

Seeler, Katherine and Edgar, *Nantucket Lightship Baskets* (Nantucket: The Deermouse Press, 1972).
Survey, with photographs.

Stackpole, Edouard, *The Sea Hunters* (Philadelphia & New York: J. B. Lippincott Co., 1953).
Much information from logs and journals.

Starbuck, Alexander, *History of the American Whale Fishery From Its Earliest Inception to the Year 1876* (Washington: Government Printing Office, 1878).
Monumental record of American whaling voyages to 1876. The classic study.

Starbuck, Alexander, *The History of Nantucket* (Boston: C. E. Goodspeed & Co., 1924). Reprinted by Charles E. Tuttle, Rutland, Vermont, 1969.
Basic history of the island with many references from primary sources.

Swan, Susan Burrows, *Plain & Fancy, American Women and Their Needlework* (New York: Holt, Rinehart & Winston, 1977).
Scholarly and readable social history of American needlework; attractive illustrations.

Vital Records of Nantucket Massachusetts to the Year 1850 (Boston: New England Historic Genealogical Society, 1925). Five volumes, two on births, two on marriages, one on deaths.
The basic source of early genealogical data for Nantucket.

Worrall, Arthur J., *Quakers in the Colonial Northeast* (Hanover, N. H.: University Press of New England, 1980).
General study of Quakerism in the northeast in the seventeenth and eighteenth centuries.

It is the intention of the authors to publish two supplements to this book to document areas which would be primarily of interest to specialists and scholars:

1. *Occupations in Colonial Nantucket.* This would be an expansion of the material in Appendix I of this book and would attempt to list all recorded occupations of Nantucketers of the 1660–1776 period.
2. *The Inventories of Colonial Nantucket.* The plan is to publish all of the inventories of the Nantucket Probate Court of the 1660–1776 period.

GLOSSARY

backstaff A kind of quadrant formerly used in taking altitudes at sea, so called because the observer turned his back to the sun.

bêche-de-mer (trepang) Any of several sea cucumbers of the southern Pacific and Indian Oceans. The dried or smoked body of any of these animals, used as food in the Orient.

becket Handle made of woven or twisted rope secured through brackets on each end of a sea chest.

bengal Applied to piece goods (apparently of different kinds) exported from Bengal to England in the seventeenth century. Silks from India, usually striped.

blockmaker One who makes a wooden or metal case enclosing one or more pulleys, called a block, which is used to increase the mechanical power of the rope running through it. Blocks are employed especially for the rigging of ships.

brasier One who works in brass.

calash A two-wheeled box wagon, usually without a cover, with a seat for the driver on the splash board.

calimanco A tightly woven glossy worsted cloth.

camlet (cambet) A plain woven cloth of wool, linen, or goat's hair used for clothing, bedhangings, and furniture upholstery.

cherryderry Striped or checked woven cloth of mixed silk and cotton, imported from India.

close-stool A chamber pot enclosed in a stool or box.

clothier In America, a man whose occupation was to full and dress cloth.

comber One whose business it is to comb wool.

cooper A craftsman who makes and repairs wooden vessels formed of staves and hoops; as casks, buckets, and tubs.

cordwainer A shoemaker; a worker in cordwain or cordovan leather.

delft or delf A style of glazed earthenware, often blue and white. Note the small *d* which denotes English delft.

diaper A linen or cotton fabric woven with lines crossing to form diamonds.

dimity A stout cotton cloth similar to fustian, is ornamented in the loom either with stripes or fanciful figures, and when woven is seldom dyed, but commonly bleached a pure white.

drug (drogue, drudge) A block of wood or crossed planks fastened to a whale line used to check the whale in its struggle to escape capture.

drugget A kind of stuff, all of wool, or mixed of wool and silk or wool and linen for making apparel. Later, a coarse woolen stuff used for floor coverings, tablecloths, etc.

earthenware A variety of coarse, porous, baked clayware.

fellmonger A dealer in skins or hides of animals, especially sheepskins.

feltmaker One who works with or makes felt, a nonwoven cloth.

firkin A small wooden vessel or cask.

fuller One who "fulls" cloth; an operator of a fulling mill where woven cloth is scoured, shrunk, and pressed to render it stronger, closer, and finer.

fustian Usually a twill-woven cotton and linen cloth.

garlick (garlix) A linen cloth first imported from Goetlitz, Silesia. "Garlick Holland" and "double fold Garlix" are specified in American records from the late seventeenth century.

gentleman A person of distinction or rank; a man of superior position in society; often one whose means enables him to live in easy circumstances. His name is often followed by the term esquire.

glasier (glazier) One whose trade it is to glaze windows.

hogshead A large cask or barrel, especially one containing sixty-three to 140 gallons.

housewright A builder of houses, especially of timber houses; a house carpenter.

huck-a-buck A stout linen fabric, with the weft threads thrown alternately up so as to form a rough surface, used for toweling and the like.

husbandman A man who tills or cultivates the soil; a married man who is head of a household.

joiner A person who makes furniture by mortise-and-tenon construction. The term cabinetmaker was not used in eighteenth-century Nantucket records.

keeler A shallow tub used for household purposes.

kersey A cheap, coarse, woolen cloth of twill weave.

lawn A fine plain woven linen.

lot-layer A surveyor.

mariner A sailor, a seaman; that is, one who navigates or assists in navigating a ship.

manumit To release from slavery; to set free; to release from bondage or servitude.

osnaburg (ozenberg) Coarse, unbleached linen or hempen cloth, first made in Osnabruck, Germany.

piggin A small wooden pail or bucket with one stave projecting above the rim for use as a handle.

pillowber Pillow case.

plate Usually, objects made of silver. The modern use of the word implies silver-plated metal.

porcelain A hard, white, translucent ceramic made by firing a pure clay and glazing with variously colored fusible materials; china.

rigger One who is responsible for the rigging of sailing vessels. The rigger sets up the arrangements of masts, spars, and sails.

romals Handkerchiefs from India.

russels A worsted damask.

saddler One who makes or deals in saddles.

shalloon A cheap twilled worsted cloth. Worsted yarn is manufactured in shalloons and other light stuffs, of which the threads are visible, not being covered with a pile.

slay An instrument used in weaving, to beat the weft.

spinster A woman who spins, especially one who practices spinning as a regular occupation. (This is the first meaning of the word in the *Oxford English Dictionary*).

stoneware This ware has a hard-pitted glaze which is the result of throwing salt into the kiln when it is very hot; sodium from the vaporized salt combines with silica and alumina in the clay to form the "salt glaze." English stoneware is usually white or buff. German stoneware is brown or gray.

swift A reel used to hold yarn as it is being wound off. Sometimes made of whalebone.

tapa A coarse cloth made in the Pacific islands from the pounded bark of the paper mulberry, breadfruit, and other plants, and usually decorated with geometric patterns.

turkey-work Turkish tapestry work or an imitation of this work.

victualler A purveyor of victuals or provisions, especially one who makes a business of providing food and drink for payment; a keeper of an eating house, inn, or tavern.

warp (in weaving) To arrange yarn or thread that runs lengthwise in a woven fabric.

(in whaling) A rope readied to use for harpooning the whale, a towline.

weft The threads that run crosswise in a woven fabric, at right angles to the warp threads.

yeoman A man holding a small landed estate; a freeholder under the rank of gentleman, hence a common or country man of respectable standing, especially one who cultivates his own land.

INDEX

Note: Page numbers in italics indicate illustrations.

C

D

E

F

I

J

K

L

Q

R

S

T

U

W

Y